MONTRÉAL
A CITIZEN'S GUIDE TO CITY POLITICS

MONTRÉAL
A CITIZEN'S GUIDE TO CITY POLITICS

EDITED BY
MOSTAFA HENAWAY, JASON PRINCE AND ERIC SHRAGGE

Montréal/Chicago/London

Montréal: A Citizen's Guide to City Politics by Mostafa Henaway, Jason Prince, and Eric Shragge, editors is licensed under a Creative Commons Attribution-NonCommercial-NoDerivatives 4.0 International License, except where otherwise noted.

Claire Morissette's chapter "Streets that Breathe: Controlling Cars" originally published in the book *Montréal: A Citizen's Guide to City Politics* (1990) is reprinted with permission from Black Rose Books.

This publication was made possible with the financial support of the Concordia University Part-Time Faculty Association (CUPFA) and the Social Justice Centre at Concordia University.

Black Rose Books No. VV425

Library and Archives Canada Cataloguing in Publication
Title: A citizen's guide to city politics : Montréal / Jason Prince, Eric Shragge, and Mostafa Henaway, eds.
Other titles: Montréal
Names: Prince, Jason, 1965- editor. | Shragge, Eric, 1948- editor. | Henaway, Mostafa, editor.
Description: Includes bibliographical references.
Identifiers: Canadiana (print) 20210223073 | Canadiana (ebook) 20210223138 | ISBN 9781551647814 (hardcover) | ISBN 9781551647791 (softcover) | ISBN 9781551647807 (PDF)
Subjects: LCSH: Montréal (Québec)—Politics and government—Citizen participation.
Classification: LCC JS1761.7.A15 C58 2021 | DDC 323/.0420971428—dc23

C.P. 35788 Succ. Léo-Pariseau
Montréal, QC H2X 0A4
CANADA
www.blackrosebooks.com

ORDERING INFORMATION:

USA/INTERNATIONAL	CANADA	UK/EUROPE
University of Chicago Press Chicago Distribution Center 11030 South Langley Avenue Chicago IL 60628	University of Toronto Press 5201 Dufferin Street Toronto, ON M3H 5T8	Central Books Freshwater Road Dagenham RM8 1RX
(800) 621-2736 (USA) (773) 702-7000 (International)	1-800-565-9523	+44 20 8525 8800
orders@press.uchicago.edu	utpbooks@utpress.utoronto.ca	contactus@centralbooks.com

Cover design by Ali Overing. The slightly modified cover photo (https://commons.wikimedia.org/wiki/File:Manifestation_d%27Alg%C3%A9riens_%C3%A0_Montr%C3%A9al_2019.jpg) by Great11 (https://commons.wikimedia.org/wiki/User:Great11) is licensed under the Creative Commons Attribution-Share Alike 4.0 International license. (https://creativecommons.org/licenses/by-sa/4.0/deed.en)

CONTENTS

Acknowledgements	ix
Preface Luc Ferrandez	1
Introduction Mostafa Henaway, Jason Prince, and Eric Shragge	5
Montréal, between Oral Tradition and Historical Archives Eric Pouliot-Thisdale	13
Power and the City Mostafa Henaway, Jason Prince, and Eric Shragge	23

PART I. NATURE AND THE CITY

Despair and Hope: A Story of Montréal's Natural Spaces Patrick Barnard	47
Montréal's COVID-19 Pandemic: A Crisis of Inequality Elizabeth Leier	57
Montréal's Changing Climate: There Is No Turning Back Joey El-Khoury	69

PART II. MOVING IN THE CITY

Debating Public Transit: What about a Regional Tramway? Luc Gagnon and Jean-François Lefebvre	83

F*** the Car: A New Vision for Transport in the   95
Montréal Region
     Jason Prince

Streets That Breathe—Controlling Cars   111
     Claire Morissette

Beyond Critical Mass: Scaling up Bike Infrastructure in   125
Montréal
     Bartek Komorowski

PART III. PLANNING THE CITY

Solidarity Architecture and Social Urbanism   137
     Christelle Proulx Cormier and Ron Rayside

The Reconstruction of Montréal's Chabanel District   147
     Mostafa Henaway and Norma Rantisi

PART IV. THE ECONOMY AND THE CITY

The City as Sweatshop   159
     Mostafa Henaway

The Social Economy and the City   171
     Jason Prince

PART V. HOUSING THE CITY

Municipal Government: Ally or Adversary of   187
Montréal's Co-operative Housing Sector?
     Jacob Ryan

Community Housing: Leveraging Our Collective Assets   199
     Jean-Pierre Racette

How to Fight Your Landlord: Gentrification and Tenant   209
Organizing in Montréal
     Jon Milton

PART VI. GOVERNING THE CITY

Power and City Hall   221
     Linda Gyulai

Consultation, Participation, or Power: What's in It and for Whom? — 233
    Eric Shragge

PART VII. SOCIAL JUSTICE AND THE CITY

Challenging Policing in Montréal: An Interview with Robyn Maynard — 247
    Robyn Maynard

Whose City? Claiming Justice for Indigenous Peoples — 263
    Christopher Curtis

Pushing Municipal Boundaries: Experiences of Montréal's Immigrant Workers Centre — 271
    Cheolki Yoon

PART VIII. UPPITY 'HOODS AND THE CITY

Milton Parc: Grabbing and Keeping Community Control — 283
    Nathan McDonnell

Pointe-Saint-Charles: Legacies and Continuity — 293
    Jocelyne Bernier and Cédric Glorioso-Deraiche

Montréal-Nord: Community Power Catalyzed by Hoodstock — 305
    Rushdia Mehreen, Mzwandile Poncana, and Will Prosper

Final Word: Prenons la Ville! — 317
    Mostafa Henaway, Jason Prince, and Eric Shragge

Author Bios — 329

ACKNOWLEDGEMENTS

The editors would like to thank the Centre for Social Justice at Concordia University for a graduate fellowship for research support that allowed Mostafa Henaway to contribute to the book and subsequently join the editorial team. We thank CUPFA, the part-time faculty union for a grant to help with executive support, translation and graphics. Thanks to Michael Nugent for graphics support and Kimberly Salt for the tramway graphic. Thanks to the 50 people who supported the book in the early stages and to finance translation. Finally we thank Patrick Gannon for his excellent editing and keeping the three editors focussed on the detail of finishing the book.

PREFACE

LUC FERRANDEZ

This letter was written May 2019.

Friends and citizens, I am announcing my departure from political life.

In May 2009, ten years ago, I began the election campaign that would lead to my victory in November of that year, together with my six colleagues at the Plateau Mont-Royal mayor's office.

For ten years, that is all I did. I regret nothing—what a great adventure.

For months I have been thinking about leaving, and a thousand reasons make me want to stay—starting with my real passion for this work and my sincere affection for my colleagues. Only one reason makes me want to leave, but it keeps coming back with more force: a feeling of imposture. More specifically, I feel that I am fooling people into believing that we are collectively taking all the necessary measures to slow the pace of our planet's destruction.

Because my environmental convictions and ability to act are well known, my presence in this administration helps reassure many people of the value of the work we are doing. By resigning, I hope to topple this image and force the group to regain the confidence of the electorate I represent.

After only two years, Projet Montréal's environmental record is far superior to that of its predecessor. The ban on oil heating by 2030, the ban on single-use plastics, and major announcements (with more to come) regarding public transit, active transport, and the acquisition of natural spaces provide evidence of constant concern and a certain capacity for action.

But these gestures will remain anecdotal if they are not part of a concerted plan to reorient and slow down consumption, and the development of the city.

As an example, a real environmental program would include at least the following measures:

Tax 100% on-street and off-street parking; tax entry to the city centre; reinvent trucking in the city, and tax foreign investment; tax waste; lobby to prevent airport expansions, and tax flights; limit the development of the port's oil activities; reintroduce tariffs on certain categories of products, and tax meat. With these revenues, we must acquire or zone all of the green spaces still available, build hundreds of permaculture farms, build the green belt around Montréal, expand parks, set up a decontamination program using phytoremediation, demineralize 10% of the streets, plant 500,000 trees, acquire and demolish houses in floodplains, strengthen wetlands, and reinvent recycling and deposits. We also need to reinvent the way that we occupy the city, block speculation in the downtown core by reducing allowable building heights; concentrate our efforts on human-scale densification in the hearts of villages throughout the city—notably by forcing the relocation of jobs, and the construction of large-scale family housing, around parks and metro stations. This construction would be done in local wood-frame buildings, with windows that open at the height of the rows of trees planted in front to temper them. Finally, and most importantly, we must focus our investments on environmental objectives, even if it means abandoning the massive investments planned for roads and the new construction projects planned for sports, leisure, and culture.

In terms of discourse, we must tackle the consumer society head-on and denounce its excesses—like a second baseball stadium financed by the real estate speculation that we will have to allow in its vicinity, and a cookie-cutter shopping and housing development at Royalmount (*"un Royalmount en carton"*).

Such a program cannot be achieved in a single mandate, nor can it be done without other levels of government. But we need to start now. We need to show our true colours and mobilize the public. Above all, we must make the environment the backdrop for all of our actions—not an isolated program.

What I am proposing is nothing less than a war effort. It is only out of the indulgence of our worst faults and their defenders that we refuse to acknowledge that extinction is worth a war, and victory is worth the sacrifice of a few hundred thousand votes.

Unable to influence the mayor (as well as the president and members of the executive committee) on the seriousness of the situation and the measures that need to be taken, I choose not to remain on this team.

However, I recognize that Valérie Plante is more representative of the population than I have ever been. I can never thank her often enough for taking power at such a critical moment in history—faced with a mayor and a party frozen in the past—she alone could do it. She has the immense responsibility of getting a progressive party re-elected in a political landscape where there are fewer and fewer progressives remaining, and I understand the difficulty of making choices in this context. I also thank her for entrusting me with projects for parks, streets, and squares that will transform Montréal.

I do not want to weaken her leadership or work for another team. On the contrary, I hope that Projet Montréal will remain strong and united and that it will win the next election.

Despite everything, I leave with a light heart. Thank you to the citizens of the Plateau Mont-Royal for these ten years of happiness.

Luc Ferrandez

INTRODUCTION

MOSTAFA HENAWAY, JASON PRINCE, AND ERIC SHRAGGE

"Cities today have a choice between becoming active forces for social change or quietly acquiescing to the whims of global capital"
(Benoit Bréville 2020)

As we write this introduction, we are living through a unique experience. The global COVID-19 pandemic has forced large parts of the economy to shut down. Many people are now working from home, with social distancing and masks the norm. When our highways suddenly emptied at the beginning of the pandemic, we also experienced the possibilities of clean air and quiet streets, with huge numbers of people out walking, jogging, and spending time with family. That is, if you were not doing the essential work of caregiving, cleaning, food production, or the sales and distribution of essential goods. Across the world, class, racial, gender, and immigration divides have come into sharp focus during this pandemic. Who stays home? Who works? Who is daily exposed to the virus, and who contracts it because of the injuries of class? All of this plays out dramatically in our city—and in all cities.

The reflections and analysis leading to this book pre-date the COVID-19 crisis, but at its core was the centrality of cities in both the exacerbation and resolution of the consequences of life after 40 years of neoliberal capitalism and ongoing environmental degradation.

As the old labour song asks: "Which side are you on?" We ask the same about cities in general, and specifically about our city: Montréal.

This project began because of the urgency of the current context and the possibility that the municipal level of government holds the key to building opposition to the existing formations of economic and political power. At the same time, the city can be the lever to support alternative forms of economic development and the democratic participation of residents. This could lead to greater collective power to counter the dominant economic and related class forces that have shaped cities in the interest of profitability and growth.

We were impressed by a number of municipal governments in the U.S. and Europe that have acted in opposition to private capital and other 'higher' levels of government; cities that have pushed various forms of economic and social innovation, both within, but also beyond, their 'local' mandates.

Benoit Bréville (2020) discussed the conflict between municipal and national governments across Europe and North America. He notes that some municipal governments have promoted greater transparency, participatory democracy, and sustainability, while central governments have become more nationalist, anti-immigrant, and explicitly pro-business (Bréville 2020).

Some cities have even bypassed central and regional governments to find solutions to contemporary problems. For example, Prague, Budapest, and some U.S. cities have challenged central governments on issues related to immigration, the environment, and the very structure of local economic development. Ironically, cities are now in competition to be the "most innovative, modern and trendy."

Here are three examples of progressive municipal governments:

- The first demonstrates how cities can take symbolic actions to resist the dominant powers of media repression. The City of Geneva erected a statue of Julian Assange, Edward Snowden, and Chelsea Manning in June 2021, in part to quash extradition proceedings against Assange, but also in defence of a free press. It was not placed in some forgotten corner of the city but at an important central location.
- The second example shows how cities can use their powers to materially improve the lives of workers. In 2014, Seattle adopted a $15 per hour minimum wage, underscoring the fact that workers were not being paid a livable wage; some were drowning in essential monthly payments for rent and food, while local corporate giants scored record profits.
- Third, cities can act in defiance of private capital and landlords. When the "Red-Red-Green coalition" won the Berlin state election in 2016, they immediately challenged the power of developers and landlords. They imposed a rent cap in 2019 (as well as a rent cap for state-owned housing companies) to take power away from speculators and landlords. However, the top court overturned the move.

Cities are the centres of population density, wealth creation, tax revenues, and poverty, but everywhere, cities have only very limited means and powers to control their own development.

While Berlin is a city that provides a template of what is possible, there are essential differences in Montréal. Berlin is one of three city-states in Germany. On the other hand, Montréal is a 'creature of the province' under Canada's current constitution. Though Berlin is a city with a rich tradition of dynamic social movements that have challenged gentrification, the climate crisis, and acted in solidarity with refugees, these movements do not always align with the goals of the elected officials at higher levels.

It is this dynamic and tension that forms a central element of the book. Cities can play a role if there is pressure from local organizations and social movements pushing against city hall. Local elected officials need to embrace these movements to become levers of change and the megaphone for our current crises, amplifying the voices of these organizations and movements.

With the election of Projet Montréal in 2017, this conflict between visions became a reality here. Legault's provincial government under the Coalition Avenir Québec (CAQ)—whose power base is off the island of Montréal—supports traditional car-based transport, along with anti-immigrant and pro-business agendas. We see a sharp dividing line between the suburban/rural areas and the city proper. Given this, what is the role of the City of Montréal and its boroughs? More broadly, what is the role of any city government? What are the possibilities and limits of any progressive municipal government? If a city can become an engine of structural change, how do we get there? These are the fundamental questions we ask throughout this book.

Finally, the role of contemporary social movements is entrenched in what are very much urban struggles. Movements that have recently come to the fore, for example, the struggles for Black Lives Matter and defunding the police, are squarely confronting structural racism entrenched in municipal power and politics. Movements of cities' most precarious workers are fighting for economic justice. Solidarity cities are demanding sanctuary for people without status. We are witnessing the intensifying effects of neoliberal capitalism, reshaping our urban landscape, with financialization and rampant speculation leading to housing precarity. However, movements against gentrification show the dynamism of resistance. The climate crisis has propelled new movements, which have mobilized millions across the globe. These movements, at times linked to progressive municipal governments, have converged. Despite the multitude of crises we face, we are witnessing a convergence of hope and solidarity within and across our cities.

THREE URGENT ISSUES

Here, we briefly present several issues that, although not necessarily within the traditional mandate of municipal governments, shape its agenda. They also allow the city to challenge other levels of government, take initiatives, and support alternatives that have the possibility of doing something concrete about these urgent problems.

The first is the climate disaster. The planet is on fire, and it is no time for half measures. Municipal governments have to play a leadership role, and in the best examples, they are playing this role. Cities are central in creating the problem, and local governments can act on solutions. For example, getting rid of cars, upgrading buildings, eliminating carbon emission sources, and protecting existing carbon sinks. Progressive cities take action on issues within their delegated mandates but also push against these boundaries.

Cities also need to play the role of critic: publicly and vocally challenging other levels of government, exposing their half-measures and backsliding on climate change, educating and mobilizing the public, and actively supporting oppositional movements and alternatives. The city is not the only level of government that can play such a role, but—especially in light of this vast political divide—local government is critical.

Second, we are witnessing the seemingly unstoppable concentration of wealth and economic polarization. This is played out mainly in cities. We will elaborate on this point in the framing chapter that follows (Power and the City) but suffice to say, cities have become sites for the investment of surplus capital, and one of the central contestations is around land usage.

Any useful land is being gobbled up by the few for their profit. Is urban land to be used for growth and profit or for the social needs of the majority? Needs such as housing, green spaces, or efficient collective transport. What land is still owned publicly by federal, provincial, or municipal governments or by public institutions like universities and churches? What role can cities play in protecting these assets? Can cities redistribute public wealth to benefit the majority—and not just land but also its spending power—through decisions on land use, distribution of public services, increased wages, and collective economic and social alternatives?

Third, which is related to the second issue, there is enormous pressure on cities to follow the dictates of the free market. Tax revenues in cities are based on land value. Property taxes are the primary source of revenue for cities—which is acutely the case in Montréal. As such, investments that increase property taxes are valued, despite the resulting gentrification and the displacement of working-class and lower-income people. This perversity—this conflict of interest between the City of Montréal and most of its residents—is of fundamental importance and is explored elsewhere in the book.

In contrast, as Gonsalvez argues (2017), cities should use their financial resources, programs, and land use policies as a means of redistribution from the wealthy to the majority as part of a strategy to challenge inequality. He argues that the progressive city should not cede to developers against the interests of their residents but rather defend them with the powers they have, with clear and explicit policies, zoning, and budgets (Gonsalvez 2017).

Dawson (2017) uses the concept of the extreme city to discuss the dual and intertwined challenges of climate chaos and structured economic and social inequality, both of which are concentrated in cities. He argues that the extreme city is a product of global capitalism run amok and harbours concentrated assets of the world's wealthiest in a physical form (Dawson 2017).

Extreme cities are the location where climate chaos will have its most potent and devastating impacts—with disparities of class determining one's chances of surviving. He writes:

> efforts to challenge environmental injustice… hinge on the most basic questions of survival … [And we must] focus struggles for climate justice on the scale of the city, where progressives can hope to win meaningful victories in a period of reaction. …cities are responsible for the lion's share of carbon emissions globally. … we are fighting for the city **as it may be** rather than the extreme city of the present (Dawson 2017, 295 [our emphasis]).

As this project came closer to completion, we began to see it more than simply a guide to politics in the city, but more as a roadmap for us as residents, regardless of our status, to take the city. *"Prenons la ville!"*

As this project unfolded, it became clear that there was an essential and urgent need to see the city as a place to bring together progressive forces under a common vision, identifying the root causes of injustice in our city.

The pieces are all there. The struggle to protect our green spaces. The fights for decent and affordable housing. The call for more public transit, fewer cars, and more bike paths. The crying need for wages that allow us to live decent lives. The common call for a just and democratic society.

The thread that allows us to see clearly, we argue, is the ongoing commodification of our city in all these ways: the city—our city—as a manifestation and realization of global and local capital in the endless pursuit of profit. The solution is to stop that and to find another path into the 21st century.

This reflection and urgency became clear in assembling the rich contemporary and historical analysis of activists, writers, and people directly involved in the most pressing issues facing Montréal. It was an impossible task to be as comprehensive as we would want to be. The issues sketched out in the following pages attempt to lay out the primary issues, examples, and organizing that are key to understanding our city.

Our first attempt is to understand the City of Montréal within a broader framework of power. The introductory chapter on Power and the City draws attention to the fact that municipal governments are shaped by the balance of forces of capital, working people, and social movements. This helps set the stage for contextualizing Montréal's trajectory, its electoral politics, and the movements that have historically shaped and continue to shape our city.

Another introductory chapter examines Montréal's colonial roots and the history and trajectories of the Indigenous peoples whose land was stolen by force and colonialism. It traces the past and current issues faced by Indigenous communities whose land this island belongs to; issues they face as a result of this history of colonialism.

A central and urgent theme of this book has been the climate crisis. Several chapters explore how Montréal has been at the forefront of movements for climate justice and the fundamental issues we confront in Montréal related to the environment and transportation. Other chapters explore the efforts to expand and preserve green spaces, the radical origins of Montréal's extensive bike network, and the present-day organizing of the Montréal Climate Coalition.

Another section of the book which deserved critical attention is the role of power in shaping urban planning. The role of planning is usually viewed solely as a technocratic process. The contributions in this book underscore how urban planning has created the architecture and backbone of the neoliberal city, but also how it can be a force to enact change from below.

Another section related to planning and power is the section on Housing and the City, which presents movements for social housing and the role of non-market co-operative housing in Montréal, as well as the challenges presented by neoliberalism and the role of the City of Montréal. This section explores the radical traditions of the co-operative housing movement in Montréal stemming from Pointe-Saint-Charles to the movements for social housing and affordable housing.

The neoliberal city has exposed the growing wealth gap through the housing crisis and gentrification but also through the trajectory of economic development in Montréal. In the section on the Economy and the City, chapters highlight the growth of precarious work as a key to understanding the city as a sweatshop. However, Montréal's economy is not completely subsumed under the logic of the market, as shown in the chapter on the development and potential that exist within Montréal and Québec's social economy.

A key section of the book rests upon understanding who has power within city hall and the participation of residents within decision-making processes. This section on Governing the City brings to the surface the mechanisms gained by movements for consultation and participation, but also highlights their limitations.

The section on Social Justice and the City is committed to discussing how structural inequality and racism are inherently urban issues and presents some of the movements that seek to address them. The section focuses on defunding the police and the politics of abolition within movements fighting against anti-Black racism, and the fights for a $15 minimum wage and sanctuary cities.

The book's final section pays homage to the legacy and ongoing grassroots neighbourhood organizing in Milton Parc and Pointe-Saint-Charles and how new urban movements in racialized inner suburbs such as Montréal-Nord have built novel institutions of counter-power and hope. These final chapters shed light on the dynamic campaigns and organizing across neighbourhoods and in this city; how they are not powerless to address the issues highlighted above but can be the embryos of broader social transformation in Montréal. As Ashley Dawson writes: "We are fighting for the city as it may be rather than the extreme city of the present" (Dawson 2017, 295).

This project, which has taken nearly two years of discussion and collaboration, has been a journey of analyzing the City of Montréal and the current juncture we face, but also of the contradictions that are present even within a moment where we have one of the most progressive city councils in Montréal's history.

Even as we live through this historical moment, why does it constantly feel as writers Jennifer Bolen and Jack Coughlin wrote in 2017: "Cities today have a choice between becoming active forces for social change or quietly acquiescing to the whims of global capital." The rest of this book seeks to grapple with this very question in our context of Montréal. To do so requires looking at the forces that shape our city beyond and within the halls of city council. In that view, we do hope to take the city and take our future collectively into our hands and neighbourhoods.

REFERENCES

Bolen, J., Coughlin, J. 2017. "Becoming a Fearless City." *The San Francisco Phoenix*, 19 July 2017. https://medium.com/the-phoenix/becoming-a-fearless-city-800b070dec4c.

Bréville, B. 2020. "The Return of the City State." *Le Monde Diplomatique* (English Edition), 13 April 2020.

Dawson, A. 2017. *Extreme cities: The peril and promise of urban life in the age of climate change*. New York: Verso Books.

Gonzalez, J. 2017. *Reclaiming Gotham: Bill de Blasio and the Movement to End America's Tale of Two Cities*, New York: The New Press.

MONTRÉAL, BETWEEN ORAL TRADITION AND HISTORICAL ARCHIVES

ERIC POULIOT-THISDALE

INTRODUCTION

Indigenous land acknowledgements have become customary at many public gatherings in recent years. They help underscore the relationships between Indigenous peoples and their traditional territories, including the cities and towns where most Canadians now live. Behind these previous eras of inter-nation diplomatic exchanges, however, lies a more complex tale of commercial rivalry, religious zeal, warfare, and geopolitics, which brought Montréal into existence as an outpost of New France in the mid-17th century, contributing, ultimately, to the establishment of three Mohawk Nation territories in the island's surroundings. Since ancient times, long before French fur traders and missionaries laid claim to Montréal, various groups of Algonquian and Iroquoian peoples periodically gathered on the island to settle disputes, trade, and socialize.

Archaeologists have suggested that the St Lawrence Iroquoians, encountered by Jacques Cartier in the 16th century, may have been dismantled by Algonquian rivals, with the few remaining survivors integrated into other First Nations communities. However, this theory is rejected by some Mohawks, who argue that they are the direct descendants of the people Jacques Cartier encountered 500 years ago. The term 'St Lawrence Iroquoians' is primarily used by archaeologists to describe the agricultural, village-dwelling people Cartier encountered shortly after he arrived in the St Lawrence River Valley in the 1530s. However, 75 years after Cartier's visit, Samuel de Champlain noted that the communities previously described by Cartier were nowhere to be found. Even though many relics were discovered around McGill University, as observed in an archaeological survey reported by the *Montréal Herald and Daily Commercial Gazette* in February 1861, until recently (2019), the physical evidence of a permanently established community has yet to be found.

Since the Oka Crisis of 1990, the Canadian population, as well as people around the world, have become better informed regarding the situations faced by Natives in North America. This has shed light on the poignant segregation that has affected Natives in Canada. This segregation has been in place since the creation of the reserves in 1851 and the adoption of the *Indian Act* in 1876. Since then, slowly but surely, many positive new developments have been taking place for Native peoples in Canada. Most recently, in Montréal, on 21 June 2019, it was announced that Amherst Street would be re-named *Atateken*—the Mohawk term symbolizing fraternity and peace. To this day, an ancestral tie to *Teotiake* (the Mohawk-language name for Montréal) remains in the oral traditions of modern-day Algonquins, Atikamekws, and Iroquois. This collective acknowledgement has led to declarations in recent years, both as opening remarks in public gatherings and included within email signatures, that Montréal is located on unceded land. This past summer (2020), with the movements created by Black communities in the United States following the murder of George Floyd by four police officers in Minneapolis on May 25, there has been a societal awakening and a North American movement to dismantle statues of patrimonial figures of those who promoted slavery and other immoralities towards Blacks and Natives.

In order to clarify the historical situation of First Nations originally living on the island of Montréal, this chapter will depict important details from both archival records and Native oral tradition.

HISTORICAL SITUATION OF FIRST NATIONS WITHIN MONTRÉAL

First, various conflicting theories have led to complexities in how the concept is perceived. For millennia, Montréal had been a neutral trading ground between the Algonquins located on the northern and western side of the island and the Iroquois located in the triangle that stretches from the Great Lakes to the St Lawrence Estuary to the north of what is now New York State. For certain, we know that Montréal was a trading area where peaceful commercial relations and exchanges took place during certain periods. However, some conflicts may also have occurred, as well as neutral periods between different factions.

Mohawks, Algonquins, and Atikamekws all claim that their ancestors are co-owners on the island of Montréal. However, their concepts of ownership are different from Western perceptions. As relations between these groups moved from neutral diplomatic periods to periods of sharing and peaceful interaction and sometimes to periods of conflict, this might explain why no permanent encampments or villages seem to have been established. Therefore, we could designate those different settlements that did occur as semi-permanent to semi-nomadic, considering the various relations occurring at the time.

Since the development of the fur trade was the most important economic objective for the European settlers, reaching the Great Lakes was their main priority. Therefore, it was essential to charm the First Nations into partnership. These partnerships were essential to allow the settlers to reach the route leading towards the western shore of the St Lawrence Estuary. However, the territory of the Mohawks of the Iroquois Five Nations Confederacy was not expected to be shared with the French, English, or Dutch settlers. It was Mohawk land, without any of the conceptual boundaries as the Europeans perceived it. This made it difficult for the settlers to impose their concept of ownership on the territory surrounding the Great Lakes and the St Lawrence Estuary.

Today, the theory of the St Lawrence Iroquoians is still not unanimously accepted by historians, whether Native or non-native, traditionalist or less-traditionalist. Anthropologists usually describe them as a "disappeared nation," while many others assert that the St Lawrence Iroquoians were the original ancestors of the current Mohawk nations of Akwesasne, Kahnawake, and Kanehsatake. It is likely that the diplomatic relations created by a defined group of Iroquois and other First Nations residing and trading along the St Lawrence River eventually developed symbiotic traditions during those years of exchanges.

MONTRÉAL IN NEW FRANCE

In an 1884 map from the City of Montréal archives entitled *"Historical Map of the Island of Montréal, Showing the positions of Forts, Redoubts and missionary chapels with the dates of their construction,"* valuable historical information is displayed. It outlines the history of forts built on the island of Montréal, indicating their date of construction.

From 1658 to 1672, eighteen were built, mainly after 1666 when the Carignan Salière Regiment was called forward. The Regiment had been called up since the Iroquois had never recognized the colonizers—neither the Dutch, English, nor French. Those structures surrounding Montréal included: Fort Ste Marie, Verdun, Pointe aux Trembles, La Montagne, Ste Anne de Bellevue, Riviere des Prairies, Lorette Mission, Pointe St Charles, Bout de l'Ile, Longue

Pointe, Saut au Récollet, and Lachine. Additionally, between 1665 and 1721, many other redoubts were built around Montréal, for example, St-Lambert, Boucherville, Laprairie, Varennes, Longueuil, and finally, the Lake of Two Mountains (*Deux Montagnes*) mission.

The map displays the location of forts and missions with a seemingly promotional note exposing that Montréal—the metropolis of the province of Québec—was founded by Paul de Chomedey de Maisonneuve in 1642 (and only later gained the right to self-government in 1832). The note reads:

> On May 18, 1642, Mr Paul de Chomedey de Maisonneuve was put in possession of the island of Montréal, which he governed for 24 years. The King gave to the settlers of the island a 250-ton boat with artillery: this was the last action made by Louis XIII in favour of Montréal; this Prince died 24 May 1643.
>
> 1643, this year, dogs were brought in, which made a great round every day in order to discover the enemies. The first combat of settlers of the island of Montréal with the Iroquois occurred where the Post office, the Bank of Montréal and Place d'Armes were built, in this fight, Mr de Maisonneuve killed the Chief of the Iroquois with a pistol. A great abundance of goods on the island of Montréal in 1649. […]
>
> Cruel wars of the Iroquois with the settlers of the island of Montréal in the years 1643-1645-1646 to 1653 and from 1657 to 1669.[1]

Other notices expose the administrative grant given to the Seminary of St Sulpice:

> Donation of the island of Montréal to the Seminary of St Sulpice, the contract of this donation was insinuated at the Châtelet [Little castle], on June 5, ratified by the King Louis XIV in May 1677 and registered in Québec City on September 20, 1677.

Next, an important reference reveals the previous denominations of First Nations establishments:

> The land on which Montréal was built was called before the arrival of J Cartier, Teiontiakons [meaning tip of the island] Tiotioake, Osera [or Asera], Hochelaga, Pitonague [Tsitonague] was located in the very place where Fort Ste Marie stood along the hillside at the foot of the current. The word Tiotiaki is still given to Montréal by the Iroquois.

Further, the text accompanying the map continues:

> 1663, on September 28, a civil and criminal justice system and a Sénéchaussé royale [Bailiwick] were established for the island of Montréal. […]
>
> 1665, Mr Paul de Chomedey de Maisonneuve left Canada for ever.
>
> 1689, August 24, 1,400 Iroquois massacred all the inhabitants living on the North shore of Lake St-Louis, from Ste Anne to Lachine.
>
> 1690, Great massacre on the island of Montréal, 20 settlers and soldiers and 30 Iroquois were killed.

---

1. This and subsequent quotations from the *Historical Map of the Island of Montréal* in this section from Beaugrand (1884); original in French.

The so-called "Great Massacre" of 1690 was the Lachine Massacre, in which the Iroquois avenged the betrayals of previous relations with both French and English settlers.

An important detail is missing from the promotional description offered on the map. One concerning what motivated the Intendant of New France to organize the arrival of the Carignan Salière Regiment in the first place (in 1665-1666). However, another map of the Five Nations, according to the Carignan Salières Regiment, was completed between 1664 and 1665 to organize their settlements; it was entitled *"Plan of the Forts Constructed by the Carignan Salières Regiment along the Richelieu River."* For the Mohawks ranging from present-day Ontario, Québec, and New York State, the perception of the Kingdom of New France was therefore non-existent. Feeling forced to join a foreign colony under the newcomer's conditions went against their principles, even though the King of France and his immediate subjects perceived everything very differently.

In fact, the King sent the Carignan Salières Regiment a viceroy, a new governor, and a new intendant, along with settlers and labourers, to resupply New France on 12 September 1665. The Saint Sebastien ship arrived in New France with Prouville de Tracy, the commander-in-chief of the troops, Rémy de Courcelle, the governor, and Jean Talon, the first intendant of justice, police, and finance. Jean Talon's duties included organizing provisions, ammunition, tools, and supplies for the maintenance of the troops, soldiers, and labourers. Meanwhile, Tracy and Courcelle were meant to protect the colony from the Iroquois. Thus, three Peace Treaties were signed in 1666 (22 May, 12 July, and 13 December) to control Mohawk families and their movements in Québec, Ontario, and New York, in a final attempt to subjugate them under the King of France.

However, on 1 September 1666 (between the second and third treaty), Talon wrote a letter to Tracy and Courcelle. His intentions were absolutely clear: the *Agnez/Agnes*, a term then used to describe the Mohawks, had to be exterminated. The letter was entitled *"1st September 1666 Memories Ojnaux* [Original] *Canada, A problem sent by M. Talon to Sirs de Tracy and de Courcelle to determine whether it is more advantageous to the King's Services to declare war on the Agnes than to make peace with them."*[2] Courcelle expresses why war seemed more advantageous than making peace, indicating that the current situation would seem extremely favourable for the annihilation of the Mohawks. The colony's primary objective was to open the route towards the Great Lakes for fur trade opportunities and resources. The letter starts by outlining a series of reasons why a war against the Mohawks should be conducted: "Problem: It is

2. Excerpts from this letter available in Pouliot-Thisdale (2017).

more advantageous in the service of the King to make war on the Agnez than to make peace with them."³

The letter continues:

> That the King, having sent a Regiment to Canada of twelve hundred men of war and troops regulated and commanded by good officers with orders to fight this Barbarian nation, which is so far delaying the establishment of the French colony. It would be more glorious to his Majesty and more useful to the country […].

Then, the strategic purpose of keeping the Algonquins and Hurons allied against the English, Agnez, and Onneiouts (Oneidas) was noted:

> […] the current conjuncture seems to be the most favourable of all those that can be experienced hereafter, because there is no time to lose for the destruction of this nation other than this one, that of the winter, or of the next spring […].

Talon weighed the advantages and disadvantages.

The opportunity foreseen by the French, like the alliance with the Algonquins, was then defined:

> […] the Algonquins and other savages will find themselves willing to return to this war, because they seemed seriously wounded from what was not left to them at the disposal of the Ambassadors taken prisoners by them. […] That the Mohawks, who seem to ask for peace with a sincere intention to maintain it well, will never want to hear it again, if they realize that we have formed a plan.

The strategic manipulation organized by the French against the Algonquins was conducted through evangelization and the return of captives. In fact, Talon demonstrated how he was able to convince the Algonquins to oppose the Mohawks:

> That the Algonquins and other savages can be commanded by authority. [For] The war or engage them in it by force of reasoning and by present, which disinterested them in the advantages they would have made of the prisoners whom they would have taken if they had agreed to it. That it is better to be at open war with the Agnez; than to have with them a weak peace of as long a duration as the most capricious of them please, considering even that it is more desirable that all the French soldiers and others regard them as declared enemies than to suppose them to be friends, since from them to us there is no more loyalty than between the most savage beasts.

Talon ended by explaining that: "The problem is that it is more advantageous to wage war against the Agnez than to conclude peace with them."

Let us not forget that what led to the Great Peace of Montréal in 1701 was more symbolic than it was effective. Through this so-called peace, the captives of intertribal conflicts related to the fur trade routes to the Great Lakes (captured since the wars of 1665-1666) were supposed to be released. Previous attempts at setting peace had not been respected, complicating voyages towards the Great Lakes. Since the start of the fur trade, those

---

3. See Pouliot-Thisdale (2017) for a complete discussion of the nine reasons outlined in the letter.

relations became jeopardized by all European colonies (English, Dutch and French). In the end, several archival documents expose numerous requests by First Nations to have their captives released, up until 1709—nearly a decade after this 'great peace.'

SULPICIAN MISSIONS

In the mid-1650s, the Sulpicians managed and financially contributed to Montréal's first religious congregations: St Joseph, Notre-Dame, and Charity (better known as the Grey Nuns). In 1663, they were officially entitled the Seigniorial Lordships of Montréal, and in 1664, the Seigniorial Lordship of Saint-Sulpice. From 1668 to 1680, taking advantage of the peace concluded with the Mohawks in 1667 following the aftermath of the so-called "three peace treaties of 1666," the Sulpicians went to Christianize the Mohawks on the shores of Lake Ontario.

Some Mohawks moved with the Sulpicians to *La Montagne Mission* (also known as *Fort de La Montagne*), located at 1931 Sherbrooke Street West, where the *Collège de Montréal du Séminaire* is currently located. A notice is engraved on top of the door stating:

> First Sulpician Mission
> de la Montagne
> Hic Evangeliz Abantur Indi [Where we evangelize the Indians]
> MDCLXXVII [roman numeral for 1677]

Other missions created during the same period included: Gentilly (1673-1676) and Ile-aux-Tourtes (1704-1721), which were eventually annexed to Two-Mountains. Mission Fort de la Montagne (1675-1705) was built around 1685 to evangelize Natives, and in 1696 it was relocated to Ahuntsic in Sault-au-Récollet (1696-1721), before finally moving to Two-Mountains (Kanehsatake) in 1721.

So, more precisely, some Algonquins, Hurons, and Mohawks followed the missionaries to *Fort de la Montagne* around 1675-1705 and then to Sault-au-Récollet in 1696-1721. They then moved to Two-Mountains (Oka) in 1721 as the Sulpicians claimed that the influences of alcohol in Montréal created devastating situations for the Natives. Of course, what was referred to as "moving of missions" by historians is still filled with speculation, considering the lack of detail regarding Mohawk families' previous locations and movements. These families would have occasionally moved their villages to access more fertile lands, avoid overexploitation of the land's resources, and respect natural cycles.

For Two-Mountains (Oka), the Mohawks' encounters with Anishnabes (Algonquins) and Nipissings clearly made them ethnologically and culturally somewhat different from the Mohawks of Southern Montréal. The number of intertribal conjugal unions observed in the Two-Mountains area is very high compared to Akwesasne and Kahnawake. Also, between 1825 and 1851, the Mohawk population of Two-Mountains represented only 30% of the total population registered at that time, with the remainder consisting of Nipissings and Anishnabes (45 to 60%), and a smaller proportion of Abenakis, Innus, and Ojibways (10 to 15%).

These Nipissings and Algonquins who were brought to Oka came primarily from the Ile-aux-Tourtes mission (1703-1726), which had previously integrated members from the Baie d'Urfe mission of 1685-1687. However, the Algonquins and Nipissings were nomadic and spent most of the year along the Temiskaming region between Québec and Ontario (this included Algonquin chief Paul Oka, for whom the mission was eventually named). As a result, they only spent a month or two each year at the Sulpician mission together with the Mohawks. Though during this time, many mixed unions were established, opening diplomatic relationships between the nations.

JESUITS: CAUGHNAWAGA

As for Kahnawake, the previous missions occasionally moved, as observed in the 1883 W. McLea Walbank collection in the Archives of Montréal. The document outlines a surveyor's plan showing the various positions occupied by the Mohawks of Caughnawaga from 1669 to 1883, compiled by the Reverend Nicholas Victor Burtin, Priest of Caughnawaga in the mid-to-late 19th century. The plan shows the locations occupied by Mohawk missions and villages in La Prairie, the Portage River, Sault-Saint-Louis, and Caughnawaga.

In 1673, about 40 Mohawks from Mohawk River (in present-day New York State) came to join. The Jesuits formally asked permission from Frontenac, the Governor-General of New France, for the organization of the Sault St-Louis mission in 1674. For several reasons, such as potential soil deterioration, the village moved several times over the subsequent years. These moves, in 1676, 1689, 1696, and 1716, brought it closer to Sault Saint-Louis, well known as the "Lachine Rapids." Still governed by the Jesuits, the village took the French name Saint-François-Xavier-du-Sault in 1676. In Mohawk, *Kahnawake* (1676) meant "at the rapids," *Kahnawakon* (1690) "in the rapids," *Kanatakwenke* (1696) "from where we left," and Caughnawaga (1716), which was reinstated as "Kahnawake" in 1980.

In 1667, around a dozen Oneidas joined St-François-Xavier-des-Pres, a small Jesuit mission newly established in the Lordship of La Prairie-de-la-Madeleine along the west side of the St-Jacques River. The Mohawks named it *Kentake*, which meant "the prairie." These were the survivors, those left on the land helpless and sick after the three so-called "peace treaties of 1666." The mission then moved five times between 1676 and 1716, each time moving further west, an average distance of about 15 km from the present-day Kahnawake. This could have been related to the populations' traditional ancestral movements, which occurred periodically until 1721.

Located between New York and Montréal, the Richelieu Valley region, Lake Champlain, and the Hudson Valley, it was located in a strategic point against English invasions. In the 1690s, several raids were carried out against the French. The Great Peace of Montréal in 1701 was meant to be the official initiator of the colonies and the western fur trade, when European expansion really started—mainly in La Prairie and St-Bernard Island. From 1730 to 1744, more than half of the Lordship of La Prairie-de-la-Magdeleine was granted to the colony. This lasted until the end of 1831, after which Montréal gained the right to self-government.

Access to the British colonies during the 18th century, and to the United States in the 19th century, contributed to creating divisions between the Five Iroquois Nations. This began during the French and Indian War (1754-1760) and the U.S. War of Independence (1775-1783). It continued in 1793 when conflict between France and Britain broke out, lasting until the War of 1812. The British did show some support to Natives but did not actually provide much substantial assistance, making their conviction contradictory.

The Iroquois posed fewer problems for Britain after the American Revolution. They were considered to be remaining within British territory, namely in Akwesasne, Kanehsatake, and Kahnawake. Compared to those from Akwesasne and Kahnawake, the neutrality of the Iroquois from Two-Mountains/Kanehsatake was noticeable during several conflicts with the newly independent United States. For example, during the War of 1812, only five to ten Mohawks from Two-Mountains took part in the *Indian Warriors* unit. This was potentially related to problems they already had with the Sulpicians who had claimed legal ownership of the land at Two-Mountains, granted by the King of France in 1717. It is the only Crown land that was managed by a religious entity.

REFERENCES

Beaugrand, H. 1884. "Historical map of the Island of Montréal, extract from Le Vieux-Montréal 1611-1803." City of Montréal, archival reference; drawing from P-L. Morin; published by H. Beaugrand, director of the Journal La Patrie newspaper, fonds VM066, S1, p005, **VM4, S1, D1**.

Bilharz, J. 2009. *Oriskany: A Place of Great Sadness/ A Mohawk Valley Battlefield Ethnography*. Fort Stanwix National Monument Special Ethnographic Report, National Park Service.

Pouliot-Thisdale, E. 2017. "War planned after so-called 1666 peace treaties." *The Eastern Door* (Kahnawake weekly newspaper), 1 December 2017. https://www.facebook.com/notes/eric-p-thisdale/war-planned-after-so-called-1666-peace-treaties-eric-pouliot-thisdale-the-easter/10155903302089266/.

Trigger, B.G. 1987. *The Children of Aataentsic: A History of the Huron People to 1660*. Vol. 2. Montréal and Kingston: McGill-Queen's Press.

Walbank, W.M. 1883. "Plan shewing the various positions occupied by the Iroquois Indians of Caughnawaga from the year A1669 to 1883D." Compiled from a copy belonging to the Rev Nicholas Victor Burtin Ptre O.M.I., and R.C. Miss. Caughnawaga. *Bibliothèque et Archives nationales du Québec*.

POWER AND THE CITY

MOSTAFA HENAWAY, JASON PRINCE, AND ERIC SHRAGGE

In this chapter, we present a framework for analyzing the forces that shape Montréal, and the counter-forces that contest them. These forces are unequal. The dominant ones are shaped by large-scale capital and business interests, often with allies in all levels of government. However, these forces have historically been challenged by unions, neighbourhood organizations, and social movements.

Most of the chapters in this book examine the tensions and conflicts that have been played out in Montréal; specific examples address housing, transport, the environment, local development, and many others. At times, Projet Montréal has responded positively to some of the demands of these movements; they have taken the initiative on creating green spaces and bike paths and on some housing issues. However, Projet Montréal, like many other municipal administrations, finds themselves confronted by the limited powers of city hall and a provincial government with opposing values and orientations. This is in addition to the competing demands of capital and local organizations.

This chapter will outline these forces. The question of power is fundamental and will be explored in this chapter and throughout the book. Our underlying assumption is that counter-power is necessary to challenge, limit, and overcome the power of capital and also the governments that support a view of urban development that prioritizes profit and growth over the environment and social and economic equality. This book is written and edited to support, describe, and encourage the movements, community groups, and labour organizations that are part of this opposition in these difficult times.

Conflict is central to understanding any city. Relations of power shape urban life, not only municipal politics. The city must be understood as the place that brings together the most critical competing and contesting forces in capitalist societies; these forces are played out in urban life. The dominant force is capital, including traditional 'productive' capital driving manufacturing industries in transportation, engineering, and agri-business in Montréal. But more important for our current time is the power of speculative real estate and finance capital, looking for ways to shape cities for the profit of their investors.

Opposition forces in cities include engaged citizens, community organizations, and social movements; working-class organizations, including unions and related groups, may also be included among this opposition. Because of their power and capacity to organize, these working-class organizations should be playing an even more decisive role at the municipal level. Conflict is shaped by contesting the direction of urban development, defined by private interests, versus the need for decent wages, housing, public services, security, and a healthy environment. These social needs are never guaranteed in a private market that prioritizes private development and profit.

PRIVATE CAPITAL AS CITY SHAPER

First, we will briefly trace Montréal's evolution to begin to examine the question of power and how urban priorities are shaped. In *Rebel Cities*, David Harvey argues that throughout the history of capitalism, the process of urbanization has been an essential means for absorbing capital and labour surpluses. This process shapes the way that the urban environment evolves. At the same time, it is integral to the accumulation of capital—the production of private wealth. The urbanization process also calls for finance capital, represented by a combination of bankers, developers, and construction companies acting in alliance to shape the "the urban growth machine" with state engagements as fundamental to its functioning (Harvey 2012).

Stein brings valuable nuance to discussing the role of capital in the urbanization process. As manufacturing capital is no longer the leading force in urban economic development politics, particularly in North American cities following the evacuation of certain manufacturing functions, real estate capital now rules. These two manifestations of capital are no longer in competition for land use in the city. This has opened up three vacuums in North American cities: a capital vacuum, a political vacuum, and a spatial vacuum. In describing the rise of the 'real estate' state, Stein notes:

> Real estate's gargantuan growth manages to overdetermine cities' economic, political, and demographic futures, pricing out certain actors and industries while encouraging

others. In the absence of any major competition, real estate dominates contemporary urban planning (Stein 2019, 34).

Stein also introduces labour and pension fund capital (more on this below), as well as criminal capital, into his fractional analysis of capital at play in our cities. He cites Vancouver urbanist Andy Yan, who describes the 'hedge city' phenomenon as the way that the wealthiest people in the world (the global 1%) have been "transforming urban high-rises from 'machines for living in' to machines for money laundering" (Stein 2019, 35). He further describes the current dynamic of real estate as "not a tide that lifts all boats, but a force that feeds off long-standing structural inequalities" (Stein 2019, 36). We see these trends as central to Montréal's development; as its economy has changed, so have the forms of economic power that shape the city.

Naylor (1990) summarizes the development of Montréal from its time as Canada's dominant economic, industrial, and banking centre, before losing ground to Toronto as head offices moved and the resource-based economy in western Canada boomed. From the 1970s to the end of the 1980s, manufacturing shifted to the suburbs, leaving Montréal as the epicentre only of unemployment and poverty. The provincial government's active role in economic development and related policies paid little attention to their impacts in Montréal.

These tendencies continued and were worsened with the shifts in production to the 'Global South' after signing "free trade" agreements. For example, Mostafa Henaway and Norma Rantisi's chapter in this book describes the changes in Montréal's textile and clothing industries as factories left the city to chase cheaper labour. Montréal Gazette business writer Hadekel updated Naylor's portrait, finding these trends have continued and evolved in the 21st century:

> as the new millennium began, more negative trends had crept in: offshoring, outsourcing, contracting out. Companies had found new ways to cut costs by sending work to places like China, India and Mexico at a fraction of local wage rates. More industrial plants began to shut their doors (Hadekel 2015).

With the havoc wreaked upon the Montréal economy by the two senior levels of government in favour of Canada's owning class, the city had to reinvent itself economically. The focus was on building a strategy for the development of the Montréal region, as declining industries, like textiles, transportation equipment, and commodities, were deeply impacted by globalization. At the time, Montréal had the highest unemployment rate in North America due to the compounding crises of the early 1980s. One pillar of the strategy was creating the third sector or social economy, described further in Jason Prince's chapter in this book.

The other pillar for Montréal's political and capitalist class was adopting the 1986 federal government-issued Picard Report, a policy document that contained the guiding principles for Montréal's transformation and economic revival (Hamel and Jouve 2008; Boudreau et al. 2006). The report concluded that Montréal's internationalization and the attraction of foreign investment were pivotal to its economic revival.

With encouragement from both the municipal and provincial governments, the city has taken a cultural turn in urban and regional development policy, with creative industries and tourism playing an essential role alongside real estate. These are in addition to Montréal's ongoing important role as an educational and life sciences hub. Montréal's local creative economy includes fashion, digital arts, film production, and videogame development, all encouraged by multimedia tax credits and directed investment into the culture and creative industries. Moser et al. (2019) argue that Montréal is typical of many cities that are responding to a post-industrial decline by trying to redefine their direction. Montréal's knowledge economy and its 21st century evolution have been driven by:

> a deliberate post-industrial transformation towards a knowledge economy and concentration of sector-specific expertise and capacity for innovation as the foundation of a new economic growth strategy (Moser 2019, 130).

This strategy has had some success, but at the same time, it creates new challenges, urban transformations, and displacements. Along with the growth of the knowledge economy and its growing need for a university-educated workforce, a primarily hidden low-wage economy within the expanding logistics, distribution, and service sector support this economic direction. The distribution and service sectors primarily draw from newly arrived immigrants and have produced an abundance of low-wage and precarious work (see further details in Henaway's chapter in this book: The City as Sweatshop). This economic development creates greater income polarization with the expansion of intellectual and creative work coupled with a low-wage sector of largely immigrant workers.

Montréal is also an internationally recognized centre for artificial intelligence research, host to some of the most surprising breakthroughs and practical applications of machine learning algorithms and other developments in this field. Along with robotics, these two vectors of change threaten to completely change the nature of work in the coming years.

Running parallel to these transitions is the ongoing role of speculative real estate and property markets, which, as we have argued above, plays a significant role in shaping the city. The neoliberal revolution has been grinding along for four decades now, and the testament can be seen in Montréal's landscape and redevelopment.

Henry Aubin's important contribution to Montréal's real estate history, published in the late-1970s, shows how the city was shaped to a large degree by foreign investment and their interests, drawing some startling conclusions:

> This story...is also a partial X-Ray of how power over a city works. It is a case history of what goes on beyond the parochial world of city hall... In Montréal's case, the bulk of influence over urban growth happens to come from outside of French Canada, even outside of Canada. Much of what the local radicals call with awe the 'local power structure' is in fact, little more than a collection of local yokels acting as agents and intermediaries for these much larger global interests (Aubin 1977, 16).

He continues:

> Perhaps the most important story told here is about one community's loss of control over the form and character of its own growth (Aubin 1977, 18).

The portrait of our city painted by Aubin has not substantially changed in the last 45 years, except for a bump in the mid-1980s when vast parts of Montréal's manufacturing sector were shuttered. Indeed, in the past 20 years, the pace has actually increased as capital searches for places to speculate on, buy up, and cash out. One change, however, is that the power of capital that is now redefining the City of Montréal has an increasing role for our own home-grown capitalist class: from finance to industry, pension funds, and even the vestiges of the powerful textile firms. These fractions of capital have continually reinvested their profits into safe havens looking for returns but have now turned inwards into our own city through real-estate development. There are many examples of how Québec-based capital is shaping the city through speculation and real estate development. For instance, AEDN is the real-estate wing of the Lieberman family, the same family which owns Lamour Inc., one of Montréal's largest garment manufacturers. Claridge Investments, another of the largest real-estate developers, is an arm of the Bronfman family, while Group Mach owned by the Saputo family has the National Bank as its majority investor.

This concentration of power over the economy and the city—over the decisions made about our very shelter, what kind of housing is built and where, about protecting our agricultural lands, the few remaining parcels of green spaces and biodiversity, about what kind of transportation system we have—these priorities are now all shaped by a handful of firms. Below are just a few of the major players:

1. Group Mach is a real estate firm valued at $10.4 billion owned by the Saputo family and the National Bank. It is involved in several controversial projects in Pointe-Saint-Charles.
2. Claridge Investments is an investment firm owned by the Bronfman family. It is recently involved in $200 million of investments with Ivanhoé

Cambridge. This covers 19 major development projects in Montréal, including projects in the Peel Basin.
3. Devimco Immobilier is a real estate developer, which was one of the major forces that gentrified Griffintown. It focuses on Transport Oriented Development (TOD) complexes and is now working in partnership with Fiera Properties and the *Fonds de solidarité FTQ*.
4. Fiera Properties manages $3.08 billion in real estate investments, including $600 million in Québec. It is a subsidiary of Fiera Capital, a private equity firm with assets of $143.8 billion that was previously a subsidiary of Desjardins capital.
5. Ivanhoe Cambridge—a "global real estate industry leader"—is owned by the *Caisse de dépôt et placement du Québec*, which receives contributions from 6 million Québecers and holds $40 billion in real estate holdings.

Examples of investors who are shaping the city

Ivanhoe Cambridge	The real estate subsidiary of the *Caisse de dépôt et placement du Québec*, which manages $365.5 billion dollars in assets. Ivanhoe Cambridge and Otéra Capital, which are subsidiaries of the Caisse, and through other partnerships, hold interests in more than 1,100 buildings, primarily in the industrial, logistics, office, residential, and retail sectors. It holds $60.4 billion in real estate assets, as of December 31, 2020.
Fonds immobilier de solidarité FTQ	Launched in 1991, the *Fonds immobilier de solidarité FTQ* promotes economic growth and employment in Quebec by strategically investing in profitable and "socially responsible" real estate projects in partnership with other industry leaders. The *Fonds immobilier* backs residential, office, commercial, institutional, and industrial projects of all sizes across Quebec. As of 31 May 2017, the Fonds immobilier reported 49 projects in progress, 45 properties under management, 14 million square feet of land and $69 million invested in affordable, social, and community housing. The *Fonds immobilier* is the real estate arm of the *Fonds de solidarité FTQ*, with $17.2 billion in net assets as of May 31, 2021. The "socially responsible" real estate component is 0.49% of the *Fonds de solidarité's* net assets.
Fondaction CSN	Fondaction-CSN invests in Quebec small and medium sized enterprises (SMEs) to help maintain and create jobs in the province, based on principles of sustainable development. It manages more than $1.7 billion in assets drawn from the retirement savings of more than 137,000 shareholders. Through its investments and commitments, either directly or through partner or specialized funds, Fondaction supports the development of more than 1,200 SMEs, including many social economy enterprises, that make a distinctive contribution to Quebec's economic, social and environmental development.
Fiera Capital	Fiera Capital is headquartered in Montreal. Fiera Capital controls over $172 billion dollars in assets. It is the 3rd largest non-bank owner of assets in Canada.

Examples of developers who are shaping the city

Devimco	Devimco, founded in 2005, is a major investor and developer in Griffintown. It has a proposed $2.5 billion dollar mixed-use development in the Peel Basin, and proposed development in Cabot Square at the former Children's Hospital. It also has an $800 million dollar Transit Oriented Development (TOD) in Longueuil. Devimco is a private firm which has been in partnership with *Fonds de solidarité FTQ*, *FondsAction CSN*, Claridge Investments, and with major investment by Fiera capital corporation.
Group Mach	Group Mach has significant investments in 6.5 million square feet of downtown Montreal office space (including the stock exchange tower and CIBC Tower). Mach now co-owns over 24 million square feet of residential and commercial properties and manages over 3,000 rental units in Quebec. Group Mach was owner of the CN Rallyards: "the initial tussle over Bâtiment 7 began in 2004 when CN Rail sold its disused property in Pointe-Saint-Charles to Groupe Mach for the symbolic sum of one dollar. The land spans 32.5 hectares – equivalent to 55 football fields, or one-quarter of the entire borough." Group Mach has major financial investments from Jolina Capital and Petra. Jolina Capital is the investment company of the real estate management firm and holding company, Group Petra. Group Petra's major investors include Jolina Capital, the family investment firm for the Saputo family. Vincent Chiara also owns several buildings with the Lieberman family, owners of Lamour Inc and AEDN Realty. They own six joint properties along Jean-Talon, east of the proposed Blue Line metro extension.
Iberville Development	Iberville Developments is owned by the Adams family. Founded by Marcel Adams, and previous CEO Sylvain Adams, the family's net worth remains at $1.5 billion.
Claridge Real Estate Investment	The investment firm of Stephen Bronfman's family, Claridge is a holding investment firm in food and beverage, renewable energy, and real estate. $200 million of equity has been deployed in 19 distinct development projects in the Greater Montreal Area and Quebec City.
AEDN	AEDN is owned by the Lieberman family (owners of Lamour Inc). They have ownership in buildings in Chabanel, Côte-Saint-Luc, Ahuntsic, and Montreal East. Their major partner has been Group Mach.
DevMcGill	Founded in 1998, DevMcGill is a major developer within downtown, Griffintown, the Quartier des spectacles, and Parc-Extension (Mile-Ex). DevMcGill has major partnerships with *FTQ Fonds de solidarité*. It was purchased by COGIR in 2018. COGIR now operates 14,000 rental units in 140 properties, with 1,500 condominium units sold, and over 50 retirement homes. COGIR sold 33% of its stake to Batipart investments, a French company headquartered in Luxembourg. Batipart is a major real estate firm which operates in Europe and Africa. Its owner, Charles Rugieri, is Frances 98th wealthiest person.
Carbonleo	Founded by Andrew Lufty (the president of large clothing retailer Groupe Dynamite and Garage), in 2012. He formed Carbonleo with two former Devimco partners who developed the *Quartier Dix30*. The company is also developing the $500-million Four Seasons Montreal in downtown Montreal, next to the Ogilvy department store on de la Montagne and Ste Catherine Streets. The Royalmount development is Carbonleo's most significant, with a cost of $2 billion. The Royalmount development is backed by L Catterton Real Estate (LCRE)—the real estate investment and development arm of L Catterton—which manages over $15 billion of equity capital. L Catterton is a joint venture between Catterton, LVMH (Louis Vuitton Moët Hennessy), and Groupe Arnault.

Recent examples showing how Montréal has been reshaped by these firms include the redevelopment of Griffintown, the massive shopping and housing complex in Royalmount and the vast spaces around Chabanel. There are also numerous other examples still the planning stages, such as the Hippodrome, areas around the Old Port, and parts of Lachine. These areas of the city have been, and continue to be, shaped by large-scale capital investment, ignoring issues of social need and the exclusion and displacement that come with profit-driven development.

GENTRIFICATION

One feature of gentrification is that it acts as a "value-capture strategy" by the rich, capturing the beauty and complexity that emerges from human efforts and in human communities. A hip neighbourhood made cool by poor artists who inhabit and breathe new life into a dead (read: cheap rent) part of the city is subsequently invaded by the rich. While displacing the poor and enriching the few, this paradoxically also threatens to kill the emergent beauty of the place that made it attractive in the first place. For example, this effect is visible in the Mile End, where lovely local shops give way to bland multinational chains.

As Jeremiah Moss (2017) in his book on New York City argues, this shift in population from working-class or poor to artists and hipsters, itself, is not gentrification. It is just the drops of blood in the water that attracts the shark, killing the neighbourhood and displacing residents with this new investment. The displacement and gentrification are reflected in how property is developed and who benefits from this development. In Montréal, the vast majority of housing built since 2000 is unaffordable to even the average household. As the last remaining available land in our central areas gets developed as high-end condos, supported by our municipal government—despite the modest limits imposed by the Projet Montréal administration—the city is quickly becoming something else.

Indeed, the gentrification process affects not just traditional working-class areas but all parts of the city. A study completed in 2012 concluded that even in Westmount, we can find gentrification, defined in that report as a situation where the current owners of the housing could not afford to buy it from themselves. The current occupants of these homes represent Montréal's upper 10% (CEGEP teachers, professors, engineers, small business owners, etc.), a group who now can only afford to live in NDG or St Henri. They are now being replaced by upper-income households from the local and international 1%. At the same time, speculative and land/property developments have faced opposition in many neighbourhoods of the city. Examples of neighbourhood opposition in this book appear in the chapters on housing and uppity neighbourhoods. Without this opposition, private capital would continue to shape the city unopposed.

Examples of who is shaping the city in different neighbourhoods

Neighbourhood	Developments
Montreal's Children Hospital/Cabot Square Four high rise condominiums over lands of the former hospital, purchased from Government of Quebec	1. Devimco has partnered with the *Fonds de solidarité FTQ* and *Fiera Capital* (FSZ-T) to build two 25-storey condo towers called EstWest. 2. High Rise Montreal, in partnership with *Batimo*, *Claridge*, and *Devimco* (*Batimo's* partners include *Claridge Investments* and *Ivanhoe Cambridge* investment) 3. 11 Atwater, by *Claridge Investments* and *Ivanhoe Cambridge* investment
Peel Basin/Adjacent Griffintown Federal government-owned 950,000 square-foot plot, slated for mixed-use development, baseball stadium, and a 2nd REM station	1. Devimco's project includes a $2.5 billion mixed-use redevelopment in the Peel Basin. 2. Claridge Investment 3. Lands now owned by Devimco, Canada Lands Company (with rights given for development)
Griffintown Redevelopment began in 2012, with City of Montreal approval for redevelopment	1. *Devimco-Fonds de solidarité FTQ*: Projet Griffin-Hexagone 1 and 2, St Anne apartments, Mary Roberts Condominiums 2. Mondev 3. *DevMcGill*: NOCA condominiums phase 1 and 2, along Lachine Canal 4. *Fiera Capital* Brickfield project: Maître Carré's 5. BentallGreenOak
Mile-Ex (Marconi-Alexandre corridor) Developments affecting Little Italy and Parc Extension	1. 6660 St Urbain: Canderel, in partnership with Claridge Inc. 2. 6795 Marconi: Microsoft research centre-Canderel, in partnership with Claridge Inc. 3. 150-53 Beaubien West: Canderel 4. Castelnau Condos: Ateliers Castelnau, Castelnau phase 3, TGTA partnership with DevMcGill 5. Mile Ex phase 1/Mile Ex phase 2: Mondev 6. 7250 Mile End: BentallGreenOak

The following section outlines the traditions of urban opposition—and its limits.

OPPOSITION

Those with wealth and power have largely shaped the development of the city. This goes back to the initial colonization and subsequent displacement of First Nations, through to periods of industrialization, more recent periods of economic redefinition, and increased financial and property speculation. With brief exceptions and some attempts at regulation, these developments have been supported and encouraged by governments at all levels. They often rationalized this with notions of trickle-down economics or by the idea that increased property values will increase city revenue—therefore, increasing services. However, power is not absolute, and contesting the direction of urban development—often based on basic needs for housing, collective goods, and green spaces—is central to understanding how the city actually develops.

Montréal has a long history of fighting back, which has taken many different forms. The chapters in the book provide many examples of community organizations and social movements, such as the environmental and housing movements, contesting forms of urban development while building alternative visions and practices to shape the city. Unions, workers organizations, community organizations, and social movements have been the vehicles that contest power. Montréal's history has seen these movements and organizations contest the power of private capital, both through labour practices and urban development speculation, as well as contesting the policies and practices of all levels of government.

Many examples in the following chapters illustrate the movements and organizations challenging power in Montréal, including those addressing housing, urban development, racial oppression, the environment, and those in specific neighbourhoods, like Montréal-Nord, Milton-Parc, and Pointe-Saint-Charles. Victories have been celebrated, where private sector development has been blocked, where co-operative and social housing has been expanded, and where green spaces have been protected. In addition, even in cases where specific gains are not made, social movements and community organizations have expanded public awareness and altered the programs and policies of both elected governments and parties in opposition.

When they are working at their finest, the potential of these organizations and movements is to form the real opposition to the established powers that shape the city: capital and its allies. Given the challenges of our time and the power of capital and its relentless pursuit of profit at any cost, we argue that our best hope is in building and maintaining alliances of these organizations and movements and using the power of city hall both to push back and stake out our ground on these urgent matters.

Urban social movements and community organizations both have their roots in contesting power. Although the two overlap, the difference between them can be understood by looking at their organizational forms and structures. Social movements tend to be broad and messy, including many different expressions; they mobilize periodically, bringing together the different components. Community organizations are place-based with a fixed structure, almost always registered as non-profits. These tend to have defined mandates (e.g. housing or anti-poverty) and can be members of coalitions or other structures like local community tables. Community organizations can be explicit in contesting power and making demands, or they may contest more quietly by creating new services and democratic spaces controlled by residents. They are a force for democratizing society and our cities and for building counter-power. Many community organizations do not engage in broader social change processes but provide a specific service to a defined clientele. Service providers do not mobilize or organize but can be part of wider coalitions that demand change. There is a dynamic relationship between broader social movements and community organizations, each supporting the other. None of this is new. There is a long history of organizing and advocacy for urban reform in Montréal and among movements of the working class. We will not elaborate on these themes and their complexity here.

MONTRÉAL'S COMMUNITY SECTOR

The 1960s brought a renewed and innovative community movement that played a crucial role in shaping urban life in Montréal.[1] Grassroots organizations in many Montréal working-class neighbourhoods formed committees, bringing together tenants, welfare recipients, and groups protesting social and economic conditions or focusing on local issues. In addition, new forms of democratic organizations were established to provide services, such as health clinics, youth organizations, legal aid programs, food co-ops, and services for women. These new initiatives were run democratically and extended a degree of control over daily life to residents. They also contested power, whether that of landlords, state organizations, or private sector business. The service components also redefined questions of healthcare, legal aid, and the patriarchal society to give local communities power to shape daily life.

At the time, many of these organizations were involved with sections of the union movement. They also got involved in urban politics with the founding of the political party *Front d'action politique* (FRAP), which contested the 1970 municipal election. Central to the FRAP platform was the idea of working-

---

1. For a more detailed description, analysis, and history of the community movement and its organizations see Shragge (2013) and Defilippis, Fisher, and Shragge (2010).

class and local power. The link between unions, working-class neighbourhood organizations, and an urban political party was unique, and threatening.

From the 1970s to today, there has been a continual growth of community organizations in every district in Montréal, not only in their number but also their importance in service provision, advocacy and organizing on many social issues such as housing and poverty. After 1990, they even branched into different forms of alternative and social economic development. Linked to their importance was the growth in their professionalism and recognition by the Québec government. This led to many community organizations receiving recurrent funding from the province. This relationship is complex, with many groups entering into a sub-contracting relation with the government to provide services. However, a few of these groups, despite receiving funding, continued to contest power.

For urban politics, there are two consequences. First, professionalization has led to a de-politicization of the organizations and a significant decline in organizing the people they serve, seeing them as clients rather than social and political actors. This, in turn, has weakened the political voice of many community organizations. Second, because the provincial government has a central role in health, social services, housing, education, and other similar sectors, the community sector sees the city as less important and does not target city hall for its demands (with a few exceptions, such as some housing groups). In addition, because funding is tied to social service provision and is linked to the provincial government, this reinforces the view that city hall is less important. At the same time, many individual staff members and volunteers from these organizations have been active in municipal political parties such as the Montréal Citizens' Movement (MCM) and Projet Montréal, bringing their experience and expertise.

Montréal has a highly organized community sector. As with other groups across Québec, it has negotiated a structure of representation and funding with the provincial government. Consequently, the community sector has a far more important relationship with the provincial government because of the wide mandate in sectors where these organizations often function as sub-contracted providers and because their primary source of funding is the province. This highly structured community sector has led to a high level of specialization, whether providing health, housing, women's services, or other social functions. Because the provincial government is the key funder and provider of these services, when community organizations do mobilize to demand benefits and services for their participants, they tend to target the provincial—and at times also the federal—government.

The main exceptions have been housing groups and environmental groups focused on increasing and improving green spaces and access to bike lanes—whose agendas are obviously "urban"—as well as some neighbourhood groups, particularly some community development corporations (CDCs),[2] attempting to control local development.

Another consequence of this highly structured development of the community sector is fragmentation and a silo effect, with greater specialization mirroring the respective departments of government at both the municipal and higher levels of government. The downside is that at the level of the city, there is no coordinated, organized community base that has the capacity to pressure the municipal government in any concerted way. Because of this, local fights remain local, and most of the formal, organized community sector does not engage with the municipal government.

PROTEST MOVEMENTS

Protest movements have had greater success in influencing city hall but primarily limited to the short-term. Two recent examples illustrate the role they can play, particularly when there is a receptive municipal government. The first is the vast mobilization to demand that the *Office de consultation publique de Montréal* undertake a public inquiry into systemic racism (see further discussion in the chapter by Eric Shragge in this book). The subsequent hearings received a large number of community interventions and briefs. The report was released in the midst of a huge international protest movement launched by Black Lives Matter. The mayor, Valérie Plante, publicly stated that the combination and convergence of these events served as a mandate for her administration to act. However, initial actions remained within the bureaucracy. This involved the appointment of a commission with an office mandated to act but then defining actions narrowly within the boundaries of the municipal government. The city was clearly not prepared to become a political ally and support an ongoing, longer-term process across the city. However, at the same time, the initial movement that pushed for the consultation and then subsequently participated in the process has all but disappeared (see the chapter on Montréal-Nord and an interview chapter with Robyn Maynard, for additional context, elsewhere in the book).

Similarly, the climate movement organized the largest demonstration in the city's history; yet, when the city announced its environmental plan in late 2020, there was hardly a response (see further details in the chapter by Joey El-Khoury). These examples illustrate the strength of these movements to mobilize and create public awareness, but also how they often fail: by

2. *Corporations de développement communautaire* (CDCs) are highly structured associations of community organizations that play an active role in many boroughs. Some have been active on issues and act as a voice for the wider community, for example, *Action-Gardien* in Pointe St. Charles and its ongoing role on housing and urban development (see chapter in this book by Bernier and Glorioso-Deraiche) and in Cote-des-Neiges on the redevelopment of Blue Bonnets. Other CDCs play a coordination role and do not engage through making public demands and advocating for them.

failing to sustain pressure on the municipal government; and by not critically monitoring responses and keeping pressure on, to hold even a sympathetic administration accountable to deliver the necessary change.

UNIONS

The role of unions and labour remains crucial to understanding power in the city. The power of capital, representing the few, is well organized and has access to extensive resources. For working and poor people in the city, trade unions remain a vital form of opposition. The city can become a space that concentrates working people and their power. In previous periods, trade unions led the fight for improved conditions and wages. The role that trades unions have played in contesting the power of capital and for a more egalitarian society has made them a major vehicle for working-class people to shape their workplace but also their political and social life. The militant trade unionism that Québec has become known for has its roots in the great workers' revolt of Montréal in 1919.

In December 1918, municipal public sector workers, from firefighters, sanitary engineers, and waterworks employees to the police, organized a united front and went on strike. In response, the City of Montréal was placed under trusteeship by the provincial government. The administration enforced strict management regulation and mass layoffs, further provoking the strike. The mainly Francophone strikers inspired other workers across the city, leading to widespread demonstrations and strikes. However, the dominating American-affiliated craft trade unions and labour council, the Montréal Trades and Labour Council (MTLC) condemned the strike. This caused a rift between new forms of local trade unions and the larger American affiliates. Workers in Montréal were also expressing their solidarity with the Winnipeg general strike and the strike movement growing continent-wide. By May 1919, more than 15,000 workers in Montréal had gone on strike.

By 1968, radicals in the Confederation of National Trade Unions (*Confédération des syndicats nationaux*; CSN) had gravitated towards the *Conseil central du Montréal metropolitain*, electing Michel Chartrand as president on a clearly socialist platform. During the 1960s, union density in Québec was roughly 35 to 45%, the highest in North America. The increase of state and para-public workers had joined the ranks of the CSN and the CSQ[3] (*Centrale des syndicats du Québec*), giving strength to the CSN as a major labour federation in Québec. By 1968 the CSN and CSQ had wholly broken from social democracy and sought a more pronounced anti-capitalist position (Güntzel 2000).

---

3. Formerly named the CEQ (*Corporation des enseignants du Québec*)

By 1968, the CSN had taken centre stage of the Québec labour movement. The call made by the document for a 2nd front was a call to action for trade unions to participate and foster radical action, along with community groups and social movements; it was a call for trade unions to be part of the growing mobilizations for social and economic equality. The radical turn in Montréal's political and social life had an enormous impact on workers' action in the city. There was reciprocity as a series of strikes mobilized support from the labour unions and allies to support striking workers.

Several dramatic examples brought out militancy and massive demonstration of support for workers, as well as confrontations with police. The taxi driver union (*Mouvement de libération du taxi*) campaign and strike against the Murray Hill company, which had been receiving favoured status for airport service. Next, there was the *La Presse* strike in 1971, provoked when Paul Desmarais purchased the paper. Attempting to transform the paper, he locked out typists to provoke further action. This backfired as unions held a mass demonstration to support the locked-out workers. Mayor Jean Drapeau had to use special powers to ban all demonstrations. The following day over 15,000 workers marched to the offices of *La Presse* (Sweetman, 2006). The common front strike of public sector workers in 1972 was played out in the streets of Montréal when over 210,000 public sector workers went on strike. Arrests of the three federation presidents led to widespread anger sparking the largest wildcat general strike in North American history in May 1972.

In 1974, a strike at the Robin Hood bread plant challenged federal government wage control policies when the Anti-Inflation Board rolled back a promised 11% wage increase. Sympathy strikes began at all flour mills in Montréal. The strike led residents of the city to hoard bread. A radical coalition of community groups supported the strike; the demonstration of 2,500 supporters was met with police repression, and eight people were shot on the Robin Hood property.

Around the same time, the 1976 Olympics were becoming a political lightning rod in the city. For Drapeau, the mega project would cement Montréal as a global city. Construction workers knew the mayor was short on time to finish the construction of the Olympic Park. Construction workers launched wild cat strikes, leading to a first decree for construction workers. At this point, Bourassa's provincial government attempted to place four construction unions under trusteeship. This resulted in a wave of action with a six-day strike at the Olympic Park. All of this was occurring within the context of a high degree of corruption and massive wealth being appropriated by the developers of the Olympics and its infrastructure. As reports from the time note: "both city and Montréal Olympic Organizing Committee officials expressed fears that a long delay could jeopardize the Games" (New York Times 1975, 72).

These examples demonstrate the historic militancy of the union movement in Montréal and the importance of working-class solidarity organizing. They also reveal the level of repression that the government is willing to enact and the direct confrontations with the city's police force that often follows.

The neoliberal offensive of capital that began reshaping Montréal in the 1980s had a significant impact on the power of trade unions. Deindustrialization led to declining membership. Then unions had to fight to maintain employment by accepting the demands of employers and government demands for investment. The role of workers organizations continues to complement new forms of opposition both inside and outside the unions.

Non-unionized immigrant workers are now leading new campaigns organizing against inequality and racism in our cities, which is a testament to the traditions of workers organizing. The campaigns for the $15 an hour minimum wage, or against abusive practices of agency work in key sectors of the economy of Montréal, show that the question of labour remains vital (see further discussion of the campaign for $15 in the chapter by Cheolki Yoon in this book). The Immigrant Workers Centre (IWC), along with other unions, such as the CSN's *Fédération du commerce* (FC-CSN), are organizing this layer of the working poor within the urban context.

CHALLENGING THE CITY ADMINISTRATION

The other fundamental role of trade unions is challenging the city administration itself. Canadian Union of Public Employees CUPE-429, representing white-collar workers, has challenged the city regarding its pension plans, wages, and work conditions. While CUPE-301 represents the vast majority of municipal employees, comprising 6,500 blue-collar workers from city services to waste management. CUPE-301 has argued that much of the deficit-cutting comes at the expense of their workers. For example:

> Last April 23 [2020], we learned that the City of Montréal would be cutting forecasted expenditures on average by 3.1% for all central services and in the 19 boroughs. It announced in the same breath that it would be asking all employees to pitch in with a $50 million contribution at a time when the City has a budget surplus of $251 million (CUPE 2020).

The union (CUPE-301) has also criticized the city's efforts to privatize some blue-collar work, for example, the outsourcing of janitorial services in 2019. Workers in the union voted to go on an unlimited strike, but it did not take place because of the pandemic hitting Montréal in 2020. However, this did lead to an eventual agreement, displaying the power of this union and the reliance of the city and its public services upon municipal workers. Workers' struggles remain central to ensuring maintenance of the public good for all residents.

A key challenge remains: how do we link (re-link) the struggles underway in Montréal's wider community and the work of the broader progressive forces fighting for social justice to that of the power of organized labour working within the city itself against the privatization of vital public services?

Trade unions also bring contradictions. As noted above, one of the largest real estate investors in Québec is the *Fonds de solidarité FTQ*, the investment arm of Québec's largest union federation (the *Fédération des travailleurs et travailleuses du Québec*). Indeed, it is the largest of its kind. According to labour researchers Ian Macdonald and Mathieu Dupuis:

> To our knowledge, no other labour movement in the world has established such a degree of control over workers' savings and taken such a large share of the venture capital market in its jurisdiction (MacDonald and Dupuis 2018, 3).

The Fonds exercises its power in newer and rapidly growing sectors of the Québec economy. For example, out of its $13.7 billion in total asset holdings, $8 billion is under active investment in Québec enterprises. The Fonds FTQ now claims to be the largest source of private venture capital in Québec (Fonds FTQ 2020).

Much of this investment is now tied up in real estate, accounting for $3.7 billion in 58 different projects. The Fonds asserted in 2017 that it had invested $115 million into affordable housing—a small fraction (3%) of its total real estate investment (see table for details). The contradiction plays out as most working people are confronted with a housing crisis due to gentrification and a lack of affordable housing. Labour should be confronting this, not profiting from such investments. The logic of the Fonds FTQ is that the returns will flow back to member-investors and create labour for some of its members—at least for a short while. However, such a strategy only erodes working peoples' ability to afford housing in Montréal.

The chapters in this book further examine this dynamic of conflict in Montréal. Whether it be in housing, green spaces, or neighbourhood development, the underlying tension is the same: Who is the city for? Who decides priorities and future directions? What are the underlying forces that shape the city? We have talked about the power of capital and the right of private ownership under capitalism, as well as the fragmented opposition, sometimes rising up in specific moments but mostly lacking organization and longer-term continuity (with the exception of some housing groups).

There have been exceptional moments when trade unions, community groups, and social movements converged to raise common demands and build a political program. The examples of the 2nd Front and the founding of FRAP were discussed earlier. Another important example was the *Sommet Populaire* in 1980. Former CSN president, Gérald Larose, describes it as follows:

> It was in this context that in April 1980 he took the initiative to organize a Popular Summit to respond to government strategies for the development of Montréal and to reorient trade union action with respect to living conditions. But above all, with this first Popular Summit, the Central Council of Montréal aimed to break the isolation between the trade unions and the people's organizations so that they could consult each other in order to identify prospects of mutual support (Larose and Hamel 1980, 141).

Subsequent collaboration between unions and the community sector has focused on provincial government policies, particularly budgets and austerity and the fight against cutbacks in social programs.

City hall has been by-passed as an important element for these struggles. This is a mistake: building power to reorient the city requires a remaking of the *Sommet Populaire*, with a convergence of demands and a program to reshape the city. Given this, what is the role of city hall? Where do the politics of the city fit in?

THE WEAK CITY

There is a fundamental challenge to Montréal controlling its own destiny. The province has constitutional power over the city, and the city faces enormous barriers under this constitutional arrangement. From Québec's perspective, Montréal is a mere office-boy gofer to the provincial government—clearing the snow and managing the garbage. The province directly determines the rules concerning municipal revenues, financing of major projects, distribution of resources to cities while also controlling health, social services, and education, among other issues. Despite some measure of municipal democracy, real political power remains outside of the city.

Dependence on the province is related to the fact that the city has little authority to raise its own revenues. Nearly 70% of Montréal's operating budget comes from property taxes, with the remainder primarily from user fees, permits, and fines. A "dirty little secret" is that commercial land use pays considerably more in municipal revenue than housing (Trent 2012). Yet, thanks to "free trade" agreements, the concentration of these commercial and industrial functions in the city have plummeted, leaving them gasping for condo development on these very lands.

There are two key barriers to the city acting as an autonomous force for change. The first is the structural limits, including the power of taxation based on wealth and income, linked to the constitution and structures of government. The second in the present period is the ideology, direction, and political base of the current provincial government. Both have an impact of creating barriers to municipal autonomy.

There are many examples of how the provincial government has used its power over the city. One example is the Turcot Interchange highway replacement project just minutes from downtown Montréal. Besides disrupting urban traffic flows for years, the massively overbuilt Turcot increases automobile flows, erodes health, spews carbon, promotes migration of residents to off-island suburbs, directly contradicting the City of Montréal's *Plan de transport*, adopted in 2008.

André Lavallée presented the perspective of the City of Montréal succinctly during the hearings of Québec's environmental review board (*Bureau d'audiences publiques sur l'environnement*; BAPE). Sitting beside Mayor Gerald Tremblay on the evening of 16 June 2009, he stated:

> I'm going to answer you as frankly and as concretely as possible. First of all, I want to use an image, very briefly. In a few days, and we were talking about this with the Mayor [of New York] before the hearing began this evening, in a few days the City of New York will close the intersection, the meeting of three major streets on Broadway at the level of Time Square. The City of New York is going to pedestrianize part of Time Square in order to provoke, because it wants to provoke a major change in behaviour towards the centre of New York. What the New York City authorities have observed is that there are 55,000 vehicles trying to pass through the Broadway intersection, there are 360,000 pedestrians, everyone is trying to pass through the same place, people are driving at 4 miles an hour, polluting the whole environment, creating a very unpleasant urban environment. I am not proposing to you this evening to close the Turcot interchange, but I think that the image I just used suggests the spirit in which we want to work.

Yet, the Québec Ministry of Transport went ahead and rebuilt the Turcot Interchange as planned—at a capacity nearly three times larger than the original design.

The city also opposed the A25 Bridge connection to Laval, as well as new off-island highway developments that funnel cars towards Montréal. This list could go on. While the city has prioritized keeping cars off the island, the province is busy bringing them in. The ideological and political conflict around transportation is at the centre of determining the direction of urban development and the municipalities' self-determination (see other chapters that discuss transport choices for Montréal in more detail).

In addition, we live in a context of the growth of right-wing nationalist governments around the world. These governments share policies that either deny or severely limit efforts to address climate change, are anti-immigrant, pro-big-business (through their tax policies or other forms of support), and support austerity measures, in particular attacking social programs.

Montréal finds itself in this situation, though less so than cities in the U.S., particularly under Trumpism. We have a pro-business, anti-immigrant government in Québec that has little representation from Montréal. It has displayed its anti-immigrant stance through Bill 21 and other policies to limit permanent immigration. Montréal is a centre of immigration, racial and cultural diversity—we celebrate our diversity every day—which has led to conflict on this question.

On issues of the environment, despite the provincial government's rhetoric, it uses its political power to prioritize building highways to move more cars into the city, in direct conflict with municipal priorities. For example, the *Fonds vert*—a $6 billion war chest for fighting climate change—has been mired in controversy since it was founded. And it has been used for anything but its core purpose. Will it be used to build the Third Link, to increase automobile use in Québec City? Should the *Fonds vert* not be turned over in its entirety to cities to reduce automobile use—especially as transportation is the principal source of greenhouse gas emissions in Québec?

Throughout this book, contributors raise a number of questions: what has the municipal government achieved and under what circumstances? What are its limits, and how has it tried to go beyond these and push both the private sector and 'senior' levels of government? What are the current burning issues, and what needs to be done next? These questions play out in many ways: around battles to protect green spaces, expand public and active transit, promote living wages, or improve neighbourhood planning and zoning; around demands for greener buildings, and action on environmental issues like climate change, and on many social issues such as urban poverty and housing. At least at the level of recognition, these issues have been major priorities for Projet Montréal, both in boroughs and at the city-level, despite limited implementation.

Given the limits of the city as the weakest level of government, both politically and financially, and given the power of capital, what is possible?

The challenge is to see municipal government as the vehicle to bring about the limited changes it can within its mandate. But it must also become an advocate for the broader changes necessary to address current challenges like climate change, racism, and inequality. The city needs to situate itself as an ally with active community groups and social movements and work in conjunction with them to further their demands. The city should carry them outside of the usual boundaries of the municipal mandate, to pressure higher levels of government, to challenge private capital, and to play a public role in educating the residents of the city on a variety of issues. David Harvey, in his book *Rebel Cities*, argues:

> the right to the city has to be construed not as a right to what already exists, but as a right to rebuild and re-create the city as a socialist body politic in a completely different image—one that eradicates poverty and social inequality, and one that heals the wounds of disastrous environmental degradation. For this to happen, the production of the destructive forms of urbanization that facilitate perpetual capital accumulation has to be stopped (Harvey 2012, 138).

CONCLUSION

The underlying question for us is: can a municipal government ally city hall with other progressive movements and organizations to transform the city? Can this alliance act as a counter-weight to the forces of capital that shape our cities and the wider ecological, social and economic disasters we face? What are the steps necessary to do this? What is the role of local organizing to build opposition and alliances, and what is the role of municipal political parties? Can local movements and community organizations be part of an alliance but also act to push Montréal toward goals that may not be part of its mandate? We do not have easy answers to these questions, but we want to explore the dimensions of this problem and approach.

Critically, we believe the time is short, given the issues described above. To be blunt, they are winning. Without a strong counter-weight, our society's current dangerous directions will accelerate.

Is it possible to build a counter-power at the municipal level? What are the possibilities and opportunities, and what are the barriers and limits? The City of Montréal represents the level of government least able to bring about these changes. But if we are to face the great challenges of our time, if we aim to bring about the changes described throughout this book, then the municipal level of government has to become part of this counter-power.

We must take the city and make the city our vehicle for change and our collective voice for the radical change we need right now. Before it is too late.

REFERENCES

Aubin, H. 1977. *City for Sale*. Toronto: James Lorimer & Company.
Aubin, H. 1977. *Les vrais propriétaires de Montréal*. Montréal: Éditions l'Étincelle.
Boudreau, J.A., Hamel, P., Jouve, B., and Keil, R. 2006. "Comparing metropolitan governance: The cases of Montréal and Toronto." *Progress in Planning* 66(1): 7-59.
CUPE (Canadian Union of Public Employees). 2020. "Money is not an issue with the City of Montréal." 28 April 2020. https://cupe.ca/money-not-issue-city-montreal.
Defilippis, J., Fisher, R., and Shragge, E. 2010. *Contesting Community: The Limits and Potential of Local Organizing*. New Jersey: Rutgers University Press.
Fonds de solidarité FTQ. 2020. "Who we are." 30 November 2020. https://www.fondsftq.com/en/a-propos/qui-sommes-nous.aspx.
Güntzel, R.P. 2000. "'Rapprocher les lieux du pouvoir': The Québec Labour Movement and Québec Sovereigntism, 1960-2000." *Labour/Le Travail* : 369-395.
Hadekel, P. 2015. "Stagnation city: Exploring Montréal's economic decline." *Montréal Gazette*, 15 January 2015. https://montrealgazette.com/news/local-news/montreals-economic-stagnation/.
Hamel, P., and Jouve, B. 2008. "In search of a stable urban regime for Montréal: Issues and challenges in metropolitan development." *Urban Research & Practice* 1(1): 18-35.
Harvey, D. 2012. *Rebel cities: From the right to the city to the urban revolution*. New York: Verso books.
Larose, G., and Hamel, P. (1980). "Syndicats et organisations populaires : élaboration d'une perspective de lutte sur les conditions de vie." *International Review of Community Development / Revue internationale d'action communautaire* 4(44): 141–145. https://doi.org/10.7202/1035052ar.
MacDonald, I. T., and Dupuis, M. 2018. "Managing workers' capital? Limits and contradictions of labour investment funds." *Economic and Industrial Democracy* 0143831X18793025: 1-26.
Moser, S., Fauveaud, G., and Cutts, A. 2019. "Montréal: Towards a post-industrial reinvention". *Cities* 86: 125-135.
Moss, J. 2017 *Vanishing New York: How a Great City Lost its Soul*. New York: Dey Street Books.
Naylor, T. 1990. "Business Prospects: Decline and Fall." In *Montréal: A Citizen's Guide to Politics*, edited by J-H. Roy and B. Weston. Montréal: Black Rose Books, pp. 70-75.
New York Times. 1975. "Montréal Olympics Troubled." May 14, 1975.
Shragge, E. 2013. *Activism and Social Change: Lessons for Community Organizing*, 2nd ed. Toronto: University of Toronto Press.
Stein, S. 2019. *Capital city: Gentrification and the real estate state*. New York: Verso Books.
Sweetman, G. 2006. "1972: The Québec general strike." *Libcom*. https://libcom.org/history/1972-the-quebec-general-strike.
Trent, P.F. 2012. *The merger delusion: How swallowing its suburbs made an even bigger mess of Montréal*. Montréal and Kingston: McGill-Queen's University Press.

PART I.

NATURE AND THE CITY

DESPAIR AND HOPE: A STORY OF MONTRÉAL'S NATURAL SPACES

PATRICK BARNARD

THE BEAUTY OF NATURE AND URBAN SPRAWL

Montréal Island and the adjacent Île Bizard rest in the middle of one of the most extraordinary ecosystems in North America. On one side, the Ottawa river, once a huge logging sluice, feeds into the Lake of Two Mountains, and on the other, the mighty St Lawrence pushes its way relentlessly from the Great Lakes to the Atlantic Ocean. The Lachine rapids—literally "the China rapids"—foam like the sea, taking their name from Jacques Cartier's mistaken assumption that he had found a Northwest passage to China.

From the beginning of its European colonization, Montréal has been shrouded in myth. The natural reality of the place has always been imposing. This environment is truly riverine: surrounded by water, the 50,000-hectare island possesses underground streams that few residents have heard of. The prevailing humidity produces abundant snow; in late spring and summer, the remaining natural spaces become incredibly verdant, almost semi-tropical. The island of Montréal lies in the heart of the region of Québec, with the province's highest level of biodiversity.

Yet, Montréal has one of the lowest amounts of natural spaces preserved per capita among Canadian cities. For thirty years—until the city's most recent administration—municipal officials have facilitated the destruction of their own natural patrimony. During this time, Canada as a whole lost 90% of its urban wetlands. Montréal is no exception to this despoliation; the attack upon nature in this supposedly "green city" has been merciless.

How is that possible when Montréal has so many single-family houses with lawns, often decorated by trees? After all, the potential threat of political separation resulted in a lower rate of economic growth than in Toronto, so Montréal, spreading out horizontally, looks more benign and nature-friendly than its densely populated urban rival. In fact, this genial suburban atmosphere outside Montréal's urban core represents, even hides, the very poison that has destroyed the city's natural environment over the last two generations.

A 2019 report shows that Montréal ranked below nearly all Canadian cities with respect to the area of parkland per capita, at a rate of only 2.4 hectares per 1,000 people (Park People 2019). The city also performs poorly when observing the percentage of parkland that is considered 'natural area' (Park People 2019).

After the Second World War, Montréal's political leaders and citizenry embraced the ideals of the 1950s without much reflection—a new car, the family home, a move from inner-city apartments to houses in the burgeoning suburbs. On the island, there were still farms and forests that offered real estate developers the land to buy, build on, and profit from. This "land uptake" process in Montréal was extremely high, as single, nuclear families occupied an increasingly large amount of previously undeveloped land. The result was an extremely high incidence of urban sprawl: uncontrolled, low-density development at the urban edge. In fact, among Canadian cities, Montréal is the champion of urban sprawl.

Here is the great suburban paradox. Households move to the suburbs to gain access to bits of greenery; however, as the process continues, they help destroy the very nature to which suburbanites feel they have escaped.

Recent research indicates the scale and intensity of the problem (Dupras and Alam 2015; Nazarnia et al. 2016). Urban sprawl "has increased exponentially in Montréal since 1951"; for example, between 1971 and 2011, it has "increased 26-fold" (Nazarnia et al. 2016, 1229). As Dupras and Alam (2015) explain, the increasing cover of urban areas has led to significant declines in the area of croplands and forest in Metropolitan Montréal and has had severe negative impacts on ecosystem services. Some of the adverse effects of this urban sprawl include: "Soil sealing, increasing scarcity of land for renewable energy and food production, increase in greenhouse gas emissions and water pollution, loss of habitats and valuable ecosystem services, lower infrastructure and public transportation efficiency, long commuting times, and reduced civic involvement in the society" (Nazarnia et al. 2016, 1230). These damaging impacts occurring in post-War Montréal reinforce each other. The end result is radical habitat loss in a unique environment whose ecology remained misunderstood and under-appreciated by its own denizens.

CITIZENS DESPAIR, HOPE, AND DESPAIR AGAIN

Interestingly, as environmental deterioration intensified in the 1970s, citizen environmentalists began to raise the alarm about what they saw happening all around them. Like elsewhere in North America, damage to the natural environment engendered pushback from civil society. A dynamic set in: ecological damage, protest, partial reparation, then more harm and more protest. The ups and downs of the Montréal environmental movement over the last 40 years reveals a tremendous amount about local politics—and the deeply negative consequences of real estate development within the framework of untrammelled and unquestioned capitalism. Many people were involved in this history. Here we will follow the journey of two particular environmentalists, Sylvia Oljemark and David Fletcher (founders of the Green Coalition—Coalition Verte).

From the late 1940s, Sylvia Oljemark has lived in the same small house in the Village of Saraguay next to the Rivière des Prairies (aka the "Back River") on the northern part of Montréal Island. The Oljemark family were amazed to be living a semi-rural life while at the same time inhabiting a twentieth-century city. Nearby were forests and farmers' fields.

By the 1970s, most of this landscape was gone, replaced by suburban development. In July 1977, the Saraguay villagers learnt that the entirety of the nearby Saraguay Forest would be razed to make way for fourteen apartment blocks, two shopping centres, Twin Towers on the edge of the "back river," and a marina.

Sylvia and her own mother worked with many others until Montréal mayor Jean Drapeau reversed the zoning change that would have permitted the forests' destruction. The *Société d'Horticulture et d'Écologie du Nord de Montréal* then promoted the conservation of Saraguay Forest as a *Parc Naturel Urbain*. In 1979, the Québec provincial government conferred rights to acquire and manage regional parks to the Montréal Urban Community (MUC), first allocating $10.5 million to fund land acquisition, supplemented by $2 million when Saraguay Forest was purchased outright. Decades later, the MUC was superseded by the City of Montréal and the Agglomeration Council; however, this breakthrough has had an ongoing impact.

Citizen action from a small locale triggered a significant change in government policy at both the provincial and municipal levels, resulting in six separate nature parks from 1979–1982: Pointe-aux-Prairies, Île-de-la-Visitation, Bois-de-Saraguay, Cap-Saint-Jacques, Bois-de-Liesse, and L'Anse-à-L'Orme. André Bouchard of the *Jardin botanique de Montréal* commented: "The campaign to conserve Bois-de-Saraguay was the catalyst for the creation of the MUC regional parks network."[1] Yet, at the same time, the acceleration of urban sprawl in Montréal was becoming more pronounced. Yes, nature parks were created, but an incredible amount of natural and agricultural space was lost. Most of the lost space, as well as that remaining, was in the western part of Montréal since urban sprawl had spread historically from east to west. However, the MUC had come into existence, and there was a new authority to allocate funds. In 1987, the MUC adopted its first *Schéma d'aménagement*—but it contained no greenspace conservation program!

At this point, many citizens gathered around Sylvia Oljemark and David Fletcher, the charismatic teacher who specialized in taking students out into nature to learn.

It was David Fletcher in the 1980s who first proposed that a vast conservation zone be created in the west of Montréal island. His vision proved to be prophetic since these very lands will become part of *le Grand Parc de L'Ouest* created by the Plante administration in 2019... 30 years later.

But the late-1980s and early-1990s were days of hope that ended in despair.

On 14 May 1988, thirteen groups invited the public to demand that the MUC initiate a Green Space Program; 3,000 people attended the event. This momentum led to the formation of the Green Coalition in 1989 and a huge battle pitting suburban mayors against their own citizens. It is important to note that suburban citizens, not their elected officials, led this fight for nature.

First, the mayors pulled a massive amount of money from the Green Program—then deep protest compelled the MUC to completely reverse itself, appropriating $200 million for what was called *La stratégie d'action pour les espaces naturels*. Serious acquisitions were made, $100 million worth, and at this point, 3.2% of Montréal's territory was protected, which was far behind the provincial target of 8% for the city. Interestingly, though the Québec government had set this target, it contributed very little funds to meet it. Another $100 million remained to continue the MUC action plan, but in 1992 the Urban Community withdrew this money and instituted a spending moratorium that would last ten years. This destructive action was led by a suburban mayor representing one of the wealthiest jurisdictions on the island. Now, mayors not only attacked environmental spending, but they also seriously damaged the very constituents they thought they were representing.

The lesson was clear: significant nature initiatives could come from the municipal structure, but what the mayors gave, they could easily take away. And citizens were always the catalysts for positive change.

---

1. Sylvia Oljemark is still a Montréal environmental activist and member of the board of the non-partisan Green Coalition. I have spoken at length to her, and, with her permission, the discussion here draws directly from her monograph, "Montréal's Green Space Story" (see Oljemark 2011).

THE DARK AGES

The next 25 years (1992-2017) was a dark age for Montréal's natural spaces. During this period, citizen activists and municipal authorities, both in the urban core and the suburbs, were at loggerheads. Two uninspiring mayors, Gérald Tremblay and Denis Coderre, served for much of this period. Tremblay's administration ended in a massive corruption scandal and his resignation, while Coderre was openly hostile to the environmental work needed.

Tremblay always wanted to seem as if he were doing the right thing. He did end the acquisition moratorium that he had inherited, saying in 2002 that Montréal needed between $100 and $200 million to purchase natural spaces. During his decade in office, he proposed an expenditure of $12 million per year, but the actual spending was only one-third of that—nearly 70% of the money set aside was never spent. Nonetheless, Tremblay managed to increase the coverage of conserved natural spaces from 3.2 to 5.2% during his tenure, an average of 100 hectares added per year, still far short of what was needed.

Coderre was worse, lacking both Tremblay's PR interest in the environment and the will to at least do something.

Consistently during Coderre's term (2013–2017), citizen advocates raising concerns for the environment were met with antagonism and contempt. His contribution to Montréal's inventory of protected natural spaces was minimal: a sum total of 61 hectares (0.12% of the island), averaging just 15 hectares a year. Nonetheless, officials at various levels of municipal government did feel a sense of shame, just as they had a generation before, so in 2015, the city's executive committee formally adopted a target of 10% for conserved natural spaces. With only 5.3% preserved at the time, this meant that more than 2,000 hectares were needed across Montréal to meet the target.

This new target was part of an important turning point—one brought about by citizen activism.

The year 2015 was significant because civil society successfully pushed to get their elected officials "above" to command a zoning change "below" to protect the natural environment. A major alteration was made at the higher planning level of the Montréal Agglomeration's *Schéma d'aménagement et de développement*. The pressure exerted by a group of citizens called *Les Amis du Parc Meadowbrook* made all the difference.

In fact, Montréal's political leaders had resisted this kind of proactive initiative, with directives from a higher planning level, precisely because it would set a precedent and clearly show what could be done if the political will to prioritize the environment really existed.

What was at stake was a unique ecological zone. Near the railway tracks in the west of the island of Montréal is a 57-hectare greenspace (Meadowbrook Golf Course) with rare trees, beautiful stretches of grass, and a stream running through it. In 2009, a Montréal Agglomeration body (the Labrecque Commission) recommended the area's "transformation into a nature park." In January 2014, the PDM (*Projet de Plan de développement de Montréal*) Commission of Montréal's Office of Public Consultation (OCPM; *Office de consultation publique de Montréal*) urged the city to formally adopt the Labrecque recommendation. However, the southern portion of Meadowbrook was zoned "residential," and an ambitious real estate developer wanted to build on it.

In November 2014, Montréal's all-powerful executive committee was still refusing to act on the advice from the Labrecque Commission (2009), the OCPM (2014) and the Agglomeration Schéma. The City of Montréal, at that point, still did not want the greenspace to be fully protected. Officials were applying the tactics of complete inertia that characterized the Tremblay-Coderre era: make promises but do not carry them out, pass appropriations but leave them unspent, leave advice unheeded, and always use the weight of inaction to paralyze the forces of change. But *Les Amis du Parc Meadowbrook* had a dynamic lawyer: Campbell Stuart, ex-mayor of Montréal West and a passionate environmentalist. Both he and the leadership of *Les Amis* knew they had to begin an intense public information campaign. A letter-writing blitz addressing key municipal politicians was followed in January 2015 by a phone campaign to all city councillors, focusing on the members of Montréal's executive committee. At the same time, the campaign was helped by the fact that a prominent municipal official had been "outed" for improper negotiations with the private company that wanted to build on the golf course.

The public pressure was intense, and it continued down to the last hour before the crucial meeting of Montréal's highest officials. On 22 January 2015, the city's executive committee voted to adopt the new plan, including changing Meadowbrook's designation from "residential" to "large green space or recreational." The path was now clear for the area to eventually become a "nature park." The citizens had prevailed.

Victory in the effort to save Meadowbrook marked a victory in what had been a protracted struggle, a rare exception during the Coderre years, which on the whole were grim for Montréal's environment. Nonetheless, the Green Coalition and others kept up the fight. They continued attending council meetings, organizing demonstrations, writing, and phoning, targeting independent municipalities, boroughs, and the City of Montréal itself.

VALÉRIE PLANTE BRINGS HOPE

In 2017, the pendulum swung back. Campbell Stuart, an environmental lawyer with *Les amis du Parc Meadowbrook*, the Green Coalition, and other activists, were instrumental in getting the municipal opposition party Projet Montréal to make a decisive commitment to nature.

Projet Montréal officially adopted an election promise to create a very large urban park radiating outwards from the existing wetlands in the nature preserve of *L'Anse-à-L'Orme* in the far west of the island. Once again, citizens played a key role. One highly active local group (*Sauvons L'Anse-à-L'Orme*) led by Susan Stacho, a resident of Pierrefonds-Roxboro, consistently raised awareness of the value of the remaining natural spaces in the western part of Montréal.

That November, Coderre was defeated by Valérie Plante, who came to office carrying a pledge to create a Great Western Park.

During the early days of the Plante administration, Nature itself had a decisive say when massive floods swept through in 2017 and again in the spring of 2019—impacting the very area described as a future *"grand parc"*. It was almost as if the Montréal landscape itself was speaking up in the environmental debate.

On 8 August 2019, Plante and her party called a press conference in Cap-Saint-Jacques, a beautiful green area of Montréal, to announce the creation of the promised *"nouveau grand parc urbain."* Much of "The Great Western Park" drew together existing protected areas into one integrated space. But additionally, she specifically mentioned the protection of 175 hectares of wet meadows previously coveted by real estate developers, and she made an unequivocal statement of her purpose:

With more than 3,000 hectares in area, the Great Western Park will become the largest municipal park in Canada. It is an historical moment that marks a major turning point in terms of the protection of wetlands and the valuing of natural spaces. This initiative is part of our desire to protect 10% of the territory of Montréal. Sue Stacho of *Sauvons L'Anse-à-L'Orme* said the announcement was "everything we've ever wanted," and "it sets a precedent for the protection of natural spaces in urban environments for the rest of Canada" (Sucar 2019).

Plante finished 2019 by announcing the $73 million purchase of the 140-hectare wet meadows owned by the real estate promoter Mario Grilli (Corriveau 2019).

Plante quite accurately stated: "In five months, our administration has acquired more natural spaces than in the last fifteen years" (Lapierre 2019). Nearly half of the purchase money came from infrastructure relief supplied by the federal government.

The wet meadows at the heart of Plante's initiative are former hayfields that now provide essential habitats and hydrological functions, acting as sponges in the spring and attracting a great number of birds along the re-naturalized hedgerows and trees. Lack of knowledge regarding the high ecological value of the land, including its essential hydrological functions, led to their neglect. But Plante and her party followed through on an election promise by purchasing them.

Now, 5,000 new suburban houses—classic urban sprawl—will not be built there; instead, a natural space has been gained for all Montréalers.

DARKNESS THREATENS AGAIN

> *"We need to ensure that not even the smallest marsh is lost."*
> Prof. Rodger Titman[2]

The story of Montréal's natural spaces is one of light and dark. Almost always, the environment comes at the very bottom of planners' lists of priorities. What is now required is a complete reversal of values. The guiding principle of an ecological city must be: The Environment Comes First. However, there is a direct conflict between that imperative and developers' obsessive need for profit.

The Plante administration was ecologically bold when it purchased the Grilli-owned wet meadows. However, as the focus of attention moves closer to the city centre and runs into entrenched economic interests, Mayor Plante and her team have become far more cautious. The much-anticipated Parc d'Anjou has failed to see the light of day. Why? Because real estate lobbyists pushed hard against the park project, and Montréal feared a host of lawsuits. Montréal's municipal bureaucrats are set in their ways and are wary of standing against vested economic interests.

A prime example of this ongoing failure to defend the environment is happening yet again in 2021, exemplified by Montréal's inability to protect the Technoparc marshes, just north of Pierre Elliott Trudeau airport. A series of unused farm fields have been re-naturalized, forming a unique system of marshes, meadows, and trees, supporting many rare birds. For the last five years, local birding expert Joël Coutu has led enormously popular walks through an area that has become the primary birding site on the island of Montréal. Along with the birds, public attention has been brought to this invaluable 200-hectare wetland; much of it owned by the Canadian government.

Montréalers, like all Canadians, have lost nearly all their urban wetlands. The Technoparc represents the last unprotected wetlands in Montréal—and now they too are threatened by destruction (Barnard 2020). Once again,

---

2. Testifying Feb. 7, 2020 in Coalition Verte v. Technoparc Montréal et Ville de Montréal et Ministre du Développement Durable, de l'Environnement et de la Lutte Contre les Changements Climatiques

citizen groups are going to bat for this vital ecosystem. Joël Coutu and the group he founded (*TechnoparcOiseaux*) joined with the Green Coalition to take the authorities to court to defend the marshes.

What happened in the Technoparc saga? Why did the pro-environment Projet Montréal refuse to budge to save a precious wetland? Why did they not take up the possibility of an out-of-court settlement in favour of the marshes? The Green Coalition's Sylvia Oljemark blames powerful economic interests constraining Plante: "The city machine is still grinding away to destroy this one great and amazing wetland left," Oljemark said, adding: "I think it is the system that is doing this, behind the scenes."

The case was finally heard before Judge Sylvain Lussier of Québec's Superior court in February 2020. Still, it took more than a year to render a technical judgment that dismissed the case. The reason for this long delay is unknown.

The highlight of the hearing was the testimony of renowned biologist Rodger Titman. He spoke quietly but eloquently about the crucial importance of the Technoparc marshes and "the biodiversity below the birds." As a result of the construction already underway, Prof. Titman said, "a significant portion of the wetland is lost."[3] He stressed the destructiveness of ecosystem fragmentation and commented about his own sense of pained responsibility for the dramatic decline of bird populations in North America.

Prof. Titman spoke the plain truth of our time: "We need to ensure that not even the smallest marsh is lost."

On the other hand, the judge insisted that the tribunal did not "have the jurisdictional, scientific or political competence to rule on the general criticisms that should be debated in other forums." At the same time, Judge Lussier nonetheless had strong views about the science he heard.

Expert testimony was presented on both sides, and the Judge offered dramatically contrasting descriptions of the specialists. A retired biologist for the city of Montréal was described positively as a man "rich in 38 years of experience." Regarding Prof. Titman and another witness for the plaintiffs, the Judge said: "the sincerity of their convictions is precisely tinging their testimony", and "the testimony of these two experts were more like advocacy than independent scientific expertise."[4]

The court dismissal was not unexpected; it fits into a long historical pattern.

The Lussier judgment includes a summary of the construction project threatening the Technoparc marshes, and the text itself reveals the faulty

---

3. Quotes in this section are either from the Lussier judgment or from the official court hearing transcription.
4. Citations are translated by the author, from the court judgment.

premise of the plan. At its inception a decade ago, planners made a false distinction between wetlands that they labelled "low ecological value" and those of "high ecological interest" (Lussier judgment #22). Whatever method the planners used to make this judgment, the fact remains that the marshes form one integrated system. There is no valid distinction between "sub-optimal" marshes, in the words of one government expert, and those that are not. That kind of thinking leads to fragmentation, habitat loss, and ultimately destruction.

Clearly, the Plante administration has changed Montréal's environmental history, but they have also been its prisoner. The still-unfolding drama holds meaning for Canada and the whole of North America since migratory birds moving across the continent depend on the Technoparc marshes and other such vital places.

On 27 September 2019, in Montréal, 500,000 people marched to demand action on climate change when Greta Thunberg visited. Most of those marchers have lived and grown up in the suburbs, where more than two-thirds of Canadians now reside. Like the people in Saraguay village fifty years ago, the suburbanites of today need to rise up and take hold of their environmental future—no one else will do it for them. The history of the Green Coalition, and others, in Montréal points in only one direction—massive mobilization, not later, but now!

REFERENCES

Barnard, P. 2020. "Pimento Report #147: Degradation of Saint-Laurent Wetlands." *YouTube*, 9 October 2020, video, 14:41. https://www.youtube.com/watch?v=xTRJPZPaDwM.

Corriveau, J. 2019. "Montréal acquiert 140 hectares pour le Grand parc de l'Ouest." *Le Devoir*, 13 December 2019.

Dupras, J., and Alam, M. 2015. "Urban sprawl and ecosystem services: a half century perspective in the Montréal area (Québec, Canada)." *Journal of environmental policy & planning* 17(2): 180-200.

Lapierre, M. 2019. "Great Western Park: Montréal acquires 140 hectares in Pierrefonds-Roxboro." *CTV News*, 12 December 2019. https://montreal.ctvnews.ca/mobile/great-western-park-montreal-acquires-140-hectares-in-pierrefonds-roxboro-1.4727876?cache=yes?clipId=263414.

Nazarnia, N., Schwick, C., and Jaeger, J.A. 2016. "Accelerated urban sprawl in Montréal, Québec City, and Zurich: Investigating the differences using time series 1951–2011." *Ecological indicators* 60: 1229-1251.

Park People. 2019. *The Canadian City Parks Report*. W. Garfield Weston Foundation. https://cityparksreport.parkpeople.ca/2019/.

Sucar, D. 2019. "Environmentalists applaud Plante's 'visionary initiative': If built urban green space would be 8 times larger than N.Y.'s Central Park." *Montréal Gazette*, 9 August 2019.

MONTRÉAL'S COVID-19 PANDEMIC: A CRISIS OF INEQUALITY

ELIZABETH LEIER

Editors' Note: This chapter was written at the end of the first wave of the pandemic. Although there are some differences with future waves, the underlying dynamics affecting the communities and their responses remain fundamentally the same.

SUMMARY

COVID-19 has had a disproportionate impact on poor and marginalized citizens. Having borne the brunt of decades of neoliberal policies aimed at defunding public services, vulnerable communities were left to face a devastating health crisis without adequate protection and support. Moreover, working-class residents were called upon as essential workers to expose themselves further, while wealthier citizens were protected by staying home. In Montréal, the notable segregation of poor residents in lower-income and diverse communities exposed the extent of the inequitable nature of this pandemic. As the crisis progressed, epidemiological maps began to closely mirror socioeconomic and sociodemographic trends, allowing for a visually striking confirmation of the links between sociological factors and health outcomes. By zooming in on COVID hotspots, it is further possible to identify some of the factors that amplified the risks of infection for poor and racialized residents. On the one hand, these residents experienced social and economic conditions that accentuated risks; on the other, they were left to bear the cost of a weakened and overwhelmed healthcare system that could not cope with the added pressure of COVID-19. However, in spite of revealing inequitable outcomes, this pandemic also exposed the degree of interdependence between citizens who inhabit a common space. In acknowledging this interdependence, Montréalers can enable themselves to reimagine their city as a space that reflects increased solidarity and social equity, effectively empowering themselves to traverse the next crisis with collective strength.

INTRODUCTION

It is hard to overstate the global impacts of COVID-19. The pandemic, which began in China in 2019, had profound and widespread consequences, which ranged from new social norms around physical distancing, border closures, mass layoffs and the adoption of government emergency powers. The pervasive discourse on the need to "flatten the curve" monopolized media coverage in the early days of the pandemic, as elected officials and experts reckoned with the clear limitations of various healthcare systems (Elliot 2020). It is worth noting that flattening the curve was not deemed urgent because it meant avoiding the spread of COVID-19 but because it would slow the virus down to avoid overwhelming healthcare services.

For years now, healthcare specialists have warned that a pandemic is inevitable (Friedman 2020). Moreover, they stressed that globalization and the ease of international travel would accelerate transmissions. In spite of this, ill-preparedness emerged as a major obstacle in mitigating COVID-19 (Drefel 2020). As a result, countless lives were lost, while others were permanently altered by the wildfire-like spread of this virus.

It would, however, be incorrect to state that this pandemic affected all people and communities equally. Despite widespread infections, those rendered most vulnerable by economic precarity and social marginalization were, as they usually are, harder hit by this crisis. Poor and racialized communities accounted for most of those infected, deceased, or otherwise negatively affected by the pandemic. COVID-19, like other major crises, very clearly exposed and accentuated the striking inequalities that characterize neoliberal societies.

Montréal, Canada's second-largest city—and the largest city in the province of Québec—presents a fertile case study of the injustices amplified by COVID-19. Though not the first major Canadian city to be hit by the virus, Montréal nonetheless became the Canadian COVID-19 epicentre and one of the world's deadliest cities (Lindeman 2020). Initially, officials brushed off this unflattering observation, pointing to Québec's ambitious screening targets and to the holiday that preceded the enforcement of travel restrictions and mandated self-isolation (Perreaux 2020). Though it would be reasonable to assume that these factors may have been responsible for the initial spread of the virus, community transmission in Montréal accelerated uncontrollably in lower-income and culturally diverse neighbourhoods. As the pandemic progressed, these areas began to systematically show up as hotspots on epidemiological maps, revealing themselves not only as areas of contagion but crucially as areas underserved and misunderstood by social and health services. The truth is, racialized, immigrant, and poor citizens were left to bear the brunt of our ill-preparedness in the face of this crisis.

BEFORE THE PANDEMIC: NEOLIBERAL REFORMS AND THE GUTTING OF QUÉBEC'S HEALTHCARE SYSTEM

For decades, Québec's healthcare system has been criticized as inefficient and costly (Siedman 2015). Despite significant public spending, the province's health service has struggled to cope with population demands, leading to wait times surpassing neighbouring jurisdictions. In addition, the difficulty in accessing a family doctor has led to the significant overcrowding of emergency rooms. When COVID-19 hit in March 2020, Québec's emergency departments had been operating overcapacity for years.

Since its creation in the 1960s, Québec's public health service has suffered a number of reforms designed to optimize its services while cutting costs (so-called austerity measures). Under the Charest government (2003-2012), then health minister Philip Couillard began a mass centralization policy, regrouping health services according to region, under a top-down administrative structure (Siedman 2015). As managerial resources increased dramatically, funding to frontline healthcare services diminished. Under this new paradigm, patients went from being recognized as members of the public to being referred to as individual clients.

The man who instigated the neoliberal reform of the healthcare system then found himself leading a Québec Liberal Party government from 2014 to 2018. Under Couillard's leadership, health minister Gaétan Barette ushered in a new set of reforms designed to micromanage resources (rendered services began to be timed by the minute) and cut any costs deemed to be superfluous. Moreover, all health services were made subservient to regional hospital services, meaning community and preventative care institutions such as long-term care homes or *centre d'hébergement et de soins de longue durée* (CHSLD) lost both funding and autonomy (Siedman 2015). This so-called "optimization" of resources also led to major cuts for the province's Public Health Agency—the institution responsible for analyzing and predicting public health trends, including but not limited to pandemic response.

Ill-preparedness in the face of a predictable and measurable public health emergency is necessarily the result of political decision-making. Amidst the warnings of the likelihood of a global pandemic, most governments stayed the course in embracing austerity measures aimed at defunding and "optimizing" public services such as healthcare. This was observably the case in Québec as a slew of managerial reforms led to a weakened healthcare service already overwhelmed by basic public demands (Valiante 2015). As COVID-19 hit, there should have been ample resources and updated protocols to rapidly quell the crisis. Instead, officials found a severe lack of equipment such as urgent care beds, ventilators, masks, gowns and so on, in addition to an already overworked and overwhelmed staff.

Moreover, it is important to note that municipal authorities had little autonomy in dealing with the pandemic. Attempts to intervene to quell the advancing crisis were cut short by the centralized public health administration. The ability of local authorities to act has been intimately tied to the provincial government's instructions and direction. In addition to having their hands tied by provincial authorities, municipal officials had to navigate the lacklustre responses of the federal government in relation to international transit and border administration. Indeed, Montréal healthcare workers made headlines early on during the pandemic as they chose to bypass the federal government in order to begin systematic interventions at the city's major international airport (Messier 2020).

Acknowledging the flagrant inadequacies of the government's response to COVID-19 is important. Austerity measures and excessive centralization may not have caused COVID-19, but they made an efficient and equitable response impossible. These measures also disproportionally and systematically impact poor and marginalized communities. The COVID-19 crisis demonstrates the amplified vulnerability of these communities. The institutional lack of foresight proves that governments are ready to tolerate greater risks when those likely to be affected are poor or racialized. As Jane Shulman, a health researcher at the University of Winnipeg wrote:

> We were told, before the virus even reached Canada in great numbers, that hospitals were not equipped to manage the pandemic with the resources available, and people might die as a result. Now we know that Black and Indigenous people, people of colour, and people with low incomes are more severely affected by COVID-19 and unattainable public health care directives. (Shulman 2020)

The negative impacts of the pandemic were the tragic culmination of years of austerity politics. In Canada, the consequences of COVID-19's collision with a weakened healthcare system were most evident in Montréal, the early epicentre of the country's pandemic. However, in addition to exposing a lack of preparedness, Montréal's COVID-19 experience has shone a light on the prominent links between socio-economic status and health outcomes.

Examining Montréal's COVID-19 outbreak highlights the compounded impacts of government policy, poverty, and marginalization in a time of crisis.

MONTRÉAL: A PATCHWORK OF INEQUALITY

Montréal is a relevant and poignant example of crisis inequity. Though all major cities deal with inequality and class struggles, Montréal presents certain analytical advantages given the clear physical distribution of communities in distinct neighborhoods and the stark contrasts visibly rendered by their unofficial borders. As such, Montréal's COVID-19 epidemiological mapping closely matches the mapping of the socioeconomic and sociodemographic status of its citizens. The areas with the highest number of cases per 100,000 residents were among the least affluent and most disadvantaged (Montréal Public Health 2020).

As the virus began to actively spread through the metropolitan community, the disproportionate distribution of infections appeared to puzzle certain officials and members of the press. For those unaware or uninterested in understanding the material displays of inequality and systemic discrimination, a striking puzzle emerged from Montréal's COVID-19 epidemiological map; namely, *why do higher income and cultural privilege have such a pronounced effect on determining the risk of infection?*

A closer look at some of the hotspots points to the undeniable importance sociological factors such as income and cultural identity play in determining the lethality of this pandemic; the number of COVID-19 cases was revealed to be *2.5 times higher in poor and culturally diverse areas* (Montréal Public Health 2020). Moreover, contrasting the contagion clusters in poor communities with the limited infection rates in wealthier neighbouring communities further supports the link between health outcomes to sociological status. Montréal's relevance as a case study lies in the fact that these contrasts are nakedly visible, even to the casual observer. The epidemiological mapping of the city's pandemic confirmed that Montréal's urban landscape is a patchwork of inequality.

What follows is an *exposé* of three of the city's early COVID-19 hotspots. Parc-Extension, Hochelaga-Maisonneuve and Montréal-Nord exemplify COVID-19's disproportionate impact on vulnerable communities.

PARC EX

The diverse neighbourhood of Parc-Extension is situated in the middle of the island of Montréal and is colloquially referred to as Parc Ex. It is one of the poorest urban communities in Canada (Halais 2019) and was one of the city's earliest COVID-19 hotspots. In contrast, the neighbourhood is bordered by some of Canada's richest areas, such as the Town of Mont-Royal. Historically home to the Greek and Italian diasporas, Parc Ex's identity has been shaped by the successive waves of immigrants that have established themselves in the neighbourhood. Today, Parc Ex is home to significant South-Asian and Muslim communities.

Given the area's connection to public transit, physical access to public services in Parc Ex is reasonable; however, there are notable barriers to accessibility owing to the diversity of languages spoken by residents. In addition, access to care requires a health insurance card issued by the Public Health Authority through proof of residency in the province. Obtaining this card can be difficult—even impossible—for those who are newly arrived in Montréal and who struggle in speaking one of the two official languages.

This accessibility issue arose when health authorities began to formulate recommendations and regulations to mitigate the spread of the virus, as many residents struggled to comprehend the rapidly changing information and daily updates. Owing to these factors, it took several weeks before authorities were able to provide adequate testing in places like Parc Ex (Carpentier 2020).

Parc Ex is home to Montréal's concentration of working poor. According to a study by the *Institut national de la recherche scientifique* (INRS), 30.7% of the population of this neighbourhood is considered workers who live below the poverty line. Many of these residents are employed in essential services (Leloup et al. 2016). Many residents in Parc Ex worked in meat processing factories known to have outbreaks, for example at Concord Premium Meats (Curtis 2020). Workers on the evening shift at Concord faced an outbreak in the summer of 2020. A lack of proper protective equipment and being forced to rely on the temporary placement agency's transportation led to the outbreak (Curtis 2020). Essential workers employed through temporary placement agencies have then increased transmission from workplaces to the community.

Given its geographic situation, Parc Ex is experiencing rapid gentrification, and families are being forced out of the area through rent increases. In fact, throughout the COVID-19 pandemic, Montréal has experienced a serious housing crisis, resulting from real-estate speculation and extreme rent hikes. In places like Parc Ex, many families were forced to move in with friends and relatives or move apartments entirely; this can have significant adverse consequences in the midst of a pandemic (Hickey 2020).

HOCHELAGA-MAISONNEUVE

In the traditionally working-class neighbourhood of Hochelaga-Maisonneuve, situated a few kilometres east from Montréal's central business district, long-time residents have also been forced to adapt to rapid gentrification. The neighbourhood is predominantly French-speaking, and many residents struggle with substance abuse issues and crippling poverty. The CISSS de l'Est de Montréal reports that 20% of residents live below the poverty line (CISSS de l'Est de Montréal 2020). Moreover, access to basic necessities like fresh produce has traditionally been difficult. Though gentrification has somewhat ameliorated this situation, quality food and products remain prohibitively priced for many residents. Consequently, epidemiological studies of residents in Hochelaga-Maisonneuve show an aging population in poor health (CISSS de l'Est de Montréal 2020).

Hochelaga-Maisonneuve's situation contrasts heavily with that of neighbouring areas, such as the highly gentrified Plateau-Mont-Royal borough. Outside of significant socioeconomic differences, both neighbourhoods share many geographical similarities, such as their proximity to the city centre and their high population density, among others. However, the Plateau's much higher socioeconomic context translated to a very limited number of overall cases (921) compared to Hochelaga-Maisonneuve, which reported more than twice as many (2325), as of the summer of 2020 (Santé Montréal 2020).

MONTRÉAL-NORD

Montréal-Nord is a neighbourhood situated in the north-east of the island, far removed from downtown and underserved by public transit. Its population presents a combination of the factors outlined in both Parc Ex and Hochelaga-Maisonneuve; it is both low-income and culturally diverse. Montréal-Nord's experience with COVID-19 poignantly illustrates the impact of sociological factors on population health, given the difficult conditions experienced by many residents who could not protect themselves from this virus adequately.

Montréal-Nord is a densely populated area of the city where physical distancing is difficult. Many lower-income residents live in high-rise buildings or multi-generational households where it is nearly impossible to physically isolate (Mckie 2020). As soon as the virus began to actively spread within the community, officials struggled to control the rate of infections.

Montréal-Nord is also distinctly underserved by public services. For example, access to most health services requires public transit, which is both notoriously inefficient and overly priced given the typical incomes in the neighbourhood. Given the challenge in accessing adequate care, epidemiological analyses of the area unsurprisingly point to a population with significant underlying health issues (CIUSS du Nord de l'île 2020).

When the city initially declared a public health emergency, it established

COVID-19 testing and care facilities in areas close to downtown, effectively rendering them inaccessible to residents unable to commute to the city's centre. In fact, many officials identified this problem as the province was unable to meet its screening targets amidst a rising number of cases in areas like Montréal-Nord. Eventually, their solution was to deploy mobile testing units set in municipal buses (Luft 2020). Residents were consequently hard-pressed to access services once they became ill with COVID-19 and the impracticality of physical distancing led to an uncontrolled spread of the virus.

Moreover, people residing in Montréal-Nord were more likely to become infected due to their roles as essential workers. As such, they were unable to work from home and shield themselves from COVID-19. Many of the area's residents are employed in the healthcare system, often working as nursing staff or orderlies (Bruemmer 2020). Though working conditions within public healthcare have steadily deteriorated, many new Montréalers had no other choice but to accept frontline jobs in a healthcare system that underpays and overworks them. As such, many resident care workers found themselves routinely dispatched to different institutions during the pandemic. This not only increased their risk of infection but also contributed to the spread of the virus in long-term care facilities such as the city's CHSLDs. This proved to be lethal for a significant number of older residents, which have accounted for the overwhelming majority of deaths from COVID-19 in Montréal.

In addition to being employed in frontline health services, many residents in Montréal-Nord work in other essential sectors, such as food retail and delivery. This means that they also faced a greater risk of infection than the general population, who could often stay at home while working remotely.

Crucially, residents in Montréal-Nord were not only more susceptible to contracting the virus but were also among the residents with the least access to health services once they fell ill. Given the housing situation in the area, as these residents returned to their communities, many were unable to isolate themselves properly from family and friends. Combined, these factors explain why Montréal-Nord experienced the highest cumulative case rate on the island and accounted for a disproportionate number of fatalities. The injustices related to economic precarity and cultural marginalization compounded the lethality of the virus.

THE CANADIAN EPICENTRE OF COVID-19

The portrait that emerges of Montréal is not a flattering one. Decades of austerity measures left a weakened provincial healthcare system already unable to cope with population needs, most significantly in lower-income and marginalized communities. As the government embraced neoliberal reforms, it systematically shunned those areas deemed to be less profitable, paving the way for uneven outcomes in education, health, and overall well-being. It should come as no surprise that neglected urban areas suffered more acutely from COVID-19.

By February 2020, more than 100,000 people had contracted COVID-19 in the metropolis; of these, more than 4,500 have died. Poor urban communities accounted for close to half of COVID-19 cases in Montréal, despite their respective populations accounting for just over 35% of the city's population.[1] It is reasonable to wonder how many of these deaths could have been prevented by an adequately resourced response to the crisis, or, to put it in other words, how many of these fatalities are directly attributable to the deliberate weakening of public healthcare. The sacrifice of public health was an implicit sacrifice of working-class and immigrant communities.

Montréal's director of public health, Dr Mylène Drouin, explicitly condemned the years of austerity policies that have left her agency severely under-resourced. In an interview with *La Presse*, Dr Drouin expressed the desire to see this crisis result in significant sociopolitical reforms, stressing the urgent need to redress inequity in society (Levesque 2020). Drouin's comments point to the undeniable links between population health and equality. In the case of Montréal, COVID-19 has clearly demonstrated that profound inequalities are antithetical to collective health.

Neoliberalization *de facto* harms those who rely on collectivized services such as public health care. By choosing to embrace neoliberal policies, elected officials implicitly sacrificed the most vulnerable among us. The neoliberal turn in healthcare has had a devastating impact on our ability to mitigate the pandemic, but these effects were more lethal for some than for others. This staggering inequity ought to make us rethink our collective accountability for the tragedy wrought by COVID-19.

The cities we inhabit are a mirror image of the social and economic conditions we create and sustain. In tolerating inequity, we accept sacrificing our fellow citizens to hardships and risks that we refuse to endure ourselves. Accordingly, though we may all face similar challenges in times of crisis, we do not experience them together in solidarity.

In Montréal, COVID-19 not only amplified deep-seated inequalities but also revealed the extent to which we all depend on one another. Those who share a common space are inevitably interdependent, even more so in a time of crisis. All Montréalers depend on the healthcare workers, grocers, and other essential members of our community, no matter where they happen to reside.

---

1. Based on calculations from *Santé Montréal* (2020) and the 2017 municipal survey (Ville de Montréal 2017).

Surely this should justify the kind of solidarity that would allow us to remedy some of the striking inequalities that plague the city.

The Marxist geographer David Harvey speaks of the potential cities offer as communal spaces of existence. In *The Right to the City*, Harvey writes:

> The question of what kind of city we want cannot be divorced from that of what kind of social ties, relationship to nature, lifestyles, technologies and aesthetic values we desire. The right to the city is far more than the individual liberty to access urban resources: it is a right to change ourselves by changing the city. It is, moreover, a common rather than an individual right since this transformation inevitably depends upon the exercise of a collective power to reshape the processes of urbanization. The freedom to make and remake our cities and ourselves is, I want to argue, one of the most precious yet most neglected of our human rights (Harvey 2008).

Though the tragedy of COVID-19 is undeniable, the disruptive nature of this crisis has opened up spaces of possibility, allowing us to disentangle ourselves from harmful neoliberal ideology and reimagine the world we wish to cohabit. As we recognize the strength of our mutual reliance, we can reimagine and redesign our communities and our cities as harmonious, equitable, and inclusive spaces. This unique moment of history could allow us to, as Harvey states, collectively remake our cities to reflect renewed forms of solidarity. Thus, when the next crisis hits, we will be stronger and better able to face it together.

REFERENCES

Bruemmer, R. 2020. "Montréal North's residents paying the price for taking care of others." *Montréal Gazette*, 30 April 2020.

Carpentier, P. 2020. "Parc-Extension community trying to contain the spread of COVID-19." *Global News*, 11 May 2020.

CISSS de l'Est de Montréal. 2020. "Portrait de la population de l'Est." Accessed 16 July 2020. https://ciusss-estmtl.gouv.qc.ca/propos/portrait-de-la-population-de-lest.

CIUSS du Nord de l'ile. 2020. "Portrait de santé de la population." Accessed 16 July 2020. https://cdn.ciusssnordmtl.ca/documents/Menu/Votre_CIUSSS/portrait-territoire/PortraitSanteCIUSSSN_2018.pdf?1570042513.

Curtis, C. 2020. "Migrant workers detail covid-19 outbreaks at warehouses and factories." *Montréal Gazette*, 29 June 2020. https://www.healthing.ca/news/migrant-workers-detail-covid-19-outbreaks-at-warehouses-factories.

Drefel, A. 2020. "Québec unprepared for coronavirus outbreak, says Montréaler back from China." *Montréal Gazette*, 11 February 2020.

Elliott, J.K. 2020. "Flatten the curve: How one chart became a rallying cry against coronavirus." *Global News*, 12 March 2020. https://globalnews.ca/news/6665558/coronavirus-flatten-the-curve/.

Friedman, U. 2020. "We Were Warned." *The Atlantic Monthly*, 18 March 2020.

Halais, F. 2019. "Gentrification under Trudeau's nose: how his electoral district is struggling with evictions." *The Guardian*, 26 September 2019.

Harvey, D. 2008. "The Right to the City." *The New Left Review* 53.

Hickey, P. 2020. Parc Extension tenants seek help to avoid evictions. *Montréal Gazette*, 15 June 2020.

Leloup, X., Desrochers, F., and Rose, D. 2016. *The Working Poor in the Montréal Region: Statistical Profile* and Spatial Distribution. Abridged Report. INRS Centre Urbanisation Culture Société; Centraide du Grand Montréal. http://espace.inrs.ca/id/eprint/4925/.

Levesque, K. 2020. "Moi, mon patient, c'est la population de Montréal." *La Presse*, 20 April 2020.

Lindeman, T. 2020. "Why are so many people getting sick and dying in Montréal from Covid-19?" *The Guardian*, 13 May 2020.

Luft, A. 2020. "Montréal to use city buses as mobile COVID-19 testing units in hardest-hit boroughs." *CTV News*, 4 May 2020.

Mckie, D. 2020. "Poverty and COVID-19: More data would help explain the connection." *The National Observer*, 12 May 2020.

Messier, F. 2020. "COVID-19 : Montréal déploie des ressources à l'aéroport Trudeau." *Radio-Canada*, 16 March 2020. https://ici.radio-canada.ca/nouvelle/1668253/voyageurs-mairesse-valerie-plante-mylene-drouin-sante-publique.

Montréal Public Health. 2020. "Unequal Toll of the Pandemic." Accessed 16 July 2020. https://santemontreal.qc.ca/fileadmin/fichiers/Campagnes/coronavirus/situation-montreal/point-sante/inegalites-montreal/Inegaux-Pandemie-Population-EN.pdf.

Perreaux, L. 2020. "Why Québec's coronavirus cases have skyrocketed." *The Globe and Mail*, 30 March 2020.

Santé Montréal. 2020. "Situation of the coronavirus (COVID-19) in Montréal." Accessed 16 July 2020. https://santemontreal.qc.ca/en/public/coronavirus-covid-19/situation-of-the-coronavirus-covid-19-in-montreal/.

Siedman, K. 2015. "Québec's health care system leads way in 'failure': researcher." *Montréal Gazette*, 2 October 2015.

Shulman, J. 2020. "'Just Don't Get Sick:' Neoliberal Health Care in the Pandemic. COVID-19 and Cultural Studies: Articulating the Pandemic Centre for Research in Cultural Studies (CRiCS)." 26 June 2020. https://www.uwinnipeg.ca/crics/covid-19-and-cultural-studies/just-dont-get-sick-neoliberal-health-care-in-the-pandemic.html.

Valiante, G. 2015. "New study says Québec needs more doctors, as opposition smells blood in health sector." *The National Post*, 18 March 2015. https://nationalpost.com/news/canada/study-says-quebec-needs-more-doctors-as-opposition-smells-blood-in-health-sector.

Ville de Montréal. 2017. "Population et démographie." *Montréal en statistiques Service du développement économique*, 14 November 2017. http://ville.montreal.qc.ca/pls/portal/docs/PAGE/MTL_STATS_FR/MEDIA/DOCUMENTS/22_POPULATION ET D?MOGRAPHIE_NOVEMBRE2017_LOGEMENTS_ARROND.PDF.

MONTRÉAL'S CHANGING CLIMATE: THERE IS NO TURNING BACK

JOEY EL-KHOURY

HALF A MILLION PEOPLE MARCH FOR A RAPID AND DEEP DECARBONIZATION

Here we were, summer 2019, with unconfirmed news circulating that young Swedish climate justice icon Greta Thunberg was considering attending in Montréal the highly awaited global climate strike. After the huge turnout for the 'Climate Spring' march earlier that year, environmentalists across Québec knew that her presence could galvanize an already effervescent local climate movement. Still, few had anticipated what the world would witness on 27 September 2019. No less than half a million people marched across Montréal's downtown for what was deemed one of the largest protest marches in Canadian history.

While the world took notice of the unprecedented climate strikes in cities across the globe, it seems that few political decision-makers took note of one of Greta's most important messages: given today's global emission levels, the remaining carbon budget to limit global warming to 1.5°C above pre-industrial levels will be gone in less than 8.5 years; this does not include already locked-in warming, ecosystem tipping points, feedback loops, and issues of social equity and climate justice; as well, recent emission reduction targets rely on currently inexistent technologies to suck 100s of billions of tons of CO_2 out of the air.

Importantly, at current rates of greenhouse gas (GHG) emissions, the Paris Agreement's 1.5°C 'safe zone' will likely be exceeded before 2030; warming may reach 2°C above pre-industrial levels by 2050 and 4°C by the turn of the century (IPCC 2018). In this context of catastrophic climate overshoot, unless a drastic shift in GHG emissions is undertaken, humanity's existence as we know it is in peril. This is compounded by the fact that the actions needed to rapidly decarbonize the global economy require such transformational scale and speed that our civilization has no documented historical precedent.

The next ten years are among the most important in our history, and climate decisions can no longer be 'kicked down the road.' There is now a general consensus that two key elements are crucial if we are to adequately respond to the climate emergency: cities and civil society actors.

The City of Montréal represents approximately 2% of Canada's and 14% of Québec's total GHG emissions. Transport represents 40% of those emissions, followed by industry (28%), commercial/institutional (16%), residential (12%) and waste management (4%). Montréal's remaining GHG emissions budget, to respect the 1.5°C limit, is 22,556 kt of CO_2.[1] This will require an annual reduction of 38%, reaching carbon neutrality by 2030.

To put things into perspective, the city has seen a (temporary) decrease of 7% since the start of the COVID-19 pandemic. The city's current (modest) GHG reduction target is 55% below 1990 levels by 2030, representing an annual decrease of 5.2%. So even if we were to dramatically halt the global economy as COVID-19 has done—and for the next decade or two—it might not suffice to limit global warming to 1.5°C. This is further compounded by the fact that the city's target is based on future technologies to absorb CO_2 from the atmosphere that do not exist today. Even if these technologies were to be deployed at the necessary speed and scale, it would require years before they could begin reducing atmospheric CO_2 at the magnitude required to avert climate breakdown.

In a nutshell: the house is on fire, and we need to act decisively—and we need to act now.

A LOOK BACK AT MONTRÉAL'S SUSTAINABILITY JOURNEY

The City of Montréal made environmental headlines in 1987 with the signing of the Montréal Protocol, recognized as one of the most successful international environmental agreements. This international treaty has succeeded in protecting the ozone layer by phasing out the production of ozone-depleting substances. Around the same time, the city witnessed the development of many of its first 'green' urban infrastructures; the first bike path network, reserved bus lanes, and the pedestrianization of some main avenues. By 1992, the year of the Rio Earth Summit, the city had its first urban

---

1. As of December 2019, with 67% chance of success.

master plan, which also included the first plan for its biggest urban green space, Mount Royal Park.

These early 'green' achievements were at the account of Jean Doré, Montréal's mayor from 1986 to 1994. Doré is credited for modernizing Montréal after the 'dark decades' of Jean Drapeau's 'one-man rule' (Katz and Roussopoulos 2017).

In 1994, Doré was defeated by Pierre Bourque, a right-leaning horticulturist and ex-director of Montréal's Botanical Garden. He initially campaigned on a vision of turning Montréal into a 'garden city,' the first 'environmental city' in North America. Despite high expectations, the city witnessed major setbacks on democracy and very little progress on the environmental front. His key achievement was creating the *'eco-quartier'* model, borough-level organizations that promote and implement environmental initiatives; they are credited for laying the foundations of the city's household recycling and composting system. However, today, this system remains sub-optimal. By 2015, recyclable waste recovery was just over 58%; while this is some improvement from the 37% measured in 2006, it is still far behind the provincial target of 70%. Moreover, the city currently collects only 26% of its organic waste (Ville de Montréal 2019), significantly short of the 2020 provincial target of 100% collection.

After Bourque came Gerald Tremblay, mayor from 2001-2012. His administration's first milestone accomplishment was the organization of Montréal's first citizen summit on 'The Future of Montréal.' From this emerged the city's Charter of Rights and Responsibilities, a first of its kind in North America. It reaffirms the city's commitments to fundamental values of citizen participation, human rights, social justice, and environmental sustainability. Following this ground-breaking initiative, and in close collaboration with dozens of civil society groups, Montréal's 2004 urban plan and 2008 transportation plan were developed. These plans considerably increased investments in the city's public transport agencies. As a result, bus and metro services improved, leading to ridership levels surpassing provincial targets. In 2010, the *Société de transport de Montréal* (STM) won the Outstanding Public Transportation System Achievement Award from the American Public Transportation Association. By 2015, 180 km of additional bus lanes had been developed, and bike lanes increased to 680 km.[2] As one of North America's most densely populated cities, Montréal is one of the most walkable, bike-friendly, and least car-dependent.

Nevertheless, it remains far behind cities like Copenhagen, where more than 70% of residents commute by public or active transport. In 2016, across

2. See Komorowski's chapter in this book for more on the history of cycling infrastructure in Montréal.

Montréal's metropolitan region, the share of car use for commuting was almost 70%. The automobile is still king in Montréal.

From the ground-breaking citizen summits also emerged Montréal's first sustainability plan (2005-2010), followed by a second plan (2010-2015) that was elaborated in conjunction with 180 civil society organizations. These plans provide specific objectives detailing the city's commitments in many areas, most notably GHG emissions (with a target of 30% below 1990 levels by 2020), but also addressing transportation, urban sprawl, water and air quality, biodiversity, and other areas.

While these plans were robust on paper, the city has rarely delivered on these promises. Tremblay's mandate ended in controversies surrounding corruption, especially in the construction sector, and has left deep scars in Montréal's urban landscape. This is exemplified by the unsustainable Griffintown neighbourhood, a best-in-class example of *what not to do* in terms of urban (re)development.

In 2004, a new 'program and membership-based' centre-left municipal party was established by urbanist Richard Bergeron: Projet Montréal. Firmly set on a vision of urban sustainability for the 21st century, its main objective is improving quality of life by reducing dependence on cars, curtailing urban sprawl, and developing human-scaled, socially mixed, and pedestrian/bicycle-friendly neighbourhoods while revitalizing the local economy around public and active transport systems. It has contributed to re-energizing urban political life by empowering progressive environmental initiatives and urban experiments driven by grassroots organizations at the 'hyper-local' neighbourhood level. Acting as an important guard-rail against 'urban development as usual,' it has been attempting to fend off the dominant car culture entrenched in Montréal's urban fabric since the 1960s.

Tremblay's time in office ended darkly. In 2013, after several years of the city being marred in scandals of systemic corruption, career politician and 'one-man show' Denis Coderre was elected mayor while Projet Montréal took power in several key strongholds in the inner city.

In 2014, a small group of Montréalers began meeting informally to discuss the implications of climate change on their city, and how the municipality needed to begin filling the climate void left by provincial and federal governments. After organizing a climate march in September 2014, followed by a 'Climate Science and Policy Teach-In' at McGill, they launched Climate Action Montréal. They leveraged Montréal's 'right of initiative' by mobilizing citizens to push the city's administration to hold a public consultation on reducing Montréal's dependence on fossil fuels.

THE 'POST-2015' MOMENT AND THE EMERGENCE OF THE MONTRÉAL CLIMATE COALITION

The adoption of the Paris Climate Agreement in 2015 was a major turning point in international climate geopolitics, one that opened the door to the possibility of envisioning a new economic model for society. At the time, Montréal joined the international network of resilient cities, and Coderre endorsed the Paris City Hall Declaration of the Climate Summit for Local Leaders. These symbolic acts gave Coderre the media attention he was seeking, while at the local level, he agreed to Climate Action Montréal's demand for a public consultation, short-circuiting the 'right of initiative' process. Immediately, Climate Action Montréal and several of its allies[3] united to push Montréal to set a goal of achieving carbon neutrality by 2042, the year of the city's 400th anniversary.

The Montréal Climate Coalition was born at a moment when the city was seven points behind on its 2020 GHG reduction target of 30% below 1990 levels. Most of the progress on emission reductions achieved by that time was a direct result of the closure of Shell's Montréal refinery in 2010 (The Canadian Press 2010).

The second phase of the public consultation on the reduction of Montréal's dependence on fossil fuel took place in early-2016. With over 3,500 participants and over ninety briefs presented, it was dubbed Montréal's most successful public consultation to date. Its final report included 15 key recommendations for the city to implement in order to rapidly reduce GHG emissions (OCPM 2016).

This year also saw the announcement of the *Réseau express métropolitain* (REM) project, a controversial electric SkyTrain that aims to connect Montréal's suburbs and international airport. The Montréal Climate Coalition argued that the REM was more of a real-estate development project than a public transport project designed around Montréalers actual transportation needs. The project's potential for reducing GHG emissions is also negligible, according to a 2018 study commissioned by the Montréal Climate Coalition and the Canadian Union of Public Employees (Gagnon and Lefebvre 2018). Designed and adopted in an undemocratic fashion, it is anticipated that the REM will be a considerable financial burden for Montréal in the future.

Grassroots organizations such as the Montréal Climate Coalition and its allies opposed the REM, arguing that a better project could be completed for less money. In contrast, more renowned publicly funded environmental organizations (some of which were founding partners of the Coalition, such as *Équiterre* and the David Suzuki Foundation) came out in favour of the project

---

3. GRAME, David Suzuki Foundation, Équiterre, Greenpeace, and CRE-Montréal.

under the argument that it was better than nothing. The REM controversy highlighted the deep-rooted divisions within Montréal's environmental movement, between the publicly funded 'moderate/sustainable development' organizations and the more financially independent 'community-based and citizen-led' ecological groups.

By the end of 2016, Montréal joined the Cities Climate Leadership Group, an international network of cities collaborating to decarbonize the world's cities. A month later, Québec's environmental review board (the BAPE; *Bureau d'audiences publiques sur l'environnement*) announced that it had major reservations regarding the REM's social acceptability, a position that was supported by the main provincial opposition parties, as well as Valérie Plante, the newly selected leader of Projet Montréal.

By spring 2017, as Québecers experienced unprecedented flooding, the Montréal Climate Coalition sued the Québec government and CDPQ-Infra[4] for disregarding the BAPE's evaluation of the REM. The court battle was lost, as the issue was deemed a difference in political vision rather than a legal matter. Nevertheless, the Montréal Climate Coalition went on to inspire the establishment of Climate Reality's 'Climate Community Hubs,' a pan-Canadian network of local citizen-led climate groups.

While the REM controversy made yearlong headlines in Québec, 2017 was also focused on Montréal's 375th anniversary, with Coderre's administration investing almost $300 million for the festivities. This investment included a few 'green' projects, such as enlarged sidewalks on Sainte-Catherine Street, a new public square over the Ville-Marie expressway facing city hall, and the creation of an 'urban promenade' connecting Mount Royal to the Saint Lawrence River.

On the environmental front, Coderre will be remembered for several disasters: supporting a massive housing development project in the Pierrefonds borough that threatened to raze 185 hectares of near-pristine grassland and wilderness, home to nearly 160 bird species; chopping down 1,000 trees in Parc Jean-Drapeau to make way for an amphitheatre; and reducing the budget for the city's transit agency, which led to diminished services, increased fares, and stagnation in ridership for the first time in decades. He also discarded Tremblay's tramway project, pushed the development of car infrastructure (such as the Laval highway), and was one of the main supporters of the Electric-Formula 1 fiasco.

By the end of Coderre's term, Montréal had several sustainability plans: the GHG emissions reduction plan (2013-2020), Climate Change Adaptation Plan (2015-2020), and the city's third sustainable development plan (2016-2020).

---

4. The contractor behind the REM project, a subsidiary of Québec's public pension fund manager (*Caisse de dépôt et placement du Québec*; CDPQ).

This included a GHG emissions reduction target of 80% below 1990 levels by 2050 (Ville de Montréal 2016). As for the 15 recommendations that had come out of the public consultation on reducing Montréal's fossil fuel dependence (OCPM 2016), they were never given an implementation plan. Similarly, while Coderre's administration had proposed increasing the bike path network to 1,280 km, no timeline was set, and no actions were implemented. Coderre's mandate has been characterized by a major disconnect between promises and actions, all 'green' talk but no action.

THE MUNICIPAL 'GREENS' ARE IN POWER

Valérie Plante began her mandate by signing the Montréal Climate Coalition's 2042 carbon neutrality declaration, and shortly after, announced that the city aimed to become carbon neutral by 2050. To advance this new vision, the city created the Bureau of Transition and Resilience,[5] which encompasses all city services and functions associated with sustainability, climate change mitigation and adaptation, sustainable transport, waste management, and green spaces. Simultaneously, it also partnered with the David Suzuki Foundation and Trottier Foundation in establishing a working group to oversee the development and implementation of Montréal's 2020-2030 Climate Plan. By early 2019, the city adopted a motion to establish a carbon budget for Montréal, one of the Coalition's key demands. While these were positive signs, they remained mere commitments.

By 2019, a survey conducted by environmental grassroots organizations gave Valérie Plante and her administration a grade of D for their environmental performance (Valois-Nadeau 2019). This also coincided with the surprise resignation of Luc Ferrandez, mayor of the environmentally progressive Plateau-Mont-Royal borough, and executive committee member in charge of large parks, green spaces, and major projects. Ferrandez's parting message amounted to this: the house is on fire, and the city is not doing enough. Individuals and groups, both within and outside the party, were beginning to express their dissatisfaction at what was all too familiar in Montréal: a persistent lack of political will for concrete transformative sustainability policies and actions. By spring 2019, as Québec witnessed a second major flood in as many years, and Canada's Prime Minister Justin Trudeau approved the controversial Trans Mountain pipeline extension project, Montréal was the scene of a major climate strike that saw thousands of students and citizens take to the streets to demand concrete actions from their governments.

As for the Coalition, around this time, it partnered with the Lachine

---

5. More info at https://montreal.ca/transition-ecologique

borough and co-organized a public consultation on the redevelopment of East-Lachine, with the vision of making it Montréal's first carbon-neutral eco-district. This has set a standard for the kind of citizen participation that is needed if we are to accelerate Montréal's decarbonization while inspiring another push for a carbon-neutral redevelopment project at the Namur-Hippodrome site and catalyzing the elaboration of an 'Eco-District' charter for Montréal (now part of the city's 2020-2030 Climate Plan).

By summer 2019, Valérie Plante made two rather ground-breaking announcements: creating one of Canada's biggest urban parks in the west part of the city and establishing a new decarbonization target for Montréal (reducing GHG emissions 55% below 1990 levels by 2030). That fall, as Canada's federal elections were gearing up, Greta Thunberg and Montréal's environmental movement took the city by storm with the historic climate march.

So here we were, at the start of 2020, with all concerned stakeholders ready for what was expected to be the year that Montréal's ecological transition would finally take off. However, nothing less than the biggest global disruption in a century—COVID-19—was about to emerge. It has reshuffled the cards entirely, transforming the rules of the game at all levels of society, from health to social stability, the economy, and the environment. While global lockdowns have catalyzed never before seen (but temporary) GHG reductions, governments are eager to restart economic growth, albeit with talks of a 'green' restart. Montréal's Climate Plan 2020–2030 was unveiled in December 2020; it contains 46 actions collected under five themes: mobilizing the Montréal community; mobility, urban planning, and urban development; buildings; exemplarity of the city; and governance (Ville de Montréal 2020). It also contains a GHG emissions reduction target of 55% below 1990 levels to be reached by 2030. As in earlier plans (Bruemmer 2015), it also encourages boroughs to set their own planning tools favouring climate change adapted urbanism.

While the plan is appealing, pertinent, and attainable, one limitation is its generality. Implementation measures are unclear, short- and medium-term timelines remain ambiguous, and financial resources are extremely limited and inexistent at the borough level. It seems that past shortfalls are being perpetuated: ambitious plans on paper but no robust implementation scheme. *Who does what? How? With what resources? And by when?* These remain open-ended questions. As an example, even though a Carbon Budget for the city has already been developed by the Rapid Decarbonization Group[6]—and was proposed to the city's administration—it was not included in the final report (nor did the city see fit to collaborate more closely with the concerned

---

6. More information at: https://rapiddecarbonizationgroup.org/

researchers). It remains to be seen which metrics and tracking tools the city will adopt to follow through on their climate commitments.

2021-2025 AND BEYOND: TRANSFORMING MONTRÉAL'S MUNICIPAL CLIMATE

Under the Paris Agreement, 2020 was the year when countries were expected to submit their new or updated Nationally Determined Contributions, with more ambitious actions, to limit global warming to 1.5°C. Climate scientists continue to depict the current decade as 'make or break'—the moment that will decide if humanity will have what it takes to avert the worst of climate chaos.

Will we rise to the occasion and avoid civilizational collapse?

In our current 'century of the city,'[7] municipal governments face the daunting challenge of implementing the kind of urban governance that can create the social conditions necessary for citizens, civil society organizations, and elected officials to co-produce ambitious justice-based urban climate policies and actions. What bold climate policy and governance mechanisms is Montréal's future city administration willing to adopt to catalyze, facilitate, and empower the kind of multi-stakeholder relationships and dynamics that can transform its urban context in ways that respond to both the climate emergency and the COVID-19 pandemic?

The people know that action must be taken now. Improved local democracy is the cornerstone for transforming Montréal into an ecological city that can respond to our century's perils. There has never been so much at stake for Montréalers in a municipal election as there is this November.

Some of the Montréal Climate Coalition's main strategies to raise Montréal's climate ambitions include consistently participating in municipal council meetings, both at city hall and at the boroughs. Through an 'issue partisan' rather than a 'party partisan' approach, it has been able to directly engage with municipal elected officials.

In parallel, it has been continuously co-developing independent 'Montréal-specific' climate research and reports that analyze and advance policy proposals for carbon-neutrality. This enables the Coalition to participate extensively in climate-relevant public consultations at various levels of government. In doing so, the Coalition is building bridges with a diversity of stakeholders, not just within the environmental movement but also with the private sector and religious communities, among others.

Another key strategy is fund-raising, to file environmental lawsuits, as they did, for instance, on the REM. This is not just about winning lawsuits to halt unsustainable urban development projects; it also serves to raise awareness

---

7. By 2008, half of the world's population lived in cities; this will likely rise to 67% by mid-century.

on various environmental issues. By elevating the political stakes around environmental issues and employing a diversity of tactics to frame the climate emergency in the urban context, it has catalyzed the creation of new local citizen groups. The Coalition has played a key role during the last five years in setting Montréal's carbon neutrality agenda.

Moving forward, if Montréal aims to accelerate GHG emission reductions, its climate plan needs to concretely 'take root' within the urban landscape, at the 'hyper-local' level of boroughs, neighbourhoods, and streets.

It is there that just, equitable, and inclusive decarbonization plans need to be co-developed and co-implemented by citizens, elected officials, and other stakeholders. Here, we touch upon an important yet historically unfilled municipal promise and the very seed of the ecological city: citizen assemblies. Thanks to a multitude of local citizen-led transition groups, the city's landscape has never been so fertile for the 'lost promise' of a human-scale ecological city to finally begin materializing. This is vital, as the city's 2020-2030 Climate Plan encourages boroughs to co-develop and co-implement climate action plans. To become a truly ecological city, socio-political and economic power in Montréal needs to be transferred to the hyper-local level.

As we look back at Montréal's past three decades, we have seen how the city has come to develop local democratic infrastructures. This is a strong base that needs to be enhanced by innovative governance mechanisms that can elevate citizen involvement from one of 'participation' to one of 'power sharing' and 'decision-making'. The time has come for Citizen Climate Assemblies to emerge across Montréal's neighbourhoods.

Montréalers remain deeply dependent on fossil fuel consumption, and their 'pusher' (the neoliberal urban development machine) continues to accelerate urban sprawl and the sale of gasoline-hungry SUVs. Tackling climate change is not just about *what needs to be done*; it is also about *what needs to stop*, *what needs to be undone*, and *what should not be done*.

In our current decade of climate reckoning, will Montréal have what it takes to fulfil the promise of a just and ecological city, one that can provide quality of life for its citizens in the face of this century's existential threats? While municipal governments need to adopt climate policies, it is more critical that the city's potential as an urban site of social experimentation, challenge, resistance, and justice is supported in order to illuminate how alternative pathways are possible (Bulkeley 2015). Montréal's upcoming municipal election is a critical turning point for the kind of urban story that Montréalers want to write for themselves and their city.

There is no turning back … *Onwards then!*

REFERENCES

Bruemmer, R. 2015. "The City of Montréal unveils its climate-change action plan." *Montréal Gazette*, 24 November 2015. https://montrealgazette.com/news/the-city-of-montreal-unveils-its-climate-change-action-plan.

Bulkeley, H. 2015. "Can cities realise their climate potential? Reflections on COP21 Paris and beyond." *Local Environment* 129(11): 1405-1409.

Gagnon, L., and Lefebvre, J-F. 2018. *Test climat : Réseau express métropolitain (REM)*. Syndicat canadien de la fonction publique, and Coalition climat Montréal. https://coalitionclimatmtl.org/wp-content/uploads/Test-climat-REM.pdf.

IPCC (Intergovernmental Panel on Climate Change). 2018. "Summary for Policymakers." In V. *Global warming of 1.5°C. An IPCC Special Report on the impacts of global warming of 1.5°C above pre-industrial levels and related global greenhouse gas emission pathways, in the context of strengthening the global response to the threat of climate change, sustainable development, and efforts to eradicate poverty*, edited by Masson-Delmotte et al. World Meteorological Organization.

Katz, S., and Roussopoulos, D. 2017. "At the Crossroads of Cultures: The Distinct Politics and Development of Montréal." In *The Rise of Cities*, edited by D. Roussopoulos. Montréal: Black Rose Books, pp. 35-92.

Latour, B. 2017. *Facing Gaia: Eight Lectures on the New Climatic Regime*. Cambridge: Polity Press.

OCPM (Office de Consultation Publique de Montréal). 2016. *Rapport de consultation publique: Réduction de la dépendance de Montréal aux énergies fossiles*. https://ocpm.qc.ca/sites/ocpm.qc.ca/files/pdf/P80/rapport-energies-fossiles.pdf.

The Canadian Press. 2010. "Shell confirms closure of Montréal refinery." *CBC News*, 4 June 2010. https://www.cbc.ca/news/canada/montreal/shell-confirms-closure-of-montreal-refinery-1.973360.

Valois-Nadeau, B. 2019. "Protection du territoire : un 'D' pour Projet Montréal." *Journal Métro*, 24 April 2019. https://journalmetro.com/actualites/montreal/2312809/protection-du-territoire-un-d-pour-projet-montreal/.

Ville de Montréal. 2016. *Montréal durable 2016-2020: Ensemble pour une métropole durable*. https://montreal.ca/articles/montreal-durable-2016-2020-8944.

Ville de Montréal. 2019. *Montréal, objectif zéro déchet: Projet de Plan directeur de gestion des matières résiduelles 2020-2025*. http://ville.montreal.qc.ca/pls/portal/docs/PAGE/ENVIRO_FR/MEDIA/DOCUMENTS/PROJET_PLAN_DIRECTEUR_2020_2050.PDF.

Ville de Montréal. 2020. *Montréal's Climate Plan 2020–2030*. https://res.cloudinary.com/villemontreal/image/upload/v1608323325/portail/esyaiwmnnhqe2w1pxcas.pdf.

PART II.

MOVING IN THE CITY

DEBATING PUBLIC TRANSIT: WHAT ABOUT A REGIONAL TRAMWAY?

LUC GAGNON AND JEAN-FRANÇOIS LEFEBVRE

THE TRAMWAY: A TOOL FOR REDEVELOPMENT

In December 2019, France celebrated the 10th anniversary of its eco-neighbourhood (*écoquartier*) program. Certainly, the concept of creating new, denser developments that focus on residents' quality of life and on reducing their ecological footprint has a long history. For example, the Vauban eco-neighbourhood in the German city of Freiburg am Breisgau dates back to the mid-1990s. However, with 600 eco-neighbourhoods now certified or in the process of being certified, the French program has become a model for other cities around the world to follow. For instance, the people of Brussels took inspiration from it for the first eco-neighbourhood in the Belgian capital, the Tivoli project.

Recently, a partnership was established between the Montréal borough of Lachine and the city of Strasbourg. This followed the arrival in Montréal of Mr Alain Jund, Strasbourg's elected representative in charge of urban planning and president of the French eco-neighbourhood commission. There was an exchange of delegations from Montréal and Strasbourg, while the City of Montréal began designing its own *ÉcoQuartier* program, inspired by the French experience.

What do many European eco-neighbourhoods have in common? For one, they have a reduction in the space occupied by cars thanks to new tramway lines. This reclaimed space allows for increased neighbourhood greening, as well as the construction of public squares and the addition of pedestrian and bicycle paths. In fact, these new developments are generally in line with the

North American concept of Transit Oriented Development (TOD). While TOD areas can be developed around existing metro or train stations,[1] the return of the tramway is essential to winning the fight against climate change. This is how Mr Jund describes the importance of the return of trams in urban redevelopment:[2]

> I am just making a parenthesis about the tram and urban development. Tram and metro are not the same thing. The tram has been in Strasbourg, as in some other cities, an extraordinary factor of urban renewal. Because it has completely changed the game [...] This has completely transformed the urban character of the city. It is a mode of transport which is certainly collective, but it is a means of transforming the urban character of a city. It is not just about mobility, it is not just about travel. It is about how we live in a city, how to transform a city and, in fact, how we feel in a city. How we share the public space, which used to be for the use of the car only, and which is now completely shared with public transport, pedestrians, and bicycles [...] And all the shopkeepers who are delighted, whereas 20 years ago they were savagely against it.

Welcome to the era of the tramway renaissance!

THE END OF AN ERA

The city of Montréal dismantled its last tram line in 1959. This followed a "modernism" movement that originated in the United States, which led to the removal of tram systems in hundreds of North American cities. A 1991 U.S. Senate committee revealed that the dismantling of the American tram system was neither accidental nor inevitable. Quite the contrary. This process resulted from decades of deliberate activity (Schwartz 2015), in addition to the systematic regulation in American cities imposing low density and the separation of functions. Some examples of the intentional acts that led to the removal of North American tram systems include:

- In 1926, President Hoover created a committee headed by the director of the Detroit Automobile Club, which produced *"The Model Municipal Traffic Ordinance"* of 1927. This ordinance transformed city streets from a mixed-use public space to one focused on exclusive use for cars. Pedestrians became confined to sidewalks and pedestrian crossings. According to Schwartz: "The real target ... wasn't the pedestrian. It was the streetcar" (Schwartz 2015, 5).
- Electricity generating companies had been banned from owning their own tram networks. Tram companies owned their tracks but had to pay for maintenance (including snow removal and sometimes even lighting) in addition to taxes. Fare rules condemned the transport companies to run at a deficit. For example, in Boston, fares had to be kept at five cents per trip

---

1. This is already provided for in the *Plan métropolitain d'aménagement et de développement* (PMAD) adopted in 2012 by the *Communauté métropolitaine de Montréal* (CMM).
2. Lecture presented by Mr Jund at UQAM on 11 March 2019.

… for 25 years! (Schwartz 2015).
- Starting in 1936, two shell companies (National City Lines and Pacific City Lines), owned by a consortium of General Motors, Firestone Tire, and Standard Oil of California, among others, bought up over a hundred tram companies in at least 45 American cities. They proceeded to dismantle all of them. They then replaced the trams with much less attractive bus services, which are consistently caught up in traffic congestion. For their crimes, General Motors was fined a paltry $5,000 (Schwartz 2015).

The era of the automobile was destined to spread, overtaking tram networks on every continent. Of all Canadian cities that previously had a tramway, only Toronto retained its lines. In France, only three cities retained them. In Berlin, only the East German part of the city had retained its trams. From this midcentury low point, there was no indication that the return of the tram would soon become one pillar of the energy transitions underway in many cities.

THE RENAISSANCE OF THE TRAMWAY IN FRANCE

In France, public commitment to the return of the tram is exemplary. By 2015, there were more than 70 tram lines with over 1,310 stations in 27 cities in France (Boquet 2017). Many of these lines are located in small and medium-sized towns with a ridership of 15,000 trips/day or more. Regardless of their ridership, these tram lines are justified since they attract and concentrate development. This reduces the social, economic, and environmental costs of urban sprawl.

The case of the city of Lyon stands out. Despite the addition of 11 metro stations over a ten-year period (1986-1995), the modal shares of public and active transport had continued to decline. The modal share of public transit declined by 4% between 1986 and 1995, while active transport (cycling and walking) fell by 1%. At the same time, the modal share for automobiles increased by 5%.

This called for a change of strategy. Over the next decade, from 1995 to 2015, the growth of the metro network was limited to seven stations, while a network of six tram lines with 92 stations was added throughout Lyon. The modal share of public transport rose by 5% over this decade, as did that of active transport (3%), while the modal share for automobile use declined significantly, falling by 9%.

Another trend that breaks with the past is the impressive decline in car ownership rates in the city. Car ownership rates fell from 0.93 to 0.75 vehicles per household between 2006 and 2015 in the central Lyon district of Villeurbanne.[3]

3. Transport survey of the Lyon metropolitan area, press file, January 2016.

THE NEW TRAMWAY

The old trams were noisy, uncomfortable, and often caught in the congestion of the cars with which they shared the track. In contrast, the new generation of trams are quiet, comfortable, and run for most of their routes on exclusive rights-of-way. Above all, they are now designed as tools for urban development (see Table 1; adapted from Bergeron 2003).

THE RIGHT MODE IN THE RIGHT PLACE

There is a consensus that public transit is essential to ensure mobility and to reduce traffic congestion. However, there is often debate about the merits of different modes, such as the metro, tram, or bus. In reality, each mode is tailored to specific needs. To provide the best public transit, at reasonable costs, you have to choose the mode that best meets the needs.

Metro: The metro is justified when there is high circulation, usually at least 100,000 trips/day. In practice, this level of traffic is found in the high urban density typical of the centre of a large city.

Tramway: When circulation is between 15,000 and 100,000 trips/day, either the tram or metro is possible. However, we can choose between 5 km of metro or 50 km of tramway for the same investment. The choice of a tramway allows us to replace ten times more diesel bus trips for the same investment.

Buses: Buses are more flexible than trams, able to take detours and better serve low-density neighbourhoods. The bus is, therefore, the logical choice for networks requiring around 10,000 trips/day. However, the modal attraction of the bus for pedestrians is low, at around 250 metres (beyond this walking distance, pedestrians may be less likely to walk to the bus). This often results in numerous bus lines with low frequency and poor off-peak service. Even with increased frequency and dedicated bus-only lanes, improvements in bus service may have little impact on urban development options. Often, the bus is perceived as a nuisance; Todd Litman of the *Victoria Transport Policy Institute* even notes a reduction in the value of homes near bus stops (Litman 2020).

Several studies confirm that metro and tram systems will attract residential and commercial development, unlike bus networks. The tram has the best performance because, for a given investment, it is possible to construct up to 20 tram stations for the cost of a single metro station. The key to the successful electrification of public transport is to increase the number of citizens living within walking distance of a station, which is enabled with the tramway. Moreover, the tram can integrate smoothly into the urban environment—which is not the case with automatic light rail or *skytrains*.

TABLE 1: OLD AND NEW TRAMWAY

	Tramway of the 1950s  Photo: Courtesy of the *Société d'histoire de Lachine*	New Tramways  Tram from Strasbourg, France (photo JF Lefebvre 2015)
Method of Implementation	Shares the road with other vehicles. The tramway was considered a nuisance for traffic. For this reason, in the 1950s, several tram networks were dismantled, including Montreal's.	Full exclusive right-of-way obtained by appropriating part of the roadway previously granted to the automobile. By this method of implementation, the public authority asserts its intention to reduce the vehicular capacity of the streets and arteries used by the *New Tramway*.
Urban Integration	No special provisions. The streets and arteries on which the tramway ran were indistinguishable from others.	A tool for the redevelopment of public space. "End-to-end" treatment to give a distinctive personality and a strong brand image to the streets and arteries used by the *New Tramway*.
Ground Infrastructure	Low-tech. The rails, which were not welded, were simply laid on the ground and embedded in the surface material, usually asphalt. As a result, the tram was noisy, and it caused unpleasant vibrations for local residents.	High-tech. The infrastructure consists of a concrete foundation resting on a gravel bed, which separates the tram system from the surrounding environment. The rails are welded together to create a continuous track. As a result, the tram is silent, and it does not cause any vibration
Power Supply	By catenaries and overhead wires. Significant overhead congestion.	By catenaries and overhead wires. Overhead congestion remains, although it is reduced. A ground power supply, similar to that used in Bordeaux, does not seem possible for Montreal.
Comfort and Security of Access	Often problematic, as tram users had to cope with car traffic.	The immediate environment of the *New Tramway* is designed to ensure the comfort and safety of pedestrians and users.
Conditions of Operation	Subject to the vagaries of traffic. Like most buses today, the tram was never faster than the cars and trucks with which it shared the streets.	Independent of car traffic for most of its route. The *New Tramway* controls traffic lights remotely, giving it priority.
Costs	A few million dollars per kilometer, in today's dollars, for the infrastructure.	Costs in the range of $60 to $80 million/km (in 2021), including rolling stock.
Rolling Stock	Rustic vehicles, without design or comfort, with a maximum capacity of about 100 passengers.	Trains from 30 to 45m in length that can accommodate up to 300 passengers (up to 600 with additional cars). Most cities opt for a distinctive design, reflecting their "personality". Among the comfort features that have become the norm today are the integral low floor (which makes access easy even for persons with disabilities), air conditioning, quiet operation, lack of lateral movement, and generous windows.

THE BATTERY-POWERED ELECTRIC BUS, A SUBSTITUTE FOR THE TRAM?

Thanks to electrification, an electric tram or bus consumes about four times less energy per passenger than a diesel bus. Some politicians, therefore, assume that the tram is no longer useful, as it will be possible to simply introduce battery-powered electric buses on a large scale. This assumption is unfounded for three reasons:

- A battery-powered electric bus must carry three or four tonnes of batteries, a weight equivalent to 50 passengers, at all times. Therefore, it has less capacity than a diesel bus and costs three times as much (see, for example, the case of Pie-IX). Additionally, the manufacturing process for these batteries is highly polluting. Not to mention that the weight of buses leads to premature wear and tear on the roadway.
- A bus network has no structuring effect, unlike the tram.
- For major networks, the tram replaces between three and five buses, with a significant reduction in operating costs.

TRAM NETWORKS WELL ADAPTED TO THE COLD CLIMATE

Some Québecers, dreaming of subways that go everywhere, say that the tram is unsuitable for winter weather. However, international experience shows otherwise. Many cities with cold climates currently use trams (think of examples in Scandinavian countries like Stockholm, Gothenburg, and Norrking in Sweden, Helsinki in Finland, Oslo, Bergen, and Trondheim in Norway, as well as cities in Switzerland like Bern, Geneva, and Zurich, and several cities in Eastern Europe, including Tallinn, Riga, Minsk, Kiev, Prague, St Petersburg, and Moscow, not to mention, closer to us, Toronto and now Ottawa). It should be noted that these cities are confident in the reliability of their trams, as many of them are constantly adding new lines.

THE IMPLICATIONS OF CHOOSING THE "WRONG" MODE

In Québec, the metro is considered the public transit option *par excellence*. However, this is an illusion given the often excessive cost of the metro. In Montréal, the 5.8 km extension of the Blue Line for **five metro stations** will cost at least $6.1 billion.[4] For a similar amount of money, it would be possible

---

[4] The failure to take metro costs into account is glaring in the *Metropolitan Montréal Metro Extension Study* (Bureau de projet du prolongement des lignes de metro 2015). The study concludes that the tramway would offer a much better service than the bus, but that the metro would provide the best, for the corridor studied. However, this study makes no mention of the much higher cost of the metro, nor of the increased number of citizens that could be served by a tram network. On the other hand, the extension of the orange metro line by two stations—from Côte-Vertu to Bois-Franc—despite its high cost, makes sense from the perspective of intermodal connection with the REM (and to reduce costs). See also Bergeron (2021).

to build at least four tram lines, with at least **140 stations over nearly 90 km**. The same is true elsewhere: according to H. Werner Franz, a transport specialist in Berlin, more than 100 km of tram lines will be added because the costs for building one kilometre of metro are at least ten times higher than for one kilometre of tramway.

As for the downtown/Montréal-Nord section of the proposed Pink Line metro project, it would clearly have served areas that are in great need, with expected ridership that could have justified the choice of metro over other modes. However, excluding the surface portion, which could be completed as a tramway for less than a billion dollars (the Lachine/downtown tram), construction of the Pink Line metro could cost between $16.6 and $23.6 billion for 21 km underground, or at least $800 million per kilometre (Chouinard and Lévesque 2020). Unless there is a significant reduction in costs, a surface network should be preferred.

It should be noted that if the metro proves to be too heavy a mode for the expected 80,000 users per day on the Blue Line extension, the Bus Rapid Transit (BRT) being developed on Pie-IX will not be enough, with its expected 70,000 trips per day. In both cases, a tram would have been preferable. In particular, we would have saved about $30 million per year by installing a tramway instead of the BRT on Pie-IX. From now on, the tram must be one of the options seriously considered.

The same observation applies to the *Réseau express métropolitain* (REM) light rail network currently under construction across Greater Montréal. The project has multiple inconsistencies: like the metro, the *skytrain* is always away from the roads, leading to significant costs; it has limited capacity due to overhead or underground stations; the project serves low-density neighbourhoods like a commuter train; large parking lots are being built which will encourage automobile use, etc. Including the Mount Royal Tunnel and the tracks on the new Champlain Bridge, the real costs for the first phase will be approximately $10 billion for thirteen new stations. This amounts to $770 million per new station, or twenty times more expensive than each station in a new tram system would cost.

It would also cost much less to serve the east end of Montréal and Montréal-Nord with tram lines than with the overhead and underground *skytrain* (REM) that CDPQ-Infra wants to impose. It is the proponent (CDPQ-Infra) who has commissioned the studies, which systematically fail to compare the costs of alternative options and the number of lines and stations that public funding would allow. Fast access to more stations within walking distance would compensate for the slightly lower speed of the tram compared to the REM, while also preventing some neighbourhoods from being disfigured by massive concrete infrastructure.

Worse, the REM is, above all, a project designed to privatize public services—for 99 years (with options for renewal). The costs charged to cities will be much higher with the REM than with public alternatives—particularly trams—and could total nearly $1 billion annually.

A judicious combination of trams and reserved bus lanes, coupled with the *Réseau express vélo* (REV), could transform the city for equivalent investments.

A *BIG SHIFT* FOR MONTRÉAL

Québec City is making an excellent choice in developing its first tramway line, as is Montréal's South Shore with its East-West Electric Link (EWEL) project (Gerbet 2020). Gatineau is also considering the development of a tram network, in order to join Ottawa's new light rail system. It should be noted that the difficulties in implementing Ottawa's light rail network did not stem from the choice of technology—widely tested elsewhere—but from a poor public-private partnership (Spears 2020; CBC News 2019).

Map 1 illustrates a proposal for the first phase of the implementation of a real tram network for Montréal. The cost of this proposal would barely exceed that of the five new metro stations for the Blue Line. This network would need to be well integrated into the existing system, while allowing for the creation of a multitude of *ÉcoQuartiers*. This first phase could include four tram lines:

1. The Lachine tram (covering the western section of Mayor Valérie Plante's proposed pink line), including the future *ÉcoQuartier de Lachine-Est* (Lefebvre, Gagnon, and Chevalier 2020).
2. The Eastern tram, which will run along Notre-Dame Boulevard to Pointe-aux-Trembles, including a north-south branch linking the metro's Green Line and the Blue Line extension.
3. The Taschereau tram, running along Taschereau Boulevard on the South Shore, going from the Brossard REM station to the Longueuil–Université-de-Sherbrooke station on the metro's Yellow Line.
4. The Côte-des-Neiges tram, as well as an extension to the north (Hippodrome-Namur-Marché Central tram), making the Hippodrome-Namur and Royalmount developments real eco-neighbourhoods (Consortium Genivar-Systra 2011).[5]

All four tram lines of this first phase could be completed within a decade. Then, a tram-cargo system should be operated during off-peak periods, offering an electrified and battery-free means of transporting goods in the city, combined with local delivery of parcels by bicycle (Lefebvre, Gagnon, and Chevalier 2020).

---

5. Thanks to Pierre Barrieau for the idea of the extension to the Marché Central.

MAP 1: PROPOSAL FOR THE FIRST PHASE OF A BIG SHIFT TOWARDS THE TRAM IN MONTRÉAL

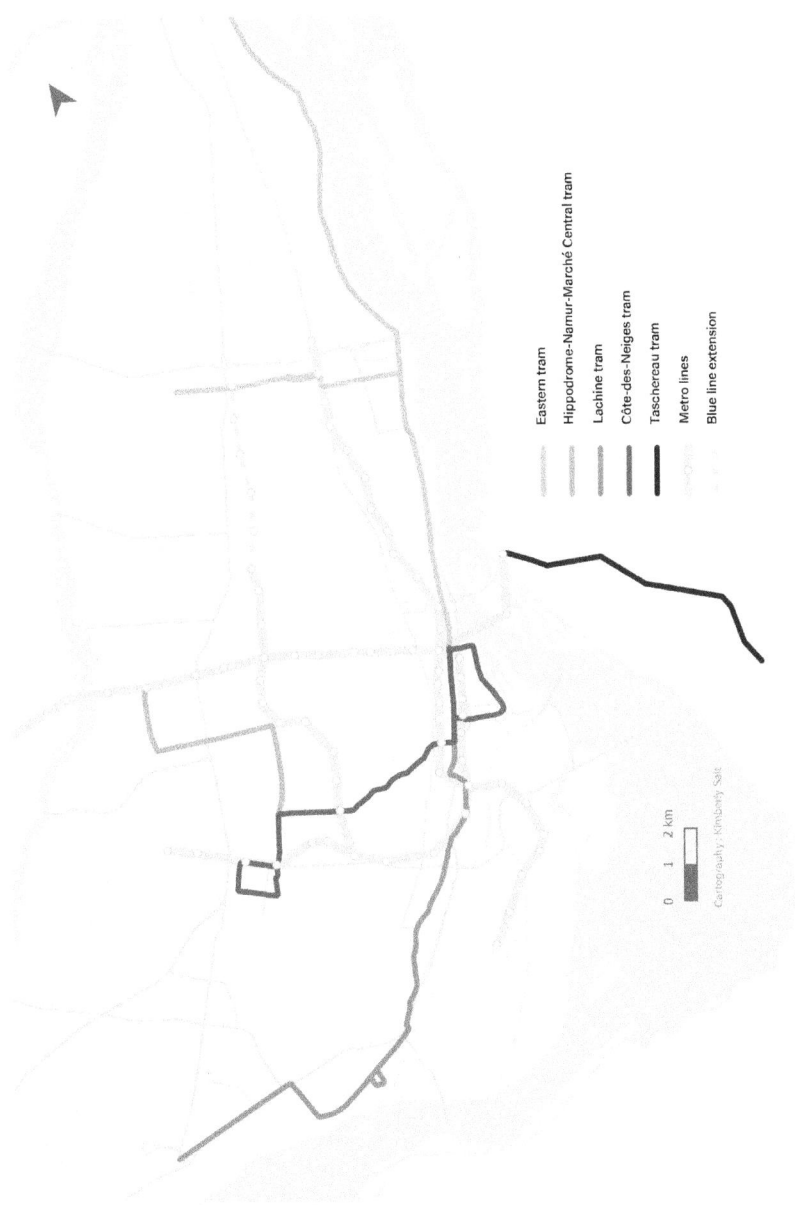

MAP 2: PROPOSED ROUTE FOR THE REM DE L'EST

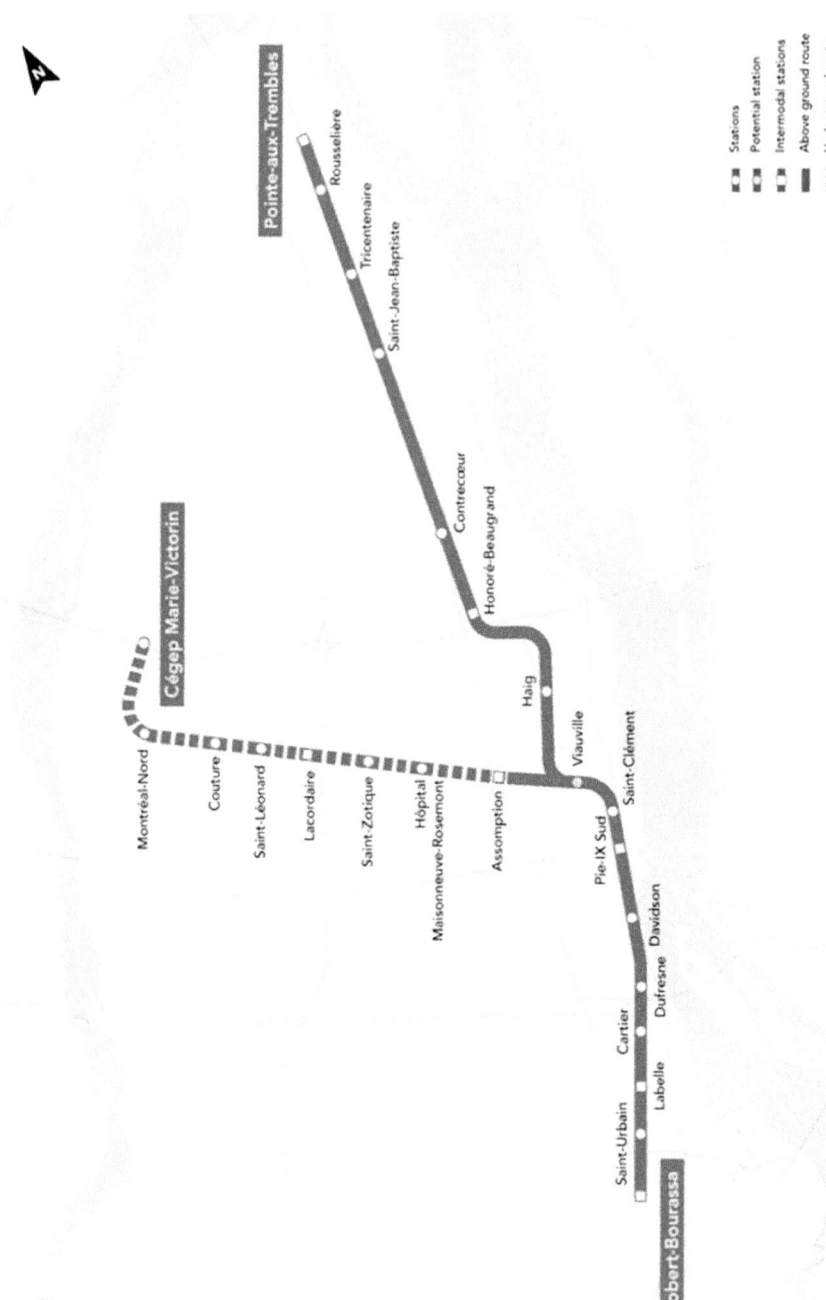

Moreover, as noted by transport and urban planning researcher Jeffrey Kenworthy, there is no incompatibility between the purchase of buses and the development of trams:

> We have found that in cities with strong rail traffic, buses are used even more per capita than in cities where public transport is based solely on buses (Kenworthy 2019).

In twenty years, nearly a dozen tramway lines could see the light of day. These could run along major arteries like Park Avenue, Newman Boulevard in LaSalle, Cavendish Boulevard, and Côte-Vertu Boulevard in the borough Saint-Laurent. This could be combined with the completion of the orange line in Laval and the extension of the yellow line into Longueuil using trams, followed by other tramway network extensions across the city.

CONCLUSION: TRAMWAY, THE MISSING LINK

In *Why Rail Systems are Essential in Creating Eco-cities*, Jeffrey Kenworthy says:

> Urban Rail Systems are the key to the renaissance in public transport worldwide and a key to reducing automobile dependence. We will not change any significant size city into a more ecological model without high quality urban rail (Kenworthy 2011).

The implementation of state-of-the-art tram networks will quickly create dozens of electrified public transport stations, universally accessible by foot and offering a multitude of destinations. Each line added to the network could encourage the creation of genuine eco-neighbourhoods while allowing buses to be better distributed to improve service in other areas. The return of the tramway is a *sine qua non* condition for a successful energy transition in our cities.

REFERENCES

Bergeron, M. 2021. "Le coût des expropriations quadruple à 1,2 milliard." *La Presse*, 10 May 2021. https://www.lapresse.ca/affaires/2021-05-10/ligne-bleue/le-cout-des-expropriations-quadruple-a-1-2-milliard.php.

Bergeron, R. 2003. *Le nouveau tramway*. Montréal: Agence métropolitaine de transport.

Boquet, Y. 2017. "The renaissance of tramways and urban development in France." *Miscellanea Geographica: Regional Studies on Development* 21(1): 5-18.

Bureau de projet du prolongement des lignes de metro. 2015. *Étude de prolongement du métro du Montréal métropolitain: Étude d'un mode alternatif au metro: Étapes 1 – étude préliminaire des modes de surface*. Project co-directed by the AMT and the MTQ, 8 May 2015.

CBC News. 2019. Public-private partnerships boast 'mixed record,' expert warns. 25 November 2019. https://www.cbc.ca/news/canada/ottawa/public-private-partnerships-mixed-record-1.5372121.

Chouinard, T., and Lévesque, K. 2020. "Ligne rose: une facture de 17 à 24 milliards." *La Presse*, 28 February 2020.

Consortium Genivar-Systra. 2011. *Tramway de Montréal, Étude de faisabilité de la première ligne* (Vol. 1 to 14).

Lefebvre, J-F., Gagnon, L., and Chevalier, H. 2020. *Le tramway Lachine / centre-ville, un outil de redéveloppement*. Study conducted for the borough of Lachine by the CDEC LaSalle-Lachine.

Gerbet, T. 2020. "Tramway Longueuil-La Prairie : ça se concrétise." *Radio-Canada*, 26 February 2020. https://ici.radio-canada.ca/nouvelle/1539708/tramway-longueuil-la-prairie-taschereau-ligne-jaune-rem-metro.

Kenworthy, J. 2011. "Why Rail Systems are Essential in Creating Eco-cities." During the keynote *Ecomobility and Urban Planning in Ecocities*. Ecocity World Summit, Montréal, 26 August 2011.

Kenworthy, J. 2019. "We should build urban environments and transport systems that are not dependent on cars." Interview with Jeffrey Kenworthy. *YIT Corporation News*, 6 November 2019. https://www.yitgroup.com/en/news-repository/news/we-should-build-urban-environments-and-transport-systems-that-are-not-dependent-on-cars.

Litman, T. 2020) *Best Practices Guidebook for Evaluating Public Transit Benefits and Costs*. Victoria Transport Policy Institute.

Schwartz, S.I. 2015. *Street smart: The rise of cities and the fall of cars*. New York: Public Affairs.

Spears, T. 2020. "Analysis: Why Ottawa's LRT is a lesson in how not to manage a major environmental project." *Ottawa Citizen*, 27 January 2020.

F*** THE CAR: A NEW VISION FOR TRANSPORT IN THE MONTRÉAL REGION

JASON PRINCE

VISION

This chapter will try to sketch out the revolution in transportation that we must achieve in the Montréal region, and rapidly, if we are to slay the many-headed Hydra we now face following 70 years of car-oriented planning. The transport sector is the principal source of greenhouse gas emissions in Québec and the only sector where they continue to grow. But there are other cascading and catastrophic problems arising from our ongoing car-oriented development. Transportation represents a substantial annual cost for the working poor and forces tough choices on these families. The proposals here attack these problems with a bold new vision for our city.

Let us start with a description of Montréal's transportation system in 2030, or what it should look like if we have succeeded in our revolution. By 2030:

- 75% of daily rush-hour trips in the Montréal region occur by collective transport. Currently, that ratio sits at under 25%, with the remaining 75% of trips by private car. In Brazil, the city of Curitiba (a city comparable in size to Montréal) managed a similar transition.
- Public transit is free for all. The Province of Québec and the City of Montréal have declared a climate emergency and are tackling it head-on.
- The Montréal region's carbon footprint is well on the way to carbon neutrality, and Montréal is recognized as a world leader in climate solutions. We are gathering and publishing the city's carbon data biannually. We use all the instruments available: regulatory powers, public pressure tactics, free public transit, taxes per kilometre travelled,

gamification strategies, car-sharing incentives, and measurably reducing space for automobiles every year. We are applying all the carrots and sticks we have—all of them.
- We have eliminated development pressure on agricultural lands and green spaces by changing our transportation patterns and completely outlawing greenfield development. The greenfield moratorium in the Montréal region has been in place since 2022. Municipalities are expropriating these spaces and putting them under *fiducie à utilité sociale*,[1] and construction now occurs only on remediated brownfield sites.
- Private car ownership rates have dropped, electric cars outnumber conventional ones, and public transit combined with car-sharing is the new norm. A convenient and effective public transit service has been extended to the suburbs, integrated with car-sharing, with particular attention paid to the "last mile problem."

SOME PROBLEMS

It is time to take the gloves off as we face the transportation question in the Montréal region. We must break our dependency on the private automobile, and we must do it decisively.

Let me provide an admittedly oversimplified framework for thinking about the transportation problem in our city.

Today, the Montréal region has roughly four million inhabitants. A stable core population of about one million residents is well-served by public transit. In contrast, the growing suburban population—now roughly three million—is more or less dependent on their automobiles. For over 70 years, this suburban population has grown—and it continues to grow.

When did our cities start to go off the rails, and why?

In 1955, the vast majority of Montréal's rush-hour trips were by public transit. But in 1959, after Montréal's tram lines were dismantled, the automobile began to grab a growing part of the modal share (the means of transportation used for morning rush-hour trips). Across North America, car, tire, and oil companies bought out and dismantled the profitable tramways, leaving them as empty husks, before selling them back to the public sector.[2]

From that moment onward, every highway, bridge, and tunnel built in the Montréal region has been justified by evoking the "problem" of congestion. The problem has always been the same, and the solution has always been: more highways.

What if we redefine the problem as a dependence on the automobile?

Three million people in the Montréal region are trapped by circumstance.

1. A Québec Civil Code tool that can permanently remove property from speculative use.
2. See the infamous Snell Report to the U.S. Congress in 1974.

They have no viable alternative to the private automobile. Many need it to go to work. They need it for groceries. They need it to go to the library and the hospital. They need it to pick up their kids. Many suburban families have two or three cars, and often, all are used at once.

These residents need a public transit solution that is faster, cheaper, and more convenient than their automobile. Not more highways, which will only make the problem worse.

The real solution is a comprehensive door-to-door alternative to the private automobile.

We currently face two distinct problems. On the one hand: what do we do about the suburbs we have already built? How can we eliminate this dependency on the private car? On the other: what must we do now to stop feeding sprawl?

Let me call one the first one the "retrofitting problem," caused by 70 years of urban sprawl. The second is the "future growth problem," weakly addressed by the regional urban plan (PMAD; *Plan métropolitain d'aménagement et de développement du Grand Montréal*), Transport Oriented Development (TOD), and projects like the driverless electric train (REM; *Réseau express métropolitain*). Any serious effort to change the way we move in the Montréal region, or any large Canadian city, must address these two very different problems.

SPRAWL: THE "RETROFIT PROBLEM"

Origin-destination data shows that while daily traffic patterns in the region continue to be primarily from the edges to the centre, large daily volumes also move between edges, from the centre to edges, and even across the island. Daily trucking flow across the island is layered on top of this. If we want to serve the three million car-dependent residents in the Montréal region with effective public transit solutions, we need a high-quality matrix approach (or spider's web) for the region, not just direct lines into the centre (which the REM proposes).

The solution is staring us in the face. Suppose tomorrow we announce the conversion of every highway in the region to dedicated Bus-Rapid-Transit (BRT) lines, with massive parking lots squeezed into the dozens of butterfly off-ramps (currently wasted urban space). In that case, we have the starting place for a radical transformation of transportation by 2030.[3] The major construction component requires building elevator access from the parking lots to the highways and dozens of comfortable stations. This can be done in three to five years.

---

3. See the transit component of Melanie Joly's 2013 electoral campaign, as a starting point. Hers was a great idea: under city control, cheap, effective, and fast.

We can start with BRT and later convert to steel (see the chapter on tramways elsewhere in this book). Of course, some lanes on the highways will be left for private automobiles and the growing number of trucks arising from the Amazon Prime Now phenomenon,[4] but there will always be congestion. Always.

POLITICAL PROBLEMS ARISING FROM THE "RETROFIT PROBLEM"

What about the politics of this dramatic change in vision?

Under Mayor Drapeau in 1960, the City of Montréal represented 90% of the regional population; when he spoke to the provincial or federal government, **Montréal** spoke. But when the City of Montréal speaks now, only representing 45% of the region's population, it is a different story. Now, "Montréal" is one big hen and a bunch of chicks squabbling and jousting. There is a pecking order of sorts, but it is messy, and the region does not speak with one voice. Unchecked, this political power will continue to dwindle.[5]

THE "FUTURE GROWTH PROBLEM"

Finally, the Montréal region continues to grow. Every year, it welcomes about 40,000 new immigrants (see chapter on the city as sweatshop to see how warm our welcome is). Including our natural birth rate, the region may grow by up to one million people, adding 300,000 new households by 2030.[6] The regional urban plan (PMAD), adopted in 2011 (despite a great deal of noise by a few of the chicks in the regional henhouse), aims to direct regional growth away from sprawl (low density, car-oriented development) and towards transit-oriented village hubs.

Let's take a closer look at this solution.

SOME SOLUTIONS PROPOSED SO FAR

THE REM AND TOD TO CONTROL FUTURE GROWTH

In 2011, the Montréal region adopted its first regional development plan (PMAD), with relatively ambitious transport-oriented development (TOD) targets to guide future development of the city around "transport-oriented villages." The REM is meant as a path to achieve this vision. Imagine the

---

4. See comedian Ronny Chieng's routine on YouTube: https://youtu.be/BGEAiUeiaKs
5. As of the last census, the median household income in the Montréal region was $61,790 while it was only $50,227 in the City of Montréal (comparing the median income for the region, excluding the city, would show an even more drastic difference). This is another aspect of the "political problem": poverty is concentrated in the city of Montréal and their political power is diluted in a regional decision-making process.
6. Depending on immigration, longevity, and other factors (see Morency, Caron Malenfant, and MacIsaac 2017). The PMAD projects 4.3 million people in the CMM by 2030 (an area slightly smaller than the region). The beyond-the-edge problem—behaviours just outside the planned area—is a serious one and needs a fix, but is beyond the scope of this chapter.

REM lines as threads in a super-saturated sugar solution. Each station should act as a catalyst. Housing and mixed-use development should cluster around each station, and the PMAD imposes an (admittedly lightweight) regulatory framework to make this happen. Assuming that the region grows by 300,000 new households over the next ten years, 60% of those new homes should appear close to REM stations or other transport hubs, according to the revised PMAD.

At least, that is the big idea.

If reports from the CMM (*Communauté métropolitaine de Montréal*) are to be trusted, the plan seems to be working, though two urban sprawl studies suggest we are heading in the wrong direction (Dupras and Alam 2015; Nazarnia et al. 2016). Even if we achieve the 60% goal, 40% of future growth will be car-oriented and continue to feed the problem. The REM, raised above highways rather than replacing them, actually increases urban sprawl by making edge development more attractive. Regrettably, many REM stations are being placed on or near 'greenfield' sites that should be protected, not developed (see Barnard's chapter elsewhere in this book). Finally, while TOD along these expensive REM lines may be intended to control urban growth and remove pressure on agricultural lands and remaining natural areas, we must remain sceptical. We need more robust land-use controls in Québec instead of simply leaving it to the 'market' or the piecemeal decisions made at the municipal level. Some municipalities still see their abutting agricultural lands just as opportunities for bungalows.

But there is another big contradiction at the core of the REM project, and it lies at the intersection of the retrofit and future growth problems.

The lure of living in an REM transport-oriented village is that you can go to work in your pyjamas. The lucky worker would walk a couple of minutes to their REM station and be downtown in 20 minutes. But if it attracts tens of thousands of workers who would drive to the REM station instead or walk or bike—another promise of the REM and a feature of the Caisse's business model—where will they park?

What exactly is that TOD village? Is it a sea of parking lots—perhaps a clutch of multi-level parking garages? Or an elite TOD village that looks like the brightly coloured towns at the base of the Mont Tremblant ski hill? It cannot be both.

THE PMAD: ESTABLISHING GREEN AND BLUE PRESERVATION TARGETS

While the centrepiece of the PMAD is TOD, it also adopts two other targets. First, raising the modal share for public transit in the region from roughly 25%

to 35% by 2030. This would hardly put a dent in our carbon emissions, as the electric revolution still a mirage.[7]

Second, to protect 17% of the Montréal region's land via *"la Trame verte et bleue,"*[8] the province, region, and City of Montréal have all established ambitious preservation targets but continually failed to meet them (also addressed in Barnard's chapter).

The City of Montréal's website whispers that we have already preserved 17% of the territory, "if one considers the protected areas within these large water bodies, which are under federal or provincial jurisdiction as appropriate." Move the goalposts, and who knows what we might be able to claim.

The PMAD is a good first step, but it does not go nearly far enough. Given real estate developers' interests at Montréal's periphery, municipal thirst for more property taxes, and the ongoing market demand for low-density suburban living, what needs to be done now? How do we fix this?

QUÉBEC'S LAND USE PLANNING ACT AND AGRICULTURAL PRESERVATION ACT

Enacted in the 1970s, these two legislative frameworks aimed to achieve two broad goals: to contain urban sprawl by directing development under a regulatory framework and protect precious agricultural land in one of the most fertile deltas in North America. Both projects have failed: the Montréal region is dying a death by a thousand cuts. The accumulation of exceptions made, each one seeming to make sense in its context and blessed by urban planners overseeing the laws, is killing our city. Notably, according to testimony from the Québec Environment Ministry at a critical court case on the *Technoparc* in early 2020, not a single certificate of authorization to destroy wetlands has been refused by the ministry since the law protecting them was adopted (Symon 2020).

NEW SOLUTIONS? SOME THOUGHTS

THE RETROFIT PROBLEM

Let's say we muster the political will to transform the highways that criss-cross the region into dedicated public transit routes with parking hubs at each butterfly on-and-off-ramp. Fluid transitions at each knot in the web are

---

7. In 2011, when approving the Turcot Interchange, Jean Charest said that 25% of cars sold in Québec would be electric by 2020. In 2020, there are still only a few hundred charging stations and just tens of thousands of electric cars in Québec (only 6.8% of new car sales, less than one-third of the 25% target).

8. See more at: https://cmm.qc.ca/projets/trame-verte-et-bleue/

created so that moving around the edge is as fast and easy as getting into the centre.

We will need engineers to recalculate regional traffic flows. The STM (*Société de transport de Montréal*) currently has 2,300 buses, operates over 200 bus routes, and serves 1.4 million users daily (pre-pandemic).[9] I have argued elsewhere that we must at least double its reach before making the public transit system free (Prince and Romano-Toramanian 2016).

The economic arguments for investing in public transit have been well documented by the *Chambre de commerce du Montréal métropolitain*, and the business community continues to argue for improvements (Goudreault 2020).

In a second phase, the most densely travelled routes can be replaced with tramways, with busses redeployed elsewhere in the network.

Transport engineers and cities must experiment with 'first and last mile' solutions that make public transit more convenient and faster than the automobile. Everything should be tried, and every trial should be evaluated. Montréal should cast itself as an 'experimental city', not afraid to make mistakes, constantly testing low-cost solutions and expanding those that work.

The transport solution for the Montréal region has to be much more ambitious than it is now.

Florence Junca-Adenot, an influential figure on transport questions in the Montréal region, once provided the recipe for success, and I paraphrase it here from memory: First, we dangle the carrots by installing appropriate collective infrastructure with the capacity to serve the region's needs—add buses and reserved lanes, build trams and REMs. We give drivers choices. Second, we bring out the sticks: tax gasoline, put tolls on bridges, charge for kilometres travelled, tax all parking lots, etc. Finally, we deconstruct our automobile infrastructure by removing car lanes, demolishing highways, and removing parking.

At this moment in the climate emergency, we may need to simultaneously implement all of the carrots and sticks. But maybe start with a target of 2,000 new buses and 1,000 km of new reserved bus lanes by 2025.

THE PROPERTY TAX SYSTEM

The municipal property tax system should be replaced with one that removes the perverse incentives that put the city in a conflict of interest with its own residents. The current system encourages it to develop high-end condos that drive a wave of unaffordability rippling through the city. Until this is challenged and changed, the city will continue to chase development and

---

9. One of Plante's missed opportunities was building a first iteration of her Pink Line, in pink paint, using dedicated bus lanes. The busses themselves could have been painted pink. Every action going forward must remove space from the private automobile and give it to other modes.

continue to gentrify, increasingly pushing middle-income residents to the periphery.

THE BARRIERS

THE MTQ

The principal enemy in transportation planning in Québec is the Ministry of Transportation (MTQ). The MTQ's approach to planning is stuck in the 1950s, and its power is deeply entrenched—'a state within a state.'[10] This ministry must be completely dismantled. Senior civil servants should be given early retirement, and the remaining civil service redeployed elsewhere in the government. A new ministry should be constructed from scratch, with its leadership drawn from the collective transport authorities. It should approach the problem with a completely new mandate and a vision based around collective transport. Engineering solutions in Québec must evolve and our new expertise exported to cities across the world.

THE GOVERNMENT OF QUÉBEC

Québec has completely failed to address climate change. It has a peculiar genius for establishing glossy laws, policies, and programs that look great on paper but include plenty of backdoors. In practice, they are systematically ignored, not only by the private sector but by the government itself.[11]

In my years watching the Québec government closely, I only once remember a politician publicly admitting that it openly lies.

When Premier Couillard announced at COP-21—the historic meeting that led to the Paris Agreement—that Québec would shut down the petroleum industry, he "misspoke", observed Natural Resources Minister Pierre Arcand while leaving a cabinet meeting.

"The Prime Minister's statements were made in a context," he told reporters. "I say to everyone: ***judge our actions*** since we've been here. The Prime Minister was present when the Stolt announcement was made, which is a natural gas project" (Robillard 2015 [emphasis added]).

Minister Arcand could easily have continued: do not judge us by our laws, plans, policies, or programs. They are magic dust we throw in electors' eyes to make them believe. To make them feel like something is being done. Meanwhile: we do what industry wants and what the lobbyists tell us to do. "Judge our actions."

---

10. As declared by retired UQAM professor David Hanna in this must-see documentary, *Cities Held Hostage*, available at : https://vimeo.com/ondemand/mainbassesurlaville
11. See Thompson's 2013 paper which exposes the contradictions between Québec's beautiful laws and it's disastrous public investments, using the Turcot Interchange as a case study (Thompson et al. 2013).

So we cannot expect leadership from Québec, whose current political base is in the regions. The current CAQ (*Coalition Avenir Québec*) government elected only two representatives out of 27 on the island of Montréal: it is completely divorced from the experience and reality of Montréalers (Valiante 2018).

If the province is not an ally, then Montréal should reach beyond Québec City to Ottawa to fund its ambitions. It must experiment more (see Prince's chapter on the social economy). It must organize a common front with smaller progressive municipalities, on and off island, for a transportation revolution that costs their tax-base nothing and improves quality of life. The plan must be built on three principles: (1) faster than the private car, (2) as convenient, with first and last mile solutions that work fluidly, and (3) free for users.

PENSION AND LABOUR FUNDS

Our pension and labour funds have become critical drivers in Montréal's "real estate state." Until they change their vision, they will continue to act against the goals outlined in this chapter. If they do change, they can become powerful allies in the drive for a truly just and ecological city. The union membership and Québec's pensioners must wake up to the greater cause and push their leadership in the right direction.

LACK OF AMBITION AND VISION IN MONTRÉAL'S CIVIL SERVICE

Montréal cannot rely on its civil service to devise visionary solutions either.

When the OCPM (*Office de consultation publique de Montréal*) conducted a public consultation on how to reduce Montréal's dependence on fossil fuels, those who participated were likely shocked by the lack of ambition and lack of vision from the city's civil service. City staff do not see themselves as agents of the Big Change that must occur if we are to do our part to steer our city, and the planet, away from the precipice of climate collapse. Proposals from city staff amounted to nothing more than rearranging the deck chairs on the Titanic.

If the city is to move forward on a revolutionary new vision, it will have to gain the hearts and minds of its civil service and incite them to show leadership in the city. Let me suggest one example: too many Montréal employees live off-island. What if we aim to change that over the next decade? What about incentives to encourage transport-oriented workforce housing? The city could set up a revolving loan fund for down-payments on homes bought inside city limits through a payroll contribution, negotiated in collaboration with the city's unions. A dime contributed for every hour worked—refundable upon retirement, a kind of forced savings matched by employer contributions—would enable the construction of thousands of permanently affordable workforce housing units over the next ten years, if constructed on a community land trust (see chapter on the social economy for other ideas).

The city's workforce must become agents of positive change if we are to enable a revolution in transportation.

THE AUTOMOBILE

The abuse of the automobile is the problem. An occasional glass of red wine may be good for your health, but two bottles a day will put you in an early grave.

Québec used to be known as Canada's 'smoking section.' It was the last province where you could smoke in restaurants and bars. What if Québec decided to get ahead of the curve this time? Yes, let's electrify the fleet of cars. But we need to make the car a shared object.

Here are two actions we can take immediately.

First, ban the advertising of private automobiles in Québec. The idea of the private automobile, as constantly reinforced by the advertising campaigns, does not exist and never did. Those highways blazing through the city are only empty during a pandemic or at 4 am, sometimes. The automobile does nothing for Québec's economy, and its fuel must be imported. Québec has made it illegal to advertise to children, so too should it outlaw private automobile ads. Mass media will find another way to survive.

Second, massive encouragement of car-sharing is needed. Government incentives. Privileged, free parking spaces in all publicly and privately owned lots. Large-scale subsidized partnerships between public transit authorities and car-sharing operations with suitable "last mile" solutions. For the next five years, every possible configuration should be tried, and each one carefully evaluated (see chapter on the social economy for additional thoughts).

Montréal is already the car-sharing capital of North America. How far can we go?

THE SUBURBAN POPULATION

Without at least the grudging support of most suburban populations to try something new, any effort will meet resistance. The solution must be built around addressing their problems. Surveys have consistently suggested that roughly a third of Canadian suburban residents would choose public transit if it were a viable option. A compelling vision and a faster, convenient, free option could get us over 50%. If not, sticks can be imposed by the city, imposing higher costs on parking and on using a car downtown.

FREE PUBLIC TRANSIT

LESSONS FROM TALLINN

The largest experiment in free public transit enacted to date is in the capital city of Estonia.

Tallinn is about the same size as Québec City and is also surrounded by little towns and suburbs. In 2012, the mayor of Tallinn proposed free transit across the city, and citizens voted overwhelmingly in a referendum to implement it. Importantly, only tax-paying residents in the City of Tallinn would get free transit, while tourists, commuters and others would pay double. At the time, the farebox recovery ratio was about 20% in Tallinn compared to 45% in Montréal (roughly half the operating cost of Montréal's system comes from the farebox as user fees). After a few years, the City of Tallinn found it actually **made money** by making transit free: commuters moved into or registered with the city to get the bonus and ended up paying their taxes to the city.

This is the first important lesson: public transit can become a powerful city-building instrument if appropriately handled. By making transit free only for residents of the city, you can keep people in and even draw them back from the suburbs. But if Montréal followed the Tallinn model, we would have to do it carefully. Such a move would put additional pressure on the existing housing stock, accelerate gentrification and displacement, and put pressure on greenfields (see other chapters in this book that deal with housing and green spaces).

Second, free public transit would immediately become a keystone to poverty reduction. Free transit would amount to about a $1,080 annual tax credit for current users of the transit system, at today's transit pass cost. That $1,080 represents a significant proportion of the yearly take-home revenue of the working poor in Montréal. Free public transit would make an immediate, measurable difference to many working families in Montréal.

The third important lesson from Tallinn is that free public transit is extremely popular. But again: the political problem. Only one in four voters in the region will be happy with that given current system.

Finally, if Montréal made public transit free, it would immediately signal that it was taking the climate emergency seriously and was prepared to fundamentally alter the structure of transport in the region. The REM would be free. The metro and regional suburban train network: free. All free carrots.

Then: the sticks come out. Mandatory car-pooling. Gas taxes. Tolls on bridges. Recommissioning highways for public transit. Demolishing the Ville-

Marie Expressway or filling it with sand to restore peaceful sunrise views from downtown Montréal.

Pierre Brisset, a long-time critic of the MTQ (and just any government agency involved in transport decisions), has often been exactly right about the transport solutions we need in the city, and he is right about this one: the REM de l'Est should NOT be placed on Sherbrooke Street East or Hochelaga Street East as currently proposed but within the existing CN right-of-way from the Assomption branch to Pointe-Aux-Trembles.

Why would we interfere in the viability of a city street when a linear wasteland is yearning for reinvention?

The downtown portion of the REM (or light rail solution) should be within the Ville Marie Autoroute right-of-way from the Jacques Cartier Bridge to the Turcot Interchange. It should replace several lanes of high-density roadway instead of being built on concrete towers in the centre of René-Lévesque Boulevard or trying to tunnel underground to the Central Station. From the Turcot to the airport, the REM would use the right-of-way provided in the Turcot project north of the CN tracks, thus completing a continuous East-West backbone of the REM system on the island of Montréal, Brisset argues.

Whatever route is chosen, it should replace highway lanes used by cars with collective transport; collective transport solutions should replace the automobile and reduce sprawl, not add to it.

IMMEDIATE NEXT STEPS (3-5 YEARS)

RESERVED BUS LANES ON ALL OF MONTRÉAL'S ARTERIALS

The city should immediately recommission its arterial roads as reserved bus lanes, with massively improved service. These should be strictly policed, with anyone found parking in a reserved bus lane getting towed: creating work for tow-truck operators year-round.[12] It must fight the province to implement permanent grade-separated reserved bus lanes on all highways criss-crossing the island.

Maybe some arterials become 'bus only'? What if de Maisonneuve was bus-only in both directions, sharing the Claire Morrissette bike path? Are there some opportunities here to explore?

And the city must call on the provincial and federal governments to make the emergency public transit funding—granted during the pandemic—permanent. Weeks after the pandemic was declared, the federal and provincial governments announced emergency operating funds for transit systems across Canada. Montréal received $400 million to cover its projected

---

12. A car blocking a reserved bus lane at rush-hour can penalize 50,000 public transit users, notes our public transit authority.

deficit, half from the federal level. Permanent funding of this magnitude puts free public transit within reach.

The city should direct its civil service to acquire all the second-hand buses available as an immediate short-term measure for increasing its transport capacity.

PARTNER WITH SHOPPING MALLS TO MAKE BUS STOPS

The parking lots of the Montréal region's shopping malls could become sites for incentive parking for suburban dwellers. Cars can park there before opening, at the farthest edge, and start to clear out before the after-work rush. Indeed, why not pick up a few things on the way home? Sales might even increase in the malls. This should be explored as a win-win scenario. Why not experiment? The STM already has the 747 express to the airport and a shuttle for the hockey games, among others. What about expanding on this concept with dedicated downtown rush-hour service from the region's shopping malls?

DOWNTOWN REINVENTED

Some observers have argued that now is the time to reimagine Montréal's downtown core completely. Only 60,000 people live in the downtown core today, but what if we push that to 300,000 or 400,000? What if we convert some office towers into social and community housing if the owners go bankrupt and the properties are up for grabs? If we better control rents, tenants will have more disposable income to spend in the local economy, bringing new life to dead commercial and cultural spaces. If hotels go belly-up, what if we convert them to fully-serviced seniors residences with a floor or two for medical supports, already fully accessible for those with mobility challenges?

Teletravail is the new norm for many white-collar workers, and we should make strong efforts to consolidate it, to reduce the need for expensive, wasteful highways, bridges, and tunnels. We should immediately cancel all new road construction and redirect budgets to collective transport. Further, any bridges or tunnels facing major renovations should be prioritized for decommissioning or retrofitting to support only public transit and bike highways. We should definitely not waste another nickel of public money rebuilding car-oriented infrastructure.

CONCLUSION

Fast, convenient, and free must be the keywords for the new hybrid public transit system in a Montréal truly worthy of our century—one that tackles climate change, sprawl, and poverty.

If the city is to take bold action, the elected city council will have to work with citizens to build a wall of anger at the staggering inaction of its civil service and the provincial and federal governments.

It will have to become an activist local government that causes trouble, organizes demonstrations, and calls for civil disobedience to block the decisions of the other levels of government (see El-Koury's chapter on the climate emergency).

A central component of a Green New Deal in Canada must include a dramatically different model for moving people in the city. Another chapter proposes the first spokes of such a system on steel wheels, considerably more efficient to operate than anything on rubber—faster, more comfortable, and made in Québec. Battery-powered electric buses are a very limited option: their batteries weigh three or four tonnes, equivalent to 50 passengers. They may be a good short-term solution, and for low density areas, but they cannot compete with trams for major transit networks.

This transportation revolution need not worry about rights of way! Too many years have been wasted worrying about how to do this when the answer is staring us right in the face: we put light rail on our highways and remove space from automobiles.

If you want to see where we need to put the light rail system of the future, the free public transit system in Montréal, grab any map of the island and a green marker and draw it yourself, right down the middle of Highway 20 and Highway 40, and all the highways and urban boulevards that cut the city like a loaf of bread. All this automobile-oriented infrastructure should be recommissioned to collective transport.

We replace the highways with rail, as swords into ploughshares, to make the Montréal of the 21st century.

And the whole system, free for all.

REFERENCES

Dupras, J., and Alam, M. 2015. "Urban sprawl and ecosystem services: a half century perspective in the Montréal area (Québec, Canada)." *Journal of environmental policy & planning* 17(2): 180-200.

Goudreault, Z. 2020. "La CCMM appelle à plus de transport en commun en périphérie du centre-ville." *Journal Métro*, 17 September 2020. https://journalmetro.com/le-choix-de-la-redac/2520788/la-ccmm-appelle-a-plus-de-transport-en-commun-en-peripherie-du-centre-ville/.

Morency, J-D., Caron Malenfant, E., and MacIsaac, S. 2017. "Immigration and Diversity: Population Projections for Canada and its Regions, 2011 to 2036." Statistics Canada. https://www150.statcan.gc.ca/n1/pub/91-551-x/91-551-x2017001-eng.htm.

Nazarnia, N., Schwick, C., and Jaeger, J.A. (2016). "Accelerated urban sprawl in Montréal, Québec City, and Zurich: Investigating the differences using time series 1951–2011." *Ecological indicators* 60: 1229-1251.

Prince, J., and Romano-Toramanian, J. (2016). "Le mouvement collectif pour une ville carboneutre." Brief presented to the Office de Consultation Publique de Montréal. https://ocpm.qc.ca/sites/ocpm.qc.ca/files/pdf/P80/7.1.40_romano-toramanian.pdf.

Robillard, A. 2015. "Arcand rassure l'industrie". *Le Devoir*, 10 December 0220. https://www.ledevoir.com/societe/environnement/457570/hydrocarbures-arcand-rassure-l-industrie.

Symon, J. 2020. "Green Coalition Calls Ministry actions "Scandalous" developers never refused certificates of authorization." *Montréal Times*, 22 February 2020. https://mtltimes.ca/life/green-coalition-calls-ministry-actions-scandalous-developers-never-refused-certificates-of-authorization/.

Thompson, U.C., Marsan, J.F., Fournier-Peyresblanques, B., Forgues, C., Ogaa, A., and Jaeger, J.A. 2013. "Using compliance analysis for PPP to bridge the gap between SEA and EIA: Lessons from the Turcot interchange reconstruction in Montréal, Québec." *Environmental impact assessment review* 42: 74-86.

Valiante, G. 2018. "Avec la CAQ au pouvoir, l'île de Montréal pourrait perdre de son influence." *Le Devoir*, 20 August 2018. https://www.ledevoir.com/politique/quebec/534846/l-ile-de-montreal-pourrait-etre-moins-influente-a-l-issue-des-elections.

STREETS THAT BREATHE—CONTROLLING CARS

CLAIRE MORISSETTE

Editor's Note: This chapter is reprinted with permission from Black Rose Books, in part to provide a glimpse into the debates of 1990 (*plus ça change, plus c'est la même chose*) but also to provide an organic link to this book by the same name. It originally appeared in the book *Montréal: A Citizen's Guide to City Politics*, published in 1990.

- Almost one quarter of Montréal's pre-World War II buildings were razed for burgeoning autoroutes, parking lots, and other car needs.
- Since 1966, urban sprawl fueled by automobile commuting has siphoned off about a quarter of Montréal's population.
- The MCM promised to reduce the space used by cars in article 7.9 of its 1986 programme. Instead it fell over itself to accomodate private autos—a stinging sight for citizens who voted for the cycling mayor.
- A May, 1988 *Le Devoir*-Createc+ poll found 84% of Montréalers believe that traffic is a serious or very serious problem, 42% believe that cars should be banned from downtown.
- The City, which furnishes Montréal drivers with free, paved parking, clear of snow and debris, drags its feet on giving cyclists parking racks.

You would have to be born on another planet not to notice that the private automobile is the major cause of environmental degradation in Montréal, as in other big cities. But few are the people, and fewer still the politicians, with the courage to look the issue straight in the face. We all know what nuisances are caused by the automobile. It pollutes, kills, makes noise, eats up space, wastes energy, pushes people into debt, crowds the streets, increases stress and aggressiveness, and promotes physical inactivity. It dominates transportation, and even our way of thinking. But the crux of the problem is that by allocating space and public transportation funds to it, pro-automobile policies prevent alternatives—mass transit and the bicycle.

We have the technology to implement the most modern, efficient, and safe mode of transportation available. Yet our current transportation system has led to a massacre whose casualty figures resemble those of a civil war: 3,992 traffic deaths per year in Canada.[1] On the island of Montréal alone, 110 deaths and 1,333 serious injuries with long-term consequences are reported.[2] Worldwide, the killing costs the life of 250,000 people every year, and millions of injured.[3]

Do fourteen women have to die in a university to attract attention and make people stop and think? On Québec roads, the annual death toll is the equivalent of seventy-eight Polytechnique massacres—eight in Montréal—normal, routine, without any media splash. At the Polytechnique, unpredictable deaths by which we were all appalled; on our roads, predictable deaths, avoidable ones, yet ones we've practically given our consent to amidst general apathy. Is that not doubly revolting? But we've got to lock up our anger and revulsion when faced with the collective refusal to acknowledge the situation. Next year more than 1,000 people, including 400 youths under the age of 25, will be killed by cars in Québec.[4] We're all signing petitions to ban semi-automatic weapons, so why not cars, which are far more murderous?

Death is not a normal and tolerable consequence of transportation. The streets—which fifty years ago were an extension of the home, a living space to play, meet neighbours, hang around, and enjoy the fresh air—have become corridors of danger, dirt, stress, and injury. The children in working class neighbourhoods are the victims of traffic accidents at almost twice the average rate.[5] The street, their immediate universe of play and socialisation, has been stolen away from them, as a sacrifice to the almighty automobile. In Montréal, we are intruders as soon as we step out our front door.

PRIME ENEMY OF THE ENVIRONMENT

The quality of urban life is affected by an incredible array of inconveniences caused by the flood of one million cars assaulting the island of Montréal every day.[6] Our air smells bad, and is bad for our health. Ground level ozone linked

---

1. Statistics Canada, 1986
2. Régie de l'assurance automobile du Québec, annual report, 1987
3. The bicycle: vehicle for a small planet, Marcia D. Lowe, Worldwatch Paper #90, September, 1989
4. 369 in 1987, op. Cit., Régie de l'assurance automobile du Québec.
5. Canadian Press, August 26, 1989
6. Every day 1,035,000 vehicles use the island of Montréal access bridges in both directions. The annual increase is about 100,000 extra trips per day: Québec Transportation Ministry, Technical

to smog (a serious threat to the human immune system[7]) surpassed acceptable limits twenty times in Montréal in 1987. An omnipresent noise surrounds us from morning rush hour until night, and we are forced to close our windows in summer to keep it out. The ground is dirty because of metallic dust and oil leaking from motors. In the Montréal area, 10 million litres of used motor oil a year are poured into the outdoors,[8] and more than 100,000 tons of calcium are spread on our streets.[9] It doesn't go away. It eventually ends up in the St. Lawrence River and in the groundwater.

No bombs have fallen on the city, yet twenty five per cent of the houses built before 1940 have been razed to make way for cars.[10] Thousands of people were expropriated, uprooted, and displaced. Parishes and entire neighbourhoods were smashed to pieces to build autoroutes. Architectural treasures and park spaces were bulldozed. Cars even invaded the smallest nooks and crannies, the wooded rows which used to line many streets were ripped up for parking lots, and alleyways were paved over. What's under the ground—after Viger Square, maybe St. Louis Square—is the new target for parking lots.

In 1990, we can no longer look our kids in the face and continue to pollute as if there were no tomorrow, leaving them practically irreparable environmental devastation. But that's what we're doing in terms of atmospheric pollution. The greenhouse effect, acid rain, destruction of the ozone layer, micropollutants, all these problems are complex and difficult to remedy. The car is guilty of the massive production of pollutants, through its worldwide fleet of 400 million vehicles,[11] and the production of forty-five million more each and every year.[12] Just imagine all those exhaust pipes and factory chimneys.

Automobiles produce a phenomenal quantity of atmospheric pollutants: almost one half of all the carbon monoxide, hydrocarbons, and nitrogen oxides in the world.[13] These pollutants accumulate in the upper atmosphere, creating a greenhouse effect, a gradual warming of the planet with all its consequences: droughts and, because of the expansion of the oceans through the added heat, flooding of coastal areas and deltas where many densely populated cities are located. If that were not enough, nitrogen oxides increase the acidity of rain,

measurements division, 1987. In 1987, there were 750,000 motor vehicles in Montréal: Montréal Urban Community, Environment division, February, 1989
7. Canadian Press, September, 1989
8. Québec Petroleum Association and Québec Automobile Club, joint brief to the MUC Standing Committee on Transportation, October 10, 1989
9. 108,500 metric tonnes, City of Montréal, Activities Report, 1988
10. *Contretemps*, #16, Spring, 1989
11. Rene Dumont, public lecture, Montréal, June 12 1989
12. 46 million in 1987, Table Rase, *Radio-Canada TV*, February 14, 1989
13. Op. cit., Worldwatch Paper #90, September, 1989

killing our lakes and forests, and eating away at the exterior of buildings. The automobile is even said to contribute to the destruction of the ozone layer in the upper atmosphere. Air conditioners, which leak and are discarded in great quantities especially in the US, also produce a large quality of chlorofluorocarbons[14] which corrode the ozone layer and expose us to higher levels of cancer causing ultraviolet rays, The next century's atmosphere will be a charming cocktail. Alarm bells have been ringing since the report of the United Nation's World Commission on Environment.[15] A radical shift is needed now towards "durable" and ecological transportation systems.

THE COSTS OF URBAN SPRAWL

Life in the city is becoming so hard that those who can afford to are fleeing to the suburbs to raise their family in more decent surroundings. Some 317,000 people have left Montréal's afflictions behind for the relative comfort of the suburbs, a loss of close to twenty-five percent of the population since its apex point at 1,293,000, in the heyday of the metropolis.[16] Yet downtown continues to be the centre of employment, especially in finance and the professions. These suburban refugees drive in daily, and *voila*—the car/bungalow/gasoline nexus is firmly entrenched, and expands continuously with disastrous consequences in terms of energy consumption and the allocation of public funds.

Suburbs lead to an explosion in the consumption of energy and other resources. The building of single homes costs four times more in terms of public infrastructure, such as new streets, sewers, water mains, lighting, phone interconnections, school bus services, deliveries, garbage collection. Densities are so low it becomes impossible to set up profitable public transit. This leads to auto madness, as two or three cars per household become "artificial" necessities of suburban life. To the energy consumption of the car, from the mining of raw materials for manufacturing all the way to disposal in a car dump, including all related costs, add the cost of road repair and police surveillance. To put it simply, when a family moves to the suburbs, it increases its energy use by a factor of ten to twenty.[17]

The exodus of the economically better-off affects Montréal's tax situation. Among the people remaining in the city (1,015,000 in 1988[18]), there is a high proportion of the poor and elderly, and concentrations of different ethnic

---

14. *The Economist*, October 7, 1989
15. Our Common Future, report of the World Commission on the Environment and Development, 1988
16. Montréal's population was 1,239,000 in 1966; it had decreased by 1987 to 1,015,000, despite the annexation of Pointe aux Trembles, (pop. 39 000), City of Montréal archives
17. Joint brief, Québec Union for Nature Conservation (UQCN) and Québec Association on Acid Rain, January 4, 1989
18. City of Montréal, Activities Report, 1988

communities caught in the poverty trap. The impoverishment caused by the exodus and the slowdown in some job sectors means Montréal has lost some of its ability to properly maintain mass transit, garbage collection, aging sewer and water main infrastructures, and provide new services to face the growing problems provoked by poverty. Life in the city is getting worse because of a simultaneous increase in poverty and decline in available city resources. It's this same pattern—the vicious circle of self-reinforcing poverty—we see in American cities, albeit with a lapse of ten years. Those cities show us only too well where we might well be headed.

A more attractive city, one less asphyxiated by cars, would encourage people to move there, or to stay instead of choosing the lawn-and-asphalt suburbs that have covered over richly fertile soil from the alluvial deposits from the ancient Champlain Sea, and which threaten irreplaceable ecological sites like the Oka forest which is so essential to preventing sanding-in. The island has the potential to absorb all the housing needs of the next thirty years, by building triplexes on the 2,400 hectares of land currently earmarked for residential purposes in Montréal Urban Community plans.[19]

LOST TIME AND MONEY

The automobile's negative impact is also linked to the financial expense it represents, especially for the poor. The private automobile is the most massively consumed non-durable, non-essential commodity in North America. It eats up as much money as housing — twenty-five to forty per cent of the household budget[20]—but must be replaced every five to seven years. It costs $5,000 per year in simple out-of-pocket expenses. It's not difficult to imagine the hardship for less fortunate families for whom the proportion of income gobbled up by the family car is greater, depriving them of other, more useful or enriching goods or activities. The automobile traps consumers in a debt cycle—a car to get to work, a job to pay for the car.

To sell its products the automobile industry spends millions to keep up an obsessive advertising barrage to create an illusion in the minds of the dominated that they control something. In fact, the dream is a nightmare. After a day chained to their desks, people get trapped in traffic, hands tied to the steering wheel, feet on the pedals, eyes on the bumper of the car in front for two hours day in, day out, for ten hours a week. The work week suddenly is discovered to have fifty hours. Without cars, a four-day work week would become possible. We could leave for short weekend trips every Friday.

---

19. Op. cit., UQCN and Acid Rain Association, January 4, 1989
20. Un char qui prend d'assaut le budget, Joliette Association coopérative d'économie familiale (consumer association), 1986

The millions of hours wasted in tiring, unpleasant, dangerous traffic jams are unpaid. For workers, it's a total loss of invisible labour.

Owning a car often has a lot to do with the attributes of power, prestige, and other deep pressing urges of drivers. They roll along in full contempt of the injustices and damage they inflict on the people in the neighbourhoods through which they drive, and they internalise the individualistic values associated with the automobile—for some to be able to drive a car, others are paralysed because they're too old, too young, too poor. Car owners love their machines, while hating the cars of others.

The automobile, which in theory should help us visit other people, has created new interpersonal distances. At the same time a result and a cause of automobile traffic, suburbs take on a special nature that divides the population according to age. Young families move away from the elderly who are then exposed to loneliness. Young people between the ages of eighteen and thirty are hardly to be seen. Those even younger no longer have a natural model for their development. By definition, residential suburbs deprive the young of any contact with the working world. Because of their spatially dispersed nature, suburbs even affect time, which becomes organized into slots: human contacts through chance meetings on the street are ruled out by agendas, and the unpredictable is out of place.

The automobile shapes our neighbourhoods and our lives. For many people, movement seems impossible without it. Even people who don't one find it hard to imagine a world without cars. Top public officials, generally highly paid people with cars, see the urban problems from behind a steering wheel, so their proposed solutions are biased towards the automobile. Politicians in turn, even when conscious of the consequences of a *laissez-faire* transportation policy, don't have the necessary political courage to challenge a wheeled electorate, seventy per cent of whose households own at least one car in Montréal.[21] There's a cultural environment whose inertia reinforces irresponsible transportation policies.

Some will claim that the right to own a car is a matter of freedom of choice. In fact, a real conspiracy, revealed by the U.S. Senate, did its utmost to impose the private automobile in North America. And it's reign is constantly reinforced by socially unbalanced transportation policies. Starting in 1932, General Motors, Exxon, and Firestone, among others, plotted together to buy out and eliminate 100 tramway companies in forty-five U.S. cities. This led to a tripling of car sales and the reduction in the number of mass transit passengers of 3 billion.[22] During legal proceedings before the U.S. Senate Anti-

---

21. La séduction de l'automobile, *Le Point*, Radio-Canada, January 17, 1990
22. Snell, Bradford C., Hearings before the subcommittee on antitrust and monopoly of the Committee on the Judiciary of the United States Senate, U.S. Government Printing Office, Washington, D.C., 1974

Trust Committee, the guilty companies were fined a grand total of $5,000 dollars for their criminal activities, some of the most disastrous of all history when one takes into account the ransom in human lives and the environmental damage that "carmania" has caused.

In Montréal, the process was roughly the same. Around 1950, municipal experts compared the speed of thirty-year old trams with that of new diesel buses. The results were respectively 14.8 km/h and 17.0 km/h[23] altogether not that bad. The City had just become the owner of the tramway system and experts convinced authorities to scrap it in favour of the noisier, dirtier, less efficient bus system, to the great discontent of citizens of the time. Today, the subway, whose enormous capital and operating costs keep public transit fees high, continues that policy of giving up the streets to private automobiles.

The automobile and petroleum industries are huge. General Motors alone has annual sales in excess of $100 billion U.S.—and maintain powerful political lobbies. Yet the auto industry, along with the defense industry, is among the least productive in terms of job creation: $1 million dollars in invested capital creates only one job.[24] The same amount invested in social services would create ten times as many jobs, of much greater use, in recycling, home insulation, education, care for the elderly, and they would be less specialised, more accessible local jobs. In 1990, politicians can no longer blindly wave the banner of job creation without a good look at the type of jobs created, their usefulness, and their short- and long-term impact on the environment.

STATE ACCOMPLICES

An examination of government policies shows governments have encouraged auto supremacy. At least $5,000 a year of public funds have squandered on each car driver in budgets for the road network, for snow removal, the police, for hospital care due to accidents and diseases caused by car pollution, and disability pensions, etc.[25] This only covers the known, quantifiable expenses. Other car-induced effects still have to be evaluated such as damage from acid rain and the warming of the atmosphere, the lack of productivity of public transit systems, and the destruction of potentially good land.

In the meantime, each mass transit user is only subsidised to the tune of $500 dollars a year,[26] or ten times less than the average driver. And public transportation authorities in Montréal are in a pitiful state. VIA Rail under the guillotine, Voyageur and the South Shore Transit Commission hit by record strikes, the Lake of Two Mountains commuter train cut in half, loss of

---

23. Dagenais, Jean-Pierre, *Ironie du Char*, Montréal, 1982
24. 26.5 hours in the United States, 19.5 in Japan, Newsweek, October 16, 1989
25. Op.cit., UQCN and Association on Acid Rain, January 4, 1989
26. *Ibid*

passengers at the Montréal Urban Committee Transit Corporation. When it comes to support for mass transit, the three levels of government are quite thrifty, but they roll out the red carpet for the private automobile. Freedom of choice? Who are they kidding?

During the Drapeau years, the automobile continued to gobble up space to the point that forty-five percent of the downtown area was devoted to it.[27] As late as 1985, then vice-president of the city executive committee Pierre Lorange proudly boasted of the city's 8,000 parking meters, and of the twenty new parking lots built downtown in the preceding five years.[28] In the opposition ranks, people were working on more intelligent policies. In its program, the MCM included proposals to place restrictions on the private automobile. The MCM won the 1986 elections in part because of its commitment to improve the quality of life for Montréalers.

On the eve of taking over the reins of power, the party's priorities were studied by the MCM General Council, but without being submitted to a party congress. Articles to rein in the automobile on city streets lost their edge, being reduced to simple measures to help fight traffic congestion. In 1989 the MCM implemented tough bylaws to cut down on double parking. Once again, the "let 'em roll" school of thought prevailed. In alleyways, the proliferation of speed bumps offered better protection to pedestrians. But on the city's streets, the speed limit remains at 50 km/hr. Requests to improve the safety by installing special lights, as in Ottawa and Toronto, fell on deaf ears.

The MCM continues to preach the virtues of public transit, yet under the MCM administration it has continued to suffer. The number of buses on the road has declined. Metro frequency has been cut, and closing time for the system is earlier. The number of breakdowns has increased, and fees—which the MCM froze in 1987, will now climb every year,[29] as if commuters' relative contribution was an appropriate item to index to inflation. The percentage of people who use the MUCTC to travel is in regression, mostly to the benefit of the automobile, and the MCM's arrival at the Montréal Urban Community has not in the least corrected this tendency.

A reserved bus lane on Pie IX boulevard finally saw the light of day. Without question, this is an important achievement. More special lanes have been announced, but only during rush hour, on Bleury Street, Côte des Neiges Boulevard, and Sherbrooke Street. Yet common sense would dictate the creation of reserved lanes on all routes where congestion has been slowing buses down, and especially downtown and on access bridges. It's inconceivable that buses carrying seventy passengers should be held up by four or five cars

---

27. Contretemps, #161, Spring, 1989
28. Pierre Lorange, in front of the Québec Roads and Transportation Association February 15, 1985
29. Transport 2000, brief to the MUC Standing Committee on Transportation, October 10, 1989

occupied by only one driver each. Why is the City allowing so much road space to be occupied by cars? In its negotiations with the province, Mayor Doré has pleaded the case for an extension of the Metro, a costly solution which will simply make the public transit debt even heavier. A Metro extension to Laval, a train to Chateauguanay, will only facilitate the exodus to the suburbs.

We have seen some movement by the MCM administration on cycling policy. First a policy statement, then, more concretely, five kilometres of new paths, the "missing link" between the island and the South Shore, and some needed modifications to existing bike paths. But for bicycle users, that's not a lot. The cycling policy has already fallen behind schedule, the City has committed too few people to working on the issue, and those who are working on it lack authority. To think that Doré campaigned for mayor riding around on his ten-speed.

When it comes to speaking out on transportation issues, Mayor Doré loves above all to talk of his tunnel idea for the Metropolitan expressway, at the minor cost of $2 billion. That's his conception of the best use of public funds when moving the shipment of goods over to rail and reducing the daily horde of single-occupant automobiles could probably replace the entire speedway with a nice urban boulevard. To sum up, as far as transportation policy goes, the MCM deserves an "F" for its lack of guts. The record indicates not only a lack of sensitivity to the fate of a city facing a daily onslaught of automobiles, but an unforgivable short-term administrative and ecological outlook.

AUTO ALTERNATIVES

The craziest thing about the situation is that it's not hard to replace the car with a much more comfortable and functional mode of transportation. If the public funds currently being devoted to supporting the private car were shifted to mass transit, and space given over to cars were given back to buses, bicycles, and pedestrians, we'd be able to afford a pretty luxurious system of trains and trams, with collective taxis and buses on demand, safe streets, and a cleaner, more attractive city.

All around the world, appropriate transportation policies are offering a variety of wonderful technologies. There are French TGV high-speed trains which zoom to 482 km/h, minibuses on demand in the Paris suburb of Ivry, collective taxis in Kingston, double-deckers in London, heated bus shelters in Calgary and Edmonton. Bombardier's product catalogue is chock full of vehicles that are as efficient as they are avant-garde. One example is the bimodal electric trolleys with fifty per cent autonomy, retractable steps, and wide doors for baby carriages.

In Europe the downtown areas of Rome, Milan, and Oslo are off-limits to cars. In Florence the city centre was closed to cars in the spring of 1988. The only complaints received were from neighbourhoods that were not included in the protected perimeter. Other innovative towns have experimented with all sorts of restrictive measures. In some places drivers are allowed into the city only every other day, depending on whether their license plate number is odd or even. Elsewhere coloured stickers allow access to the city only on a given day of the week. Sometimes stickers give access only to legal residents. In Singapore electronic counters installed inside the cars calculate toll fees according to mileage. In Burlington, Vermont parking is very expensive for a car with a single occupant, and rebates are offered to people in a car pool. Special lanes are reserved for car pools on Washington and Los Angeles freeways.

Whether mass transit can become a vastly more advantageous system than the private automobile is above all a question of space allocation. The success of reserved bus lanes in generating higher passenger densities no longer needs to be proven. Montréalers are already showing an affinity for the bicycle as a mode of transportation. In the Netherlands, where the governments devote some ten percent of the overall transportation budget to cycling, the bike path network is used for up to fifty percent of all trips, along 13,500 km of roads, in an area smaller than the Gaspé.[30]

An equitable redistribution of public funds could provide citizens with a greatly improved free mass transit service, if only we would make drivers pay the true costs of their preference — roughly double what they pay at the moment. Many countries impose a gasoline tax according to the principle of polluter-pay: 245 percent in the Netherlands, 355 per cent on gas and 186 per cent on the purchaser of a car in Denmark.[31] In Stockholm, car owners must first buy a monthly bus pass before being allowed onto inner city streets. Those are just some of the sources of substantial funds that can be made available for the development of attractive alternatives.

DEAD-END DRIVERS

Preaching virtue isn't good enough. The city administration has a responsibility to take a stand against the root of the problem, and to introduce ways to reduce the massive car use, especially by people driving alone in their car, a flagrant abuse whose time has passed. Let's limit their rights in the city, let's forbid them access to the island. Once and for all, the right of Montréalers to a better quality of life should prevail.

In the summer of 1989, there was a telling event in Montréal. Autoroute 20 was shut down. Special lanes were created for bus lines 90, 190, 211, and 212 to

---

30. Op.cit., Worldwatch Paper #90, September, 1989
31. *Ibid*

the Metro, transit authorities increased the capacity of the Rigaud commuter train, which managed to attract twenty-six percent more passengers than usual. Thousands discovered appropriate transit. This experiment should be extended to all areas, and expressways should be reserved for carpools and goods shipments as an incentive to single occupant car owners to switch, even if this means a temporary increase in traffic congestion.

Cars are like cigarettes: a social phenomenon, a lethal danger, and a costly habit which is hard to give up.[32] To beat the car habit, we need the same kind of strategy as that used against smoking: education campaigns coupled with restrictive measures to limit space used by cars. 84% of Montréalers believe traffic is a serious or very serious problem, and forty-two percent want all cars banned from downtown Montréal.[33] In the 1990 municipal election campaign, citizens have every incentive to closely scrutinise the transportation policies of all parties running. Citizens may judge whether the parties have the honesty to propose solutions to the plague which is asphyxiating the city and the planet.

New Zealand, with a population of 3 million, stood up to the American nuclear superpower. The small town of Irvine, California adopted a law banning CFCs. Montréal has no excuse not to adopt vigorous ecological policies. If they don't do their utmost to correct the many aberrations from which our city suffers, of what use are municipal politicians?

Going beyond the election debate for a moment, we each have some personal choices to make. The transportation revolution must not only be a matter for public decision-makers. Not owning a car is already a form of refusal to participate in the destruction of the biosphere, a refusal to create nuisances for neighbours and fellow citizens. It is also a way of integrating theory and practice, to prove to oneself and others that it is possible to live differently. It is in the parking lot that we can judge the sincerity of public figures on the environment. Using public transit and riding a bicycle keeps up our sincerity, and sustains the radicalism of our demands. They keep alive our consciousness of the frustrations imposed upon us, frustrations that convince so many people a car is the only answer. Sooner or later, the private automobile will have to yield. The idea is to help viable transportation solutions to fruition and end the tyranny of Gasosaurus Rex.

BICYCLE POLICY

Bicycles are not toys, to be accommodated if a city administration can find the time. The bicycle is the best adapted mode of transportation for distances under ten kilometres, which represents three in four trips in cities. The bicycle is environmentally irreproachable and is already the choice of a significant and

32. Groupe de recherche appliquée en macroécologie (GRAME), Non aux autoroutes, 1989
33. Poll by *Le Devoir-Createc*, *Le Devoir*, May 16,17, 1988

growing proportion of the Montréal population. Bike users expect real and tangible support, in the form of safe bicycle paths, as they never cease to repeat. The only thing missing is an enthusiastic response from the city.

The Danish, Dutch, and Chinese examples demonstrate the potential of bicycle paths, even when bicycle use is reduced by harsh winters. Here, only three to four months are less favourable to cycling. Despite this the number of winter cyclists is on the rise. In the Netherlands, where ten percent of the transportation budget is devoted to the bicycle, the 13,500 kilometers of bicycle paths are used for half of all trips.

In Montréal, there are currently 121 kilometers of bicycle paths. Half is protected from street traffic through physical barriers, the other half is only identified by lines on the pavement or by street signs. In three years, the MCM has added only five kilometres of new paths, four of which are along Rachel Street. That project, slated to go ahead in 1986, was delayed for two years before starting again in 1989, then being dug up. With the exception of the Rachel Street path, no other short-term initiatives were announced.

In the summaries of district planning priorities made public in mid-January of 1990, there is an uneven level of interest in the question of the bicycle as a mode of transportation. In some districts, even existing paths are ignored. As for any future projects, forget it. In other district summaries, there's some discussion of the odd extension to be built here or there, but there is no attempt to promote the idea of a complete, interlocking grid of bicycle paths.

In November 1988 the City adopted a bicycle policy. It was a good document, outlining needs for infrastructure, safety, and promotion, as well as for coordination. But the ten-year timetable makes one wonder. Already there are major delays, even on many of the short-term proposals.

Under pressure from cycling lobbies, the Québec government has shown itself open to the idea of providing financial assistance in the $10- to $20-million range to expand bicycle paths. The promise was reiterated in the 1989 provincial election campaign. The City instead went to the government with hat in hand, to beg $40 million for the biodome. This brings back memories of 1975, when Drapeau was building his $75-million Olympic Velodrome, a project most cyclist lobbyists decried as a useless prestige object.

Some repairs and modifications have been brought to existing paths. Traffic lights were installed on the Chrisophe Colomb-Berri Street path at the Brébeuf-Rachel and Brébeuf-Mont-Royal intersections. But mobilisation by local cyclists, a petition, and the antics of Monsieur SOSO (a local TV personality) were needed before concessions were granted. At the Brébeuf-Rosemont and Brébeuf-Jean-Talon intersections, where lights are a real need, nothing has been done. It is almost as if the City wants to battle it out intersection by intersection.

As for the "missing link" of path between the island of Monreal and the South Shore via the St. Lawrence Seaway, the City has made a remarkable financial effort. It will provide $300,000 of the $550,000 needed for the project. The rest will come from the provincial ministry of recreation, hunting, and fishing. The link is to be completed by the spring of 1990, just in time for the opening of the Ile Notre Dame beach-park. But Le Monde à Bicyclette, which has been pursuing the issue "inch by inch" as it were, has noticed a total lack of leadership on the part of the city administration. No one has been put in charge of the project, which has been relegated to the bottom of the priority list, and civil servants in the concerned departments didn't even know of it. If the citizens' group had not grabbed the bull by its proverbial handlebars, the link would no doubt still be missing somewhere.

In June, 1989 a bicycle-parking policy for commercial districts was announced and then almost immediately postponed. Work on a prototype for a bicycle stand was behind schedule and the very high demand for the service required further analysis. Le Monde à Bicyclette informed merchants of the new policy, and more than 100 requests were filed. The bike-o-crats at city hall were quickly overwhelmed. A new bicycle support prototype designed for high-density parking, which is needed along commercial arteries where two or three bicycles are now often locked around the same parking meter.

For residential parking, according to its bicycle policy the City intends to propose a bylaw obliging contractors to provide a certain number of parking spaces for bicycles in new and renovated buildings, the number being proportional to floor-space. It would have been wonderful if it were only shown to be true. Another problem which remains unsolved is that of parking spaces in triplexes, where available interior space is limited. A motion from the Plateau Mont Royal/South-Centre District Advisory Council requested that the City provide street parking places in dense neighborhoods. The request was taken under advisement, but people were told it was not a priority. Yet the City provides plenty of free parking for cars along almost all residential streets, and spends a large portion of its annual $90 million street maintenance budget on paving, sweeping, and snow removal.

Who was it who once said that it's in their driveway that one can judge the sincerity of public personalities on environmental issues? Some forty thousand cyclists take to the streets every summer for the annual Tour de L'Île rally, thousands more get around every day on a bike. Bicycle users have sufficient weight to get results. But on the whole, the MCM administration doesn't assign enough people to cycling issues, and those who do work on the issue are not given enough power to get things done properly. Cycling is not seen as a high enough priority by the concerned departments, and no municipal councillor has provided strong leadership when it comes to the interests of the cycling population.

The councillor who was the assistant to the official in charge of bicycle policy in 1987 and 1988 subsequently turned down requests for a meeting saying the issue now fell directly under the authority of the city executive committee, without any special political attaché. Finally—and this is a major root of frustration for cycling enthusiasts and activists—the city does not seem to attach any importance to transparency vis-a-vis bicycle users and their associations, even though the official policy calls for the creation of an extended task force including private and public groups involved in bicycle transportation issues.

BEYOND CRITICAL MASS: SCALING UP BIKE INFRASTRUCTURE IN MONTRÉAL

BARTEK KOMOROWSKI

Montréal is one of North America's coldest and snowiest major cities. Oddly, it is also among the most bicycle friendly. This chapter will provide a look at the history of cycling in Montréal, particularly the last 50 years, to provide some insight into how this came to be. Three themes emerge that offer some explanation: first, establishing a strong and effective bicycle advocacy community; second, a history of political allies in or in proximity to the mayor's office; and third, the population's wide embrace of cycling.

THE FIRST WAVE

The early history of cycling in Montréal is similar to that of cities across North America. The first proto-bicycles (*velocipeds*) arrived in 1869—four decades before the Ford Model T rolled off the assembly line. The bicycle's initial popularity as a mode of urban transportation peaked near the end of the 19th century.

This popularity began to decline when a new, cheap transportation alternative was introduced: the electric streetcar. The proliferation of mass-produced automobiles further precipitated the decline. As their numbers and speeds increased, they made streets increasingly unpleasant and unsafe for the remaining cyclists.

Post-WWII urban development focused on single-family housing and a new lifestyle centred on private automobile use, further undermining the role of the bicycle. It was ultimately relegated to the realm of children's play and sport for men in tight clothing, to be practiced on quiet countryside backroads, not in the city. It was no longer seen as a mode of transportation for serious, self-respecting adults. Those who dared to pedal on Montréal's thoroughfares were regularly subjected to verbal abuse and intimidation from motorists.

THE TURNING TIDE

The tide did not begin to turn until the 1973 oil crisis. By then, Montréal was thoroughly car-dependent, its modest underground metro and commuter train systems notwithstanding. In older, pre-war neighbourhoods, streetcar tracks were torn out or paved over. Tree-lined sidewalks and planted promenades were removed to allocate space to cars. Whole swaths of urban fabric were destroyed to make way for freeways, fragmenting neighbourhoods and making life increasingly difficult for the dwindling non-driving public. The oil crisis temporarily suspended this automobile-driven orgy of destruction. It was in this context that the bicycle slowly began to reappear in the urban landscape. Two very different grassroots organizations came to the fore through their complementary efforts to foster the rebirth of the bicycle as a mode of transportation.

One was a ragtag group of environmentalists and cycling enthusiasts, brought together in 1975 by a shared "cyclo-frustration"—the inability to safely ride and park bicycles around the city. They called themselves *Le Monde à bicyclette* (MAB), a double entendre in French, meaning "people on bikes" but also "the world on bikes". Their objective was to foment a "velorution"—to demonstrate that bicycles are not merely for sport but rather *trans*port, an alternative to dirty and dangerous cars. "We're not just talking about a change," Robert Silverman, one of MAB's founders explained, "we're talking about the reconquest of the city, taking it back from the private car and making it a quieter, cleaner, healthier and friendlier place for people" (Montréal Gazette 2019).

MAB had two prominent figureheads: the aforementioned Silverman (aka "Bicycle Bob") and Claire Morrissette. The duo shared a penchant for the poetic and dramatic, and masterminded a string of theatrical protests. The first of these "cyclodramas" was a 1976 "die-in" during which a few hundred cyclists played dead in the middle of the intersection to raise awareness of the dangers faced by cyclists forced to share roads with cars and to demand that spaces free from cars be created for cyclists. Another would feature MAB-led protesters riding down streets draped with car-shaped frames, highlighting the absurd amount of space occupied by cars. Perhaps the most legendary of MAB's stunts involved Silverman costumed as Moses leading a group of bicycle-riding Israelites to the riverbank, where he attempted to part the waters of the St-Lawrence. This was MAB's way of calling attention to the need for a cycling link across the river to the burgeoning South Shore suburbs.

The local news media loved reporting on these colourful protests, making MAB extremely effective at getting politicians' attention. They helped catalyze the construction of cycling facilities in Montréal and, later, cycling links to the South Shore. They also helped to get city regulations changed. For instance, they helped convince the transit authority to lift its ban on bicycles in the metro in the early 1980s. First, bikes were allowed on weekends, then by the early 1990s, they were allowed at all times except weekday rush hours, as is still the case today. MAB also helped persuade the regional commuter rail operator to allow a modest number of bicycles on trains, stowed in purpose-built cabinets.

THE OTHER TEAM

Another small local organization founded a decade earlier, the *Fédération québécoise de cyclotourisme* (FQC), also advocated for cycling as a means of urban transportation. Whereas MAB excelled at drawing attention to cyclists' daily struggles, the FQC focused on proposing technical and regulatory solutions.

The FQC organized meetings and conferences and submitted briefs to government committees in the hopes of exposing public servants and elected officials to new ideas on planning and designing cycling facilities. One of their significant early achievements was convincing the Québec Ministry of Transportation (MTQ) in 1979 to rewrite certain nonsensical rules pertaining to cycling in the provincial Highway Safety Code. These included absurdities like having to keep both hands on the handlebar at all times while also being required to use hand signals when turning and stopping. MTQ bureaucrats were so impressed by one Vélo Québec brief that they invited its author, Michel Labrecque, to join the advisory committee studying updates to the code. This boosted the organization's credibility in the eyes of local and provincial decision-makers.

Recognizing that its activities had expanded beyond the realm of bicycle touring, the FQC changed its name to Vélo Québec.

THE DAY THAT CHANGED EVERYTHING

Every year from 1977 to 1983, MAB and Vélo Québec organized a mass bike ride on World Cycling Day in early June, the last few drawing up to 800 people—which seemed big at the time. But Vélo Québec had its eyes on a bigger prize: organizing a mass bike ride on streets closed to traffic, modelled on the Five Boro Challenge, the annual 80-mile ride through New York City launched in 1977.

In 1985, with MTQ funding, the city was completing construction of a 60 km cycling route encircling the eastern half of the island of Montréal. The

MTQ approached Vélo Québec to organize a public event for its inauguration. Vélo Québec proposed a mass bike ride along the new route. The free event, financed by the MTQ, was planned for mid-October. The public was enthusiastic: 7,000 people signed up to participate. Thus, was born the *Tour de l'île*.

Unfortunately, the day of the event was cold and rainy. Still, some 3,000 people showed up on their bikes. It was not the great success Vélo Québec had hoped for, but not a complete failure either.

The following year, Vélo Québec decided to organize a similar *Tour de l'île* but moved it to early June to ensure better weather. However, the election of the Québec Liberal Party in December 1985 led to the cancellation of their funding. The core team did not have the resources or experience to do it on their own, but somehow, they managed to pull it off, at great personal cost to employees. Montréalers were stoked—close to 11,000 signed up.

On the day of the event, bad luck struck again, with torrential rain—though at least this time it was warm. Much to the surprise of Vélo Québec staff, 8,000 people had arrived on site by start time; thousands more joined later, bringing the tally to 15,000. Vélo Québec's current CEO Suzanne Lareau says it was the day that changed everything, not just for Vélo Québec but for cycling in Montréal in general. The crowd's size and diversity demonstrated eloquently and irrefutably the extent to which Montréalers had adopted cycling.

Over the following years, the *Tour de l'île* snowballed, becoming an annual Montréal tradition and a major tourist draw. Participation doubled by the fourth edition (32,000) and stabilized at around 45,000 participants between 1992–1997. It is still held today, and still draws sizable crowds. Its success vaulted Vélo Québec from a small grassroots organization to an institution—a colossus of the cycling advocacy world.

In the 1990s, Vélo Québec set up new headquarters (*La Maison des cyclistes*) in the Plateau, at the crossing of two of the major bicycle paths built in the 1980s. It offered services to the cycling public on its ground floor (café, information kiosk, bicycle travel agency), with the organization's swelling workforce occupying offices on the upper floors.

Vélo Québec remains active and influential, yet too far from its grassroots origins, according to some in the cycling advocacy community. MAB, for its part, faded away in the late 1990s.

THE GROWING NETWORK

Montréal's cycling network started developing in the 1970s, spurred initially by the continent-wide bicycle boom. The first modern bikeway was a 12 km path built along the length of the Lachine Canal, shortly after the area was turned into a federal park. The next significant project came during the last mandate of Jean-Drapeau, whose final executive committee president, Yvon Lamarre, pushed through some of the earliest cycling network projects, namely the aforementioned 60 km East Island loop.

Drapeau's successor, Jean Doré, was overtly in favour of cycling. His Montréal Citizens' Movement (MCM) had big ambitions: a grid of cycling facilities created, to put every Montréaler within 1 km of the cycling network. The MCM ran into some political turbulence and never even got to the drawing board. Nevertheless, some new cycling facilities were constructed under their eight years in power. In particular, a fully separated bicycle path built on Rachel Street, linking Mount Royal, Jeanne Mance, La Fontaine, and De Maisonneuve parks. Paths were also built within parks and along riverbanks, particularly on the western half of the island of Montréal.

All of these early facilities had one thing in common—they were intended primarily for recreational use.

By the mid-1990s, the island of Montréal had about 200 km of these recreational, mostly off-street paths, putting it ahead of the curve in North America, though the development of the cycling network began to stagnate. A recession in the early 1990s was followed by austerity measures imposed by the provincial and federal governments. Among various cost-cutting measures, they transferred ownership of much infrastructure to municipalities. The added burden limited Montréal's capacity for new investment, let alone properly maintaining existing infrastructure.

Montréal started getting back on its feet politically and economically in the early 2000s. The provincial government forced a merger of the municipalities on the island of Montréal in 2001. A large public consultation, the *Sommet des montréalais*, was held the following year, setting the stage for a new city master plan. Participants overwhelmingly expressed support for developing the cycling network and a desire for the city to consider cycling as a mode of transportation.

Gérald Tremblay's administration then undertook a significant expansion of the cycling network. In particular, implementing many km of inexpensive, paint-only bike lanes on streets, including lanes that allowed cyclists to go against the direction of traffic on one-way streets—unheard of in North America at the time. At last, a grid of utilitarian bikeways as envisioned in the 1970s started taking shape.

The Tremblay administration also advanced another of MAB and Vélo Québec's long-time dreams: a bicycle path through the downtown core. The 3.5 km de Maisonneuve Boulevard bike path (from Berri to Atwater) was completed in 2007. MAB's Claire Morissette cut the ceremonial ribbon just weeks before passing away of cancer. The following year, the city decided to posthumously name the path after her, recognizing her great contribution not just to cycling but mobility in general in Montréal. In the waning days of MAB in the late 1990s, Morissette's other great achievement was the founding of *Communauto*, Montréal's ever-popular car-sharing service, which she hoped would reduce private car ownership (Lalonde 2008).

The Claire Morissette bike path brought Montréal back to the forefront of urban cycling in North America. Along with Vancouver, it was among the first cities to provide a fully separated bikeway through the middle of a central business district. It was also a bold move politically, requiring the removal of all on-street parking (some 400 space) from one side of the street. Yet surprisingly, it generated very little blowback—or "bikelash" as cycling activists like to say. Perhaps this is because the lost spaces were a drop in the bucket compared to thousands of underground parking spaces along the same corridor.

In 2008, Montréal was an early adopter of another new trend: bike sharing. At the time, automated bike sharing systems existed only in a few European cities. Paris had recently implemented *Vélib*, with around 20,000 bikes across almost 1,500 stations. In North America, the only example was in Washington DC, with a mere 120 bikes and ten stations. By the spring of 2009, BIXI—a contraction of bicycle and taxi—opened in Montréal with 3,000 bikes across 300 stations. It was an instant hit with Montréalers and became a door opener for bike sharing in North America.

BIXI was also a catalyst for increased cycling in Montréal. Data from automated counters on bike paths showed a sustained surge in bicycle traffic after BIXI opened.

CALMING DOWN

The growth of cycling in Montréal cannot just be attributed to the provision of dedicated infrastructure. The extensive deployment of traffic calming measures on local streets has played an underappreciated role in creating a more favourable environment for cycling.

The densely inhabited Plateau-Mont-Royal borough played a pioneering role. At the behest of local organizations, notably the community action group *La Maison d'Aurore*, it became the first neighbourhood to systematically deploy traffic calming measures. Since the late 2000s, a succession of borough councils further pursued measures to calm local streets, ultimately blanketing the entire borough with physical measures such as speed humps, curb extensions, raised crossings, and street narrowing. Under Borough Mayor Luc Ferrandez, robust measures were adopted to prevent through-traffic on residential streets, namely by changing the direction of certain blocks on one-way streets for cars while providing a counter-flow bike lane, so cyclists are not affected. The Plateau-Mont-Royal also became the first borough to impose a 30 km/h speed limit on all local streets.

These measures came to be strongly associated with the Plateau—so much so that when other boroughs started deploying the same traffic calming measures, detractors began accusing them of "Plateau-ization." Physical traffic calming measures have spread throughout many of the other 18 boroughs in recent years. Thousands of speedbumps and curb extensions are being implemented annually; these slow cars down at intersections and create shorter pedestrian crossings. The 30 km/h speed limit was recently adopted as the baseline limit for all local, residential streets citywide.

Traffic-calmed streets are not only more pleasant to ride on, but they have likely also helped make the city safer. Montréal outperforms all large North American in terms of traffic-related deaths, with a collision mortality rate of 1.3 people per 100,000 residents in 2019, the same as Copenhagen—but behind Scandinavian Vision Zero pioneers such as Stockholm (0.7 per 100,000) and Oslo (0.9 per 100,000). Cyclist deaths in Montréal have declined from an average of five per year a decade ago to less than two per year (and none in 2019), all within a context of exploding rates of bicycle use (Ville de Montréal 2019).

THE NEW FRONTIER

The Tremblay administration adopted a far-ranging transportation master plan in 2008, which called for doubling the size of the cycling network, to over 800 km, within a decade. The plan also called for the creating a "white network" (*réseau blanc*)—a subset of bicycle facilities that would be maintained in the winter. Winter cycling was not new *per se*—members of MAB and Vélo Québec had been practicing and promoting it since the late-1970s (Vélo Québec 2017); however, this constituted the first official city document to recognize the practice and also propose accommodations for it.

By the early 2010s, however, only a few fragmented bits of the cycling network were being maintained during winter, and in a very inconsistent manner. A new kind of *velofrustration* started setting in among the increasing number of year-round cyclists in Montréaler. A Facebook group (*Vélo d'hiver – Montréal*) emerged, where the growing and enthusiastic winter cycling community could exchange tips, organize group rides, and vent their frustration at the city's inaction regarding winter maintenance. It rapidly became the biggest Montréal Facebook group dedicated to cycling.

The *Vélo d'hiver – Montréal* page, with over 11,000 members at the time of writing, is a rallying point for citizen efforts to push Montréal and other municipalities to improve conditions for winter cycling. For example, a neighbourhood cycling group in Notre-Dame-de-Grace joined with a group in Westmount to continuously monitor the state of their respective stretches of the Maisonneuve bike path. On a daily basis, volunteers took photos and filled out a simple report describing surface conditions at selected locations along the bike path. These reports were sent to public works officials and politicians. It was an effective campaign, as maintenance of the western section of the Maisonneuve bike path has become far more consistent.

Another example has been the push for winter maintenance of the Jacques-Cartier Bridge. For several years, the *Piétons et cyclistes du Pont Jacques Cartier* (PCPJC) have held protests and lobbied federal authorities to keep this crucial link between central Montréal and Longueuil open year-round. PCPJC have an advantage that MAB never had: sympathetic mayors on both sides of the bridge. It also helps that the current federal Minister of Infrastructure, Catherine McKenna, is a winter cyclist in equally cold and harsh Ottawa. PCPJC's years of efforts and patience paid off: mere weeks before the writing of this chapter, it was announced that the Jacques-Cartier Bridge pathway would remain open to cyclists this winter (2020-2021). The federal government has also decided that the bike path on the recently completed new Samuel de Champlain Bridge will also be open year-round.

Vélo Québec has engaged in two different fronts in the winter cycling fight. On the public encouragement front, it pushed winter cycling guides on how to dress, how to adapt one's bicycle to the rigours of winter, and how to ride in various conditions, via its newsletter, magazines, website, and social media accounts. It also hosted winter cycling workshops at *La Maison des cyclistes* for those curious to try.

To get more people riding, and to grab the attention of elected officials and the media, Vélo Québec adopted a strategy from its old *Tour de l'île* playbook. Four winters in a row, it organized mass winter bike rides, dubbed *Vélo sous zéro*. The first edition, held mid-February 2014, was an unqualified success. Participation surpassed the registration cap of 500, and the ride went off without a hitch, even though many were first-time winter cyclists. Attendance varied at the following three editions, mainly due to extreme cold conditions. Nevertheless, the event's goals were met: the media and politicians came, and reporting on the event was favourable.

The second front involves efforts to persuade the city to make winter cycling easier, for example, by improving winter maintenance. Vélo Québec convinced the city to commission a study, investigating winter cyclists' needs and the city's capacity to meet them with existing winter maintenance practices. Case studies of winter maintenance practices in other cities were compiled to illustrate possible avenues for improving local practices. In a similar vein, Vélo Québec hosted the fifth edition of the international Winter Cycling Congress. The hope was that local engineering professionals and city staff would rub shoulders with foreign experts and gain new knowledge and inspiration.

There has been a recent change in the media discourse around winter cycling. In the years before the *Vélo sous zéro* events, there was always a slew of negative coverage about those crazy and irresponsible cyclists on Montréal's icy streets, risking their lives and impeding cars. This type of coverage has largely disappeared; these days, local news outlets have turned to assessing how well boroughs are maintaining their bicycle facilities and have started reporting sympathetically on the frustrations faced by winter cyclists (Magder 2016).

Many challenges remain. Cycling traffic volumes between November 15th and April 1st, when a significant share of the cycling network still shuts down for winter, are only 10 to 15% of the summertime average. Although more than half of the network is nominally open year-round, the majority of "four seasons" facilities are nothing more than painted lines. They are ploughed insofar as the roads are ploughed. Only a small fraction of the year-round network consists of physically separated bike lanes that undergo dedicated maintenance operations. If more Montréalers are to keep riding through the winter, there will ultimately need to be more of these well-maintained, separated lanes.

GOLDEN AGE AHEAD?

Montréal has been fortunate to have several administrations in a row that have been sympathetic to the cause and who have continued to expand the network. However, bold moves like the construction of the Claire Morrissette bike path have been rare. There has been a preference for projects that rely on recovering leftover street space, avoiding the need to remove lanes or on-street parking. As a result, hardly any space has been carved out for cyclists on destination-rich thoroughfares, despite sustained lobbying.

This appears to have changed with the election Projet Montréal, a progressive municipal political party with a strong mobility platform, which currently controls city council and several borough councils. Mayor Valerie Plante and her council have initiated the *Réseau express vélo* (REV, which sounds like "dream" in French), a network of wide, separated bike lanes on arterial roads. At the time of writing, the first of these projects is under construction on the iconic Saint-Denis Street. Two out of four traffic lanes are being removed to make way for the wide bike lanes, though on-street parking will remain.

There is, of course, opposition to this bold project. Some local merchants are furious. Two-thirds of merchants, however, are in favour, though half would prefer that construction be postponed until after COVID-19. Groups representing persons with disabilities have also expressed concern, if not outright opposition. They worry about the loss of accessibility to bus stops along new separated bike lanes. Anti-gentrification activists have also come out against some proposed bike lanes, which they contend are driving up housing prices.

Those who voice concerns or oppose new cycling network projects show where cycling advocates need to direct their efforts or with whom they need to establish coalitions. The further development of cycling in Montréal depends on the reallocation of street space. To make the political case for these reallocations, more than just cycling advocates will have to get behind them. Merchants, people with disabilities, anti-gentrifiers, and others need to be convinced that they too stand to benefit from increased space for bikes and less space for dangerous, polluting cars. The success of the future REV lines and other bold cycling projects will require a bigger tent than that which covers only the needs of cyclists.

REFERENCES

Lalonde, M. 2008. "A bike path for Claire." *Montréal Gazette*, 3 June 2008. https://montrealgazette.com/news/local-news/a-bike-path-for-claire.

Magder, J. 2016. "Winter cyclists gaining more respect on Montréal bike paths." *Montréal Gazette*, 23 February 2016. https://montrealgazette.com/news/local-news/winter-cyclists-gaining-more-respect-on-montreal-bike-paths.

Montréal Gazette. 2019. "History Through Our Eyes: Oct. 12, 1976, 'Bicycle Bob' Silverman." 12 October 2019. https://montrealgazette.com/news/local-news/history-through-our-eyes/history-through-our-eyes-oct-12-1976-bicycle-bob-silverman.

Vélo Québec. 2017. "Vélo d'hiver: Vélo Québec acteur et témoin d'une évolution." 1 December 2017. https://www.velo.qc.ca/par-thematique/histoire-du-velo/velo-dhiver-velo-quebec-acteur-et-temoin-dune-evolution/.

Ville de Montréal. 2019. "État de la sécurité routière 2019." https://ville.montreal.qc.ca/visionzero/.

PART III.

PLANNING THE CITY

SOLIDARITY ARCHITECTURE AND SOCIAL URBANISM

CHRISTELLE PROULX CORMIER AND RON RAYSIDE

INTRODUCTION

To be meaningful and sustainable, architecture and urban planning should not be reduced to the production of environments built according to standardized orders and technical constraints, as is too often the case. Despite the disconcerting lack of boldness and innovation we see in Montréal, formal originality should not guide the design of spaces and buildings either. Instead, architectural or urban planning projects should be an inclusive, flexible, and even formative process; one that responds to social, historical, territorial, and political realities. Obviously, in a world where everything is accelerating, from the climate crisis to growing social and economic inequality, it may seem risky to devote a precious resource such as time to understanding these contextual elements and to accompanying members of civil society so that they become actors of change and project leaders. However, this is the atypical path chosen by Rayside Labossière.

Founded in 2000 by Ron Rayside, Rayside Architects is a continuation of its founder's philosophy, inherited from the 1970s. It is based on the principles of social, community, and urban development. Following the appointment of Antonin Labossière as a partner in 2011, the company became Rayside Labossière. It now has 35 employees. Recognized for its unique involvement in the Montréal community, the firm carries out hundreds of architectural and urban planning projects each year. Among the most well-known are: Le Mainbourg Community Centre, Cactus, Les Habitations Sainte-Germaine-Cousin, Chic Resto Pop, and Théâtre Paradoxe.

Rayside Labossière is a firm that supports, unifies, equips, and speaks out; a firm that practices "solidarity architecture" and "social urbanism."

SOLIDARITY ARCHITECTURE

Since the beginning of the great social movements that emerged from the Quiet Revolution and the Church's disengagement from providing public services, it has partly been the responsibility of civil society—in particular, community groups—to initiate and implement a variety of projects that guarantee the adequacy of services offered to meet the real needs of the population. These organizations have a subtle understanding of local realities and are able to propose projects and spaces that contribute to maintaining social harmony. In this way, they offer each person the resources and spaces to find their place and flourish in our society.

Many remember that in the 1970s, the commitment of a small number of architects led to the creation of technical resource groups (GRTs; *groupes de ressources techniques*), who provided training and support to community groups and other organizations. These GRTs quickly became professionalized to specialize in the development of social housing projects. However, apart from standardized frameworks for social housing production and, more recently, early childhood centres (CPE; *centres de la petite enfance*), there are no permanent programs to support the development of architectural projects of a social nature.

Whether or not permanent programs exist, the development of social projects inevitably has the appearance of a long quest strewn with many pitfalls. It is necessary to define the project itself, work out all aspects of its implementation and, above all, obtain the required approvals and funding for its implementation. Perseverance is essential, as the process often takes many years. Flexibility is also needed to adapt the project to the context and opportunities that arise, navigate complex processes, and play the necessary political games.

Since its creation, Rayside Labossière has been committed to moving beyond the "classical" architectural practice, supporting the initiatives of social developers. The firm has supported many projects. Sometimes projects may take more than five or even ten years; often, no lines are drawn for years, though the firm, together with the leading groups, pushes the projects until they materialize. The search for opportunities, mobilization, production of substantial project documents, evolving financial arrangements, and political arguments represent the bulk of the work. Agility is undoubtedly a key to success for this type of initiative. Several dozen, perhaps even more than one hundred, social spaces have been created. Projects sometimes give a new vocation to elements of our collective built heritage: churches, monasteries, schools, obsolete industrial buildings, and other places with unique characteristics. In the eyes of private developers, these are difficult to "make profitable." With all their might, organizations are taking over these spaces and bringing them back to life.

Some groups have begun to fully embrace their role as social developers. They have successively carried out several projects, sometimes working outside of their primary area of activity. In recent decades, we have seen the professionalization of community organizations and their increasing participation in constructing our collective built environment. Now, the commitment and support of government authorities for these initiatives should further reflect the importance of the roles of community organizations.

SOCIAL URBANISM

These same social actors, increasingly aware of the positive impact of their interventions, are becoming more involved in the discussions concerning the consolidation of our communities and living environments. They now participate significantly in urban planning processes. Involved voluntarily with various social and community networks in Montréal's central neighbourhoods, Rayside Labossière is often called upon to reinforce this sense of competence in the urban planning field, by refining the actors' understanding of the territory, by provoking reflections on the issues observed, and by building consensus on elements of vision.

Involvement in the creation of the *Table pour l'aménagement du Centre-Sud* (TACS) began in 1996. This was followed in the early 2000s by the mobilization of organizations wishing to position themselves for the establishment of institutions of importance to Ville-Marie, including the *Centre hospitalier de l'Université de Montréal* (CHUM) and *Bibliothèque et Archives nationales du Québec* (BAnQ). Rayside Labossière and its founder, Ron Rayside, quickly found themselves participating in dozens of working committees, coalitions, groups, and neighbourhood roundtables of all kinds.

Generally speaking, the first decade of the 21st century was characterized by an awakening of civil society to urban planning issues. An ever-increasing number of neighbourhood roundtables carried out reflections. They were even involved in concrete actions on select urban issues, ranging from citizens' mobility to neighbourhood greening and from the development of complete living environments to maintaining local employment centres. Because of the firm's approach, which could be described as "accessible" (discussed below), Rayside Labossière is regularly solicited and participates in several of these processes, as a member, as a facilitator at citizen forums and ideation workshops, or as a collaborator on specific issues.

At the same time, public consultation and citizen participation in Montréal have now become inseparable from good urban planning practices. Rayside

Labossière seizes these opportunities to influence the transformation of living environments alongside social partners by provoking debates and exchanging ideas. From all these approaches and all these movements, the gains the firm has facilitated are tangible and visible. Some examples include:

- Construction of nearly a thousand social housing units (several approaches).
- Conversion of several churches and monasteries for social use.
- Development of several dozen community facilities.
- Development of numerous CPEs (childcare centres) in the heart of living environments.
- Coalition for the CHUM downtown: the downtown site was selected.
- Coalition for the Grande Library downtown (BAnQ): the downtown site was selected.
- Mobilization of local stakeholders regarding the transformation of the *Société Radio-Canada* site; this involved the formation of an advisory committee of local stakeholders (working in collaboration with public authorities and the developer), the inclusion of social, affordable, and family housing in the project, integration of principles for the development of quality public spaces, etc.
- Implementation of an inclusive approach for the creation of a new living environment on the Louvain site (mobilization of local players by *Solidarité Ahuntsic*).
- Review of the City of Montréal's Social and Affordable Housing Inclusion Strategy (*Habiter Ville-Marie* representations).
- Prohibition of a left turn on Ontario Street to access the Jacques-Cartier Bridge (part of efforts to revitalize Ontario Street).
- Dozens of recommendations made by the *Office de consultation publique de Montréal* (OCMP) were directly influenced by the ideas formulated in the many briefs submitted (different working groups for different participatory approaches: the regional urban plan [PMAD; *Plan métropolitain d'aménagement et de développement*], numerous PPUs [*programs particuliers d'urbanisme*], Sainte-Catherine West, etc.).
- And many more.

Thanks to the democratization of urban planning, civil society is gaining influence in the process. Because we are now facing new significant challenges, this new place for civil society in the sphere of power is valuable and essential.

VISION, THE CRUCIAL STEP

Like the economy, the city is constantly looking to grow and develop. Quickly. This mad quest for growth, combined with short-term (four-year) electoral cycles, leads to a proliferation of programs, an increase in the number and scale of projects under development, and accelerated growth in property and construction costs. Added to this is a set of complex social and environmental issues, which we claim to want to address, but do so ineptly. These include an aging population, the exodus of households to the suburbs, lack of an adequate labour force, the impacts of climate change, repeated flooding, among many others. These issues have ramifications in all spheres of our society. Yet, the current impulse is often to attempt to address individual problems—the ends of these branches—without treating the system as a whole. In the face of the increasing complexity of our environments, it is necessary to take a step back and view the system holistically. It is this step back that Rayside Labossière likes to take and for which the firm is regularly solicited.

To position ourselves regarding the planning of the territory or propose a project that really meets a need, it is necessary to have a good understanding and an overview. This is true for architecture; it is also true for urban planning. Therefore, it is imperative to take the time to understand and analyze the broader context, the dynamics and associated actors, and the needs of the population concerned. We have to play with the scales and see the bigger picture, go from micro to macro, to come back to the scale that concerns us. We need to establish a clear picture of the situation, understand the many issues observable in the territory and their interrelation. Even when the data available on these issues is partial, discussing them will always be preferable to not thinking about them at all. It stimulates thought. Only then is it possible to move on to the vision stage and, finally, the project stage.

The vision. For Rayside Labossière, this is a bit of a keystone. The impacts of our choices have long-term repercussions, and it is precisely this long-term horizon that should guide our actions. Therefore, the vision exercize allows us to project ourselves into the future, to define what our living spaces and neighbourhoods could become in several decades.

This exercize raises several questions to consider, focusing on the type of environment we want to see created: Who will be the users of the spaces we are developing, what will their needs be in ten, twenty or fifty years, and how will they be able to continue to occupy the buildings and neighbourhoods we are developing today? For example, do we want to live and work in more comprehensive, greener, more accessible, and livelier environments? What are the opportunities today and tomorrow for implementing the vision we are setting out? And what complementarity with other urban components and various sectors can we already foresee?

Answering these questions in a holistic manner allows the implementation of more adequate and, thus, more sustainable measures. To legitimize the approach, it is also necessary to be able to listen, to recognize the experience and expertise of others, and to open dialogue with a diversity of actors. These reflexes must be developed quickly and by all of us: planners, decision-makers, organizations, and citizens.

TOOLS TO DEVELOP A VISION

Every opportunity to deliver their message, to share their project, must be seized by social developers to achieve their goals. They need to be mobilizing, as partnerships often account for much of the credibility they project. Through its involvement and support of various groups, Rayside Labossière has acquired tools that have proven effective in enabling civil society actors to move forward in this vast exercize of analysis and vision and ultimately take a stand and make a concrete contribution to building their community. Moreover, these tools facilitate the structuring of almost any approach related to a development project or urban issues.

Mapping, for example, is a great tool: very effective, democratic, and accessible. It allows the overlay of quantitative and qualitative data, but also ideas and courses of action. Mapping allows us to see the territory from another perspective and contextualize a problem by playing with scales. Rich maps, the ones that "speak," inevitably unravel languages and generate relevant discussions. They are also ideal for initiating collective and inclusive reflection, such as through a thematic round table.

In addition to cartography, visuals have a prominent place in all documents and presentations. Photographs, diagrams, plans, and maps are always more abundant than text because they facilitate understanding the issues and solutions. Still, more importantly, even in a summary or preliminary version, they stimulate thinking and progress like few other tools.

In a more or less formalized framework, the round table often enables Rayside Labossière's team to bring together a diversity of actors who otherwise have little or no contact with each other: local and regional actors; elected officials and municipal civil servants; representatives of many sectors of civil society such as health, social housing, schools, heritage, property developers, merchants, community organizations, the cultural sector, etc. In this context, it is necessary to work with a wide variety of viewpoints and to identify lines of convergence.

Indeed, by exchanging observations and ideas on the same theme or subject, we generally quickly see the emergence of avenues of consensus, which contribute to the development of a unifying vision. This vision can then be formulated in a brief or presentation document to facilitate representations. In fact, the printed document is unrivalled when it comes to presenting findings, ideas, and projects, or convincing and demonstrating the strength of a mobilization. It serves at the same time as a report, as a business card for performances and as a reminder during participatory processes.

More structured than ever and better equipped to speak the language of real estate and urban development, social actors today are ready to become true allies of governments in constructing cities and regions that are more comprehensive, more sustainable, and more adapted to the needs of their population.

ROLES AND CHALLENGES OF PUBLIC AUTHORITIES

By being better able to participate in the ongoing discussions around current and desired urban transformations, civil society now has more expectations of public authorities. But, with their current structures, do public authorities really have the means to implement what is expected of them? Not yet completely, it would seem.

First, what priority challenges should they address? From all the approaches, events, reflections, and work that Rayside Labossière has had the opportunity to participate in over the last few decades, a few clear objectives emerge:

- Ensuring the maintenance and consolidation of comprehensive, inclusive, and mixed-living environments.
- Developing public and active transport networks in line with urban planning goals.
- Combating urban sprawl.
- Mitigating and adapting to climate change.
- Supporting civil society initiatives.

Important legislative changes have recently been made to recognize the status of cities as local governments and give them more responsibility in this respect. This is a very welcome advance. But to tackle the targeted problems head-on and give themselves the means to achieve the objectives mentioned above, all public authorities will undoubtedly have to continue to review their roles, responsibilities, and tools.

Municipalities are always trailing behind the private sector when it comes to achieving the vision of a territory, no matter how coherent and unifying the vision may be. In fact, it is the private developers who, with their financial power and agility to use regulations to their advantage, who generally control implementation. Municipalities are still far too dependent on the investments of private developers. Yet, these investments only partially meet the needs of the population. Indeed, current urban planning processes and laws leave municipalities with little capacity to steer a real estate project to ensure that it is appropriate to the realities of an environment. The guidance and support that planning professionals can offer to social developers make sense to counterbalance this reality.

CONCRETE ACTIONS FOR GOVERNMENTS

In the current context, where economic and environmental imperatives require rapid action to meet these demands, four principal duties must be carried out by government bodies:

1. All levels of government need to create and share an overview and a detailed understanding of the issues and problems experienced in the territory, at both the national and local levels.
2. A coherent and clear planning vision must be defined. This could be set in the form of a national policy, referred to by each level of government to guide its actions and grant funding for future projects.
3. Planning tools and regulations that give municipal governments the agility to guide development in line with this vision and reduce their dependence on private project revenues must be put in place.
4. Civil society actors should be given the means to become real developers and partners of public authorities by relying on their specific skills and in-depth knowledge of living environments, social realities, and environmental issues.

FOR GREATER SYNERGY

In conclusion, experience has shown that architects and urban planners today have the opportunity to play a critical role. This can be achieved by architects and urban planners offering reimagined support to social actors to participate effectively in planning processes; designing projects that make significant positive contributions to the development of the city; and participating in broader collective reflections on urban and social dynamics.

Thus, if public authorities, planning professionals, and civil society actors combine their respective expertise to make a sensible, multi-scale diagnosis of the territory, to develop a coherent and unifying vision for each of them, and to implement appropriate and promising projects for communities, together, they will be able to make a concrete contribution to the construction of more resilient, inclusive, and sustainable living environments, for the benefit of all.

REFERENCES

Corporation de développement communautaire Action Solidarité Grand Plateau, Coalition communautaire Milton-Parc pour l'accès au logement et à la santé, & Comité logement du Plateau Mont-Royal. 2019. *Communauté Saint-Urbain : Plus qu'un toit, une communauté. Projet en développement.* http://www.rayside.qc.ca/wp-content/uploads/2021/04/Communaut%C3%A9-Saint-Urbain191202_Rayside-Labossi%C3%A8re.pdf.

Corporation de développement communautaire Centre-Sud, and Rayside Labossière. 2020. *Rapport-synthèse des midi-concertations.* Comité d'accompagnement des grands projets du Centre-Sud. http://www.rayside.qc.ca/wp-content/uploads/2020/02/SYNTH%C3%88SE-GAGPCS_MIDI-CONCERTATIONS-PPU-des-Faubourgs-Octobre-2020.pdf.

Corporation de développement communautaire Centre-Sud, and Rayside Labossière. 2020. *Document de présentation.* Comité d'accompagnement des grands projets du Centre-Sud. http://www.rayside.qc.ca/wp-content/uploads/2020/02/2020-01-21-CAGPCS-Document-de-pr%C3%A9sentation-du-comit%C3%A9.pdf.

Corporation de développement communautaire Côte-des-Neiges, and Rayside Labossière. 2016. *Site de l'ancien hippodrome Blue Bonnets – Orientations de développement issues de la communauté.* http://www.rayside.qc.ca/wp-content/uploads/2015/08/DOCUMENT-BLUE-BONNETS-2016-CDC-CDN-RAYSIDE-LABOSSI%C3%88RE.pdf.

Table de concertation du quartier des Grands Jardins, and Rayside Labossière. 2017. *Les CIVIC COMMONS du quartier des GRANDS JARDINS. Guide de réflexion.* http://www.rayside.qc.ca/wp-content/uploads/2020/02/Civic-Commons-Guide-de-r%C3%A9flexion.pdf.

THE RECONSTRUCTION OF MONTRÉAL'S CHABANEL DISTRICT

MOSTAFA HENAWAY AND NORMA RANTISI

At the heart of Montréal's role as the economic centre of the Québec and Canadian economies in the post-war period (1940s-1980s) was its significant position in the garment and textile sector. For much of the latter half of the twentieth century, Montréal was the third most important city in North America for garment production, trailing only Los Angeles and New York. At its height, the industry employed well over 100,000 workers in Montréal. Much of the heartbeat of the industry centred along Chabanel Street in the northern end of Montréal. Until the 1990s, the street was the premier location for fashion and apparel in the country, populated with large bustling factories. The area surrounding it—also referred to as Chabanel—would come to be known as the 'garment district' (*Cité de la mode*). But Montréal's garment district, like many across North America, would undergo major restructuring in the context of neoliberal globalization—one marked by trade liberalization and offshoring—and a consequent plummeting of employment. Today, the garment industry's decline manifests in the empty sidewalks, boarded-up facades and vacancies of the massive concrete buildings that line the main street. Chabanel's restructuring is also manifest in new initiatives by local actors to revive the district based on speculative real estate development and the luring of new 'creative' industries and a cosmopolitan 'creative class.' In this chapter, we examine the evolution of Chabanel by considering its rise and decline as a garment district in the context of neoliberal globalization and how local public and private actors are shaping its 'rebirth' through property-led forms of redevelopment. We conclude by reflecting on the kind of planning needed to (re)orient development towards the service of people over profit.

THE RISE AND DECLINE OF CHABANEL

Chabanel emerged as a central hub for the textile and garment industry in the mid-1960s. It was primarily farmland until becoming a site for manufacturing and streetcar maintenance in the 1920s and serving as a site for armament production for the two world wars (District Central 2020). Its transformation to a garment district coincided with other key developments. The first was the northward migration of garment and textile factories. In the early-20th century, the industry was concentrated in downtown Montréal, along St Catherine Street and lower St Laurent Boulevard (the 'Main') in mainstay buildings such as the Belgo (Gatensby 2019). After the 1920s, the industry would gradually head northward along St Laurent Boulevard , following the residential settlement pattern for new immigrants, mainly Jewish immigrants (in the Plateau) until the Second World War, then Southern European immigrants (in the Mile End) afterwards. Other developments included constructing highways and the rise of a major commercial district, *Marché Central*, to the west of Chabanel.

Chabanel's footprint would begin to take form in 1964 with the construction of the first large factory, occupying 500,000 square feet, at 99 Chabanel Street. At the time, the area was considered to be on the city's outskirts; consequently, there were large, empty tracts available. A 1 km stretch of land along Chabanel Street, between St Laurent Boulevard and Meilleur Street, would soon see seven other massive concrete factories erected. By 1984, over 5 million square feet of industrial space was built, centralizing the garment industry in this one location. Chabanel remains the most extensive land footprint on the island of Montréal outside of Place Bonaventure (a downtown shopping and office centre). By the 1990s, there were roughly 100,000 workers in the district (Gatensby 2019). Chabanel represented one of the major employment centres on the island of Montréal, outside of Dorval (airport/logistics centre) and the central business district (Shearmer 2006). Even as many of the major manufacturing and finance firms relocated to Toronto in the 1970s, the garment industry continued to thrive in Montréal.

The eight large industrial buildings situated along Chabanel Street have served as home to major Canadian apparel firms, such as Lamour, Tricot, Reitmans, and Tristan, housing significant activities such as production, wholesale operations, and offices. There is also a slew of smaller apparel firms and small and medium-sized companies focused on pleating, button-making, zipper production, sewing machine repair, leather, and fabric supply—constituting the Montréal garment and apparel industry ecosystem, which made the area an internal market that manufacturers could readily access. Chabanel also served as a major shopping artery. The ground-level, street-facing sections of buildings served as highly visible retail stores; however, 90% of the district's production was geared towards the United States. At the time, it was a vibrant district, with lots of foot traffic and local cafés and restaurants brimming with workers and buyers. However, this would change drastically in the era of neoliberal globalization that brought major changes to the garment industry's spatial organization.

MONTRÉAL'S GARMENT SECTOR GOES GLOBAL—DECIMATING LOCAL COMMUNITIES

Despite its position as the epicentre of the garment industry—for Montréal and Canada, more generally—Chabanel was not able to withstand the winds of change in the global economy, as heightened international competition and the integration of the Global South into broader free trade agreements became the hallmarks of neoliberal globalization. The first mark of change was the North American Free Trade Agreement which entered into force in January 1994, after which the industry would witness declining employment. The next critical markers were China's entry into the World Trade Organization (2001), the signing of a 2002 Organization for Economic and Cooperation and Development (OECD) agreement which would favour the development of LDCs ('less' developed countries) through access to export markets, and the 2004 expiration of the Multifibre Arrangement, which had imposed quotas on developing countries' exports of products like yarn, fabrics, and clothing (Trichur 2011). Canada was instrumental in the latter, with former Prime Minister Chrétien announcing a "Least Developed Countries (LDCs) Market Access Initiative" at the 2002 G8 Summit in Kananaskis.

The initiative was geared towards stimulating LDC economies through the 'trade-not-aid' approach, which allowed Canadian corporations to take advantage of supply chains in Bangladesh, India, China, and other countries in the Global South, removing decades-old tariffs on clothing and textiles from 48 of the world's poorest nations (Vasil 2002). By 2015, local garment manufacturing employed just 6,305 Montréalers, down from nearly 22,000 a decade earlier and a sharp decline from nearly 100,000 workers in the 1990s (Gatensby 2019).

THE ROLE OF LOCAL ACTORS IN CHABANEL'S DECLINE AND 'REBIRTH'

The profit-oriented nature of the capitalist economy necessarily involves rounds of 'creative destruction'—the destruction or abandonment of that which is seen as less profitable (in monetary terms) alongside the creation of new activities or spaces from which to derive greater gains. This logic can be seen in the strategies pursued by many of Chabanel's garment firms—and, as we shall later see, public actors—in the face of a new global economic reality. While rising imports would play a significant part in declining employment in the industry following trade liberalization, the trend toward outsourcing on the part of local manufacturers was another major determinant. One that would have severe repercussions for local workers' livelihoods, the vitality of the Chabanel district and consequences for the Montréal economy, more generally.

Lamour, for example, is a case that exemplifies this transformation. Established in 1952, Lamour Inc is a sock and sportswear manufacturer in Montréal; at its heyday Lamour produced almost 50% of all sports socks in Canada. The company has contracts with major buyers, such as Wal-Mart and Canadian Tire, and a licensing agreement with Joe Fresh. In the 1960s, the company constructed its office headquarters at 55 Louvain. This large nondescript edifice just one block above Chabanel in the heart of the garment district resembles "brutalist soviet-style architecture." By 2008, the company began offshoring production to suppliers in Bangladesh and Pakistan, ironically the same places from which many of their Montréal-based workers had immigrated. Within six months, nearly 500 workers lost their jobs in a succession of layoffs. Were these layoffs due to a decline in business? Did the company go bankrupt? Quite the opposite: Lamour was becoming more profitable. It was also able to avoid the stigma associated with sweatshop labour or regarding the quality of production, owing to perceptions that it was a Canadian manufacturer; 'country of origin' laws only require that garment makers produce 20% of the product's value in Canada to qualify for the 'Made in Canada' label. Rather than experience decline, Lamour has continuously expanded, opening several new divisions, and growing at 7% per year with employment at 1,100 workers (Niedoba 2019).

As for the laid-off workers, the consequences were dire as they were given no compensation from the company. As Patrick Riga, account manager for the Bank of Montréal in the textile industry, stated: "A lot [of] people were working for 30, 35 years at the same corporation and ended up the next day with nothing—no pension from the company … It created a hardship on a mainly immigrant community, especially in Québec" (Trichur 2011). Many workers subsequently sought support for their fundamental rights with the Immigrant Workers Centre (IWC) in Montréal; a campaign was initiated around the broader decline and drew attention to the lack of state support for textile and garment workers.

For the district itself, the decline has meant that the large, overpowering towers of Chabanel have been hollowed out, and the buzz of thousands of circulating workers has dissipated. The outsourcing of production and the rise of imports led to significant employment and spatial vacancies turning the district into a ghost town in the 1990s and 2000s, which affected not only garment manufacturing operations but also the range of supplier and distribution services. With many workers living in proximate neighbourhoods, such as Parc-Extension, the economic effects would ripple to other locales.

Chabanel's decline, however, would also prompt a rising chorus of calls to redevelop the area. This included calls from established business interests (i.e., the Chamber of Commerce), real estate owners, garment manufacturers, and crucially, public actors and para-public actors. In line with the approach advanced by Richard Florida, which posits creativity and innovation as key drivers of economic growth, these actors have sought to remake the district as a centre for 'creative' activities and the so-called 'creative class' workers who could motor these activities, with property redevelopment being viewed as both a means and desired outcome of such reconstruction. More specifically, these actors would seek to uphold the district's status as a fashion centre, but with greater emphasis on boutique manufacturers and designers, as well as head office functions (i.e., marketing, design, and the coordination of production in Global South) for the larger apparel firms. Simultaneously, they would also seek to attract other creative or knowledge-based industries along with residential development. A closer look at the actors and investments that seek to remake the district as a 'creative hub' can provide insight into what property-led redevelopment means for Chabanel's future—along with who stands to profit and who is excluded.

CHABANEL'S RECONSTRUCTION AS STATE-LED PROPERTY REVALORIZATION

In 2004, the City of Montréal held consultations for a new Master Plan. Among the early advocates for incorporating Chabanel's redevelopment was the Montréal Chamber of Commerce and Board of Trade, a central actor with Québec Inc.[1] The Chamber submitted a response to the consultations, suggesting key factors that the city should consider: "For this difficult exercise, we suggest two reference criteria to make it easier to determine priority interventions: their impact on the city's competitiveness and their ability to generate more wealth" (Chamber of Commerce 2004, 4). More specifically, they emphasized:

> The development of the l'Acadie-Chabanel (Detailed planning area 4.16) area, a zone with major economic potential that could quickly be stimulated by redeveloping municipal 6 infrastructures and access roads. This area is home to, among others, the Cité de la mode, a strategically important area for the Montréal and Québec economy. Indeed, 587

1. For more information about Québec Inc, see discussion in the chapter Power and the City.

companies and 11,350 jobs in the l'Acadie-Chabanel area depend on the fashion industry. At a time when this industry is undergoing major structural changes and where quality, creativity and added value are becoming key factors of competitiveness, improving accessibility to and enhancing the quality of the public realm are important initiatives to further (Chamber of Commerce 2004, 5-6).

Chabanel is depicted as a strategic area, with its historic role as a garment centre providing a basis for renewal. But this renewal would be oriented to more 'creative' and 'added-value' activities within the industry, in addition to other uses.

At this time, real estate investors also began to notice of Chabanel, due to its large tracts of vacant space—hence potential as a site for speculation. Radical geographer David Harvey has observed that when the possibility for profits accruing from traditional production activities runs dry, capitalists will invest in the built environment (e.g., speculative real estate) as an alternative site from which to generate profits—an investment practice that he refers to as a 'secondary' circuit of capital.[2] The case of Chabanel is no exception. Many private and institutional actors have sought to take advantage of this potential. Starting in 2005, for instance, Groupe Dayan (a major Montréal-based real estate developer) partnered with PSP Investments (the crown corporation that manages federal government employees' pension funds) to purchase seven buildings in the district for nearly $120 million. This purchase included five buildings along Chabanel Street[3] and represented 35% of Chabanel's real estate stock, at roughly 10 million square feet. Groupe Dayan had an ambitious plan to convert some into commercial (shopping) and residential uses (Dubuc 2017) and create an 'international fashion centre.'

Factions of manufacturing capital have also been central in the speculative redevelopment of the district. The Liebermans, the family that owns Lamour Inc, also have stakes in Chabanel real estate through their company AEDN Realty, while the APP Group, which owns designer brands Mackage and Soia & Kyo, purchased a building in the district in 2010.

The city took heed of this bourgeoning interest—and lobbying—on the part of business and property interests. In the mid-2000s, city officials worked with the Borough of Ahunstic-Cartierville to develop plans for the area's revitalization—with a commitment of over $18 million and a focus on enhanced access and beautification, along the lines proposed by the Chamber of Commerce. In 2006, the first phase was initiated with the construction of a commuter train station (Chabanel), along with beautification strategies, such as a bike path, widened sidewalks, and landscaping. Later, the borough would relocate its town hall to Chabanel, and a second commuter train station

---

2. The primary circuit is associated with production processes (Harvey 1982).
3. 99, 125, 225, 333, and 433 Chabanel Street.

(Ahuntsic) would be constructed. More government offices are expected to open as the city plans to centralize municipal services there.

In 2006, public officials also collaborated with local businesses, designers, and real estate owners to establish the *Regroupement pour le développement et la promotion du quartier Chabanel*. This group would function as an advisory committee to government, proposing design enhancements, greening initiatives, fashion events, and the promotion of greater commercial offerings (e.g., cafés and restaurants) to alter the district's image from that of a worn-out, industrial sector to that of a hip quarter. To quote Stéphanie Cardinal, an urban planner and architect who has served as a spokesperson for the group: "… like the meat-packing district in New York City that became a trendy place. We have the same vision for Chabanel" (Marotte 2010).

Beyond this, government bodies at different scales would also play a formidable role in shaping Chabanel's evolution. As noted above, federal government employee pensions (through PSP Investments) serve as a key source of real estate investment in the area. The provincial government has contributed to industry restructuring by supporting the adoption of new technologies by garment firms and funding (in collaboration with the city) a new high-technology textile research centre in the district. At the metropolitan scale, the *Communauté métropolitaine de Montréal*, working in concert with Montréal International,[4] approved the formation of *Grappe mmode*, a metropolitan fashion cluster, in 2015. The cluster represents 250 members from different sub-sectors of the industry. It has a mandate to promote the industry's growth and competitiveness in Montréal and Québec, including the promotion of Chabanel as a site for fashion design, high-end manufacturing, and fashion technology.

Indeed, as in the case with other traditional garment districts in Montréal, like Marconi-Alexandra (aka 'Mile-Ex') or Mile End, government (at multiple scales) plays a pivotal role in what Hackworth and Smith (2001) term 'state-led gentrification' (see also Sprague and Rantisi 2019 on state-supported displacement in 'Mile-Ex'). This refers to a process whereby the state proactively steers large-scale, place-based investments into 'profit-oriented' uses with the effect of displacing existing uses. For Chabanel, this has involved altering its urban design features to facilitate investments in new commercial and residential uses as well as shifting the focus from garment-related employment to so-called 'value-added' (i.e., non-manufacturing) activities. This intervention is justified based on Chabanel's perceived advantages: two nearby highways, rents that are one-fifth the cost of those in the downtown core, and buildings with ample floor space for varied uses, such as large loft

---

4. Created in 1996, Montréal International is a private-public partnership, aiming to attract foreign direct investment, international organizations, and high-skilled workers to greater Montréal.

condominiums or offices. Yet, to date, investment has been slow. The district lacks the 'coolness' factor (e.g., artists and bohemian establishments) that has facilitated the transformation of other former working-class textile districts (e.g., Mile-Ex or Mile End) and accessibility (e.g., the lack of subway stations) still presents a challenge.

While the state is steering investment, local businesses have come together to oversee the fine print of economic development strategies for the Chabanel district and the rest of the borough of Ahuntsic-Cartierville. In 2016, a new business association was established and approved by the city, called the *Société de développement commercial* (SDC) District Central. The SDC seeks to emphasize Chabanel's locational advantages to potential investors and position it as a rival to the downtown by rebranding it as 'District Central.' There are currently 1,800 businesses affiliated with this SDC. It also collaborates with the City of Montréal, *Grappe mmode*, and property owners on events, branding, and promotional campaigns. By promoting co-working spaces, the SDC and property owners also seek to attract artists and designers to the area and enhance its profile as a creative zone. For its part, the city is also directly investing in the area by consolidating its municipal services there by 2022.

CHABANEL TODAY—AND TOMORROW?

Today, the district continues to serve as a critical nucleus for the apparel industry; it still serves as home to the head offices of major companies (e.g., Reitmans, Lamour, SSENSE, and Tristan), prominent high-end designers (such as Marie St Pierre) have moved to the area, and luxury apparel producer Canada Goose is investing in a new plant (Deschamps 2019). However, it is no longer defined exclusively by apparel; it is also home to a major condo development and a growing cluster of technology companies and other service and production activities (District Central 2020).

The gradual transformation of Chabanel raises questions about who benefits and who assumes the risks from the roulette wheel of property development. In 2013, Groupe Dayan completed the conversion of the building at 125 Chabanel into condos, with help from the *Société d'habitation et de développement de Montréal* (SHDM), a para-municipal corporation that guaranteed 100% of the operation. However, questions of collusion emerged, as the chairman of the SHDM board of directors, Jean-Claude Cyr, was previously a consultant for Groupe Dayan (Dubuc 2017). In 2015, PSP Investments sold 225 Chabanel, for twice the cost at which it was acquired, to its former partner Groupe Dayan, citing the building's unprofitability. And in 2017, PSP sold a further three properties (99, 333, and 433 Chabanel) to Howard Szalavetz Properties, specialising in residential properties. While one building (333 Chabanel) was sold at a capital gain of 20%, the other buildings (99 and 433 Chabanel) were sold below the price at which they were purchased in 2005, underscoring the risks of using public sector pension funds for speculative ventures.

Changes in the district also reflect the privileging of so-called creative, high-skill work at the expense of semi-skilled manufacturing. To quote Canada Goose executive Dani Reiss:

> Montréal's Chabanel district was once a central part of apparel manufacturing in Canada, but this has been eroded by the shift offshore in pursuit of [profit] margins. Some brands only have their headquarters in the city, and they are missing the great history and potential this area has (Deschamps 2019).

Indeed, as in the case of Brooklyn and more recently Sunset Park in New York City, establishing new innovative and creative hubs in long-standing manufacturing districts generally has the effects of crowding out important employment sources for low-income and racialized workers (Hum 2017). The inclusion of the condominium development—rather than social housing—as a part of the broader transformation reinforces Chabanel's function as a for-profit, speculative bubble that caters to the so-called 'creative class.'

Within the broader context of neoliberal globalization and the neoliberalizing state, the current COVID-19 pandemic has exposed the heightened inequality, labour precarity, and poor housing conditions residents in Montréal face. Yet, like many other projects across the city, the current redevelopment trajectory of Chabanel is one that ultimately serves the interests of real estate developers, corporate investors, and a newly coined 'creative' (read: elite) class. While on the surface it may appear that the city has limited tools to counter this trend, the city and other levels of government have been instrumental in shaping the course of development through their master plans, planning regulations, infrastructure investments, use of pension funds, and municipal land. It should also be noted that a large parcel of land in the heart of Chabanel is municipally owned. This raises critical questions about what the city should be doing. Chabanel presented an opportunity to repurpose vacant buildings to nurture collectively controlled local manufacturing operations and provide social housing. Yet neither of these have materialized. The city did not use its recently instituted 'first-right-of-refusal,' which gives it the right to make the first offer on a property that is on the market to use the property for social housing within the district. As of yet, the city has not adopted a similar approach to secure affordable spaces for collectively owned industrial enterprises, even as such a tool is greatly warranted in a city with a strong legacy of manufacturing employment. While Chabanel has always had a limited residential population, and by extension, a limited base for local neighbourhood mobilization, previous generations of worker organizing has shown the urgency of building a neighbourhood that reflects the needs of the people rather than speculators and large textile companies-cum-investors. The city must be a part of such an endeavour. And as opposed to using public finance for private wealth accumulation, the city should carry out its mandate to improve its residents' general well-being by using state funds, resources, and tools to provide more equitable sources and spaces for livelihood.

REFERENCES

Chamber of Commerce. 2004. *Making the City of Montréal's Master Plan a major development tool for the City*. Brief of the Board of Trade Metropolitan Montréal concerning the renewal of the City of Montréal's Master Plan, to the Office de consultation publique de Montréal. https://acclr.ccmm.ca/documents/docRaccourcis/plan-urbain-en.pdf.

Deschamps, T. 2019. "Canada Goose to open new factory in Montréal, reports Q4 profit up from year ago." *CTV News*, 14 February 2019. https://www.ctvnews.ca/business/canada-goose-to-open-new-factory-in-montreal-reports-q4-profit-up-from-year-ago-1.4296706

District Centrale. 2020. "The history of our neighbourhood." https://district-central.ca/en/about-us/.

Dubuc, A. 2017. "La Caisse de retraite PSP retire ses billes de Chabanel." *La Presse*, 6 March 2017. https://www.lapresse.ca/affaires/economie/immobilier/201703/06/01-5075908-la-caisse-de-retraite-psp-retire-ses-billes-de-chabanel.php.

Gatensby, J. 2019. "By a Thread." *Maisonneuve*, 7 March 2019. https://maisonneuve.org/post/2019/03/7/by-a-thread/.

Hackworth, J., and Smith, N. 2001. "The changing state of gentrification." *Tijdschrift voor Economische en Sociale Geografie* 92(4): 464-477.

Harvey, D. 1982. *The Limits to Capital*. Chicago: University of Chicago Press.

Hum, T. 2017. "Get Ready Sunset Park, Brooklyn Is Coming: The Real Estate Imperatives of an Innovation Ecosystem." *Progressive City: Radical Alternatives*. https://www.progressivecity.net.

Marotte, B. 2010. "Montréal's rag trade gets Cinderella makeover." *Globe and Mail*, 30 December 2010. https://www.theglobeandmail.com/report-on-business/montreals-rag-trade-gets-cinderella-makeover/article1321712/.

Niedoba, S. 2019. "Lamour Group: Canada's Best Managed Companies." *Canadian Business*, 28 February 2019. https://www.canadianbusiness.com/lists-and-rankings/best-managed-companies/lamour-group-canadas-best-managed-companies-2019/.

Shearmur, R. 2006. "Travel from home: An economic geography of commuting distances in Montréal." *Urban Geography* 27(4): 330-359.

Sprague, M., and Rantisi, N.M. 2019. "Productive Gentrification in the Mile-Ex Neighbourhood of Montréal, Canada: Exploring the Role of the State in Remaking Urban Industrial Clusters." *Urban Research & Practice* 12(4): 301-321.

Trichur, R. 2011. "The high-tech rebirth of Canada's textile industry." *Globe and Mail*, 18 June 2011. https://www.theglobeandmail.com/report-on-business/economy/the-high-tech-rebirth-of-canadas-textile-industry/article583631/.

Vasil, A. 2002. "Roots Runs Away." *Now Toronto* 23(24). https://web.archive.org/web/20140714134510/http://stage81.nowtoronto.com/news/story.cfm?content=140356.

PART IV.

THE ECONOMY AND THE CITY

THE CITY AS SWEATSHOP

MOSTAFA HENAWAY

On 23 March 2020, Montréal was placed into a broad economic lockdown, except for workers that were considered essential. The lockdown exposed two parallel cities. Those who could remain at home, working remotely and ordering out, and those who remained working, risking their lives, working in textile factories, meat processing plants, kitchens, or greenhouses, as delivery drivers, warehouse workers, cleaners, orderlies, or domestic workers, performing building maintenance, security, or renovations; working almost every crucial job that makes our city function. This tragedy came to the fore with Marcelin Francois' death, a 40-year-old refugee claimant from Haiti who died from COVID-19 complications on 14 April 2020 (Boisvert 2020). Marcelin lived in Montréal-Nord, working full-time in a textile factory and on weekends as a *Préposé au bénéficiaire* through a temporary placement agency. His wife worked for Cargill Meats, which witnessed one of the largest outbreaks during the pandemic. She worked ten hours a day for minimum wage through a temporary placement agency, where she was shuttled by school bus day in and day out. They both worked in areas of 'essential work' but were disposable workers. They worked without fundamental rights and protections, not even knowing if they would have work the next day. Yet, they would both work alongside workers who were unionized and paid decent wages. Their tragic story is unfortunately not an isolated example but is the reality for immigrant workers. Ironically, these workers remained invisible; they were called heroes and guardian angels, yet at the end of the day, for them, the city remained a sweatshop.

Many workers have been rendered vulnerable, paid poverty wages working in precarious jobs through temporary placement agencies, without protections and without organization. These workers are central to the ways our cities function and how inequality is shaped. Corporations used outsourcing and offshoring to sweatshops of the Global South to ensure their profits; now, they are replicating the same strategies within our cities, creating a form of 'insourcing' that is driving the unprecedented inequality and polarization in the cities where we reside. In the end, the result is the same: the city itself becomes a sweatshop. The difference is that the final product is not a t-shirt, but the ability of cities to sustain themselves.

PRECARIOUS WORK REQUIRES PRECARIOUS WORKERS

Montréal's transition away from manufacturing, as a centre of industries such as textiles and garments, is witnessed by its scarred landscape of empty factories along the Lachine Canal or the silence in Chabanel, once vibrant with the humming of sewing machines. The new epoch of globalization increased calls for capital mobility, competition, flexibility, and the embrace of new dynamic sectors of the economy. This transition to a service economy has been fueled by a permanent stream of immigrant labour. Migration allowed employers access to cheap labour and the capacity to undermine wage pressures from unions. This new stream of cheap labour became crucial to fill the growing demand for workers in new service-based industries in the urban centres of the advanced economies with the transformation of global production, which began in the 1970s (Sassen 1996). Immigrants became a central tool for employers to maintain a flexible, cheap, and precarious workforce in Montréal.

In Canada, temporary work is now the fastest growing form of work. Corporations operating in health, food, retail, construction, and every sector of the economy can profit from such work, reducing labour costs by accessing a cheap, exploitable, and disposable workforce lacking job security. Increasingly, part-time work, temporary work, or the misclassification of work have become the new norm. Many of these workers are new immigrants; they constitute nearly 26% of the total workforce, yet account for 35% of Canada's accommodation and food services sector (Statistics Canada 2018). Of these, 300,000 (1.7%) are temporary foreign workers, arriving through the Temporary Foreign Worker Program, most occupying low-skilled, low-wage jobs. Moreover, the Royal Canadian Mounted Police estimates that between 200,000–500,000 people live in Canada without status, constituting a large segment of vulnerable workers (Choudry and Henaway 2012).

A crucial way that employers in Montréal and surrounding areas have turned the city into a sweatshop is through the use of temporary placement agencies. According to the CNESST (*Commission des normes de l'équité de la santé et de la sécurité du travail*), there are 436 temporary placement agencies operating on the island of Montréal. These agencies are not all the same. Some that we call "fly by night" agencies operate in the shadows with no accountability; they can open and close in an instant. They often pay their workers in cash, under the table. These agencies can be found in working-class immigrant neighbourhoods such as Parc-Ex, Saint-Michel, or along St Hubert Street. They provide a steady pool of workers: those who are the most vulnerable, living without status. In Montréal, an estimated 50,000 people live and work in the shadows.

Larger established corporate agencies are the other type of temp agency. They rely on the thousands of new immigrants, who arrive as refugee claimants; while awaiting their decision, they can legally work. After the election of Donald Trump, the flow of refugee claimants through Roxham Road[1] saw nearly 42,000 seeking protection between 2017 and 2019, from Haiti, Nigeria, Guinea, El Salvador, and Yemen. For refugee claimants, temp agencies are the main avenues to seek employment in Montréal. Employers that demand 'Canadian experience' force immigrants to seek work through temp agencies for their first jobs. The industry is large, with a revenue of $14.5 billion in 2017, up 6.8% from the previous year (Statistics Canada 2017). This workforce does not just fuel marginal parts of the economy often associated with sweatshops, but through temp agencies, subcontracting has become increasingly central to our city.

FROM FARM TO TABLE

At 6 am on any given day outside of Saint-Michel or Parc Metro stations, hundreds of workers wait to get on yellow school busses; they are taken to work as day labourers in greenhouses or meat processing plants or other parts of the agri-food industry. The agri-business sector accounts for $8.2 billion of the GDP in Greater Montréal, directly employing over 42,000 workers, on top of those working in sales, retail, and restaurants (Montréal International 2019). The agri-food industry, from large grocers (Maxi, Provigo, Metro), to restaurants, processing companies (Olymel, Cargill, Saputo, Vegepro) and the farms themselves, produce and process food that is marketed as local. All these workers share common experiences. They work through 'fly by night' agencies, and many are paid below minimum wage, facing wage theft and serious accidents. Companies use these agencies to subvert basic labour standards and health and safety regulations. Workers experiencing wage theft are often unable to claim their wages because the agency can simply close up shop and reopen under another name. This was the case of agency workers in

1. Former Canadian port of entry along the border of Québec and New York state, approximately 60 km south of Montréal.

a Montréal chicken processing plant. After a 2010 *Radio Canada* investigation, the agency which did not pay its workers (one of them facing a major accident) closed and reopened at the same location under a different name.

During the COVID-19 pandemic, the Immigrant Workers Centre (IWC) focused on a chicken processing plant in St-Eustache, Concord Premium meats. Its workforce is mainly recruited from Parc-Ex, where agency-run school busses ferry them out to the plant. One worker described the conditions as "horrific." In one case, a worker had died after having a stroke in the workplace. Other times, workers came together to raise money for colleagues who had lost their hands in workplace accidents. These workers live and work in the shadows, working 12 hours a day for $8 to $10 per hour, with no access to health and safety. In 2019, one Haitian refugee working for a large meat processing plant (Olymel) and its subsidiary Sherrington Cold Storage could only find work through a temporary placement agency while awaiting his work permit (Stevenson and Bernstien 2018). Like many other non-status workers, he was paid below minimum wage and suffered a significant accident (Stevenson and Bernstien 2018). These agencies often exploit those with precarious status, knowing these workers cannot file complaints out of fears of deportation.

A member of the Temporary Agency Worker Association explains how critical invisible labour is in the food sector: "these aren't 'guardian angels'—but Québecers still eat every day. When you see the grocery stores full of fruits, vegetables, and meat, you have no idea the number of people that made them that way" (Lindeman 2020). For two years, Bénédicte worked 80 to 90 hours a week as a Temporary Foreign Worker while being denied access to her cellphone. She is not alone; Québec temporary foreign workers face constant abuse and low pay without access to their rights because they are on closed work permits. This gives employers a sense of impunity because workers are afraid to stand for their rights in fear of losing their jobs and, therefore, their status.

These workers do not simply work for Madame and Monsieur small farmer. The example of local tomatoes provides a unique insight. Savoura Tomatoes, and its owner Stephane Roy (the "Tomato King"), has consolidated as the most prominent greenhouse tomato grower in Québec. Savoura produces 240,000 kg of tomatoes weekly, and has secured its prominent position as a result of supplying the major grocers. Currently, 72% of the national market share for grocery retail is shared among the four largest food retailers (Loblaws, Metro, Empire [Sobey's] and Safeway), meaning they are able to place pressure on key suppliers such as Savoura.

As a result of changing work habits and people working longer hours, we have relied on dining out more often; we now spend around 30% of our budget on restaurants. To keep restaurant food costs low, food production costs must be kept low. This results in poverty wages and sweatshop conditions, while agri-business and larger grocers remain highly profitable enterprises. As a city that prides itself on a gastronomic tradition of local food, this corner of the labour market represents the most egregious sweatshop conditions.

THE RISE OF MONTRÉAL'S OWN AMAZON MODEL

If one company exemplifies the modern-day sweatshop, it is Amazon. Marked by gruelling labour conditions, managed by algorithms, firing temp workers *en masse*, and bent on keeping any unions out, Amazon has been widely criticized. What is essential about Amazon is the fundamental shift and importance of distribution and logistics as a critical sector in our economy, particularly within cities. Montréal had embraced a model of high speed, low wages, and low costs in the logistics sector well before Amazon arrived in the city in 2019. The shift towards just-in-time distribution had become part of major corporations' competitive edge, and the logistics sector was seen as an economic development strategy for the city.

Montréal's capitalist class aimed to secure the city's position as one that can act as a significant distribution and logistics hub within North American and European markets. "The fact that logistics has been brought on to the agenda in planning documents reflects the idea that public actors in logistics are an economic and strategic asset which supports Montréal's position as 'a transportation hub for goods', and therefore underpins its place in corridor goods trade and international trade" (Debrie and Heitz 2016, 8).

The Montréal region is an intermodal hub, with a capacity for air, rail, water, and road transportation. In 2012, Montréal International formed CargoM; "its mission is to bring together all the players in logistics and transportation of goods in Greater Montréal whose activities support the Montréal hub with common goals and concerted action, to promote cohesion, competitiveness, growth and expansion" (CargoM and KPMG 2014). The logistics and transportation sector, according to Montréal International, is well-positioned despite the competition from other Canadian cities and in the United States due to the access to 100 million consumers in a one-day radius (CargoM and KPMG 2014).

According to Montréal International, Montréal has the lowest annual salary of warehouse workers in North America, despite higher unionization rates. The average yearly salary for a warehouse worker in Montréal stands at $27,000 (CDN) per year compared to Chicago, which is $33,000 (CDN) a year. The attempt to lower costs and speed up distribution creates an ever-larger pool of exploited and vulnerable workers. In greater Montréal, 120,000 people work for some 6,000 companies in logistics and distribution, from driving trucks and providing last-mile delivery to working in warehouses and ports. Across these supply chains are high precarity, high speed and low pay. Warehousing and storage employment has nearly doubled over the past decade (CargoM and KPMG 2014). This predates Amazon, but it is at the heart of the story of inequality. The e-commerce and logistics revolution, an outgrowth of the retail revolution, has only further propelled major retailers like Wal-Mart and Amazon. Montréal's own capitalist class has benefited immensely from this emerging model.

DOLLARAMA IS OUR AMAZON

At De La Savane Metro station at 3 pm, one can witness a sight like no other. Hundreds of workers, all immigrants from India, Haiti, or West Africa, pour onto the sidewalk exhausted after working in one of the city's most gruelling distribution centres, tucked away off the Décarie expressway. This is the future of work. This is the story at the heart of one of the most powerful families and companies in Montréal.

Dollarama was founded by the Rossy family, owners of the Rossy variety stores. Neil Rossy remains CEO of Dollarama Inc and a minority shareholder. Dollarama grew from a small company in the early-1990s to one that now has over 1,300 stores and 26,000 employees. The Rossy family forms part of the bedrock of Québec Inc and Montréal's ruling class. It is the eighth richest family in Montréal, with a wealth of over $2.52 billion (Canadian Business 2017). The warehouse and distribution centres here in Montréal are the new sweatshops. They employ over 1,000 workers; though none of them works directly for Dollarama—they are instead employed through several temporary placement agencies. Before the pandemic, all workers made less than $15 an hour, facing high injury rates. There was no training or access to health and safety equipment because, under this model, it is the agency that accepts the risks, not the employer.

The agencies ensure Dollarama can continue their gruelling pace, where workers are treated worse than robots—required to move upwards of 20 kg boxes every 20 seconds to ensure their daily quota. This centre is responsible for direct distribution to all stores in Canada. The breakneck needed pace to fulfil quotas leads to a significant number of accidents, but for Dollarama, this represents no extra costs as the responsibility is downloaded onto the agencies. In fact, for companies like Dollarama, their workers are disposable; agencies ensure a constant workforce to replace them. Dollarama workers are not alone; there are roughly 36,000 warehouse workers across the island of Montréal employed by temp agencies. Due to the growth of e-commerce, warehousing work is seeing a significant increase.

In Québec, as much as 45% of the population shops online. Amazon has opened two major facilities, with a third announced for Laval. The conditions in warehouses such as Dollarama or Amazon are not unique to these companies but are now central to this trend of warehouse work premised on just-in-time distribution. In a 2019 report compiled by the IWC on warehouse work, 90% of workers were employed by a temporary placement agency, and many of them faced unsafe work conditions. These realities are by no means coincidental. They illustrate how the logic of profit-making pervades and determines who is employed and the working conditions they face. While e-commerce and online shopping represent one of the significant ways our economies are transforming, it has been part of a broader trend of 'disruption' by the new titans of the global economy alongside Amazon: the 'platform' or 'gig' economy.

SWEATSHOP 2.0

On Friday, March 29, a taxi driver is live on Québec television. At the end of the interview, he said, "Legault he has no heart," then began to self-mutilate, in protest to Bill-17, which would further deregulate the taxi industry and open the door to unregulated 'ride-sharing' companies such as Uber and Lyft (CTV 2019). In New York City, eight taxi drivers committed suicide under the pressures of immense debt and the taxi industry's decimation at the hands of Uber and similar companies. The story of the traditional taxi industry's demise is not just about a struggle between a group of Luddite small business owners pitted against the innovation of the platform economy, but very much about the future of work and the conditions faced by many immigrant workers. These taxi-drivers, already precarious workers without pensions—except perhaps the value of their taxi plates (if they owned them)—had become decimated by a now publicly traded multi-national corporation with sales of $92 billion, operating under the guise of 'ride-sharing' or the 'platform economy.'

The story begins after the 2008 financial crisis, as a new type of economy had taken hold, particularly in the urban context: the platform economy (Jamil 2017). Firms such as Airbnb, TaskRabbit, Deliveroo, and Foodora now dominate traditional industries. The gig economy only became more substantial in 2016 when Uber was permitted to operate in Québec. The state support for dismantling regulated industries in favour of the free market would only further deteriorate the conditions of working people. On 20 May 2019, the day Uber went public on the New York Stock Exchange, a global day of action by Uber drivers took place. In Montréal, nearly half of the 25,000 Uber drivers participated. The demands were clear: "according to Rafik Hanna, a member of the Professional Association of Uber Drivers, the company has been consistently scraping more and more of a given driver's fares per ride. And with drivers responsible for their car's insurance, lease payments, toll and permit fees, gas, and maintenance, it is easy to see why drivers might be angered by any cut to their fares" (Sahnoune 2019). Workers were demanding a guaranteed wage of $18 an hour, among other demands. According to Statistics Canada, a worker's median net income in the gig economy in 2016 was only $4,303 annually (Statistics Canada 2021). Workers in the bottom 40% of the annual income distribution were about twice as likely to be involved in gig work (Statistics Canada 2021). Also, 10.8% of new immigrants participate in the gig economy, almost twice the rate (6.1%) for all Canadian males (Statistics Canada 2021).

One Montréal gig worker, working for several apps, explains the reality of this precarious work: "I didn't have anything to lean back on. I did not have paid time off. I did not have health insurance; I did not have any benefits. I didn't even have someone to cover for me" (Yoon 2020). Platform companies advocate the success of their model; since these workers are 'their own boss', they are free to choose their work schedules, etc. Uber, now the largest taxi company on the planet, does not own a single car. Workers are driven into even more precarious and subservient positions.

In the recent U.S. election, proposition 22 was on the ballot in California. This proposition would determine whether gig workers (like those working for Uber) should be treated as employees rather than self-employed independent contractors; Uber and similar other platform companies spent over $200 million to defeat the referendum. This comes after the defeat of Uber in court in the United Kingdom, which deemed Uber drivers to be workers. Workers have little autonomy or choice in their work conditions but bear all the costs. They also have increasingly little choice about whether or not to participate in the gig economy due to its massive expansion to various parts of the economy. The platform economy represents "neoliberalism on steroids." The ethos of the gig economy does not lead to some post-capitalist future and is the opposite of a 'sharing economy.' Instead, it leads to a city where workers have no benefits, no stability, no unions, and operate in a continuous race to the bottom. All while profits continue to soar for companies like Uber, Airbnb, and Foodora.

THE CITY AND REGULATING SWEATSHOP LABOUR

In the 1960s and 1970s, unions represented a major political force for working and poor people in Montréal, and across Québec, as drivers for progressive change, particularly the *Conseil Centrale Metropolitan Montréal* of CSN. The power of labour has been in decline, resulting from changes in work and attacks on private-sector unions where much of this sweatshop labour occurs. As David Harvey writes, "the biggest employers of labour today are McDonald's, Kentucky Fried Chicken and Walmart. Back then, the factory was the centre of the working class, but today we find the working class mainly in the service sector. And why would we say that producing cars is more important than producing hamburgers?" (Harvey 2006, 270). To confront the fault lines in the neoliberal city, we now need to organize workers from the vantage point of the urban level, which allows people to rethink strategy and their power and tie these to future progressive politics. Today, the divides between community and workplace struggle fade away; new forms of labour organizing are essential for labour's renewal as a means to build a just city.

The neoliberal turn has created a re-concentration of urban workers, central to the making and maintaining of our cities, but the city administration itself also takes up such practices. As municipalities such as Montréal are pressured to do more with less, they have quietly enacted the same neoliberal models through sub-contracting and the use of temp agencies for municipal waste treatment, recycling, cleaning, and other public services. The city itself needs to become a voice for working people to challenge inequalities apparent in our city. Can the municipality enact a policy to refuse sub-contracting in any public contract? Can it restrain the titans of the gig economy? Can we collectively remake Montréal into a city that belongs to its workers—not the employers?

One organization at the heart of labour renewal within the City of Montréal is the Immigrant Workers Centre (IWC). Grounded in the neighbourhood of Cote-Des-Neiges, it has been organizing with precarious immigrant workers, regardless of their status, as a hybrid community-labour model. It seeks to unite workers outside the workplace, to bring together temporary placement agency workers to fight for permanent jobs, against sexual harassment, and for better health and safety. The temporary agency workers association has successfully fought campaigns for improved wages at Dollarama. It has supported and built a committee of undocumented women temp agency workers fighting for status, giving them a voice, and challenging their employers. The IWC intervened in 2018 regarding changes to the Québec Labour Standards. It campaigned for equal pay for equal work to ensure all agencies are registered with the Ministry of Labour to ensure 'fly by night' agencies can no longer disappear leaving workers without their pay.

The IWC also does outreach by the bus stops these workers access daily to shuttle them to workplaces, in order to build relationships, organize workshops, and defend their rights. While the IWC is a small organization, leadership grounded in various workplaces and communities is a testament to the urgency and need for such organizing. Organizing precarious workers is not only about challenging the sweatshops in our city—it is about something broader.

Building a broad-based and grassroots organization of immigrant workers fundamentally means confronting those same forces and capitalists who use their profits for speculation, put profit over need in housing, and limit real solutions to our climate crisis. The solutions are rooted in shifting power away from Uber, Amazon, or Québec Inc to working people in the city. While the city may be a sweatshop, workers can have power through new forms of organization. Working-class organization is needed not just at the workplace level but in the community, neighbourhood, and city. It must be tied with other movements to build a city that is not a sweatshop but one based on true social and ecological equity.

REFERENCES

Boisvert, Y. 2020. "Il s'appelait Marcelin François." *La Presse*, 8 May 2020. https://www.lapresse.ca/covid-19/2020-05-08/il-s-appelait-marcelin-francois.

Canadian Business. 2017. "Canada's richest people: The complete top 100 ranking." 9 November 2017. https://www.canadianbusiness.com/lists-and-rankings/richest-people/100-richest-canadians-complete-list/.

CargoM, and KPMG. 2014. *Profile of the Logistics and Transportation Sector in Greater Montréal*. http://www.cargo-montreal.ca/pdf/CargoM-KPMG-Rapportfinal-2014-en.pdf.

Choudry, A., and Henaway, M. 2012. "Agents of misfortune: Contextualising migrant and immigrant workers' struggles against temporary labour recruitment agencies." *Labour, Capital and Society/Travail, capital et société*, 36-65.

CTV. 2019. "Montréal taxi driver harms himself on live TV in anger over ride-hailing Bill." 29 March 2019. https://www.ctvnews.ca/canada/montreal-taxi-driver-harms-himself-on-live-tv-in-anger-over-ride-hailing-bill-1.4357939.

Debrie, J., and Heitz, A. 2016. "The Location Of Logistics Activities In Metropolitan Areas As An Issue Of Urban Planning: A Comparison Of Paris and Montréal." In *World Conference on Transport Research*, July 2016 Shanghai, China.

Harvey, D. 2006. "Consolidating power." *Roar Magazine* 0: 267-282. https://roarmag.org/magazine/david-harvey-consolidating-power/.

Jamil, R. 2017. "Drivers Vs Uber–The limits of the Judicialization: Critical review of London's employment tribunal verdict in the case of Aaslam Y. & Farrar J. against Uber." *Revue Interventions Économiques. Papers in Political Economy* (58).

Lindeman, T. 2020. "Who's Essential And Who's Not? Asylum Seekers In Québec Speak Out." *Chatelaine*, 18 August 2020. https://www.chatelaine.com/living/essential-workers-refugees/.

Montréal International. 2019. "Greater Montréal: Epicenter of the food processing industry of Québec." https://www.montrealinternational.com/en/publications/.

Sahnoune, Y. 2019. "Uber in Montréal. An uncertain future." *The Bull and Bear*, 29 May 2019. http://bullandbearmcgill.com/uber-in-montreal-an-uncertain-future/.

Sassen, S. 1996. "Beyond sovereignty: immigration policy making today." *Social Justice* 23(3 (65)): 9-20.

Statistics Canada. (2017). "The Daily: Employment Services-2017." Last modified 14 February 2019. https://www150.statcan.gc.ca/n1/daily-quotidien/190214/dq190214c-eng.htm.

Statistics Canada. (2018). "The Canadian Immigrant Labour Market: Recent Trends from 2006-2017." The Immigrant Labour Force Analysis Series, 24 December 2018. https://www150.statcan.gc.ca/n1/pub/71-606-x/71-606-x2018001-eng.htm.

Statistics Canada. 2021. "Measuring the Gig economy in Canada. Using administrative data." Analytical Studies Branch Research Paper Series, 16 December 2019. https://www150.statcan.gc.ca/n1/pub/11f0019m/11f0019m2019025-eng.htm.

Stevenson, V., and Bernstien, J. 2018. "How a Haitian asylum seeker was swept up in a shadowy industry of temp agency work." *CBC News*, 28 May 2018. https://www.cbc.ca/news/canada/montreal/temp-worker-accident-1.4594744.

Yoon, J. 2020. "Montréal Gig workers have to hustle, despite lack of labour protections." *CBC News*, 26 February 2020. https://www.cbc.ca/news/canada/montreal/montreal-gig-economy-1.5475729.

THE SOCIAL ECONOMY AND THE CITY

JASON PRINCE

*"What is fundamentally social in the social economy is the **capital**."*

Most recent progressive thinkers position the social and solidarity economy as a promising vector for controlling our economy and achieving an ecological and socially just city.

It is obviously not that simple. The same day that a half-million Montréalers marched with Greta Thunberg to fight for action on climate change, a small solidarity march blocked traffic in downtown Ayer's Cliff, Québec, population 1,100. The only vehicle that day was an oil delivery truck—operated by a cooperative.

Labour is deeply entwined in extractive and destructive industries. One of the most powerful unions remaining in the U.S. represents auto workers. Closer to home, unions have fought against forest protection in Québec's North.

But some unions are facing the contradiction with bold solutions. Canada's postal workers, together with Ottawa workers at a then-closed GM plant, pushed for the creation of a worker-controlled factory to produce electric delivery vans for a reinvented post office. At the end of 2020, General Motors—perhaps in an effort to defuse this project—promised to rehire up to 1,700 workers in a revamped pick-up truck plant.

Noam Chomsky hinted at a missed opportunity when the U.S. government owned the stock of the Big Three car manufacturers following the 2008 financial crisis, provoked by Wall Street gamblers. Had the Occupy movement peaked a few years earlier, at the moment Obama was deciding what to do with this stock, and had they shaped a specific political demand to cede factory ownership to the workers with a mandate to deliver mass transit solutions to U.S. cities, we would be living in quite a different world today. This kind of moment may come again, he suggested, and we should be ready for it.

And what if Montréal pushed the social economy as a solution to some urban problems? What would that city look like? Allow me to play out some scenarios of what would it look like if the City of Montréal were to implement the appropriate dynamics and incentives today.

By 2042, half of Montréal's housing has been taken off the private market and is held within community land trusts. These trusts protect individual housing cooperatives and non-profit housing by providing the training and financial support needed to maintain them. Perhaps 50% of these land trust apartments employ a "shared equity" model so that residents can use their housing as savings banks, but not for speculation. The land is collectively owned and community-controlled, using an anti-speculative land stewardship model. The best example of this kind of community land trust was founded while Bernie Sanders was mayor of Burlington, Vermont, in the 1980s.[1]

By 2042, Montréal's 400th anniversary, dozens of worker co-ops for public works, each with between 20 and 200 workers, have been established. These worker co-ops have garnered over half of the municipal contracts for road work and sidewalks. They compete with the private sector by producing better quality public works, more quickly. The City of Montréal appreciates that their books are made publicly available, part of their commitment to transparency and public trust. Citizens better understand how public works are built since materials and labour costs are also tracked publicly. Indeed, since 2025, construction delays have diminished as open data has made the approval processes more fluid. These public works are always branded as 'co-operatively made' using brass plates embedded in the concrete, with the date and engineer's stamp clearly indicated. Some of those worker co-ops are just a few years old, the latest ones formed with support from the construction unions and encouraged by the City of Montréal.

Importantly, construction workers' wages and quality of life have improved, and they feel greater pride in their work. So far, there is no evidence of corruption and collusion in this industrial innovation, partly due to enhanced transparency.

In 2042, food production in the Montréal region is co-managed by a para-municipal agency that operates arms-length from the City of Montréal, with a complex governance structure and a single appointee from city council. The body, created in 2022, was tasked with optimizing the links between greenhouses, farms, and food distributors in the region, to reduce dependency

---

1. The best source of practical information about community land trusts is found at the Burlington Associates web site. An ambitious translation project would make this material more readily available to Montréalers. See: https://burlingtonassociates.com/clt-resources/

on carbon-intensive imported foods and reduce food waste. The board and key staff of the organization were drawn from the robust social economy enterprises working on food security in the inner-city. Guaranteed operating funds helped structure the new body during its first years of operation while also improving wages and work conditions for a more equitable internal food supply chain. The *Société de production et de sécurité alimentaire de Montréal* (SPSAM) is self-financed after five years of operations. It achieved this by doubling the volume of fresh food produced in the Montréal region, principally through the development of rooftop farms on municipal property and strategic partnerships with private owners via import substitution.

By 2025, the SPSAM has also piloted comprehensive organic waste collection and is well on its way to meeting the provincial target of 100% collected; currently, Montréal only collects 26% of its organic waste (Ville de Montréal, 2019). SPSAM has also started producing agricultural grade compost that it uses in its rooftop greenhouses. In 2026, Montréal won a United Nations Sustainable Development Goal (SDG) Action Award for its innovation in food security and waste management for a resilient city.

Similar worker-controlled initiatives were adopted in waste management, snow removal, and the co-management of public parks in partnership with community-controlled non-profit organizations mandated by the city to maintain public assets. This last effort was initiated in part after parents revolted against an inner-city borough that persistently closed wading and swimming pools in August, even as the hot weather season was getting longer every year thanks to global warming.

The City of Montréal took the lead in creating these community and collective entities. Wise municipal leadership helped co-construct resilient legal, financial, and governance models with the best minds in the social economy. The designers also added built-in safeguards to prevent hostile or private interests from destabilizing these models while ensuring that they were robust enough financially not to depend on recurring government grants.

Each of these social economy structures was tailored using the wisdom, techniques, and financial and governance models already well-known in Montréal in 2021. Each was built with great care and with strong municipal leadership, financing, and support. They drew from existing well-functioning models, learned from experience, and pushed at the edge of what a municipal government should do, as mandated by the province.

So how did we get there? What were the models that inspired us? Why would any city embark on such a road to undermine the private housing market and booming condo development that (given our municipal tax structure) seemed to be an endlessly growing source of revenue from property taxes? Why would Montréal (or any city) care if the people buying the condos were happy voters, buying quality housing they could afford, as long as each unit sold paid its 'welcome tax' and annual property taxes? Why would any city challenge the private food production and distribution systems that have created a situation where 50% of our food is dumped in the garbage?

Why would any city try to manage its public works better when the system seems to work just fine (though it certainly does not)? These questions are at the heart of this chapter, and some are at the heart of this book.

Why, and how, would any city prioritize the social economy and collective models of ownership and stewardship to build and maintain the social functions of the city?

Community housing, food security, childcare, eldercare, and many other social functions in the city have long been sectors that the social economy has delivered. For decades, social economy organizations have managed city-owned assets like community centres and neighbourhood gyms, with voluntary participation from citizens and users in the governance.

This second wave social economy[2] in Montréal was incubated over thirty years under a local control paradigm called community economic development (CED). As practiced, CED can emphasize either community, the economy, or development. In all three approaches, the goal is to acquire some real control over the local economy. In its best examples, CED can be situated in anarchist traditions and municipal socialism. Active forces at a neighbourhood level define their own master development plans and create the community they collectively want. Tangible outcomes of this approach result in collective solutions that meet real community needs. Our achievements in community housing, daycares, seniors supports, and food security bear witness to this.[3]

The social economy—defined as social-mission-driven enterprises whose growing equity is collectively owned and cannot be privatized—has proven itself to be a viable, robust component of Québec's economy. This chapter will argue for an extended definition that would include arms-length para-municipal entities with property, complex governance structures, and that can self-finance—entities initiated directly by the city but independent from it.

2. The first wave was composed of the huge Québec co-operatives in credit unions, milk, forestry, and agriculture.
3. The abolition of CED in Montréal in 2015 under the neo-liberal government marked a shift from community-led local development to a more isolated support for social economy and private companies. CED as practiced in Montréal for three decades—although it had its weaknesses—was an attempt to have local organizations plan and build a collective voice on how boroughs should and could develop economically, parallel with, and at times against, the free market. It was a model that had the potential of becoming local economic democracy. According to Eric Shragge, activist and author on the Montréal experience, our CED experiments failed for a number of reasons principally due to centralized bureaucratic vision and control, before it was shut down: "Early on, people like Marie Bouchard, Benoit Levesque, Nancy Neamtan and Margie Mandell shifted the discussion from CED to collective entrepreneurialism but without the wider notion of community control of economic development. Community control of economic development versus social enterprise is the issue [...] social enterprise should be subsumed under community control but we lost it."

But how far can we take this model? Are there any natural limits to this approach? What are some of the frontiers that should be explored actively in the next three to eight years, particularly those directly under the responsibility of the municipal level of government? How can the City of Montréal support such a development if we agree to go in this direction? The following pages will explore these questions and attempt to formulate some clear and distinct propositions for going forward.

PORTRAIT OF THE SOCIAL ECONOMY OVER THE PAST 30 YEARS

Two studies have been key reference points for understanding the social economy, and both have attempted to define and measure the size of the social economy in Montréal and Québec. The first was a 2008 study led by INRS professor Marie Bouchard. It continues to be an essential reference. At that time, ten years into the second wave, there were 3,590 social economy enterprises on the island of Montréal, excluding the banking and finance sectors. These social economy enterprises operate primarily in the health and social services sectors, housing, and arts and culture; however, there are also experiments in food production, food security, geothermal energy, and specialized knowledge industries. By 2008, there were already no limits on what could be tried using the non-profit and cooperative business model.

Bouchard's framework for situating the social economy, in a slightly modified form, is reproduced on the following page.[4]

In 2018, the *Institut de statistiques du Québec* (ISQ) produced the first official portrait of Québec's social economy, using a different methodology than the Bouchard study. As of 2016, there were an estimated 11,200 social economy enterprises in the province (ISQ 2018).

For the most part, social economy enterprises are anchored in their communities, with a large majority of them serving populations that are physically close to their headquarters. As of 2016, 75% were non-profit organizations (8,400), while the remaining 25% were cooperatives of one form or another: non-financial (2,410), financial cooperatives (320), and mutual insurance companies (30) (ISQ 2018).

Québec has a few large social economy enterprises, but most are small: 65% have fewer than ten employees and only 2% count 100 employees or more. Nearly 40% have existed for more than 30 years; 46% are 10 to 30 years old; 15% are under ten years old.

---

4. While this framework has been adjusted over the years by its author, and other such frameworks exist for the social and solidarity economy, it remains a useful quick-and-easy way to situate the social economy within other easily recognized parts of our communities and economies.

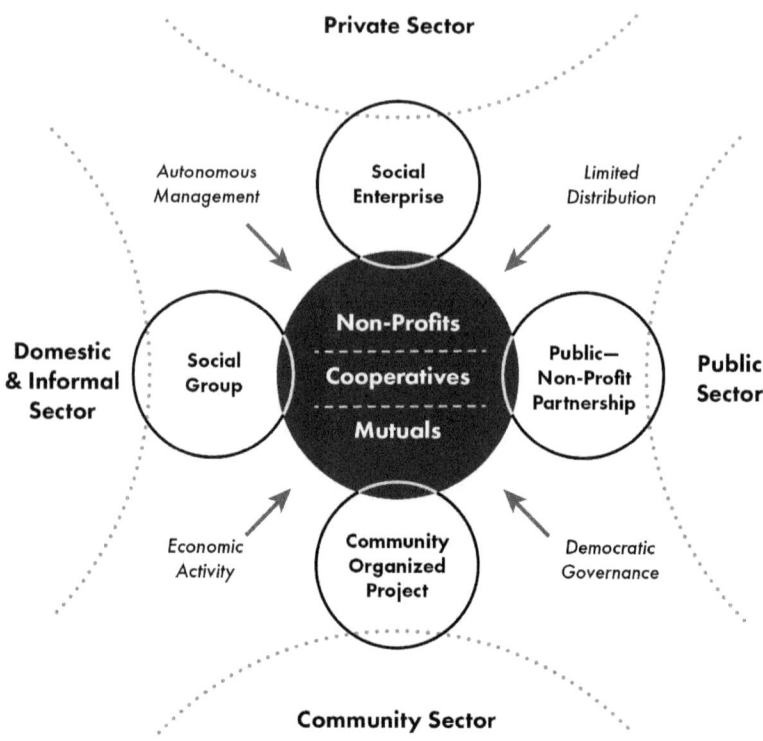

Components of the Social Economy

Bouchard, Ferraton, Michaud, 2006a. Adapted from H. Desroche, 1983

The social economy in Québec generates $47.8 billion annually (nearly 15% of Québec's GDP), and 90% of this revenue is generated by the sale of goods and services or membership fees. A vast part of this revenue is in the financial and insurance sectors: the *Mouvement Desjardins*.

While often thought of as just another bank, the *Mouvement Desjardins* takes its role as a motor of economic and community development seriously. For example, in 2017, it launched the *Fonds des regions* with $100 million to support employment, education, and economic development in the regions and in Montréal. In 2020, it launched the *Fonds du grand mouvement* with $150 million.

The *Caisse d'économie solidaire*,[5] and to a lesser degree the *Caisse de la Culture*, actively support the social economy. By pooling savings, the *Caisse d'économie solidaire* actively invests more than $650 million in Québec's social economy; it counts 21,687 members, including 4,000 non-profit organizations,

---

5. Initiated as a fusion of seven smaller credit unions in the early 1970s by the *Confédération des syndicats nationaux*, Québec's socially progressive union federation

cooperatives, and unions, as well as an additional 17,687 individual members (Caisse d'économie solidaire n.d.).

Nearly 75% of social economy enterprises have a membership larger than the board of directors. Indeed, Québec's social economy enterprises count 13 million members. While half of those are members of the *Mouvement Desjardins*, roughly 5% is composed of other organizations, most often other non-profits.

The participation of other non-profit organizations in the decision-making is considered best practice for protecting the mission.

Indeed, it is essential to **complexify the governance** of all social economy enterprises to protect against hostile takeovers. To further buttress the movement, the **collective property itself should also be complexified**, as has been done at Milton-Parc, for example. This cannot be overemphasized.

A significant portion of social economy enterprises in Québec are located on the island of Montréal. The sector is actively grappling with how to scale up, including the suitable financing instruments to allow that.[6]

It should be noted that over the past ten years, the social economy has seen experimentation in the fields of urban planning, law, architecture, and engineering, with start-ups providing professional services in these fields. Some of these are value-based decisions, while others have chosen a non-profit model to distinguish themselves from the private sector, particularly in the wake of the Charbonneau Commission. There are now non-profits and co-ops experimenting in municipal public works, social housing renovation, geothermal district heating systems, and large-scale neighbourhood development (*Société de développement Angus*).

A consortium of non-profit housing owners hopes to leverage its assets to develop thousands of new non-profit housing units by 2030 (see Racette's chapter on this non-profit housing initiative elsewhere in this book). A network of 50 non-profits and co-ops working in housing and urban planning is organizing a summit in 2021 to explore new ways to collaborate over the coming years. And a non-profit in Milton-Parc has been created to oversee the development of 650 units of co-op and non-profit housing on a publicly owned parking lot.

The Blue Bonnets site in Cote-des-Neiges, just minutes from the metro and owned by the City of Montréal, could include thousands of units of non-profit community housing. Could the entire site be turned over to a community land trust—following the model of the Champlain Housing Trust in Burlington, Vermont—so that 100% of the units developed are anti-speculative? This

---

6. TIESS (*Territoires innovants en économie sociale et solidaire*), a think-tank for the social economy, has produced some excellent material on scaling in the social economy and new financing tools. Explore their site at: https://tiess.ca/obligations-communautaires/

would make it the largest community land trust in the world, a true '*îlot d'abordabilité permanent*' in a sea of high-end condos?

Michel Bouchard, current director of the social economy team at PME MTL Centre-Ville, is recognized as the *doyen* of the social economy in Montréal. His career started in Pointe-Saint-Charles in the 1970s as a militant and organizer. Now, after decades of work in the cooperative movement, community sector, and social economy, he provides the following paradoxical definition of the social economy: "What is fundamentally social in the social economy is the **capital**."

Taken as a whole, the social economy represents a vector of economic development that permanently removes part of the formal economy from the private sector and the public sector. As this third sector grows and strengthens, can it take on ever-larger parts of the formal economy under a stewardship model that creates quality, well-paid jobs, over which workers and citizens have more control?

OBJECTIVES FOR THE NEXT DECADE

Let us assume that the bold vision put forward in my opening remarks becomes our collective target. What would our strategic objectives for the next three to eight years?

What we do now can set the pattern for the next decade and sow the seeds for another possible future.

As I write these words, Montréal and cities worldwide are being forced to rethink their futures once the pandemic lifts. Some may want to go back to the pre-pandemic "normal," but most Canadian cities were struggling prior to the arrival of COVID-19. A 2020 study based on a broad survey of downtown users, with follow-up interviews for a subset of them, concludes that post-pandemic, the spending population of the city's downtown core will be significantly and permanently reduced by *teletravail* (Shearmur et al. 2020). The twin threats to a viable downtown—online shopping and big-box malls—which already threatened Montréal's core and its main streets, may have been delivered the proverbial nail in the coffin by this pandemic.

But maybe not. Maybe there is another path for Montréal's downtown. Perhaps we need 300,000 new residents downtown—there are currently about 60,000. We could achieve this by encouraging *teletravail* and reinventing some office towers as cooperative and non-profit housing.

Montréal's main streets will also morph. In Québec and elsewhere, boroughs and cities have been changing their regulations to allow more restaurant licences on the streets to bring life back to main street. They hope to allow for a market response to change the mix of uses and keep these retail spaces open and paying taxes.

Maybe we should let our privately owned main streets die—or expropriate them from speculators. We can then reinvent them as main street land trusts that preserve the creativity of owner-occupied shops by permanently controlling rents. Seattle's Pike Place Market could be a model.

Over the past 30 years, the property tax base of Canadian cities has been shifting from manufacturing to housing. (Imagine all those bustling factories in the South West, Plateau, Ahuntsic, and elsewhere, paying taxes! That manufacturing land use paid much higher taxes, and it disappeared for a couple of decades after Brian Mulroney signed those free trade agreements!). Montréal's commercial tax base looks like it will take a further hit in the coming years, but owners of the main streets will fight the city to reduce their share of taxes, protect their investments, and keep their profits coming. Pressure to minimize commercial tax rates has already been put on the city by main street monopolists like Cromwell, Shiller, and Sergakis, and this pressure will likely continue to increase.

Maybe it is time to consider a completely different approach to our main streets—one without these main street monopolists.

The city should learn from its own history as it faces the next four years. During the late-1980s, Montréal faced a significant collapse in the property market after the first free trade agreements were signed. The city set up several para-municipal organizations to take advantage of the moment, and it bought hundreds of properties within a few years, each one for a song. The SHDM (*Société d'habitation et de développement de Montréal*) is the only easily recognizable para-municipal that continues to operate from that period. It owns about 5,000 units of de-commodified housing, and the rents in those units are below market rate. At the time, the SHDM was a revolutionary innovation in housing, owned by a city 'crown corporation.'

We need that kind of bold creativity now. Since the other levels of government seem to be dragging their feet, the City of Montréal must confront the major issues of our time directly and forcefully, using its creativity and financial power to shape our destiny. Let me sketch out possible directions in three foundational areas: energy, transportation, and housing.

HYDRO MONTRÉAL

A handful of Québec municipalities manage their own electricity by purchasing wholesale from Hydro-Québec and reselling it to their residents. The City of Westmount has been doing this for decades and bills its residents from Hydro Westmount. The City of Montréal should follow this model. Four outcomes will be immediately apparent. First, the city will immediately have a new source of revenue to buttress its property taxes: user fees and fines. Second, the city will now be in a position to directly target those still using fossil fuels, using incentives (carrots) and sticks to encourage them to convert to cleaner options. Third, Hydro Montréal could use pricing to encourage beneficial efforts (e.g., cheap energy for the Metro system and rooftop farms) and discourage negligent actors (e.g., downtown buildings that have not improved their energy efficiency). Finally, the city could explore diversifying its energy sources, directly investing in wind, solar, geothermal, or other sources, to reduce its dependence on Hydro-Québec and increase its margins.

The rapidly dropping price of other energy solutions suggests it is now becoming cheaper for cities to produce their own energy. The future of energy is small-scale and highly networked. Maybe the city needs to get ahead of the curve on this one. Can this be initiated via an arm's length non-profit organization operating in partnership with the city or even a new para-municipal entity? Are there non-profits on the ground today that have solutions that the city should recognize, valorize, and fund so that we can accelerate this transition process immediately?

TRANSPORTATION

Dozens of ride-share applications have been created, and it is time for the City of Montréal to recognize a few of them as the best way forward, as complementary to our public transportation system. Some of these solutions are in the social economy. The city should privilege ones that promise an equitable revenue sharing model for workers, operate transparently (read: publicly share their financial information, data acquisition and storage policies), and whose model will significantly reduce dependency on single-occupancy private vehicles. Car-sharing social enterprises like Communauto should be granted evermore space in the city. They should expand their integration and co-marketing with bike share and public transit systems, with ever more enticing and publicly-supported financial incentives. The city must experiment constantly and evaluate the results in close collaboration with Montréal's universities. These are not system-changing proposals but can be quickly implemented right now using city powers and funds. For systemic changes in transportation, see the chapters in this book on public transit (by Prince) and trams (by Lefebvre and Gagnon).

PUBLIC LANDS AND THE SOCIAL ECONOMY

All three levels of government own property within the confines of the City of Montréal. So do other ancient institutions, such as universities and religious groups. All of this property is either public or quasi-public, having been paid for directly or indirectly by governments and the collectivity. Together with parks, roads, highways, bridges, tunnels, and on-ramps, these lands represent a significant percentage of the usable footprint of our city.

We need to reconceptualize this public property and reimagine its function in the city of the 21st century. Several principles should be adopted to guide any future development.

First, the City of Montréal should immediately declare a moratorium on the sale of any publicly-owned land or real estate, be it a former hospital, parking lot, residual building, or contaminated port land. Some lands are owned by the city, and this moratorium could come into effect immediately. For public lands and buildings not owned by the city, it should issue "right of first refusal" notices under its new powers.

Such an announcement would signal the land crisis in the City of Montréal and the housing affordability problem and make it politically difficult for other levels of government to sell publicly-owned property.

Given rising land costs, we cannot allow the loss of another square inch of public property if we are to hope that Montréal remains an affordable city. We must act now before it is too late.

The private condominiums developed over the past 20 years are unaffordable for the vast majority of Montréalers. The overnight sale of the publicly-owned Montréal Children's Hospital to a well-connected developer, which was then flipped just a few months later for a windfall profit, cannot be allowed to happen anymore. And when a couple of years later, the city faces extortion when it tries to extract community benefits from the developer to create vital community spaces on that same site, we have entered the ridiculous and laughable.

The city must act now to create a comprehensive public inventory of all public lands, categorized, arranged, and organized, with all data placed in the public domain in a machine-readable format so that we can analyze and track it. Wherever possible, the city should register liens, rights of first refusal, or a simple *avis aux acheteurs* in the land registry file of all these publicly-owned assets.

In partnership with the city, using the public land database as its DNA, an arms-length social economy enterprise inspired by Heritage Montréal should be created and funded, but with a mission to protect all public property from privatization.

The city should fund this organization's start-up immediately. Its business model should rely on development charges as it "buys" public land for a dollar and redevelops it as community-owned assets in the social economy. It would assure that any land or buildings subject to this property transfer be carefully protected using state-of-the-art complex ownership, financial, and governance models to guarantee they remain in the social economy while not being reliant on recurring subsidies.[7]

The flagship project could be at the Blue Bonnets site—owned by the City of Montréal. It would target the construction of several thousand housing units on a community land trust with at least 50% as non-profit and cooperative housing. In contrast, 50% could be anti-speculative "piggy bank" homes that allow families to use their home to save some money, but not to resell for a profit. Community land trusts are stewards of **permanent affordability**, not just for first-time buyers, as currently practiced by the city's 'affordable homeownership' tax credits and the SHDM's 'Acces Condo' model.

The municipal protection of public land is particularly important to do **right now**, as the Federal government plans to sell off residual lands over the coming months and years in the port and eastern Montréal to pursue

---

7. Given the current economic context, there may also be other opportunities to remove property from the private market.

its National Housing Strategy. If the city does not take a leadership role in protecting this land from privatization, it will fall to private condo developers who will continue to build unaffordable units that most Montréalers neither want nor need.

The current administration knows it has a housing crisis, yet four years later, it is still fiddling with its 20-20-20 bylaw[8] that, once implemented, will only put a band-aid on the problem. We need big, bold billion-dollar solutions to our housing affordability crisis.

MONTRÉAL: THE SOCIAL ECONOMY CAPITAL OF NORTH AMERICA?

To conclude, let me suggest that although the vision put forward in this chapter is bold, it is doable. I have worked for years supporting the social economy and have continually been impressed by the energy and vision of those who dare to build a world differently. The projects proposed in this chapter up the ante for those who battle every day in the social economy simply to keep their projects afloat.

But suppose the City of Montréal were to get behind a bigger bolder vision of the social economy as a vector of fundamental change in the city. In that case, we might be surprized at what we can achieve collectively and the kind of hope we might be able to construct for ourselves and our children.

And what if we made Montréal the social economy capital of the world?

---

8. See further discussion of the *Règlement pour une métropole mixte*, including its 20-20-20 mandate, in Jake Ryan's chapter in this book.

REFERENCES

Bouchard, M., and Hudon, M. 2008. *Se loger autrement au Québec. Le mouvement de l'habitat communautaire, un acteur du développement social et économique*. Montréal: Éditions Saint-Martin.

Burlington Associates in Community Development. 2012. "Community Land Trust Resources." https://burlingtonassociates.com/clt-resources/.

Caisse d'économie solidaire. n.d. "Qui Nous Sommes." Accessed 17 May 2021. https://caissesolidaire.coop/qui-nous-sommes/mission-et-valeurs-2/.

Davis, J.E. 2014. *Manuel d'antispéculation immobilière. Une introduction aux fiducies foncières communautaires*. MontréalL: Écosociété.

ISQ (Institut de la statistique du Québec). 2018. "L'économie sociale au Québec : Portrait statistique 2016." www.stat.gouv.qc.ca.

Prince, J., and Sorin, V. 2021. "Financing tool: the Community Bond experience in Montréal, QC (working title)." In *Innovations in Social Finance: Transitioning Beyond Economic Value*, edited by T. Walker, J. McGaughey, S. Goubran, and N. Wagdy. Palgrave MacMillan.

Shearmur, R., Ananian, P., Lachapelle, U., Parra-Lockhorst, M., Paulhiac, F., Tremblay, D-G., and Wycliffe-Jones, A. 2020. "L'avenir du centre-ville de Montréal : Impact immédiat de la COVID et perspectives post-COVID. Montréal." Université McGill, UQAM, TÉLUQ.

TIESS (Territoires innovants en économie sociale et solidaire). 2021. https://tiess.ca/obligations-communautaires/.

Ville de Montréal. 2019. *Montréal, objectif zéro déchet: Projet de Plan directeur de gestion des matières résiduelles 2020-2025*. http://ville.montreal.qc.ca/pls/portal/docs/PAGE/ENVIRO_FR/MEDIA/DOCUMENTS/PROJET_PLAN_DIRECTEUR_2020_2050.PDF.

PART V.

HOUSING THE CITY

MUNICIPAL GOVERNMENT: ALLY OR ADVERSARY OF MONTRÉAL'S CO-OPERATIVE HOUSING SECTOR?

JACOB RYAN

INTRODUCTION

Québec—particularly the city of Montréal—is often viewed as a rare North American example of a well-functioning social democracy with a broadly progressive political climate. This reputation can be attributed to various factors, including the high provincial rate of unionization, nationalization of some major industries, the 2012 student movement that helped keep tuition among the lowest in the country, and the success of progressive political parties such as Projet Montréal and Québec Solidaire. Québec Solidaire has been described as "arguably the most left-wing party with seats in a Canadian legislature" (Loriggio 2018). Whether in the popular press or academic publications, the proliferation of this reputation can obscure the damaging impacts of austerity imposed by right-wing politicians, legally enshrined racism under the guise of secularism, and the burgeoning housing crisis currently facing Montréal. Likewise, there is often a lazy tendency to attribute Québec's positive qualities to some sort of vague "European" sensibility, invisibilizing the hard-fought gains that social movements have won through decades of grassroots community organizing as well as the many challenges that still lay ahead. With this in mind, I offer a critical overview of the state of co-operative housing in Montréal—not just its successes but also its shortcomings. I will also discuss how municipal government—even when led by progressives—can stand in the way of realizing a more just system of urban housing.

In short, housing co-operatives are legal entities that provide at-cost housing for their members. These members are residents of the co-op who vote within its governance structure to determine how the co-op is operated, filling the role of a landlord in more common forms of housing tenure (CHF Canada n.d.). The governance structure of co-operatives is guided by a set of international principles that encourage voluntary membership, democratic member control, cooperation among different co-operatives, and community involvement. Co-operative housing is distinct from other forms of social housing in that it is operated by its members rather than the state or non-profit entities. While both co-operative housing and other forms of social housing (e.g., public housing) provide opportunities for affordable living that are not tied to the real estate market, co-operatives are unique in providing a high level of autonomy and responsibility to their residents. In co-operative housing, residents participate in everything from building maintenance and gardening to drafting policy and by-laws via an elected board of directors.

In Canada, the co-operative housing sector grew throughout much of the 20th century with the support of lobby groups such as the Co-operative Housing Federation of Canada, a number of federal and provincial government programs, and special purpose community organizations. Throughout the 1970s and 1980s, many co-operatives were financed by the Canadian Mortgage and Housing Corporation (CMHC), which provided start-up funding and secured mortgages for co-operative housing projects. A political turn toward austerity in the 1990s resulted in these programs being cut. The federal government ceased its support of co-operative housing in 1992, and most of the provinces followed suit in the ensuing years.

Québec was an exception to this trend, with co-operative housing supported by the provincial government through a cost-sharing arrangement with the Government of Canada (Co-operative Housing International 2019). It is then no surprise that in terms of individual housing co-operatives, Québec leads Canada's other provinces by a wide margin.[1] Québec is home to more than 1,100 currently active co-ops, more than half of all housing co-ops in Canada. Out of the more than 28,000 individual units of co-operative housing in the province, more than half are located in Montréal (CQCH 2017). In Québec, independent non-profit organizations called Technical Resource Groups (GRT; *groupes de ressources techniques*) provide training and support to co-op members, community groups, and other organizations in the development of co-operative and non-profit housing; they also serve as intermediaries between these groups and public administrators, architects, engineers, and other involved parties (AGRTQ n.d.).

During the retraction of the welfare state and federal funding for social

---

1. Ontario leads the country in terms of individual *units* of co-operative housing. Those in Québec tend to be smaller.

housing, Québec's public sector increasingly partnered with the "third sector" (community groups, non-profits, co-operatives, etc.) to administer social housing when simply purchasing and converting housing stock became increasingly difficult (Vaillancourt et al. 2001). In Montréal, the creation of these partnerships, many of which persist today, came about largely during the two terms of the Montréal Citizen's Movement (MCM), a progressive municipal political party and coalition of union members, community activists, intellectuals, and radicals.

Notable among Montréal's housing co-operatives are those within the *Communauté Milton-Parc* (CMP), which collectively accounts for one of North America's largest housing co-op projects and is an oft-cited example of the political, legal, and economic potential of this model of housing. The CMP was the product of years of struggle by community members, pushing back against a developer that sought to demolish and redevelop much of the Milton-Parc neighbourhood. This redevelopment would have displaced many of Milton-Parc's residents, replacing low-rent housing with high-rises, hotels, and office towers. Following years of non-violent direct action, including sit-ins and occupations, members of the Milton-Parc community were able to broker a deal involving several non-profits and the CMHC, to purchase and convert buildings slated for redevelopment or demolition into co-operative and other forms of social housing. Residents who became members of co-operatives were able to own and control their places of residence in common, preventing displacement and safeguarding the community from the speculative real estate market; rents in the CMP remain affordable to this day (Kowaluk and Piché-Burton 2019).

The unique potential for provincial funding, the support offered by GRTs, a sympathetic municipal government, and the precedent of successful large-scale co-ops, such as those within the CMP, are factors that have put Montréal's co-operative housing sector in a position to play a significant role in addressing housing issues facing the city's low-income residents. Despite this, there are still many barriers to realizing the full potential of co-operative housing in Montréal.

THE STATE OF CO-OPERATIVE HOUSING IN MONTRÉAL

To better understand Montréal's co-operative housing movement and its entanglement with municipal politics, I spoke with John Bradley, a community organizer who has worked on questions of housing and urban health in Montréal for decades.[2] Bradley was a key figure in the development of housing projects in the *Communauté Milton Parc* (CMP), in particular the development

2. Interview was conducted in March 2020.

of co-operatives and other non-profits. Bradley also worked with the *Société d'habitation et de développement de Montréal* (SHDM), a municipal housing agency, to develop non-profit housing across the city. In addition to a professional connection to co-operative housing, Bradley spent fifteen years living in co-operative housing in Verdun, one of the city's southwest boroughs. Although affordability is a key benefit of co-operative living, Bradley also spoke of its social and community-building potential, pointing to the "good friendships and sense of solidarity" fostered in co-ops and how they can present "an opportunity for cooperation on a democratic level with other people."

During our conversation, Bradley contrasted his early days developing social housing with the CMP and SHDM to the more challenging circumstances that characterized the housing movement in the later years of his career, during which he worked for a GRT. In the 1980s and 1990s, through his work at the SHDM, Bradley participated in purchasing and converting thousands of units into community housing at a reasonable price. During this time period, Québec was unique among Canadian provinces in that the majority of its social housing was the result of renovating existing buildings rather than the result of new construction (Vaillancourt et al. 2001). Bradley notes that this purchase-and-conversion method had "become almost impossible over the last years [of his career]". He describes fruitlessly running and re-running budgets through his work at a GRT in the early 2000s, noting that "not much would work". Bradley attributes much of this budgetary difficulty to skyrocketing costs of purchasing and renovating property in addition to insufficient government budgets.

In addition to the difficulties in securing new units, many existing co-ops are now in dire financial situations and physical disrepair. In Montréal, 26 co-operatives totaling 575 units have almost no chance of survival, according to a 2018 report from the *Fédération des coopératives d'habitation intermunicipale du Montréal métropolitain* (FECHIMM 2018). Another 75 co-ops are "en difficulté" (in trouble) and may not survive without significant intervention (FECHIMM 2018). A 2017 study by the *Confédération québécoise des coopératives d'habitation* (CQCH) shows that across the province, 20.5% of co-operative housing units require major repairs (CQCH 2017); this represents a significant increase from the 12% in need of major repairs in 2004 (Gaudreault 2004). In Montréal, the number is even higher, with 25% requiring major repairs. These figures are considerably higher than the overall percentage of rental dwellings (of any type) that require major repairs in Québec—just 7.2%, at the time of the 2016 census (Statistics Canada 2016).

In Montréal, several organizations exist to help insulate co-operative housing projects from these and other problems. Chief among them is the aforementioned FECHIMM, which provides resources, support, and political representation, for the hundreds of Montréal-area housing co-operatives that it counts among its membership. Some other key organizations include UTILE (*L'unité de travail pour l'implantation de logement étudiant*), which helps develop and promote student housing co-operatives in Québec, and FRAPRU (*Front d'action populaire en réaménagement urbain*), a Montréal-based housing rights organization that is a strong advocate for co-operatives and other forms of social housing. Despite the work of these groups, plus the support of GRTs, many co-operatives in Montréal—and beyond—can be insular. They are often isolated both from the communities in which they are situated as well as from broader political movements. Bradley stresses that although co-operative housing projects present an alternative to the private housing market, they are "not necessarily schools for socialism or social change". Many co-operatives struggle just to keep up with day-to-day operations, making it difficult to put pressure on local politicians or to forge links with community groups.

In an earlier piece written by Bradley, he compares the neighbourhoods of Pointe-Saint-Charles in the city's southwest and Shaughnessy Village in downtown Montréal (Bradley 2013). In Pointe-Saint-Charles, decades of work by GRTs and community groups, including *Action-Gardien*—a community roundtable of over twenty citizen-controlled groups—has resulted in the creation of thousands of units of non-profit housing, accounting for approximately one-third of the neighbourhood's housing stock. This work included occupations, demonstrations, and a long pressure campaign targeting local councillors. Meanwhile, in Shaughnessy Village, where there are few community groups and a largely transient student population, just 1.3% of the housing stock is non-profit. Without significant community mobilization, rezoning has empowered developers to move forward with luxury condo projects, gradually displacing the neighbourhood's low-income residents. As speculation continues relatively uncontested in neighbourhoods like Shaughnessy Village, the prospect of increasing the supply of social housing, either through purchase-and-conversion or new construction, becomes increasingly dim.

RÈGLEMENT POUR UNE MÉTROPOLE MIXTE: DOES IT GO FAR ENOUGH?

For many housing advocates, the 2017 Montréal municipal election was a cause for optimism. Projet Montréal, a broadly progressive municipal political party founded on the principle of "sustainable urbanism", defeated the centre-right incumbent Denis Coderre and his eponymous political party, Équipe Denis Coderre. Among its campaign promises, Projet Montréal promised "affordable and quality housing for all"; they also spoke of the benefits of social housing, including co-operatives.

In 2019, Projet Montréal announced the *Règlement pour une métropole mixte*, a planned by-law that aims to make good on this promise. This by-law would mandate that all future developments larger than 450m² include 20% social housing, 20% affordable housing, and 20% family housing. Although this is an improvement over the city's previous housing policies, which only incentivized developers to build social housing through subsidies, a number of housing groups have pointed to significant issues that arise from the measures proposed in the *règlement*. FRAPRU, for example, takes aim at the city's criteria for affordability, which is calculated using the market value of housing stock rather than the incomes of Montréal's tenant population (FRAPRU 2019). In the proposed *règlement*, Projet Montréal defines their ceiling for affordability as equal to or slightly lower than the market price for "modest" units (Ville de Montréal 2019). However, what is considered modest by market standards may not be modest compared to the income of the average Montréal renter. According to the *règlement*, a one-bedroom apartment in the city's downtown and central neighbourhoods must have a rent of no higher than $1,040 to be deemed affordable. Following market averages, this ceiling decreases for new developments in the city's *périphérie*[3] and *extrémités*.[4] As the median income of renters in the city's central neighbourhoods ranges from $19,629 to $26,796,[5] this would leave the typical renter in these neighbourhoods paying between 47% and 64% of their annual income on so-called "affordable" housing. By contrast, the CMHC's threshold for affordability is a 30% shelter-cost-to-income ratio. By choosing market-based—rather than needs-based—criteria for affordability, Projet Montréal has bent to the interests of speculators and is complicit in pushing low-income renters to the city's *périphérie* and *extrémités*.

Beyond opposing the *règlement*'s criteria for affordability, FRAPRU is also pushing the city to increase the inclusion threshold for social housing from 20% to 40%. They argue that social housing is the only way to meet the needs of the nearly 180,000 Montréalers who spend more than 30% of their income on housing, a group whose median annual income is only $18,812 (FRAPRU 2019). For developments on publicly held land, FRAPRU goes even further, recommending 100% social housing.

Although the *règlement* is often described as "mandating" developers to build affordable, social, and family housing, a significant loophole is built into

---

3. A broad category that includes the boroughs of Montréal-Nord, Saint-Leonard, Anjou, Mercier-Hochelaga-Maisonneuve, Verdun, LaSalle, and Ahuntsic-Cartierville in addition to partial sections of other boroughs (see map in Ville de Montréal 2019, 16).
4. The boroughs of Rivière-des-Prairies–Pointe-aux-Trembles, Pierrefonds-Roxboro, and Île-Bizard–Sainte-Geneviève.
5. Based on 2016 census data for Peter-McGill, Centre-Sud, Villeray, Hochelaga-Maisonneuve, Plateau Mont-Royal, and Rosemont. Data ordered from Statistics Canada by FRAPRU (see FRAPRU 2019).

the policy. Instead of building social housing into their projects, developers may choose to contribute to a city fund that would finance the construction of social housing off-site, effectively buying themselves out of the obligation to do so themselves.

In a study conducted by Business and Professional People for the Public Interest, a Chicago-based housing and community development organization, mandatory inclusionary housing policies were found to be considerably more effective than voluntary policies in producing affordable units in greater number and with more uniformity (Brunick et al. 2003). This study reviewed cities that had switched from voluntary to mandatory inclusionary housing policies, including Cambridge, MA, Boulder, CO, and Irvine, CA. In each case, the new mandatory inclusionary housing policies made swift improvements over the previous voluntary policies. The voluntary approach was deemed to be ineffective at producing affordable units, as well as overly confusing for developers, elected representatives, and the public alike. In 2016, mandatory inclusionary housing policies were introduced in New York City, the heart of real estate speculation in North America. These policies apply to any area that is rezoned for housing growth and are currently in place in a variety of neighbourhoods across four of the city's five boroughs (Carroll 2019). If mandatory inclusionary housing policies have a proven track record and can be effectively implemented even in housing markets with high degrees of speculation like New York City, why are they not part of Projet Montréal's housing plan?

The "inclusion" framework that serves as the foundation of the *Règlement pour une métropole mixte* is itself subject to criticism. This model takes cues from the concept of 'social mix', which pervades much of contemporary urban planning. Proponents of social mix posit that it is inherently preferable to have different socio-economic classes co-habiting, either in the same neighbourhood or same housing development. For Projet Montréal, this means including a token number of low-income renters in new developments, including those that would otherwise cater solely to the wealthy. John Bradley compares this to the 19th century notion that too many poor people living in close quarters would be generative of social problems. Bradley highlights the one-sidedness of "social mix" by describing his neighbourhood in Verdun:

> I look out the window and the person down the street from me is a welder, the person who I know over here who walks their dog is on old-age pension, the person across the street is a waitress at the corner store, and if I look at the census statistics, 90% of the people here have incomes under $50,000. So, is that socially mixed enough for you? ... I would be in favour of quote "social mix" in Verdun after Westmount and Outremont [two neighbourhoods symbolic of wealth in Montréal] open up 30% of their units for people on low-income.

In a brief written by Bradley on the subject of the city's Namur-Hippodrome project—a proposed carbon-neutral neighbourhood to be developed on the site of a former horse racing track—he cites British economist Paul Cheshire on the fundamental flaw of social mix: "The problem is poverty—what makes people poor and what keeps them poor – not the type of neighbourhood in which people live. Trying to create mixed neighbourhoods costs substantial resources that could be used directly to relieve poverty" (Bradley 2020). Bradley sees the Namur-Hippodrome project, which is situated on public land in Montréal's Côte-des-Neiges neighbourhood, as an opportunity to develop co-operative and other forms of social housing on a large scale, similar to the CMP. He believes the Namur-Hippodrome development would lend itself well to a land trust model, where land is bought by non-profits, taken off the real-estate market, and developed into affordable housing, including co-operatives, in addition to other social enterprises. Bradley, like FRAPRU, believes that 100% of housing developed on public lands, such as the Namur-Hippodrome site, ought to be social housing. The CMP, a non-profit condominium that operates in a manner similar to a land trust, serves as proof that this model can be viable and long-lasting in Montréal. This model works well when large, contiguous areas of land are up for redevelopment, as was the case in Milton-Parc and is currently the case with the Namur-Hippodrome project.

In Toronto, the recently formed Parkdale Neighbourhood Land Trust (PNLT) is in the process of purchasing property in one of the city's most rapidly gentrifying neighbourhoods with the aim of developing affordable housing. The PNLT conducted a comprehensive study that found that in Parkdale, 28 rooming houses have been lost to conversion and upscaling in the last ten years; another 59 will face a similar fate without intervention (PNLT 2016). The PNLT seeks to use the community land trust model to counter the displacement and homelessness that stem from this loss of rooming houses and from gentrification in general. Most recently, the PNLT helped with the purchase of a $7.2 million heritage building on Toronto's Queen Street West, taking it off the real estate market and ensuring affordable housing for its occupants in perpetuity. The co-operative housing movement in Montréal should look both to its own history and to emerging land trusts like the PNLT, and not only during the public consultation phase of significant projects like Namur-Hippodrome.

CHALLENGES AND OPPORTUNITIES IN A CONTEMPORARY CONTEXT

Montréal is a city of renters (see the map on the following page). Among census metropolitan areas (CMAs) in Canada, Montréal ranks last in terms of home ownership rate (Statistics Canada 2017).

CITY OF RENTERS
PERCENTAGE OF RENTERS IN EACH BOROUGH AND CITY

THE ISLAND OF MONTREAL HAS 522,140 RENTERS, OR 60% OF ALL HOUSEHOLDS ON THE ISLAND.

THE CITY OF MONTREAL IS 63% RENTERS.

- 56% MONTREAL EAST
- 66% MERCIER–HOCHELAGA MAISONNEUVE
- 36% RIVIERE-DES-PRAIRIES–POINTE AUX TREMBLES
- 56% ANJOU
- 65% ST LEONARD
- 72% VILLERAY ST MICHEL–PARK EXTENSION
- 73% VILLE MARIE
- 66% SOUTHWEST
- 47% WESTMOUNT
- 63% VERDUN
- 72% MONTREAL NORTH
- 61% AHUNTSIC CARTIERVILLE
- 46% OUTREMONT
- 72% LE PLATEAU–MONT ROYAL
- 33% MONT ROYAL
- 73% COTE DES NEIGES – NDG
- 33% HAMPSTEAD
- 22% MONTREAL WEST
- 60% LASALLE
- 51% ST LAURENT
- 51% COTE ST LUC
- 57% LACHINE
- 40% DORVAL
- 24% DOLLARD-DES-ORMEAUX
- 30% PIERREFONDS-ROXBORO
- 30% POINTE CLAIRE
- 6% KIRKLAND
- 26% BIZARD ISLAND–ST GENEVIEVE
- 6% BAIE D'URFE
- 10% BEACONSFIELD
- 46% ST ANNE DE BELLEVUE
- 11% SENNEVILLE

SOURCE: Population and Demography, November 14, 2017. Montréal in Statistics, Economic Development Department.

Inspired by: righttothecity.org

More than two-thirds of the city's population rely on the rental housing market and must contend with rising prices, a plummeting vacancy rate, and the whims of discriminatory landlords. With more than 40,000 renters in Montréal—twice the population of the City of Westmount—spending 80% or more of their incomes on housing (FRAPRU 2019), it is clear that the need for social housing is urgent. In Montréal, co-operative housing has proven effective in keeping rent affordable for long periods of time and on a reasonably large scale. However, this model requires tremendous collaboration between local government, community groups, non-profits such as GRTs, and tenants, in order to remain viable. When this coalition cannot come together, disrepair and bankruptcy loom as threats to co-operative or social housing projects. We cannot simply demand co-operative or other forms of social housing. Instead, we must understand what allows these models to succeed and work to ensure these conditions are in place and sustained.

Municipal government, especially when sympathetic to the co-operative housing movement, can present a seemingly simple avenue to achieving housing justice. However, the reality is that most public money remains in the hands of the federal and provincial governments, who have much broader powers of taxation. Even within their limited purview and limited spending power, municipal governments—including those that are relatively progressive on housing issues—can fall short. Therefore, they must be constantly pushed by the public to meet the housing needs of Montréalers, particularly those of the most vulnerable. Just like co-operative housing itself, the municipal government must be viewed as just one of the many tools that can be used on the path to the decommodification of housing.

Regarding Montréal's current municipal administration, there is still room for optimism. In late 2019, Projet Montréal councillors in the borough of Rosemont-La Petite-Patrie voted to place a moratorium on the conversion of duplexes into condos, renewing an old struggle from the 1980s. This will help counter the displacement of low-income renters in Rosemont-La Petite-Patrie, where the vacancy rate is just 1.5%, even lower than the already very low city average of 1.9% (CBC News 2019). Even more recently, Mayor Valérie Plante announced that the city will exercise its right of first refusal—the pre-emptive right to acquire property granted under the new Metropole law—to purchase 300 properties to develop them into social housing. This initiative will target areas such as Parc-Extension, a predominantly working-class, majority-immigrant neighbourhood, where a new *Université de Montréal* (U de M) campus currently under construction has caused concerns about gentrification. Indeed, rents here have been rapidly increasing even prior to the U de M campus. It also happens to be within Prime Minister Justin

Trudeau's federal electoral district. Like Projet Montréal, Justin Trudeau has spoken about the importance of housing issues, even declaring that "housing rights are human rights" in a 2017 press conference (Tasker 2017). As his second term as Prime Minister continues, and as life in Canada's major cities becomes harder by the day for low-income renters, the emptiness of his words is clear.

Despite the challenges presented by a speculative real estate market that has pushed the supply of affordable housing to the brink of crisis, a number of paths forward present themselves. Strategies can be found in both the history of Montréal's housing movement—initiatives like the *Communauté Milton Parc*—as well as in emerging models in other cities, for example, community land trusts and mandatory inclusionary housing policies. Combining these strategies with further intervention on the part of Montréal's municipal government (e.g., exercising the right of first refusal, banning condominium conversion, etc.) and a strengthening of the relationship between the public and co-operative sectors can be a potent formula for combatting the effects of the speculative real estate market and ensuring the survival and growth of housing that helps build a more just city for all.

REFERENCES

AGRTQ (Association des groupes de ressources techniques du Québec). n.d. "Qui sommes-nous?" https://agrtq.qc.ca/lagrtq/quisommes-nous/.

Bradley, J. 2013. "Urban Space – Who Gets What … and Why?" *Montréal Serai* 26 (1).

Bradley, J. 2020. "La Santé Et Le Logement: Deux Enjeux Et Deux Droits Collectifs." Mémoire présenté à l'Office de consultation publique de Montréal sur le dossier du futur quartier Namur-Hippodrome. https://ocpm.qc.ca/sites/ocpm.qc.ca/files/pdf/P107/8-1_john_bradley.pdf.

Brunick, N., Goldberg, L., and Susannah, L. 2003. "Voluntary or Mandatory Inclusionary Housing? Production, Predictability, and Enforcement." *Business and Professional People for the Public Interest*.

Carroll, L. 2019. *Mandatory Inclusionary Housing in NYC*.

CBC News. 2019. "Rosemont–La Petite-Patrie Borough Forbids Condo Conversions for Duplexes." 20 December 2019. https://www.cbc.ca/news/canada/montreal/rosemont-duplex-condos-1.5403864.

CHF Canada (Co-operative Housing Federation of Canada). n.d. "About Co-op Housing." https://chfcanada.coop/about-co-op-housing/.

Co-operative Housing International. 2019. "Canada Archives – Co-operative Housing." https://www.housinginternational.coop/co-ops/canada/.

CQCH (Confédération québécoise des coopératives d'habitation). 2017. *Enquête Sur Le Profil Socioéconomique Des Résidents De Coopérative d'Habitation – 2017*.

FECHIMM (Fédération des coopératives d'habitation intermunicipale du Montréal métropolitain). 2018. *Rapport Annuel 2018*. https://cdn.fechimm.coop/uploads/documents/document/406/Rapport-annuel_FECHIMM-2018_web.pdf.

FRAPRU (Front d'action populaire en réaménagement urbain). 2019. *Montréal: Métropole Inclusive Ou Exclusive?*

Gaudreault, A. 2004. "Le Potentiel De Financement Autonome Des Coopératives d'Habitation Du Québec." *Confédération québécoise des coopératives d'habitation*.

Kowaluk, L., and Piché-Burton, C. 2019. "Milton-Parc: How We Did It and How It Works Now." In

Villages in Cities: Community Land Ownership, Cooperative Housing, and the Milton Parc Story, edited by J. Hawley, and D.I. Roussopoulos. Montréal: Black Rose Books, pp. 24-35.

Loriggio, P. 2018. "Upstart Québec Solidaire Turns Campaign Momentum into Election Gains." *The Globe and Mail*, 2 October 2018.

PNLT (Parkdale Neighbourhood Land Trust). 2016. *No Room For Unkept Promises, The Impact of Real Estate Speculation, Upscaling, and Conversion on Rooming House Loss in Parkdale*.

Statistics Canada. 2016. "Housing Highlight Tables." Last modified 2 Novemer 2017. https://www12.statcan.gc.ca/census-recensement/2016/dp-pd/hlt-fst/housing-logement/index-eng.cfm.

Statistics Canada. (2017). "Housing in Canada: Key results from the 2016 Census." Last modified 27 October 2017. https://www150.statcan.gc.ca/n1/daily-quotidien/171025/dq171025c-eng.htm.

Tasker, J.P. 2017. "Trudeau Says Housing Is a Human Right—What Does That Mean Exactly?" *CBC News*, 5 December 2017. https://www.cbc.ca/news/politics/trudeau-housing-rights-human-rights-1.4414854.

Vaillancourt, Y., Ducharme, M-N., Cohen, R., Roy, C., and Jetté, C. 2001. "Social housing: A key component of social policies in transformation: The Québec experience." *Caledon Institute of Social Policy*.

Ville de Montréal. 2019. *Règlement Pour Une Métropole Mixte | Résumé*.

COMMUNITY HOUSING: LEVERAGING OUR COLLECTIVE ASSETS

JEAN-PIERRE RACETTE

BACKGROUND TO THE CREATION OF THE ALLIANCE OF NON-PROFIT HOUSING DEVELOPERS OF GREATER MONTRÉAL

In 2014, after more than 25 years of existence, and with a housing stock of approximately 1,500 units located in seven Montréal boroughs, the *Société d'habitation populaire de l'Est de Montréal*, commonly known as SHAPEM, initiated an important strategic shift by taking a critical look at its history, and also at the evolution of the social housing sector in Québec.

Over the years, SHAPEM's unique approach, its exchanges and collaborations with numerous players in the fields of housing, advocacy, and economic development (both solidarity-based and more traditional), and in the academic world, have led it to take a detailed look at socio-economic development and the strategic role of housing in the development of major urban centres.

It is in this context, by sharing its analysis and vision, that SHAPEM initiated a conversation with several important players in Montréal's housing sector, such as the general management of the SHDM (*Société d'habitation et de développement de Montréal*), the City of Montréal's housing department, the management of the OMHM (*Office municipal d'habitation de Montréal*), and certain social economy organizations such as Inter-Loge, the Mainbourg Corporation, and SOLIDES (*Société locative d'investissement et de développement social*).

Very quickly, this conversation, which was enriched by the participants' input, created a great deal of enthusiasm that led the senior management of the Chagnon Foundation, the *Chantier d'économie sociale*, and TIESS (*Territoires innovants en économie sociale et solidaire*) to concretely support this strategic and operational collaboration aimed at changing the scale of these organizations and the collective impact of their interventions. This has led to two specific actions:

1. Initiating a process of **strategic alliance between non-profit housing developers in the greater Montréal area**;
2. Soliciting the CMHC (Canada Mortgage and Housing Corporation) and Minister Jean-Yves Duclos to share this vision and provide financial tools to match the ambitions of this vision, for example, by creating a **co-investment fund for the Greater Montréal area**.

In terms of the **alliance process**, the actions have resulted in the agreement of a common vision and the formulation of a declaration of alliance (presented in the next section). This has been received with great enthusiasm by the organizations involved in the process. In 2021, the Alliance should be incorporated and begin its activities.

Regarding the actions directed at the level of the **CMHC and Minister Duclos**, all of the activities regarding the Alliance's vision seem to have influenced CMHC's National Housing Strategy and the new financial tools resulting from it.

Finally, these activities have also made it possible to raise the awareness of several decision-makers, including the City of Montréal, the City of Québec, and the SHQ (*Société d'habitation du Québec*), to take an interest in this initiative. Significant gains have already been made, leading us to believe that this alliance approach will soon see the light of day and deliver the ambitious benefits desired by its creators.

The following sections present the "declaration" of alliance and the "constitution" document of the Alliance of Non-Profit Homeowners of Greater Montréal. The "declaration," drafted in 2017, was essentially a political 'manifesto,' outlining the vision, a socio-economic and political analysis, and a value system. The "constitution" document was more operational and drafted later than the declaration. This "constitution" document led to the formation of a five-member steering committee. Since then, we have narrowed the membership to only include owner-developers, with a view to pooling and creating financial tools specific to the nature of our organizations and our vision/ambition. In February 2020, we took formal steps to incorporate this Alliance, but the pandemic caused us to postpone this action. The work will be resumed shortly.

PREAMBLE TO THE 2017 DECLARATION

Considering the scale of the challenges and issues at stake—from global warming to the reconfiguration of inequalities and the political, environmental, and refugee crisis—and given the conclusions and consensus emerging from the United Nations climate conference in Paris (2015), and given the urgency to take action, it is clear that the majority of actors and populations feel powerless to take on the overwhelming responsibilities and the scale of the solutions required. **It is clear that a new stance must be adopted**, which implies turning our backs on the dominant developmentalist model based on economic growth that is both unequal and predatory on environmental resources. But how?

The call for innovation, consultation, and profound change is widely shared, but it cannot be the concern of a single actor, a single sector, or a single institution, however significant they may be. No stakeholder has a monopoly on solutions, nor can they play the free-rider when it comes to the actions that need to be taken. This collective action cannot be taken for granted.

While the need to take stock, build consensus, and take action is widely expressed, it is not without its problems:

- the presence of a shared leadership;
- the joint construction of an in-depth analysis of the foundations and causes, both structural and cyclical, of the issues and challenges to be faced;
- the formulation of a common vision on the actions to be undertaken, based on the definition of an inclusive common interest, notably on the ecological dimension;
- the presence of efficient mechanisms for coordinating social actors, allocating required resources, and effectively monitoring the actions already taken or conducted in the future.

At present, the civil society actors are watching each other out of the corner of their eyes. They are reluctant to take the first steps towards a rapprochement that would make it possible to define the contours of a social bloc based on common interest and living well together. In each civil society sector, the actors express themselves more through monologue than in the dialogue needed to produce a 'new narrative'—one on which the redevelopment of institutional arrangements could be based.

THE DECLARATION (2017)

ALLIES(H)[1] FOR BUILDING SUPPORTIVE, INCLUSIVE, AND SUSTAINABLE COMMUNITIES IN A PROSPEROUS AND INNOVATIVE GREATER MONTREAL (3 DECEMBER 2017)

We are the Alliance of Non-Profit Housing Owners and Managers of Greater Montréal, and we declare the following:

1. **Our vision of the role of housing in economic development**
Whereas:

I. **Housing is a central element of the socio-economic development** of urban centres, and even more so for large urban centres. Our globalized economic system and the fierce struggle of la**rge urban centres that are the primary creators of wealth** in industrialized countries are **also the creators of poverty and social exclusion** concentrated in certain urban areas. This weakens social balance and compromises economic development. **This dynamic is systemic and must be treated as such.**

II. **Housing**, in a **coherent and strategic approach, can become an extremely potent instrument** for promoting solidarity, social inclusion, cooperation between diverse populations, and the creation of new alternative forms of economic wealth. **Housing and habitat encourage social roots**, a prerequisite for identification, belonging, and investment in living. **All of this is necessary for the construction of communities.**

III. **In the process of innovation, and in the actions that we have collectively carried out over the last 20 years, our view of the role of housing has evolved**:

a. Housing to 'help' people;

b. As a tool for urban and social revitalization, with partners, in struggling urban areas;

c. As a process, together with the population and actors of struggling urban areas, to build communities of solidarity and inclusion;

d. A vision at the scale of large urban centres to build a collaborative ecosystem of large non-profit housing owners who would share resources and expertise to innovate and have a strategic impact across the entire urban landscape.

---

1. Alliance for Innovative Social Economy Rental Housing (*Alliance pour le logement locatif innovant en économie sociale*). The "H" is for the consistency we should have when talking about homes (*habitation*) rather than housing (*logement*). Should we use the acronym "AHLIES" instead: *Alliance pour l'habitation locative innovante en économie sociale*? Other names have been suggested by Laurent Levesque of UTILE (*Unité de travail pour l'implantation de logement étudiant*) since our November 10th meeting, including: "ACHAT" (*Alliance communautaire pour l'habitation abordable et transformatrice*; Community Alliance for Affordable and Transformative Housing) or "CHIC" (*Coalition pour l'habitation innovante et Communautaire*; Coalition for Innovative and Community Housing).

2. Our identity

Whereas:

I. We are non-profit housing owners and managers responsible for 30,989 units[2] in the Greater Montréal area. For several decades, we have housed more than 60,000 people[3] (families, couples, and singles) who are often very low-income and vulnerable.

II. With minimal means, our organizations have succeeded in providing decent housing, significantly improving quality of life, and promoting socio-economic inclusion. To achieve this, we have had to innovate, forge many partnerships, and explore new fields of action

3. Fundamental structural transformations leading to an observation

Whereas:

I. Today, with the significant and profound transformations that our economies have undergone over the past 40 years, our housing challenges have become immensely more complex. They take much more acute forms and extend beyond the space of the dwelling or the building. They are embodied in the landscape and arise more in terms of social dynamics than in terms of "real estate."

II. Moreover, these structural changes that we are all facing are accelerating and amplifying, generating socio-economic disruptions that will only increase.

III. Faced with this state of affairs, it is becoming increasingly evident that we will never change this socio-economic dynamic on our own.[4] More than ever, we must unite!

4. Joint statement[5]

With this alliance, we declare that we are taking a new look at our organizations and our ways of doing things. From now on, to achieve strategic impacts, both at the level of territories and specific populations, we commit ourselves to collaborate, strategically and operationally, by sharing expertise, experience, resources, and networks. We will forge links and create alliances with other groups of actors, particularly in the areas of social economy, environment, sustainable development, health, and inclusive citizenship.

---

2. This includes: 23,017 units for the OMHM (*Office municipal d'habitation de Montréal*), 4,700 units for the SHDM (*Société d'habitation et de développement de Montréal*), and 3,272 units for other owners according to the *"Portrait financier d'OSBL d'habitation du grand Montréal"* by Allan Gaudreault (7 July 2017).
3. Assuming an average of 2 persons per dwelling.
4. See Appendix A in the original declaration for a reading of the current socio-economic and environmental situation according to a significant proportion of granting foundations in Canada.
5. This statement is largely based on the Urban Forest Alliance Declaration.

5. Mission of the Alliance

With this alliance, we want to create a space for innovation and collaboration, both strategic and operational, between owners and managers of non-profit housing, aiming to change the scale of our action and enabling us to go beyond the "simple" implementation of projects to obtain results with constructive impacts on the urban landscape or with vulnerable or marginalized populations.

The alliance:

Aims to use our building stock, in an approach based on social innovation and **common interest**, to achieve societal objectives of environment, sustainable development, social inclusion, and solidarity-based economic development.

Mobilize other ecosystems of actors in a collaborative approach, enabling us and other ecosystems to better achieve our societal goals.

Promotes the development of member organizations, both in terms of the volume of activities, skills development, and organizational development.

Calls, in particular, on grant-making foundations, workers' funds, pension funds, and insurance companies to invest significantly, and responsibly, to create new financial tools complementary to existing social housing programs and adapted to the specific nature of the Alliance members.

Counting on the critical financial support of governments and the City of Montréal, because it is about fundamental issues of concern for socio-economic development, the inclusive future of our large urban centres, and contribution to the success of the environmental transition underway.

Wishes, from a research and development perspective, to evaluate the impacts of our actions, to adjust them to the evolution of our environment and to transfer our results to other ecosystems and other urban centres.

This declaration is supported by the following founding members:

Mainbourg Corporation; Habitations La Traversée; Habitations populaires de Parc-Extension (HAPOPEX); Inter-Loge; Office municipal d'habitation de Montréal (OMHM); Société d'habitation populaire de l'Est de Montréal (SHAPEM); Société de développement et d'habitation communautaire (SODHAC); Société locative d'investissement et de développement social (SOLIDES); Unité de travail pour l'implantation de logement étudiant (UTILE)

THE CONSTITUTION: ALLIANCE OF NON-PROFIT LANDLORDS OF GREATER MONTRÉAL PRESENTATION DOCUMENT

1. BACKGROUND

Large urban centres are places of significant wealth creation but also of poverty and social exclusion. Moreover, this phenomenon of poverty and social exclusion is unevenly distributed across the city. It tends to be concentrated in certain urban areas that are rapidly deteriorating, both economically and socially. Such deterioration significantly undermines the development of the population's welfare and the urban centre as a whole, and in turn, to the economic development potential of the urban centre.

Non-profit homeowners contribute to building supportive, dynamic, and inclusive communities. Their action is part of a perspective of social transformation and socio-economic development. A sizeable social housing stock can then become a matrix for social innovation. The existence of several social housing real estate parks that closely collaborate, in the same urban centre, by defining a common vision and sharing resources and expertise will allow for the realization of urban development activities.

2. OUR VISION

Support the integrated development of urban areas and help reduce social exclusion by supporting collaborations and resource-sharing in the social and community housing sector of Greater Montréal, while respecting each other's respective mission. Promote innovation and knowledge transfer within the network and position housing as a key player in urban development.

3. OUR MISSION

The Alliance facilitates the creation of strategic and operational collaborations between non-profit housing owners in Greater Montréal and promotes synergy with other players in the housing sector and with other players involved in the development of the territories where they operate. To encourage a change of scale in response to the population's housing needs, the Alliance creates conditions favourable to the sharing of expertise and resources among its members and supports the development of new tools when necessary, with a view to solidarity, development, and innovation.

4. OUR VALUES

Collaboration; Openness; Transparency; Innovation
Solidarity; Development; Sustainability

5. COMMON VISION OF THE ORGANIZATIONS IN THE ALLIANCE

Our approach aims to enable/facilitate a change of scale[6] in response to housing needs in the Greater Montréal area by identifying the needs of community housing actors and by building a support system adapted to the shared vision and ambitions, both in terms of financial tools and the sharing of resources and expertise.

6. GUIDING PRINCIPLES

- *Principle 1*: Engage in shared leadership by recognizing the expertise of each of the participating organizations.
- *Principle 2*: Commit to a process aimed at developing affordable, social, and community housing in Greater Montréal.
- *Principle 3*: Collaborate with other actors in Greater Montréal to carry out structuring actions in the region, mainly in the field of housing.

7. MEMBERS

To promote the implementation of strategic actions, the Alliance has three categories of members.

Active Members: Active membership is open to **non-profit housing owners** in the Greater Montréal area who intend to continue their development, adhere to the Alliance's declaration and guiding principles, and are approved by the Steering Committee.

Associate Members: Associate membership is open to **housing sector organizations that contribute to the development of community housing** in the Greater Montréal area that subscribe to the Alliance's declaration and guiding principles and are approved by the Steering Committee.

Supporting members: Sympathizing members may be **partner organizations that wish to collaborate in the development of community housing** in Greater Montréal and are approved by the Steering Committee.

8. OUR ACTIONS

The Alliance is based on a global vision of social and community housing.

---

6. With the aim of increasing the social impact of the actions undertaken by social and community housing organizations, the Alliance supports the deployment of strategies that aim to change the scale of member organizations, i.e., strategies that contribute to increasing the scope of their work and their activities in order to benefit more people.

The Alliance aims to strengthen the conditions and tools necessary to develop social and community housing within a broader vision of building sustainable communities. Thus, the Alliance supports the organizational capacities of its members to facilitate the development and management of new housing units. It contributes to the organizational development of member organizations to accompany the change of scale in community housing and allow the realization of structuring actions on the territory of Greater Montréal. The Alliance also promotes networking, pooling, and sharing initiatives that support the achievement of common objectives.

9. STEERING COMMITTEE AND WORKING COMMITTEES

In order to support the decision-making process and in the interests of efficiency, the Alliance has chosen to set up a steering committee and working committees that meet according to the priorities determined by the active members during the Alliance. The **Steering Committee** comprises five members chosen by, and from among, the active members.

The priorities identified should fall into one or other of these categories:

Mutualisation: Pooling resources to facilitate member operations, including management, communications, safety, greening, and energy savings.

Financing: Setting up financial tools and partnerships in line with members' development and investment needs and contributing to the adjustment of existing products.

Components of the Housing Ecosystem

Environment
Urban Agriculture
Sustainable Development
Research and Development
Urban Forestry
Energy Saving

Finance & Housing
Funding
Refinancing
Housing Affordability
Dedicated Acquisition Funds
Organizational Development
CMHC Construction & Renovations
Resources for Mutualisation
Community Advocacy

**Mutualisation of Management Practices
& Collaborative Economy**
Tenant Relations
Property Management
Partnership & Territorial Approaches
External Communications
Human Resources

Innovations Transfers Addressing Poverty & Social Exclusion Environment Territorial Revitalizations

HOW TO FIGHT YOUR LANDLORD: GENTRIFICATION AND TENANT ORGANIZING IN MONTRÉAL

JON MILTON

INTRODUCTION

Montréal, today, has a reputation as being the most affordable major city in Canada for tenants. While that dynamic is being complicated by accelerating gentrification, rental apartments in the city remain significantly cheaper than elsewhere in the country.

This is good news for residents of the city—nearly two-thirds of whom are tenants (Ville de Montréal 2017). Renting in Montréal is concentrated in the city's interior boroughs and makes up a higher proportion of housing in lower-income neighbourhoods. Cote-des-Neiges, a low-income community with a significant population of new immigrants, has the highest proportion of renters, at nearly three quarters (Ville de Montréal 2017). Meanwhile, Kirkland, an anglophone suburb in the West Island, has the lowest proportion of renters, at 5.5% (Ville de Montréal 2017).

Like in many other sectors, social movements have played a significant role in the history of landlord-tenant relations in Montréal, and the province of Québec more broadly. This chapter will examine the history of tenant organizing in Montréal. In particular, it will detail the history of the *Front d'action populaire en reamenagement urbain* (FRAPRU) and *Regroupement des comités logement et associations de locataires du Québec* (RCLALQ), two advocacy coalitions of neighbourhood-based tenant organizations in Québec.

The chapter will examine various tenant-led housing campaigns in post-Quiet Revolution Québec. It will provide insight into the changing nature of tenants' demands, from social housing to landlord-tenant relations. In doing so, it will show how movements dynamically respond to changing political and economic conditions from the boom years of the welfare state through neoliberal restructuring.

The chapter will draw from various sources, including archival material provided by FRAPRU and RCLALQ and interviews with tenant organizers such as Maxime Roy-Allard, an organizer with RCLALQ interviewed by the author in the Spring of 2020.

By providing an overview of the history and present of tenant organizing, the chapter will help guide ongoing tenant struggles, and provide an idea of how the future of tenant organizing in Montréal may look.

THE BIRTH AND GROWTH OF THE TENANTS MOVEMENT

RCLALQ and FRAPRU are both coalitions of housing organizations, and their membership overlaps. In Montréal, most neighbourhoods have their own "housing committees," focused on tenants' issues. For example, the *Comité BAILS*[1] in Hochelaga-Maisonneuve, *POPIR*[2] *comité logement* in the Sud-Ouest, or *Comité logement Rosemont* in Rosemont. RCLALQ and FRAPRU were born out of attempts to federate these neighbourhood tenant organizations into province-wide associations capable of engaging in broader struggle and winning positive reforms, rather than simply fighting against individual abuses by landlords and developers.

Maxime Roy-Allard, an organizer with RCLALQ, says that "the big difference [between FRAPRU and RCLALQ] is that FRAPRU mostly demands social housing, while we at RCLALQ demand more protections for tenants on the private market. FRAPRU is also larger, it's not just housing committees, it also includes groups that build social housing."[3] Both federations were formed in 1978. It was the tail end of the Quiet Revolution era, where much of the social movement infrastructure in Québec can directly trace its roots.

It is important to note that there was not only one "Quiet Revolution," but multiple facets of a dynamic social upheaval that occurred both from above and from below. Typically, the story of the Quiet Revolution in Québec is told as the story of the top-down reforms of the Liberal Party of Québec (and, later, the Parti Québécois), which took power following the death of long-time authoritarian leader Maurice Duplessis. The Liberals, in this telling, fundamentally reshaped Québec society—away from one where social services were managed mainly by the Catholic Church and toward secular capitalist modernity. Québec's francophone majority, long boxed-out of the local elite,

---

1. *Base pour l'action et l'information sur le logement social.*
2. *Projet d'organisation populaire, d'information et de regroupement.*
3. This and subsequent quotations from an interview with Maxime Roy-Allard (18 June 2020).

seized the reins of the economy. The welfare state was expanded dramatically, and institutions like Hydro-Québec were born.

While this story is true, it leaves out the massive changes occurring on the ground, particularly in Montréal. In *The Empire Within*, a study of radical social movements in that era, Sean Mills writes that "seeing the 1960s in Québec only through the lens of capitalist modernization is to succumb to what Kristin Ross calls a 'teleology of the present'" (Mills 2010, 20). Rather, Mills notes that it is useful to examine how the era's social movements fought for something larger than simply secularization and modernization. Movements during the era advanced transformative visions of revolutionary social change in workplaces and neighbourhoods, articulated in the popular language of national liberation and decolonization and against patriarchy and racism (Mills 2010).

It is no coincidence that the institutions of today's tenants' movement were born at the tail-end of that period of radical politics. Roy-Allard points out that RCLALQ was "heavily influenced by Marxism-Leninism" in its early days. "You can see it in our archives; the aesthetics were very communist."

Born first as the *Regroupement pour le gel des loyers*, RCLALQ emerged during an era when the city of Montréal was undergoing a vast infrastructure modernization program; entire neighbourhoods were being targeted for demolition to be replaced with skyscrapers and highways (RCLALQ 2018). Neighbourhood housing committees had been fighting pitched battles with the city over these measures. Tenants in the Plateau neighbourhood squatted in 1975 after receiving eviction notices in an attempt to prevent the city from demolishing their homes to build a public works yard (Saillant 2018).

The "Angus shops" in Rosemont were one of the movement's most important victories in these early years. These train part factories, which had also built munitions during the Second World War, became the site of a years-long struggle in the 1980s. During the wider process of deindustrialization, the factories were decommissioned and closed. The land was then sold to a developer with plans to build thousands of luxury housing units (Saillant 2018). By 1990, after a long struggle led by neighbourhood housing committees with participation from FRAPRU and RCLALQ, around 1,000 units of social housing were built on the site; roughly 40% of the total units built (Saillant 2018).

The 1980s were also a time of structural change for the tenants' movement. Roy-Allard describes how this was the decade where community organizations like RCLALQ began to receive financial support from the provincial government. He notes that these financial incentives progressively moved the organization away from its revolutionary communist origins: "we're still somewhat restrained because we're financed by the state. There's also a tension between being combative and making pressure on the elites, but also being accessible for the base. We want everyone to feel included."

Regardless, Roy-Allard says, "we in the housing movement are some of the more combative organizations in the community sector today." Today, that combativeness manifests itself in various ways, ranging from regular demonstrations to the occupations of ministers' offices to the squatting of vacant buildings to demand they be transformed into social housing.

In addition to being a time of change for the tenants' movement, the 1980s were also a boom period for construction in Montréal, complete with attempts to demolish large sections of the city to build luxury housing. Overdale, a small downtown neighbourhood near Concordia University with 107 apartment units, was set to be demolished in 1987 to build 650 luxury condos (Saillant 2018). Tenants squatted and blocked demolition crews from entering the neighbourhood. The city responded by sending riot police to lay siege to the neighbourhood and fulfill the eviction order (Saillant 2018). As a result, the neighbourhood was partially demolished and the tenants were fully evicted; however, the condo project was abandoned. The demolished site became a parking lot, until 2012 when it was sold to a developer. At the time of writing, the site is currently under construction and will eventually house 850 luxury condos (Saillant 2018).

With the recession of the early 1990s, massive development projects slowed down (Saillant 2018). It was also a decade of austerity, notably in federal funding for social housing—which was cut down to zero in the Liberal Party of Canada's 1993 budget (FRAPRU n.d.). After years of tenants' campaigning on the issue, the government of Québec announced its own new social housing financing scheme in 1997 (FRAPRU n.d.).

During this era, FRAPRU was focused on ensuring that government funds directed toward housing would be placed specifically in social housing, rather than the more nebulously defined "affordable housing," which often translates to subsidies for the private sector.

Social housing in Québec is divided into three categories: *Habitations a loyer modiques* (HLM), co-operatives, and non-profit housing. HLMs are directly managed by the government and generally include rent subsidies which ensure that tenants do not pay more than 25% of their household income on rent. Co-operatives are structures that are democratically managed by tenants, and non-profit housing is managed by non-profit organizations (NPOs). FRAPRU advocates for all three types of social housing (FRAPRU n.d.).

For its part, RCLALQ spent much of the 1990s advocating for universal rent control in the private market. It allied its campaign with anti-poverty groups organizing in the city (RCLALQ 2018).

Things began to take a turn in 21st century, with the onset of widespread new large-scale development projects and the rapid gentrification of Montréal.

GENTRIFICATION

"We can define gentrification as class struggle on an urban level," according to Roy-Allard; "gentrification is one class attempting to replace another."

By most accounts, gentrification is the meta-struggle that structures all other housing struggles in Montréal today. "Everything is related to it," says Roy Allard, "the rent increases, the evictions, these are the effects of gentrification." Main street monopolists. Private condo development.

Geographer Samuel Stein writes in *Capital City* (2019) that gentrification results from shifting material conditions for the economies of cities. The conditions for capital accumulation, and therefore urban planning priorities, inside metropolises like Montréal, have been fundamentally altered due to deindustrialization and neoliberalization. Prior generations of planners had to contend with the often-divergent interests of different forms of capital. In particular, heavy industry such as manufacturing holds different—and sometimes conflicting—interests than real estate when it comes to municipal level planning.

Stein describes how manufacturing capital has historically viewed real estate as a cost rather than an asset. This creates a demand for lower real estate costs that emerge from capital, rather than labour, and an "inter-capitalist feud" with real estate capital (Stein 2019, 37). These industrial capitalists also maintain material interests in the creation of low-cost housing since a lower cost of living can justify lower pay for workers.

However, this has changed in recent decades as industrial capital has largely moved away from dense urban areas and towards exurbs. In this context of industrial migration, real estate capital has come to occupy an unquestioned dominant role in municipal political economy within major cities like Montréal. Stein refers to this constellation as the "real estate state" (Stein 2019, 5).

Stein focuses much of his writing on city planning—the process whereby municipalities plan their infrastructure projects, including housing—as a key site of struggle against gentrification. Within city planning, Stein identifies two contradictions that planners in the real estate state must navigate. The "property contradiction" relates to how capital accumulation requires planned economic interventions (such as roads, sewage systems, and so on), even though capitalists are inherently suspicious of government intervention. The second, the "capitalist-democracy contradiction," emerges from this first. Since planning sits at the nexus of local capital accumulation and municipal democracy, city planners must simultaneously ensure the conditions for economic growth are met while also providing some semblance of transparency and openness. As Stein writes: "the people must have their say, but their options must be limited" (Stein 2019, p.30-31).

In Montréal, the rise of the real estate state is most visible along the Lachine Canal, where the factories and warehouses of the twentieth century have been converted to luxury condominiums. Beginning in the early 2000s, these industrial sites were bought up, one by one, by luxury real estate developers. The plans are the subject of anti-condo campaigns by tenants, such as the failed campaign against the 450-condo *Quai des eclusiers* project in the city's Sud-Ouest borough (Saillant 2018).

Then there's Griffintown, the most flagrant example of gentrification in the city. This neighbourhood sits at the eastern end of the Lachine Canal, just south of downtown. Here the formerly industrial area was razed to the ground and built anew in the span of just a few years. To date, at least 7,000 condo units have been built in Griffintown (Saillant 2018).

The developments along the Lachine Canal provide a stark contrast to the Angus shops in Rosemont—that victory of the tenants' movement in the 1980s. Both are examples of decommissioned industrial zones which were converted into residential units. And both were the subject of significant campaigning by tenants in the city, advocating for the building of social housing rather than luxury condos. But where tenants succeeded in fundamentally reshaping the plan for the Angus shops, the Canal developments ended up becoming a playground for the rich. The contrast between these two development projects—broadly similar but separated by time—shows the extent to which real estate capital has consolidated power in the city in recent decades. In Montréal, as elsewhere, the real estate state dominates city planning.

Such power also translates to increased prices and therefore profits for developers. In Montréal, as of 2017, the cost of a home or condo was 16.6 times the median income for people living in the city (Gaudreau et al. 2020). In 2002, it was only 9.8 times the median (Gaudreau et al. 2020), almost doubling in only 15 years. Between 2014 and 2019, home sales valued at over $500,000 also increased significantly, particularly in neighbourhoods that are hotspots for gentrification (Gaudreau et al. 2020). In Hochelaga-Maisonneuve, the neighbourhood with the steepest increase, those sales increased 321% for single-family homes (Gaudreau et al. 2020).

The massive construction of new luxury housing has spillover effects into the broader housing market. For the nearly two-thirds of Montréalers who are tenants, such price inflation has translated to increasing rents. In 2017, the average apartment in Montréal cost $835 per month; today, the average rent is $1,044. This represents an increase of nearly 25% in just over two years

(Ville de Montréal 2017). The average rent for a new unit in Montréal, as advertised on Kijiji, is now 30% higher than the Canada Mortgage and Housing Corporation (CMHC) average for the city (RCLALQ 2020). The CMHC tracks the average price of housing in large population centres across the country in an annual report. For large apartments with three bedrooms or more, the cost is 32% higher than the CMHC average (RCLALQ 2020). Across Québec, one-third of tenants now pay more than 30% of their income towards rent,[4] while 14% of tenants have rents costing more than half their income (RCLALQ 2020).

Such dramatic increases in rent are accelerated by financial speculation in the real estate sector. Investors, both domestic and global, increasingly see real estate as a key sector to invest in, creating rapid price inflation and financial bubbles. "If we don't want Montréal to become the next Toronto or Vancouver," Roy-Allard says, "we urgently need measures to slow down this speculation."

Montréal's nominally progressive city administration, under the administration of Mayor Valerie Plante and *Projet Montréal*, has only begun to talk of taking action against gentrification in the second half of its mandate. One of the measures on the table is the "20/20/20" regulation.[5] This proposed by-law would require all new housing construction to contain at least 20% social housing, 20% affordable housing, and 20% family units. As this chapter is being written, the regulation has not yet been enacted, and the Office of Public Consultation (OCPM) is recommending that it be re-written in May 2020. The city has also begun to exercise its "right of first refusal" on properties for sale—meaning that specific designated properties must first be offered for sale to the city rather than on the open market. That power would not only be used for housing but could also be used for the construction of schools, parks, and so on.

In the meantime, according to Roy-Allard, tenants do have rights that they can exercise when faced with an intransigent landlord. And knowing those rights is an important piece of preventing abuses.

REFORMING THE REGIE, SOCIALIZING HOUSING

The *Commission des loyers* was Québec's original rental board and had been in place since the 1950s. The *Commission* was created as a temporary measure following the withdrawal of federally mandated universal rent control in the 15 largest Canadian cities, between 1940 and 1951 (Saillant 2018). The *Regie du logement*, Québec's current rental board, replaced the *Commission des loyers*

---

4. The CMHC threshold for affordability is a 30% shelter-cost-to-income ratio.
5. *Règlement pour une métropole mixte.* See further discussion in Ryan's chapter in this book.

in 1980. In the summer of 2020, it was renamed the *Tribunal administratif du logement*, (but will continue to be referred to in this chapter as the *Regie*.)

When the *Regie du logement* was established in 1980, it was a sign of hope, according to Roy-Allard. The Parti Québécois government of the period, led by René Lévesque, authored a report regarding its desire to create a more favourable legal environment for tenants, compared to the previously lopsided system that overwhelmingly favoured landlords. The hope was that the *Regie* would embody that program. Landlords also saw that potential. As such, in 1981, they launched a failed attempt to strike down the *Regie* as unconstitutional and initially attempted a boycott of the rental board (RCALQ 2018).

While the *Regie* may have been a hopeful development at first, Roy-Allard says that by the early 1990s, RCLALQ was denouncing the board as a fraud. By 1985, a reform package brought in user fees that saw the previously free tribunal now require payments to open a case. In the five years following the 1985 reforms, not a single case for unjustified evictions resulted in repercussions for the landlord (RCALQ 2018). "The *Regie* gave people hope, but it was a false hope," says Roy-Allard. "In the end, the *Regie* became a tool to evict tenants in precarious situations."

The *Regie du logement* (now the *Tribunal administratif du logement*) has multiple responsibilities. It is a tribunal that tenants and landlords can call upon when conflict arises, which can then mandate specific actions taken to resolve the conflict. These actions can range from forcing landlords to make needed repairs, to evicting tenants for late payment of rent. The *Regie* also sets a suggested rent increase rate every year based on the rate of inflation. For Roy-Allard, the suggested rent-increase rates are something of a smokescreen. "We have this myth that the *Regie* does rent control," he says, "but really, it's up to the tenant to know their rights and contest abusive increases." Tenants can refuse rent increases, but they need to be aware of that right and how to exercise it.

In place of this system, RCLALQ advocates for a system where landlords would be automatically forced to justify increases above the suggested rate to the *Regie*. The board, in this view, would have a publicly accessible list of all rental prices, updated every year, and if a landlord attempted a significant price hike, they would be required to argue its justification. Such a system, Roy-Allard says, places the burden of justification on landlords rather than tenants—and leaves less room for manoeuvring for landlords who seek to raise rent dramatically.

The *Regie* also mandates that landlords present, upon request, any previous leases to new tenants. This allows the new tenant to see how much the rent has been increased between tenants and to contest any abusive increase. However,

Roy-Allard points out that since tenants must request this information from their potential landlord, it often just leads to landlords simply refusing to rent to people who exercise this right. Instead, RCLALQ argues that there should be a publicly accessible database of all leases in the province, run by the *Regie*, so that tenants could find the information privately without going through their potential landlord (RCALQ 2018).

If these measures were adopted, it would not be the first time that RCLALQ and other tenants' organizations won province-wide reforms from the *Regie*. In 1995, RCLALQ won a long campaign to legally mandate that all landlords use a standardized lease form; previously, they had been drawing the forms up themselves and often included illegal clauses in the lease contract (RCALQ 2018).

The measures that RCLALQ is advocating will undoubtedly relieve some of the pain associated with rapid gentrification and price increases. But Roy-Allard points out that they remain only partial measures and they operate within a context of the private market, a system which "does not respond to the need for a right to housing." In the long term, like FRAPRU, RCLALQ "definitely wants to see the socialization of housing" and its removal from the market.

As Roy-Allard concludes: "the private market doesn't respond—and can never respond—to the need for housing."

REFERENCES

FRAPRU (*Front d'action populaire en réaménagement urbain*). n.d. "Historique."
  https://www.frapru.qc.ca/a-propos/historique/.
Gaudreau, L., Hébert, G., and Posca, J. 2020. "Analyse du Marché de l'Immobilier et de la rentabilité du logement." *Institut de recherche et d'informations socio-économiques*.
  https://cdn.iris-recherche.qc.ca/uploads/publication/file/Logement_2020_WEB.pdf.
Mills, S. 2010. *The Empire Within: Postcolonial Thought and Political Activism in Sixties Montréal*. Montréal and Kingston: McGill-Queens University Press.
RCLALQ (Regroupement des comités logement et associations de locataires du Québec). 2018. *40 ans de luttes pour le droit au logement*. https://rclalq.qc.ca/wp-content/uploads/2019/07/40ans-de-luttes-du-rclalq-pour-le-droit-au-logement.pdf.
RCLALQ. 2020. *La flambée des loyers*. https://rclalq.qc.ca/wp-content/uploads/2020/06/La-flambée-des-loyersVF.pdf.
Saillaint, F. 2018. *Lutter Pour un Toit : Douze batailles pour le logement au Québec*. Montréal: Écosociété.
Stein, S. 2019. *Capital City: Gentrification and the Real Estate State*. New York: Verso Books.
Ville de Montréal. 2017. "Population et démographie." *Montréal en statistiques Service du développement économique*, 14 November 2017. http://ville.montreal.qc.ca/pls/portal/docs/PAGE/MTL_STATS_FR/MEDIA/DOCUMENTS/22_POPULATION ET D?MOGRAPHIE_NOVEMBRE2017_LOGEMENTS_ARROND.PDF

PART VI.

GOVERNING THE CITY

POWER AND CITY HALL

LINDA GYULAI

PROJET MONTRÉAL'S SHIFTING APPROACH TO DEMOCRATIC REFORM

Richard Bergeron was barely six months into his first term as a city councillor in April 2006 when he and several members of Projet Montréal, the political party he had co-founded two years earlier, packed into a rental and drove to Ottawa for the day. Their mentor, André Cardinal, a former councillor with the defunct Montréal Citizens' Movement (MCM), which had instituted democratic reforms while in power from 1986-1994, had suggested the field trip. Bergeron, the only elected member of Projet Montréal, and six members of the party's steering committee would see first-hand how a democratic city functions. The excursion to Ottawa was an opportunity for the Projet Montréal crew to witness the democracy plank of their inaugural platform in action.

The media covering the 2005 municipal election introduced Projet Montréal as an anti-car party—its keystone, a plan to bring back the tramway to Montréal. What was less known was the party's 20-page program for democratic reform (Projet Montréal, 2005). It formed the first chapter of the party's 2005 election campaign platform. It offered to reorganize some of the structures created since the 2002 municipal mergers, but also to enact electoral reform and the kind of governance changes that were long called for by the municipal left yet not promoted by any party in the city in nearly a decade.

For starters, Projet Montréal promised to abolish the city executive committee that met weekly in secret and where the city's power had been concentrated for most of the last century. The cabal, composed of the mayor and about a dozen hand-picked councillors, awarded millions of dollars in city contracts, decided what items went on the agenda of monthly city council meetings, set the city's annual operating budget, and established the allocation to be given to each borough to pay for local citizen services. The resolutions passed by the executive committee were rendered public—but never its discussions.

As an alternative, Projet Montréal proposed the Ontario municipal model of powerful standing committees that formulated all policy orientations at public consultations and brought recommendations directly to the city council for a vote. The committees were divided by theme—e.g., transit, environment, and planning—and involved all council members. A kind of super-committee presided over by the mayor existed, but only to coordinate other panels' work and prepare the city budget through two phases of public consultations each year.

Montréal had standing committees of council, but their recommendations went to the executive committee, where they could be ignored. While Montréal's committees were legally required to hold a minimum of four public meetings a year, in addition to their in-camera sessions, most rarely attained even that low threshold—and with no consequences for failing to do so. Indeed, with more members of council than available committee seats, Montréal mayors tended to use appointments to the extra-remunerated committee posts as a reward or punishment for acts of personal loyalty or betrayal.

The platform also pledged to drag the city into the sunlight by promising to legally require council committees and other bodies to hold all meetings in public. It is illegal for Ontario municipal bodies to meet in-camera, except under a few conditions, like discussing a personnel matter or contract negotiations. In Québec, such bodies routinely met behind closed doors.

Projet Montréal also committed to electoral reform, promising to lobby the province to legislate for proportional representation (PR) to replace Montréal's traditional first-past-the-post system. PR would better reflect the electorate's will and enable all parties to be represented equitably on council, according to the platform. Moreover, it noted a Projet Montréal administration would undertake a "vast popular education campaign" to explain to citizens how PR would make up for the "democratic deficit" in Montréal's electoral system.

Several promises gave citizens a say in municipal decision-making. For example, a Projet Montréal administration would entrench the right of citizen participation in the city charter and extend a new right to citizens to initiate public consultations. It would also create a *"Place citoyenne,"* a forum for citizens to advise elected officials.

The platform also laid out plans to create a council committee on democracy that would launch a public debate on the mechanisms needed for citizen participation. It would also rethink megacity governance, from the division of responsibilities between the city and boroughs to the number of councillors and boroughs. It would also study changes to party financing rules. Another new council committee would verify that contract tendering rules were respected.

Projet Montréal's platform also invoked Cardinal's old MCM with a proposal to establish neighbourhood councils to foster "co-management" between citizens and city councillors. The neighbourhood councils would help prepare a participatory city budget with citizens, among other tasks. The platform also pledged to institute these participatory budgets.

WHAT HAPPENED TO THE PARTY FOUNDERS' MANIFESTO TO STRENGTHEN MUNICIPAL DEMOCRACY?

By 2017, the year Projet Montréal was elected under its new leader Valérie Plante, the party's thoughts on democracy had been whittled down to three pages (Projet Montréal 2017). The 2005 pledge to entrench the right of citizen participation in decision-making in the city charter was gone, as were the neighbourhood councils and other mechanisms of participation. Whereas the 2005 platform had committed to electoral reform and creating a more participatory kind of democracy, the 2017 platform offered an ambiguous promise to "respect the will of Montréalers for any change in the governance or the electoral framework of Montréal."

How were Montréalers supposed to uncover a collective will for change in governance and electoral reform if the city did not offer public education and forums where these issues might be raised and discussed?

A Projet Montréal administration would also "respect the local democratic bodies of borough councils," (Projet Montréal 2017) though without explaining what that meant. The 2005 commitment to institute a participatory budget process became a three-word notation in 2017: "Promote participatory budgets."

And what about the promise to abolish the all-powerful executive committee? It morphed into a pledge to transfer "certain current responsibilities" of the executive committee to council's standing committees. The platform did not specify what responsibilities, and the Plante administration has not ceded any executive committee power since taking office.

The administration has carried through on one promise—city council's public safety committee has organized more public meetings than before.

The contrast between Projet Montréal's first program and the one it ran on in 2017 shows how drastically the party shifted over four elections. The 2005 version defined citizens as "co-managers" of the city with their elected representatives. The 2017 platform treated the citizen as a consumer of municipal services, and as a spectator rather than participant in decision-making. It helps explain why promises in 2017 to improve municipal services were dropped into a chapter purportedly about democracy, with pledges to "ensure that city services are provided to citizens at the nearest location" and "ensure that citizens get quality service and answers to their questions."

The 2017 democracy plank also made several promises to provide information to the public but offered little opportunity for citizens to help shape it. For example, a Projet Montréal administration would "continue and accelerate the sharing of city data" and "continue and accelerate" the internet broadcast of council meetings. The 2017 platform also offered to "enhance the channels for citizen engagement and input on development projects or zoning changes" and to "put in place a pre-consultation process for large-scale real estate projects."

But the Plante administration has not followed through on either promise; neither has it fulfilled another 2017 promise to "encourage the introduction of co-design processes with citizens and users" when building sports, cultural and recreational facilities, parks, and local street development projects.

Whether the battle is over bike paths, roadwork, banning cars on Camillien-Houde Way, or police station closings, Montréalers are voicing the same complaint about Plante as they did with her predecessors: "We weren't consulted."

Nearly 20 years after the municipal mergers, the city is still in the clutches of two long-standing dialectical forces: citizens expecting greater accountability and a say on the issues that affect their daily existence, and political parties with electoral ambitions and no desire to share power.

TRANSPARENCY IS NOT DEMOCRATIZATION

A few measures have been introduced over the past 20 years to make Montréal politics seem more transparent. Among them, opening the city executive committee's weekly meetings to a public audience in 2012 might appear as nothing short of a breakthrough. Overnight, the mayor's "cabinet" went from deciding most business for the island of Montréal behind closed doors to holding large portions of its deliberations in public via webcast.

Who was responsible for forcing the body that symbolized Montréal's long-standing culture of secrecy into the light? Was it a political party with a reform agenda? Or a crusading mayor committed to greater transparency?

No, it was interim mayor Michael Applebaum, seven months before he was arrested on corruption charges. Applebaum was elected interim mayor by his fellow city councillors in November 2012 to replace Gérald Tremblay, who had abruptly resigned amid allegations of corruption surrounding his party. Applebaum's first move was to start broadcasting executive committee meetings online. He then made executive committee meeting agendas publicly available before meetings instead of only afterwards. He also appointed members of the opposition to the executive committee, creating a coalition cabinet.

But transparency is not democratization. Without accountability and participation, transparency is just window-dressing. While the web offers convenient access, the ability to watch meetings online does not replace the democratic experience of debate and interaction between elected officials and citizens.

The open-door policy for executive committee meetings, and the appointment of opposition councillors, remain only gestures since neither has been entrenched in Montréal's constitution, the city charter. Section 29 of the Charter, which is provincial law, still states that "meetings of the executive committee are closed to the public" except when it decides otherwise.

Like the Applebaum measures, most changes initiated by Montréal mayors in the past 20 years were responses to crises, and none were comprehensive governance reforms. Tremblay obtained new powers for the boroughs in 2003 only after defections temporarily cost him his majority on city council. Councillors representing the suburbs-turned-boroughs had quit his party to sit as independents, accusing him of reneging on a promise to remain neutral ahead of the 2004 de-merger referendums. To prevent further departures, Tremblay asked Québec to grant the boroughs additional powers, including control over local hiring. He also convinced Québec to replace the borough chairperson, appointed from among a borough's councillors, with an elected borough mayor; they would have equivalent powers to a municipal mayor, but on borough turf.

In 2013, Denis Coderre campaigned on a promise to create an inspector general to investigate city contracts, as the province was in the grips of a corruption crisis. He appointed Denis Gallant, deputy chief lawyer of the Charbonneau commission, as Montréal's first inspector general. However, real estate transactions and zoning changes, large areas of municipal activity, are not within the inspector general's purview.

Plante was three-quarters of the way through her term when she created an anti-racism commissioner after an *Office de consultation publique de Montréal* (OCPM) report concluded the city had long ignored racism and systemic discrimination by the police and municipal departments. The report, which landed amid global Black Lives Matter protests spurred by the police killing of

George Floyd in Minneapolis, was based on public hearings that the city only held because 20,000 Montréalers had signed a petition legally obligating it to do so.

The province has also fostered a false impression that Montréal's political system has undergone substantive reform, notably with the grand gesture of bestowing the status of metropolis on the city—twice.

In 2008, the provincial government formally recognized Montréal's "special" status as the metropolis of Québec in the city charter and conferred "historic" new taxation powers on the city. Tremblay obtained some cash from the province and powers to tax swimming pools, cars, and other goods and to collect tolls from vehicles entering the island. But the city has made little use of these financial levers. Bridge tolls are costly to implement, and the political price of imposing new taxes is perceived to be higher than the revenue they would generate. So, the city remains dependent on property taxes to fund two-thirds of the municipal operating budget.

In 2016, the province announced it was conferring the status of metropolis on Montréal, apparently forgetting it had already done so. Under an agreement dubbed *"Réflexe Montréal"* negotiated by Coderre, Montréal again obtained some cash and "historic" new powers. The city was granted a right of first refusal, giving it first dibs to acquire private property at market value to create new social housing. The legislation was passed just weeks before Coderre lost the 2017 election. But the power to reserve a pre-emptive bid is only as valuable as the cash available to buy and build. While the city under Plante has registered the right of first refusal on about 300 properties, social housing projects still hinge on available provincial and federal funding.

Of course, the province's legislated mergers of the 28 municipalities on the island of Montréal and in other regions across Québec in 2002 was a major reorganization of municipal structures. But here again, it is worth examining what the shake-up actually changed in the way power is exercised in Montréal. The Parti Québécois government used the pre-merger city's governance system as the template to create the megacity. They added a sub-tier of boroughs with some spending autonomy to deliver local services and with boundaries corresponding to those of the pre-merger suburbs and the administrative districts of the former Montréal.

The creation of boroughs was presented as decentralization, except that the province did not endow the new structures with tools for citizen participation (Cliche and Levy 2005). Moreover, although the boroughs are home to over 85% of the island's residents, they control just 15% of the $6 billion municipal operating budget. Just because borough councils meet closer to their constituents than city council does not mean they are any more willing to listen to residents.

The borough councils operate the same way that city council has since the time of Jean Drapeau, says Marcel Sévigny, a left-libertarian who served as city councillor for Pointe St-Charles for 25 years until the mergers (Sévigny 2009). Councillors nearly always vote along party lines. Citizen participation is left to the discretion of the borough mayor, who chairs the meetings and can rule citizen questions out of order.

The 2006 de-mergers, removing almost half of the island suburbs forced to merge in 2002, led to another stopgap change. The agglomeration council was invented to manage services financed by Montréal and the re-constituted suburbs, such as public transit, police and fire services, wastewater treatment, and regional parks. The council consists of the Montréal mayor, 15 Montréal councillors named by the mayor, and 15 elected representatives from the de-merged suburbs. Votes are weighted according to a municipality's portion of the island population, which gives Montréal's representatives 88%.

Cliche and Levy describe the agglomeration council as an "antidemocratic structure" (Cliche and Levy 2005, 251). Under its baffling operating rules, Montréal city council votes on every agglomeration resolution before the agglomeration council. Montréal's 15 representatives are obligated to vote in favour of any resolution passed by a majority of Montréal city council—even if they had voted against them at Montréal city council.

The Montréal Urban Community (MUC), which managed island-wide services before the mergers, had its shortcomings, but at least it permitted debate and compromise. It was composed of the mayors of Montréal and the suburbs, plus all of Montréal's city councillors. On some MUC resolutions, the suburbs and Montréal were pitted against each other. On others, Montréal opposition councillors aligned with suburban mayors against the mayor of Montréal.

The Québec government has also granted mayoral requests for various amendments. For example, in 2008, the province agreed to Tremblay's wish to give the mayor of Montréal greater control over the economically vital downtown Ville-Marie borough. As a result, the mayor of Montréal is automatically borough mayor of Ville-Marie and appoints two councillors from other boroughs to serve on the Ville-Marie borough council. The anti-democratic nature of the change was evident in Coderre's 2013 victory. He ran a distant third in the popular vote in Ville-Marie, but nevertheless became its borough mayor; *Équipe Denis Coderre pour Montréal* was elected to a minority on city council and failed to win any of the three elected seats in Ville-Marie. Yet Coderre appointed two councillors from his party to join him on the borough council. With three of the six seats on the borough council, Coderre had control of Ville-Marie, because the vote of any borough mayor counts twice when there is a tie.

Montréal's notorious roads offer an analogy for the way its political system has evolved since the mergers. Occasionally, the province provides fresh asphalt to fill potholes on a road built 20 years ago, on top of crumbling infrastructure laid a century ago.

MAYORAL SUPREMACY AND MONTRÉAL'S 'BOSS' POLITICIANS

The piecemeal adjustments have contributed to one substantive change in Montréal's governance that has never been a stated objective: absolute power is concentrated in the mayor's hands. Elsewhere in Canada, mayoral powers are barely defined in provincial legislation. The mayors of the country's biggest cities tend to impose their leadership by force of personality and through the media.

The same could be said of mayors in Québec, except that mayoral supremacy is also a statutory right. The *Cities and Towns Act* declares any mayor in Québec to be "the executive head of the municipal administration." According to section 52, "The mayor shall exercise the right of superintendence, investigation and control over all the departments and officers or employees of the municipality, except the chief auditor." Since it was adopted in the 1970s, the article has been amended to exclude the auditor general from the mayor's purview. As "CEO," the mayor has the right to "lay before the council such proposals as he [sic] may deem necessary or advisable, and shall communicate to the council all information and suggestions relating to the improvement of the finances, police, health, security, cleanliness, comfort and progress of the municipality." The sections are reproduced in the Montréal city charter, where they also apply to borough mayors.

Montréalers have a long tradition of electing "boss" politicians. Just think of Drapeau or Camillien Houde. Tradition has become institutionalized, and lately, it has been reinforced through repeated legislative tweaking.

The most radical changes were introduced at the time of the mergers. The charter of the megacity, adapted from the pre-merger Montréal charter, gave unilateral power to the mayor of Montréal to appoint and remove members of the executive committee. Previously, the mayor's appointments and expulsions required city council ratification. In fact, until 1999, the charter allowed executive committee members to be removed only by death, resignation, or incapacitation. When the courts blocked Pierre Bourque's attempt to fire two members for alleged disloyalty in 1997, he lobbied the province for an amendment to allow removal on the mayor's recommendation.

The mayor's legislated supremacy exposes a certain incoherence in the *Cities and Towns Act* and the city charter since these statutes also uphold the executive committee's century-old pre-eminence. The Montréal executive committee was created in 1921 and was intended, ironically, to introduce a check on the mayor's power. The province had placed the city under trusteeship in 1918 due to over-spending and patronage scandals, and the creation of the executive committee was a necessary condition for the province to end it (Linteau 1992).

Under the city charter and the *Cities and Towns Act*, the executive committee continues to control everything in the city's jurisdiction, including drafting bylaws, the budget, personnel, contracts, and real estate transactions. It prepares whatever is submitted to city council for final approval.

So, Montréal's mayor controls the body that controls most decision-making. Since the de-mergers, the agglomeration council is also controlled by Montréal's executive committee. So, the mayor of Montréal also controls the body that controls all island-wide services. As about half of the reconstituted suburbs' municipal budgets go to the "agglo," it means that a portion of their residents' property taxes, and critical services, are controlled by a mayor they cannot elect. By contrast, the MUC had its own executive committee composed of representatives from Montréal and the suburbs, which was headed by a chairperson elected by a two-thirds majority of the MUC council.

The Montréal mayor's sphere of influence was also extended off-island at the time of the mergers with the creation of the *Communauté métropolitaine de Montréal* (CMM), which oversees regional planning for 82 municipalities. The Montréal mayor is chairperson of the CMM council, names 14 Montréal councillors to the 28-member body and gets a dominant vote.

The executive committee has been likened to a prime minister or provincial premier's cabinet. However, Montréal's political system (unique in Canada) lacks the parliamentary system's checks and balances. It has no provision for a non-confidence vote that would bring down an unpopular city government. Moreover, unlike a prime minister or premier, the mayor of Montréal is elected directly by all voters across the city, more like a U.S. president. Yet a Montréal mayor cannot be impeached or face a recall election like in the U.S. While the president is head of the executive branch of government, enforcing laws enacted by Congress, Montréal's 'presidential' mayor gets to wield executive power and hold sway in the legislative branch as a voting member of the executive committee and city council.

The most important element of reform is that "the mayor of Montréal cease having quasi-dictatorial power" (Cliche and Levy 2005, 262).

Québec's municipal parties are another source of boundless mayoral dominance. In practice, power shifted to the mayor when Drapeau invented the municipal party in 1960. The advent of legislated supremacy notwithstanding, mayors still use party discipline and the financial inducement of discretionary committee appointments to control the executive committee, city council and, indirectly, borough councils.

Plante booted Sue Montgomery, borough mayor of Côte-des-Neiges-Notre-Dame-de-Grâce (CDN-NDG), from Projet Montréal in 2019 when Montgomery refused the order to fire her chief of staff. Montgomery also lost her seats on two council committees. After Julie-Pascale Provost, a Projet Montréal borough councillor in Lachine, voted against her party's plan to convert the Lachine marina into a waterfront park—a decision known to be favoured by Plante but under the jurisdiction of the Projet Montréal-dominated Lachine borough council—she too was expelled from the party and kicked off a council committee. Projet Montréal blamed the councillor's "lack of collaboration and solidarity" for her expulsion.

Arguably, a city can only be as democratically run as the party that is elected to run it. But most municipal parties in Québec are assembled by career political organizers as an election vehicle for a mayoral hopeful rather than by a grassroots base that chooses a leader. As further confirmation, most are branded with their *raison d'être*'s name, as in *Équipe Denis Coderre pour Montréal*, *Équipe Bourque*/Vision Montréal, or *Équipe Labeaume* (the party of the Québec City mayor). Between elections, their function is limited to fundraising.

A few parties have been formed by a common allegiance to principles—notably the MCM and Projet Montréal—or to fight a common enemy—as in the Montréal Island Citizens Union, which came together as a "rainbow" coalition of anti-merger suburban mayors and opposition Montréal councillors to defeat Bourque, the instigator of the mergers. But even municipal parties with a rank-and-file can become allergic to dissenting views and internal policy debates.

Christine Gosselin, a councillor in Rosemont-La Petite-Patrie, said as much when she quit Projet Montréal to sit as an independent in late-2020. Accusing Plante of "retrograde and authoritarian" management of the city and the party, Gosselin said Projet Montréal had become too centralized, discouraged disagreement, and lost its soul.

All the 'tweaks' to the system seem to have devolved into a tale of unintended consequences.

Consider Tremblay's decision to enhance borough powers before the de-merger referendums. The reform created elected borough mayors with ginned-up powers, replacing borough chair-people with no special legislated authority. The changes gave rise to hegemonic battles between city mayors and borough mayors, often over hyper-local matters.

Coderre twice fired the Île-Bizard-Sainte-Geneviève borough director only to have the borough mayor rehire her. Boroughs, after all, are in charge of their personnel since the Tremblay reform. Coderre also obtained a legislative amendment in 2016, making it easier for the city to repatriate borough powers.

Similarly, the epic Plante v. Montgomery battle was sparked by a report from the city's comptroller general concluding that Montgomery's chief of staff had harassed two borough employees. The comptroller general barred the chief of staff from contact with the two employees. Montgomery refused the directive, saying she had not been permitted to see the report. A Superior Court of Québec judge later agreed with Montgomery that the city had overstepped its bounds.

Montgomery's own displays of mayoral supremacy were not easily digested by others. Her adversaries passed borough council resolutions overturning her unilateral decisions, including an edict requiring all their communication with the borough director to pass through her office. Montgomery, in turn, used her mayoral veto to block resolutions passed by the five other members of the CDN-NDG council. The five then overrode her veto by adopting the same resolutions a second time. The tit-for-tat manoeuvres spawned complaints that the borough had become dysfunctional under Montgomery.

However, borough mayoral power was largely uncontroversial before the CDN-NDG case largely because borough councils are usually dominated by one party. In CDN-NDG, no party has a majority. A system of governance should be strong enough to withstand incompatible personalities. The situation in CDN-NDG seems to reveal that the system itself is dysfunctional.

WHERE DOES ALL THIS LEAVE DEMOCRATIC REFORM?

Reasonable minds might conclude the public is consulted less than before. Coderre, for example, imposed a bylaw banning pit bulls without public discussion. And Projet Montréal's long-promised "participatory" budget has been reduced to an anonymous online poll.

Even transparency appears to have taken a step backwards, and not just in Montréal. In early 2021, councillors in different Québec municipalities, including Lachine borough's Provost, founded a coalition demanding transparency called *Cartes sur la table*. They want Québec to adopt Ontario's rules forcing municipal meetings, including caucus meetings, to be open to the public.

But what is required is a rethinking of municipal governance—one that attempts to balance transparency, accountability, and public participation. The only comprehensive reflection on democratic reform in the last 20 years came from Projet Montréal. But even they started backing off long before reaching power.

Cliche, a co-author of the party's 2005 democracy manifesto, questioned whether Projet Montréal still had a "progressive fibre" left when the party dropped electoral reform from its 2013 platform. Still led by Bergeron, the party had gone the way of other social democratic parties, putting electoral success ahead of principle (Cliche 2012). "This objective is far from reprehensible because the seizure of power is the raison d'être of any political party," Cliche wrote, "but it becomes so if, in its upward journey, a formation sacrifices its democratic ideals" (Cliche 2012).

Projet Montréal is not the party it was in 2005. Shortly before the 2017 election, it changed its name to *Projet Montréal-Équipe Valérie Plante*.

REFERENCES

Cliche, P. 2012. "Projet Montréal évacue le scrutin proportionnel." *L'Autre Journal*
Cliche, P., and Levy, A. 2005. "La démocratie à Montréal: toujours dans l'ombre de Jean Drapeau." *Possibles*
Linteau, P-A. 1992. *Histoire de Montréal depuis la Confédération*. Montréal: Les Éditions Bor.
Projet Montréal. 2005. *Refonder la démocratie sur le pouvoir citoyen*, version préliminaire pour discussion et adoption par le Congrès des 10 et 11 septembre.
Projet Montréal. 2017. "Democracy chapter." In *Projet Montréal 2017 Electoral Platform*.
Sévigny, M. 2009. "Et nous serions paresseux?" *Les Éditions Écosociété*.

CONSULTATION, PARTICIPATION, OR POWER: WHAT'S IN IT AND FOR WHOM?

ERIC SHRAGGE

Cities offer the potential of implementing structures that provide citizens—defined to mean all residents—with collective power to shape their daily lives, their neighbourhoods, and to some degree, the city as a whole. How has Montréal done in relation to this possibility? Democratizing the city through the decentralization of power and the involvement of citizens in decision-making is a key urban issue. One that has a long history. Is participation symbolic, or does it actually increase power and control over everyday life?

During the 1968 worker and student rebellions in France, a political poster produced by the *Atelier populaire* of Paris' *Ecole des beaux-arts*, presented a conjugation of the French verb *"participer,"* but concluding with *"ils profitent."* It was a biting critique of state instances that welcomed different forms of participation from citizens but without changing relations of power.

Is it possible to shift these relations?

This chapter reviews some of the histories of these debates in Montréal, and its institutions of participation and consultation with residents, while keeping in mind the critiques presented in the poster from 1968.

We begin with a discussion of the trajectory of these ideas of urban democracy as they evolved over the past 50 years. It will not be a detailed history, but will focus on key directions as they emerged from FRAP (*Front d'action politique*), the MCM (Montréal Citizens' Movement), and later through the Tremblay administration and Projet Montréal.

The key questions underlying the discussion will relate to issues of power and control. Who has it, and how does it influence urban change? What insights can be gathered about local organizing and power in relation to these municipal instances?

FRAP (FRONT D'ACTION POLITIQUE)

During the 1960s in Montréal, activism and organizing were expressed through building local associations on many social issues. Residents and organizers in working-class neighbourhoods established health clinics, tenants' associations, legal aid clinics, youth centres, and welfare rights groups, among others. Many were experiments in direct democracy in which citizens themselves were the decision-makers, determining the direction of the organizations or committees.

Underlying these groups was the idea of building counter-power to the established economic and political order. This counter-power was based on the capacity of these groups to develop four tasks.

The first was organizing and mobilizing residents to collectively challenge power, occasionally causing disruption through actions such as sit-ins and street blockades. Acting collectively to promote their demands was a key element. The second task was to create new forms of social service and economic development. The 1960s were an intense period during which many community clinics and forms of mutual aid were organized, such as food cooperatives and daycares, in addition to a variety of other practices such as advocating for welfare rights and providing housing information services. The third task was to understand the social issues they faced, with a critical analysis of the social and economic forces that created them, leading to a radical analysis of how wealth and power operated within capitalism. Finally, and critically, the organizations and groups identified closely with their neighbourhoods. Localism was an important element; engaging local residents in and around their organizations was a vital component. Local power, based on the collective actions and involvement of citizens, built strength in working-class neighbourhoods throughout the 1960s, with the hope that these organizations and unions working together could build a counter-force to capital.

FRAP, the *Front d'action politique*, was a municipal political party founded in 1969 by those coming out of these neighbourhood associations, and coalitions of groups including trade union activists (Roussopoulos 1982). They had an underlying belief in the common agenda of neighbourhood and workplace struggles. The origins of this radical municipal initiative were based in organized neighbourhoods supported by trade union activists committed to social transformation. This was to be the core element of FRAP and its ideas of decentralized neighbourhood power. Despite its short history, the link between decentralized neighbourhood power, democratic community initiatives, and urban politics was clearly established.

For this brief but intense moment, the notion and the practice of urban democracy were direct and built on locally organized communities. The next iterations became increasingly diluted.

MCM (MONTRÉAL CITIZENS' MOVEMENT)

The founding of the Montréal Citizens' Movement (MCM) before the municipal elections in 1974 continued some of the traditions of FRAP. It was a wider coalition than FRAP, both in terms of the party's base and its ideology. It included not only trade union members, organizers from community groups, and activists from both English and French-speaking communities but also active members of progressive political parties from the provincial and federal levels. One element of continuity from FRAP was a commitment to a decentralized vision of the city, with local decision-making power at the neighbourhood level. However, within the MCM, the role of neighbourhoods and local power was contested. The conflict and positions in the MCM are important because they reflect differing positions on urban democracy and the role of local power.

The initial position of the MCM, adopted at its founding in 1974, argued for the creation of neighbourhood councils. Elections to these councils would be held every two years, would provide a direct link between citizens and their councillors, would have some power over zoning, city permits, and approvals, and be an integral part of the city's administration (Katz and Roussopoulos 2017). The left of the party shaped a new position and promoted the idea that neighbourhood power was part of a more global social struggle:

> Born of struggle of citizens against the deformation of urban life, these neighbourhood councils will bring together the politicized citizens and increasingly enable them to resist the forms in which capital is transforming their neighbourhood... in this way citizens will acquire a taste for and experience in the democratic management of their city... (Roussopoulos 1982, 215).

The vision contained in this perspective revolves around power and contestation. Neighbourhood councils would become the extension of local organizing and give it formal power at the local level. Elements of direct democracy and challenging power are explicit parts of this approach.

If such neighbourhood councils were working today, in Saint Henri, for example, the local council would have much more say over condominium development along the Lachine Canal. It would be able to negotiate more directly the kind of housing built and the community benefits that could be extracted from the developers by signing development agreements with more teeth in them. Such neighbourhood councils would give the local population much more power in shaping the neighbourhood that they want.

After an electoral setback in 1978, the party's left—which had previously succeeded in getting the above position adopted—was pushed to the side. The party then went through a process of adopting a 'pragmatic' approach that they hoped could lead to an electoral victory. In fact, they had to wait eight more years before finally winning a huge majority under the leadership of Jean Doré in 1986.

By the time the MCM was elected, its vision of neighbourhood power was more symbolic, and it defined itself within the traditional parliamentary framework. In addition, locally organized community groups that had formed the core of FRAP and had been at the core of the radical vision of the MCM in the late 1970s, were transformed; many had either disappeared or become more highly professionalized, and the capacity to mobilize and contest power within the urban framework was diminished (see Shragge 2013). Doré and company were able to implement largely symbolic and administrative reforms. "District Advisory Councils" became the means by which certain functions were determined locally, but with ultimate power remaining in the hands of local councillors and bureaucrats. Local councils had the power to hold hearings, but they were largely advisory to the city's executive committee—centralized power that was a hold-over from the Drapeau era.

One small victory during the Doré years was the creation of the *Bureau de consultation de Montréal,* opening the tradition of public consultation in the city. However, it was subsequently closed by Pierre Bourque following the defeat of the MCM in 1994.

The trends from the Doré years left a legacy. First, decentralization was to be limited and framed within clearly defined administrative structures. Power was contained and not to be shared with the wider community. Power remained centralized, with the executive committee controlling decision-making. Similarly, the process of consultation was limited. At the same time, the counter-power of the community movement was not as strong as it was in the 1960s and 1970s, and it did not challenge the limits of these reforms.

The election of Gérald Tremblay in 2001, and the reforms brought in after the merge-demerge debate, opened new structures, with limited decentralization and increased processes of public consultation. The borough system was formalized and extended to decentralize decision-making and local planning. It added the position of borough mayor and opened borough council meetings to the public. Executive power at the borough level is concentrated in the mayor's office, with legislative acts taken by the borough council and not shared with the wider community. At city hall, power remained centralized, with the mayor-appointed executive committee still controlling decision-making. Similarly, the process of consultation was to be limited.

With the creation of the borough structure, opportunities were seized by some boroughs to introduce innovations in housing, forms of local participation, and greening. One example was the implementation of a limited participatory budget under the leadership of Helen Foutopolos, borough mayor in the Plateau during the Tremblay period in the mid-2000s. The three-year capital budget in the borough was opened to a process of resident participation. With technical support from borough staff and guided by an expert in participatory processes, hundreds of residents participated. This resulted in prioritizing allocations of the capital budget for neglected parks rather than a major cultural infrastructure in one neighbourhood. However, some elected officials questioned the process, arguing that their role had been displaced by the participatory process (see Patsias et al. 2016).

Some years later, with the election of Projet Montréal in some central boroughs, more experiments with decentralized borough power were attempted, allowing for more dramatic strategies in neighbourhood greening, prioritizing bikes and pedestrians over cars in transportation decision-making, and others. However, even with these gains, the borough structure as a form of participatory democracy is limited. This is in contrast to the propositions of FRAP and the more radical versions of the MCM, in which representation in urban decentralized structures was broader than just city councillors.

COMMUNITY INITIATIVES

In the past 20 years, urban activists, organizers, and the city itself have all taken initiatives to create opportunities for citizen participation in urban processes to define the direction of the city's development. Between 2001 and 2009, five citizen summits were initiated, led by the Urban Ecology Centre. The last summit, in 2009, attracted more than a thousand participants. These summits were able to attract and influence Montréal politicians, especially Mayor Tremblay.[1] The city also conducted its own summits; the most important one was held in June 2002, after borough-level and sectoral mini-summits, which determined priorities for Montréal. One outcome of this summit was the introduction of the Office of the Ombudsman that same year, which was mandated to investigate complaints of Montréalers.

The Taskforce on Democracy, an attempt to institutionalize democratic rights, was also launched in 2002. After meeting for two years, it succeeded in proposing the Montréal Charter of Rights and Responsibilities, which was adopted by the city and came into force on 1 January 2006.[2] The Charter outlines the city's commitment to participation, human rights, dignity, diversity, inclusion, social justice, equality, sustainable development, and respect for the environment. Importantly, the Charter allows for a citizen-initiated referendum, which mandates the *Office de consultation publique de Montréal* (OCPM) to conduct hearings on a given question. The Charter and the Office of the Ombudsman—which offers "the only available recourse to ensure the respect" of the Charter, according to their website—both formally redefined the relationship between the city and its residents and opened up some possibilities for urban democracy and citizen participation. However, they can be seen as largely symbolic unless they are made part of wider, broad-based campaigns for change.

The most significant change that has allowed direct participation of citizens is the OCPM:

> The OCPM was established in 2002, following the report of the commission chaired by Mr. Ge´rald Tremblay, which had been given a mandate by the Bourque administration to consult Montréalers on the urban planning consultation policy. The report underscored the importance of establishing an independent mechanism in Montre´al, in accordance with the rules of the art and relevant ethics, to structure public debate concerning projects of metropolitan scope. That mission was written into section 75 of the city charter, allowing the Office to carry out mandates entrusted to it by the Montre´al

---

1. Mayor of Montréal from 2002-2012.
2. Not to be confused with the Charter of Ville de Montréal, c-11.4, which defines the powers of the city.

executive committee and city council by making any relevant recommendations to elected officials following its consultations (OCPM 2017).

The OCPM builds on earlier initiatives to develop links between citizens and the municipal government, including the consultation on the redevelopment of the Old Port in 1985 and the creation of *Bureau de consultation de Montréal* in 1989, among other initiatives. There are many other examples of public participation and a wide range of issues pursued in these consultations. They range from the redevelopment of housing in Benny Farm to the proposed improvements of Percival Molson Stadium and the large-scale general discussion over the direction of the city in 2002—the *"Dialogue sur la vision et les grands plans – Sommet Montréal."*

Examples of citizen-initiated consultations that evoked the power in the Montréal Charter include one on urban agriculture (in 2012) and one on fossil fuel dependency (in 2015), which mobilized support from thousands of Montréalers. However, this last one was short-circuited by Mayor Denis Coderre[3] when he mandated that the OCPM conduct the consultation.

I will use the recent public consultation on systemic racism—the third and last one that evoked the "Right of Initiative" in the City Charter—as an example of both the potential and the problems of these processes. The OCPM's commission of systemic racism is both timely—it was released during the Black Lives Matters protests in the Spring of 2020—and because it was a response to a process of community mobilization. A group of community activists, led by Balarama Holness, launched a petition calling for a public consultation on the question of systemic racism, with the intent to use the Charter mechanism. The petition was signed by 22,000 people and was submitted to the *Service du greffe* in August 2018.[4] The city's executive committee subsequently mandated the OCPM to undertake the public consultation, which ran from August 2018 to December 2019. The group that initially organized the petition challenged the initially narrow mandate as crafted by the executive committee. The mandate was subsequently broadened to include an intersectional approach. This was meant to address issues like the necessity of a city framework on racism and systemic discrimination, employment in municipal services, racial disparities in employment and income, the need for the integration of racialized youth into municipal employment, and issues such as racial profiling, support for community services, access to housing, and support for culture. The public hearings and submissions drew an impressive 7,086 participants. It is clear that the demand for, and the actual consultation itself, was an opportunity to mobilize both

---

3. Mayor of Montréal from 2013-2017.
4. Of the 22,000 signatures received, 16,700 were validated; this is much higher than the number required.

younger and older members of racialized communities and also the many organizations concerned with these issues. There is an important potential with this process, creating a strong voice challenging the city to move forward on questions of systemic racism.

The OCPM released its report, *Racisme et discrimination systémiques dans les compétences de la Ville de Montréal*, on 3 June 2020, amid the large-scale demonstrations in Montréal and worldwide in response to the murder of George Floyd. The report is both broad and comprehensive, but as the title suggested, it is circumscribed by the city's limited powers. The report acknowledges the city's non-recognition of systemic racism and discrimination. It also raises the particular racism faced by Indigenous peoples in the city. The themes it raises and its recommendations cover many issues, including employment in the city, racial and social profiling—particularly by the police—culture, urban planning and housing, land use, and participation in city hall.

The city responded quickly. Like many governments—except the provincial government of Québec—it acknowledged systemic racism exists and appointed Cathy Wong, an executive committee member, to lead the fight against racism. In an interview with CBC News, Wong said that she is working on an "ambitious plan," which would include hiring targets for visible minorities and anti-discrimination training for city managers, "making sure that in every level and in every service, we talk about racism and discrimination" (CBC News 2020). She has committed the city to create an action plan and move forward rapidly. The city followed by announcing in October 2020 that it will hire a commissioner with three employees tasked with fighting systemic racism. One of the employees will be tasked with tackling the issue of racial profiling by the police. The process of consultation and the subsequent report raised substantial challenges and presented recommendations that, if realized, will make a difference. The city's first steps acknowledge the systemic nature of racism. In January 2021, the city selected Bochra Manai, a long-time community organizer and activist, as commissioner for the fight against racism and systemic discrimination.

However, as always, the 'devil is in the details.' For example, can the city intervene in housing, urban planning, and land use to make a difference? Can it hire more racialized minorities? These are not easy questions given the vested interests of property owners and landlords on the one hand and collective agreements with decentralized hiring processes on the other. One major challenge is to control the ongoing conflict between the police and racialized communities and bringing some degree of control and accountability to the SPVM (*Service de police de la Ville de Montréal*).

Will the groups that effectively mobilized to demand the consultation, which then pressured the city to redirect its mandate and subsequently showed up to present briefs to the OPCM in such vast numbers, now continue the campaign? Or will the responsibility be passed to the city politicians and bureaucrats to implement the recommendations of the report? Will they see the OCPM report and the city's initial response as the first steps and continue to monitor, critique, and pressure the city to move forward? Or will they now demobilize, assuming the city will follow through on its commitments?

The lesson from history is that without continued activism and pressure directed at both elected officials and city departments, the demands and initial energy of the mobilization will disappear into the maze of bureaucracy. Importantly, the principal weakness of the OCPM process is that while there is a promise to listen to citizens, there is no promise to act on the recommendations.

The above process reflects contemporary forms of activism. The process combines mobilization using social media but without building ongoing organizations or structured coalitions of existing organizations. The leadership around such moments are individuals who can be described as 'entrepreneurial activists.' At best—as shown in the process leading up to the consultation on systemic racism—there was a high level of success in initiating and mobilizing impressive participation. But since there is little over-arching organizing process that can develop a functioning structure over the longer term, the power of the initial process is dissipated and lost.

Projet Montréal's initial response to the OCPM report was positive but restrained within the boundaries of its mandated activities. What happens if the response slows or if Projet Montréal loses the next election? If there is no organization on the ground with accountable leadership, there will not be the power to influence an ongoing process. Holness, who led the initial push, has political ambition. He may be elected in this November's municipal election and could work to represent the movement within city hall, but as a consequence, could further demobilize the base. The issues are far too important to be left in the hands of political figures, regardless of their personal commitments. Ongoing organization and pressure are the only means of moving this issue, and others, forward.

WHERE DO WE GO FROM HERE?

I would like to add a personal anecdote to contrast and question the role that boroughs and structured consultation play in effecting positive change within the city. In the mid-1970s, I was involved with a coalition of neighbourhood organizations in Pointe-Saint-Charles, Verdun, and NDG (Notre-Dame-de-Grâce). One of the campaigns was the demand for 20 mph zones in front of schools and parks. The primary concern was safety, which could be addressed by slowing traffic. Local actions were organized in each of the neighbourhoods. Joint actions were also undertaken, including an occupation of city hall and the city-owned (at that time) restaurant on (then) St Helen's Island. The latter action led to a meeting and direct negotiation with the vice-chair of the city's executive committee, Yvon Lamarre. The city introduced the reform shortly after that meeting. Clearly, the power of organizing was played out through direct confrontation and negotiation.

What would have happened if a similar campaign were launched today? The borough would have entertained questions during the appropriate question periods, as would city council. There might be some kind of response—or not—depending on the borough. There could be a public consultation if there were enough signatures gathered, though this would have taken time. Even if the city were to be in favour of the demands, the subsequent report may or may not be adopted.

The impact of this process does two things. First, it leads to demobilization. It is difficult to sustain a citizen-led campaign through bureaucratic processes and long periods of waiting. Participation in the borough council and OCPM tends to favour 'professionals' who represent the community rather than citizens themselves. The growing complexities of intervention do not favour broad-based mobilization and direct action and generally acts to demobilize local communities. Second, the structures of the borough council and the consultation processes act to shield decision-makers from meeting directly with citizens and being accountable directly to them.

Put bluntly, because of this, the final report of any public consultation must be treated as the very beginning of the fight for change at city hall, drawing material not only from the recommendations of the report but also from the most powerful and articulate briefs that are submitted. Sometimes, the clearest articulations and solutions during a consultation are drowned out in the sea of words generated. These can be amplified and weaponized post-consultation in the political process, if and only if there is an organization to carry them. The process put in place by the city has acted as a mobilization-demobilization process. The process acts at the beginning to raise hopes of citizen power, but the outcomes tend not to fulfill that hope. There should be lessons about how power operates in this process, but the initial energy does not necessarily lead to organized power to shape the city.

Progress on the formal, public participation processes in Montréal's municipal government has increased over the past decades. The OCPM, borough councils, city ombudsman, question periods during city council meetings, and the live-streaming of council meetings, as well as the opening of executive committee meetings to the public, have all been celebrated as transforming urban democracy, making it more transparent, and giving residents of the city a greater voice in shaping urban policies and issues.

But with all these opportunities to participate, have we really altered things fundamentally? *Ils profitent toujours.*

How can we analyze the situation and what actions should we advocate? The first issue is the question of power: who has it and how does it operate? To discuss this question, we need to analyze how citizen power is generated and how it can operate in an urban context dominated by finance capital and the limited powers of the municipal government.[5]

Collective action in a variety of forms, including mass mobilization, community and labour organizing, and coalition-building, is the basis of urban opposition and the promotion of agendas of change. In Montréal, housing, environmental, women's and neighbourhood organizations have been the major forces in promoting alternative policies. The instances of public participation create strategic opportunities for these movements and organizations to promote their agendas and to hold politicians accountable. However, the formal structures such as borough councils and the OCPM, in and of themselves, are not accountable to citizens. In the case of the borough councils, participation is limited to question periods and no further.

Similarly, with the OCPM, groups and movements can petition for consultation and can participate in processes related to new developments, but recommendations from the OCPM are only that: recommendations. Ultimately, elected officials and the executive committee of the city have the power to make the decisions. The executive committee is not even required to follow up on OCPM recommendations, and they rarely do.

We have to continually return to the questions raised in the introduction of this book: who has power, and how does it operate? Who ultimately makes decisions, and who has real influence in the processes of urban development? What is the role of groups who are traditionally excluded, and how can they organize themselves? Under what conditions can local power be amplified and maximized? Are the instances described in this chapter merely symbolic, or can they be used to bring about social and economic change that benefit residents of local communities and a social-economic and green agenda that does not work in the interests of developers and capital?

Two key elements must be in place. The first is active and organized citizen movements and organizations that can push for their issues. The borough councils, OCPM, and city council only represent stops on the road and never the end of the journey. They can increase pressure, force public debate, and present alternatives, but they guarantee nothing.

The processes of organizing and mobilizing are ongoing, and that is the

5. See further discussion in the introductory chapter on Power and the City.

means to build power. In addition, while a more environmentally and sympathetic government in city hall is a potential ally, it cannot be the answer in and of itself. Municipal governments face enormous pressures from capital and related interests, who are also trying to shape the city. Ongoing organizing and pressure are needed to counter the forces of capital; consultation and participation have to be seen as merely a tactic in a longer-term strategy.

REFERENCES

CBC News. 2020. "Cathy Wong to lead Montréal's effort to curb racism, discrimination." 17 June 2020. https://www.cbc.ca/news/canada/montreal/cathy-wong-montreal-executive-committee-racism-diversity-1.5615504.

Katz, S., and Roussopoulos, D. 2017. "At the Crossroads of Cultures: The Distinct Politics and Development of Montréal." In *The Rise of Cities*, edited by D. Roussopoulos. Montréal: Black Rose Books, pp. 35-91.

OCPM (Office de consultation publique de Montréal). 2017. *S'approprier la ville-les cahiers de l'OCPM participation sans exclusions: Rétrospectives des 15 ans de l'OCPM*. https://ocpm.qc.ca/sites/ocpm.qc.ca/files/pdf/publications/fr/encart_-_15eme_anniversaire_de_l039ocpm-fr.pdf.

Patsias, C., Latendresse, A., and Bherer, L. 2013. "Participatory Democracy, Decentralization and Local Governance: the Montréal Participatory Budget in the light of 'Empowered Participatory Governance.'" *International Journal of Urban and Regional Research* 37(6): 2214-2230. doi.org/10.1111/j.1468-2427.2012.01171.x

Roussopoulos, D. 1982. "Introduction: from then to now." In *The City and Radical Social Change*, edited by D. Roussopoulos. Montréal: Black Rose Books, pp. 11-34.

Shragge, E. 2013. *Activism and Social Change: Lessons for Community Organizing*. 2nd ed. Toronto: University of Toronto Press.

PART VII.

SOCIAL JUSTICE AND THE CITY

CHALLENGING POLICING IN MONTRÉAL: AN INTERVIEW WITH ROBYN MAYNARD

ROBYN MAYNARD

An interview between the Editors and Robyn Maynard

The Black Lives Matter movement has been the stimulus for organizing in Montréal and beyond. What are your thoughts on the state of this organizing and mobilization?

We are living in a really exciting time, one marked by stunning possibilities. The thunder of the #DefundThePolice movement and the broader abolitionist thrust of organizing in Montréal and across North American cities is exhilarating to witness, even over and against the backdrop of the enduring and overlapping crises of the pandemic, policing/incarceration, and racial capitalism.

But the political terrain has shifted, and the demands have become more precise: an agreement is being forged in our streets and communities, that yes, we need to end police violence now and in the long-term. But what this looks like—the "how" of ending police violence—has become more nuanced. That is to say, that in these times, it is understood that to end police violence, we need to end policing as a practice, an institution, and as a central way of organizing society.

So, the wording matters: the shift across mass movements from demanding justice, more abstractly, toward the specificity of the #DefundThePolice demand is significant. And of course, I, being one of many voices in a growing refrain, have continued to re-iterate, the demand to *defund the police* is part of a broader strategy to abolish the police, to abolish prisons, and the kind of society that requires them.

Social movements—everyday people—have succeeded in de-naturalizing (at least!) the long-standing presumption that policing is a natural, normal, and inevitable way to manage society. That is to say, the long-standing presumption that policing is, and should remain, a legitimate way to manage the *people* who dominant classes have deemed unruly.

I live in Toronto now, but I have spent, until recently, most of my adult life in Montréal. Being away, it's been surreal witnessing the birth and ongoing expansion of the Defund the Police Coalition, made up of 57 community groups, including so many organizations I've been a part of over the years: Stella, Head and Hands, Black-Indigenous Harm Reduction Alliance, BLM-Montréal, and Justice for Victims of Police Killings.[1]

Right now, people are taking the struggle to new levels: an organized, critical, and brilliantly executed campaign to #DefundTheSPVM. I've been so inspired by Black queer radical organizers like Marlihan Lopez of BLM-Montréal, Frankie Lambert of AQPSUD (*Association Québécoise pour la promotion de la santé des personnes utilisatrices de drogues*), and so many more, demanding an end to criminalization—the criminalization of sex work, of drug use, of poverty; the criminalization of Black, Indigenous, mad, and disabled life! And highlighting, crucially, the need for non-police-based supports.

These demands are making invaluable interventions into the political climate of the city!

This work, and that of the entire coalition, is part of this cross-city, cross-border abolitionist movement and is drawing attention to the ongoing racial and gendered violence that is constitutive of policing. And, at the same time, it is building real power in and across communities to insist that those who have been subject to what Gilmore calls "organized abandonment" in the city—Black, Indigenous, migrant, sex working, and drug-using communities—collectively deserve better.

What is just as exciting is how many Montréal residents currently recognize the importance of this demand and the movement behind it. A recent Ipsos Reid poll found that 57% of Montréalers surveyed favour defunding the police.

Of course, it has been difficult to see this work be deliberately ignored or undermined, even by those who are nominally understood to be "leftists" or "racial justice advocates." It shows how the power of police and police unions have left us with deeply compromised leadership across the political spectrum.

Because, despite the popularity of the #DefundThePolice movement, no

---

1. For more information, including a full list of organizations involved in the Defund the Police Coalition, see https://www.defundthespvm.com/contact

one in the city government supports this effort. Valérie Plante and Projet Montréal have failed to take an ethical position on a campaign that could have significant material impacts on marginalized populations in the city. Similarly, self-styled "racial justice" advocate Alain Babineau, an ex-police officer working at CRAAR (Center for Research-Action on Race Relations), spent the last year trying to discredit Black Lives Matter organizing and working to undermine the #DefundThePolice movement.

And he has now been employed to advise the city's new commission on racism and policing. Those who have chosen to double down on injustice in the wake of a global movement for Black lives will not be remembered kindly when we look back on the who, what, and how of this moment of racial reckoning.

Can you provide some context on the history of policing and Black communities in Montréal, based on the research you published in *Policing Black Lives*?

Absolutely. Multiple studies show us that Black communities are subject to intense profiling in this city. It's important to remember that it is not only police killings that are violent: policing itself is violent.

When I used to work with Black youth, in my capacity at Head and Hands and as a co-founder of Project X^2—a group that we created about a decade ago to support Black and racialized young people in NDG around police harassment and profiling—one of the main issues that Black teenagers brought up was that whether they were walking to school, playing basketball in the park, or just waiting for the bus with a few friends, the police would stop them, question them, and sometimes force them to separate, under the pretext that they were "under suspicion of being a gang."

This was not an occasional occurrence: the experience of being policed is part of the fabric of everyday Black life in the city.

Police and media continually work together to whip up hysteria to justify the profiling of Haitian, Jamaican, and other Black teenagers as "gang members," as perpetrators of violence, as threats to "everyday" people. This has been happening for decades, even though these are the people who are measurably being targeted for harm in the form of police stops, arrests, and jail time.

As I described in my book, a 2002 study highlighted how in 1996, the Montréal police force (SPVM; *Service de police de la Ville de Montréal*) declared over a thousand teenagers, including Jamaican, Haitian, "Asiatic," and Latino youth, as an "organizational priority" (Symons 2002, 117). I noted, too, that the communities chosen as a *priority* by law enforcement—a priority to target for

2. I am no longer a part of Project X but they continue to do important work in NDG.

surveillance repression, that is—has little to do with the reality of incidences of what is called crime and even less to do with harm. Instead, this is about a pro-active choice to profile particular populations of young people, and anti-Blackness is central to this choice.

In 2010, *Le Devoir* reported that the SPVM's own documentation had found that street gangs made up less than 2% of reported crime in the preceding year (Myles 2010). But they had spent the prior decade massively intensifying and proactively policing possible "street gang" involvement in neighbourhoods like Montréal-Nord and Saint-Michel. A 2009 study showed that police stops had risen 91-126% between 2001 and 2007 (Charest 2009). Around 40% of young Black males had been stopped and carded in just one year (2006-2007), as compared to 5% of young white males! As I wrote in *Policing Black Lives*:

> [T]he fabricated profile of young Black people as possible dangerous gang members allowed for entire Black neighbourhoods to be militarized by near constant police surveillance… The ongoing scrutiny of Black life practised by law enforcement—and the cataloguing the Black population into massive law enforcement databases—has significant impacts on the psychological well-being of Black communities. It must be seen, and addressed, as a form of state violence (Maynard 2017).

So, we can see that policing is always violent, with acts of violence and killings that disproportionately impact our communities and are among the most acute and egregious on the spectrum of what Black communities are continually exposed to. The global #DefundThePolice movement is based on an understanding of police and policing as a form of violence, and working to diminish the scale and scope of this violence; to build safer communities for all of us.

You have previously written about the importance of grounding our analysis within a historical perspective on resistance to racism; can you elaborate on this perspective, and more specifically, as it relates to Montréal?

Funnily enough, living in a place where one of the official mottos is *"je me souviens"* (I remember), the commitment to memory is selective, and partial.

As the great Haitian historian Michel-Rolph Trouillot has famously reminded us, power silences certain voices from the annals of history: some of us have to fight to be remembered. "Any historical narrative," he writes, "is a bundle of silences" (Trouillot 1995, 27).

These silences are often intentional: they are being reproduced every day.

For example, when I was organizing the book launch for *Policing Black Lives*, we had to move it to the *Bibliothèque Nationale*, because there were so many confirmations. My excitement about the launch was tempered, though, when I received a phone call from the librarian booking the event, expressing a desire to cancel. They thought, she had noted, that they had booked an event for a book about *history*. They did not want to hold an event that centred, in her words, on *"la cause de noires."* What was palpable, between these words, of course, was discomfort with a less palatable local history and the concomitant desire to keep it obscure, and obscured.

We fought back, of course. I patiently explained that the history of slavery, the long-standing and ongoing legacy of police brutality against Black residents of Montréal, this too, was *real* history. It is Montréal's history, and Québec's history, and Canada's history, far more than it is my history, or "Black history."

It is not *Black* institutions, after all, which were responsible for organized racial subjugation and violence. After some pushback, the event went on. But I will never forget this exercise in authority over whose stories, which carefully curated parts of history, are allowed to be seen as legitimate. It was a real-time display of the ongoing silencing of Black women's voices, the attempt to shutter our scholarship from the annals of "real" history, and one that I will not forget anytime soon.

I also think that movement histories always have a lot to teach us about where we are going, and where we have been before. We need to work harder to document these histories. Part of this, to me, is an ethical necessity: working to counter the ongoing institutional erasure that we are subject to, as I have just highlighted.

Remembering movement histories, remembering purposefully and with intention, is one way of responding to the way that political leaders and the media like to freeze us in the present. In this view, there is no history either to our work or to our political and intellectual traditions. This erasure serves a political function, of course.

Firstly, it helps make our movements appear to be less credible, less grounded, more reactive. Secondly, the erasure also makes it possible to maintain a kind of plausible deniability, one that allows those in power to cling to the illusion of innocence. Because, if our communities are only just now, for the first time, raising the issue of the egregious harms we experience at the hands of the SPVM, then political leaders can feign surprise! They can act as if no one, in particular, is to blame; they can commit to "studying the issue" rather than taking action (as if there are not already decades of buried reports that have shown us, time and time again, the situation of ongoing brutality against our communities).

But of course: *we have been here before.*

Black communities *have been* waging organized and spontaneous protests against police violence, police killings, and other forms of ongoing racial violence at the behest of the state. This has been the case since at least the mass Black protests of the 1960s dubbed "the Sir George Williams Affair," documented so well in *Let the N*ggers Burn!* And in the streets, too, demanding better for our communities. Black feminists like Brenda Paris, and so many others, took part in Black community organizing after Anthony Griffin (who was just a teenager) was killed in 1987.

And of course, keeping some account of movement history has a lot to teach us about the present; it keeps us from making missteps.

I'll share an example that highlights what I mean. We are probably aware of what just happened in Minnesota: a police officer named Kim Porter killed 20-year-old Dante Wright, the Black father of an infant child. It should be noted that Porter, as it was reported, began yelling "taser, taser" all the while reaching for and firing her gun on Wright.

Of course, it has since been addressed by critics that a taser feels and looks nothing like a gun. So, of course, the notion that this killing could have been an "error" is a ludicrous proposition.

But what I want us to remember is that even if she had reached for her taser, *this would still have been an egregious act of racist violence*. And an act that very well could have been deadly.

Tasers are in-and-of-themselves violent weapons that can kill. And we know this because, in part, of Montréal legacies of anti-police organizing—and specifically Black families' struggles against policing. These histories have a lot to show us about the Porter case. In 2007 in Montréal, a Haitian man named Quilem Registre was killed by the police: he was tasered six times during a traffic incident in Saint-Michel.

The taser is hardly an innocuous weapon. The killing—and it was that, a killing—led to a massive pushback against the use of tasers that was led by Quilem's father, mother, and his sister Francine. Their struggle was part of a broader struggle against policing and police killings in the city over the years to come. His family became increasingly vocal in demanding an end to the use of tasers, highlighting that tasers are, in fact, deadly weapons in and of themselves. This was partly in response to then-mayor Gerard Tremblay, who had recently articulated that *more* police officers should carry tasers to avoid police killings.

If we are not careful, the ruling class will continue to sell us these types of "reforms" that expand, rather than reduce, the arms, scope, and militarization of the police. Surrounding tasers, in fact, we continue to hear officials around the country make this claim. Yet, the Registre family's struggle should not be in vain. As I said, we have been here before, if only we care to look. This is part of Black Montréal organizing history that can help us to create a more liveable space.

Going back further, Delice Mugabos's invaluable research brought out the organizing of Also Known as X (AKAX) and Black organizing in Montréal in the 1990s, where you had a thousand member-strong organization working against policing in Côte-des-Neiges.

Concordia professor Ted Rutland, right now, is looking into policing and the organizing against it in 1980s Montréal. This is crucial work. So often, for many of us here in Montréal, these histories are cut off and hidden from us, even from many of us involved in movement work.

Like all cities across North America mired in anti-Blackness, such erasure is critical to reproducing anti-Blackness across our state and cultural institutions.

So, it becomes imperative for us to continually draw upon and hold up these histories. Movement history helps us to come up against a framing of perpetual newness, in which each violent act against one of our community members is seen as ahistorical, a shock.

The narrative of perpetual surprise and novelty is still powerful.

Can you speak, from your own experience, about how earlier forms of organizing against police in Montréal informs or anticipates the defunding work that we see today?

I am happy to share here, although, of course, memory is always partial: I hope others will, in time, fill in anything I may have missed.

Before the #BlackLivesMatter movement, the period of 2005 into the early-mid 2010s was the last time there was a powerful crescendo of organizing around police killings in Montréal. This was a period of robust community response by movements, marked by strong collective labour and the presence of the families of loved ones killed by police.

In 2005, Mohammed Anas Bennis was shot twice and killed by a police officer, Constable Yannick Bernier. His sister began to mobilize, supported by what became the Coalition for Justice for Anas Bennis.

In 2007, as I'd mentioned earlier, we saw the family response to the killing of Quilem Registre. Things really began to shift in the public life of the city in the summer of 2008, when a Latino teenager, Fredy Villanueva was killed by SPVM officer Jean-Loup Lapointe, and two other teenagers were shot and injured. All of this simply because they were playing dice in the park in Montréal-Nord. This horrific act of violence against racialized young people led to a mass uprising in Montréal-Nord—what some described as a "riot."

This groundswell—this refusal to accommodate the police's war on Black and racialized communities—led to the creation of neighbourhood-based racial justice organizations such as Montréal-Nord Republik (MNR),[3] and

---

3. See chapter by Mehreen, Poncana, and Prosper in this book for more on MNR

indelibly disrupted the city's (manufactured) public identity as a place free from the racism that plagues, for example, the U.S. and France.

Montréal-Nord, which is home to one of Montréal's largest Black populations, is a gorgeous community rich with cultural production, home to an incredible array of Haitian and West African musicians and artists, cultural and community workers, and poor and working-class people of all stripes who are essential to the functioning of the city.

Yet, due to rampant economic discrimination in the city and province and ongoing police surveillance and harassment, it had been under enormous pressure from both state violence and state neglect in the years preceding Fredy's murder by the police. His killing became emblematic of the routinized violence and humiliation that police had been waging against the city's Black and migrant populations. And so, these uprisings became a cornerstone that breathed new life into anti-police organizing in a variety of ways across the city. After Fredy was killed, for example, the police collaborated with CBSA (Canada Border Services Agency) to begin a process of trying to deport his brother, Dany Villanueva (who had witnessed his brother's killing), to Honduras—a country he had not to been since he was a child.

This led to a confluence between migrant justice and anti-police organizing in the city, and I was working along with members of No One Is Illegal, *la Coalition contre la répression et les abus policiers* (CRAP), and *le Collectif opposé à la brutalité policière* (COBP) to fight against Dany's deportation.

At the same time, we launched a campaign against the "double punishment" of racialized migrants and drew attention to the police profiling of Black and racialized communities as a direct line to our community's deportation from the country. This kind of campaign was relatively rare at the time, where many North American cities' migrant justice movements continued to fight for regularization with the message that "migrants are not criminals."

We took a different approach out of necessity. What about the migrants that are, in the eyes of the law, "criminals"? Some migrants are *criminalized* (criminalization itself is a violent and racist process), and we can't support all of our community members unless we critique both the police *and* a racist immigration system.

This was also an era where the city was rife with artistic and cultural interventions against the police, highlighting the ongoing killings of our community members. In 2009, some people came together to do a street-art-based memorial for Montréalers killed by the police in an anonymous public art project against policing, called *"flics assassins"* (killer cops).[4] The project used stencil art to intervene into the way that the deadliness of policing was continually erased in the city.

---

4. You can still see some of this at the website flics-assassins.wordpress.com.

Street art went up in one night; stencils spray-painted with the names of the deceased and the insignia *"tué par la SPVM"* (killed by the Montréal police), but with the SPVM logo altered so that a gun was placed on top of it (see the image below). The stencils were placed as close as possible to the places where people had been killed. In the end, approximately 40 sites went up commemorating residents killed by the police. They became temporary sites of mourning, collective loss, and rage, placed in locations of violence that are always haunting our city but held out of sight.[5]

Here is an image of where Anthony Griffin was killed in 1987—where he was killed by the SPVM.

5. It was put together, using the research assembled by COBP that documented the over 40 people killed between 1987-2008.

This next image was taken in the park where Fredy Villanueva was killed (which organizers and his family are still working to have renamed Fredy Villanueva Park).

Another valuable organizing moment was the Forum Against Police Violence and Impunity, which took place in 2010. This served as a kind of fulcrum of anti-police organizing at the time: it brought together a wide assortment of communities impacted by, and working against, policing across the city. Participants included Black and Filipino/a community youth organizations, drug users, sex workers, migrants, and family members of people killed by the police, to name just a few.

In many ways, this historical event can be seen as a precursor to the present-day abolitionist coalition-based organizing that is happening in a variety of ways. The forum was organized on a minimal budget, put together by mostly Black and racialized organizers, with the support of various grassroots campaigns in Montréal and beyond.

While the event was mostly intended to link various local grassroots struggles, we also invited Brooklyn-based Sista II Sista because of their powerful abolitionist skills. We wanted them to share lessons in their much-lauded work building up grassroots neighbourhood responses to domestic violence that worked explicitly on a politic of no police involvement.

The work of Sista II Sista addressed the "ways we can empower our communities to create our own structures of accountability and justice, while dealing with issues of violence without resorting to the state and the police." Organizing against domestic violence while working *against* police and policing; we knew we all had something to learn from this praxis. And so we fundraised in order to be able to do so.

The forum featured a panel titled *"No justice no peace*—Why people leave the police." Three ex-police officers who went into the police thinking they could be the change, Gaby Pedicelli, Marcel Sévigny, and Will Prosper, spoke about how their lives as police, or officers in training, led them to understand the role of police more accurately in society, and the need to leave policing entirely and become organizers and activists.

Gaby, who had attended police training with the intention on "being one of the good ones," realized the impossibility of being a 'good' officer when the entire structure was violent. She went on to write a fabulous book about the experience.

Ellen Gabriel, then-executive director of the Native Youth Sexual Health Network, along with Jessica Yee, of the South Asian Women's Community Centre, and organizers with sex workers organization *Stella, l'amie de Maimie*, spoke at a workshop about the gendered nature of police violence.

There was also a panel that I facilitated that brought together different youth organizations to discuss ways to fight the criminalization of young Black and racialized people in Montréal's neighbourhoods. I am going into such detail here because it shows us at once the multiple ways that policing enacts harm on different marginalized populations across the city, as well as, I think, the kaleidoscopic horizon of what abolition needs to look like.

The most critical part of the forum, though, was a panel that brought together the family members of victims of police killings, called "Never again! Families speak out against police killings and impunity."

The panel featured Bridget Tolley, an Algonquin great-grandmother from Kitigan Zibi, whose mother was killed by the *Sûreté du Québec* (SQ) in 2001, Francine Registre, the sister of Quilem Registre, Julie Matson, daughter of Ben Matson who was asphyxiated by the Vancouver police in 2002, Lilian Villanueva, Fredy's mother, and Najlaa Bennis, the mother of Anas Bennis, who was killed in 2005. It was facilitated by Nargess Mustapha from Montréal-Nord Republik.

The family members of people who the police had killed shared with one another and with the audience the ways that their loved ones were demonized by the police and media, and blamed for their own deaths afterwards; how difficult it was for them to learn even the basic facts about the last moments of their loved ones' lives. They shared, too, how even public inquiries or coroner's inquests that they had had to fight for—and not all of them had even been able to have these—were often, in fact, weaponized against families and used to demonize those they were grieving. They told one another, and those of us in the audience, about the multiple ways they had been punished for their calls for justice for their loved ones.

Their words and the stories they shared, and the kindness and solace they offered one another, though many had only just met for the first time, demonstrated what mutual aid and grassroots heroism can look like.

Afterwards, the family members expressed a desire to continue to organize together, to support one another, and to take action to ensure that no more families would lose loved ones to the police, and an organizing committee was created. Justice for Victims of Police Killings was a collective made up of family members and a few supporters, including me and a few other individuals, coalescing around a fairly simple consensus: that nobody should lose a loved one at the hands of police. This led to a coalition, organized by the families of the victims of police killings and their supporters, who organized a vigil and/or march every 22nd of October, starting in 2010, in solidarity with the October 22 Coalition to Stop Police Brutality, Repression, and the Criminalization of a Generation, which began in 1996.[6]

We also worked to document police killings and death in police custody, which we kept on a website that we were running for several years. For a time, ours was, I think, the most comprehensive publicly available list of those who have been lost to the police's ongoing war on our communities across Canada.

This has changed, of course. We are talking about a time before the media had taken an interest in covering this topic; before the CBC had done their major "Deadly Force" investigation that looked into the 462 deaths in Canada between 2000 and 2017. This is now probably the most thorough investigation on police killings in Canada, and I think it should be read alongside Desmond Cole's recently published blog post, "Remembering Black, Indigenous, and racialized people killed by Canadian police" (Cole 2020).

One of the key areas of concern raised by family members was the absolute impunity that those who had taken the lives of their loved ones were protected by. Police continued (and mind you, continue still) to kill with absolutely no consequences, and families had to struggle enormously even to find out how their loved ones had died.

Bridget Tolley, in particular, has for decades been an under-recognized leader in the long-standing struggle to end the practice of police investigating police. Her brilliance and courage here need to be on the historical record for this work. When her mother was struck and killed by an SQ car in 2001,

---

6. See more at: https://www.october22.org

the investigation was completed, she notes, by the *brother* of the officer whose car had ended her mother's life. All that she has wanted, she continues, were answers. She has continually brought to the public's attention the fact that the forces that regularly kill—and justify the killings of—civilians should not be responsible for overseeing investigations of other forces who regularly kill and justify the killings of civilians.

Toward ending impunity, we tried to be very careful in the way we framed our demands. We knew how the state had co-opted the demand to end the practice of police investigating police who killed.

We knew, for example, how in 1980s Toronto, the Black Action Defence Committee (BADC) had tried to push for the creation of a non-police investigation body for police killings, and then ended up with what can only be described as a false civilian oversight board, the Special Investigations Unit (SIU), which ended up being staffed mainly by ex-police.

Despite this, though, what happened was predictable. In 2016, a new, and purportedly neutral investigation body, was formed called the *Bureau des enquêtes indépendantes* (BEI). However, far from being independent, the large majority of the BEI members are former police.

Perhaps we should have been more careful, more nuanced. The reparations framework, for example, that organizers were able to mobilize in Chicago, articulated clear, and un-co-optable demands; for example, that officers involved in violent acts be *fired*, that the families of loved ones harmed received *reparations*.

We can only go forward, though, and do more when we know more.

At the same time, some of the demands forwarded at that time closely anticipated the demands of the more contemporary movement to #DefundThePolice.

Julie Matson came into abolitionist demands from lived experience and used firsthand knowledge as a means to forward a call for the disarmament of the police in Montréal and across Canada.

Julie Matson's father, Ben Matson, was killed by the Vancouver police in 2002, from what was described as "restraint-associated cardiac arrest." Though he had been severely beaten and asphyxiated to death in police custody, a Coroner's Office inquest ruled the death accidental. A young woman at the time, Julie had to work against the full arsenal of police and their lawyers just to learn what had happened. Her experience taught her a lesson that she would share with other family members who had lost loved ones to police: neither the criminal (in)justice system nor the putatively "independent" investigative bodies—mechanisms like coroner's inquests or public inquiries—are going to end police killings. Neither did they have the capacity to bring justice to the families of loved ones whose lives had been decimated by senseless violence.

Julie Matson (left) and Bridget Tolley (right) at the first vigil and commemorative march, 22 October 2010.

In 2011, Julie was arguing that it was essential "to care for vulnerable people rather than meeting them at with weapons and violence." At a press conference outside of the Montréal Police Brotherhood on Laurier St, in front of a line of armed officers, she forwarded a demand to *disarm the police*.

She has repeated this demand every year since. Her calls for disarming the police—now a major demand of the defund movement shaking North America—was not picked up by the press, even though she has courageously made this call to the media, often in front of a line of heavily armed officers, every year for over a decade.

Abolitionist demands, this shows, are not dreamed up by idealists with no sense of reality. We have this longer trajectory right here in Montréal that shows us that abolitionist praxis is borne of real-life experience. The people coming together after experiencing policing and the violence of the carceral state are trying, and sometimes succeeding, in moving toward non-carceral options and supporting our community safety.

The mother, father, and sisters of Quilem Registre holding a photo of Quilem and the "Justice for Victims of Police Killings" banner at the first vigil and commemorative march in 2010. Photo credit Kinneret Sheetreet.

And of course, today, while I'm no longer a member since my move to Toronto, Justice for Victims of Police Killings is part of Montréal's Defund the Police Coalition.

But looking back allows us to see, in an earlier generation of struggle, the politics and organizing that anticipated the more formal "Defund/Dismantle/Disarm/Abolish" movement that we see today. It is essential to excavate this history because there is so much that happens between and across movements; nothing that comes about is brand new. If we look to grassroots histories, we begin to see the forms of abolitionist world-making that were always already present, if unidentical, in moments that precede the now.

So, you can see here that in many ways, this modest but powerful conference brought together individuals and movements to help us to make better sense of all the various forms in which criminalizing takes place and has harmed us, and to plant seeds for future organizing, future coalitions that would emerge in the months and years to come.

I think it's important not to forget the role played by mutual aid between multiple family members—several more families joined the yearly events and marches, with more joining every year. Every organic movement grows out of conditions that were set in place by the people and actions that came before, whether or not we are aware of it.

As engaged scholars and organizers, we are, all of us, working not only to secure more liberatory presents and futures but also necessarily working against a violent process of institutional erasure and of a purposeful, curated forgetting.

By engaging with movement histories, we can be forwarding counter-narratives that refuse the story, told and retold by the political elites, that our movements are somehow inauthentic or are imitating the United States.

Black and multi-racial struggles against the racial/gendered violence that is policing have long histories that are central to, if continually displaced from, the story of the political, intellectual, and cultural life of Montréal.

REFERENCES

Charest, M. 2009. *Mécontement populaire et pratiques d'interpellations du SPVM depuis 2005 : doit-on garder le cap après la tempête?* Montréal: Section recherche et planification, Service de police de la Ville de Montréal.

Cole, D. 2020. "Remembering 27 Black, Indigenous, and racialized people killed by Canadian police." *Cole's Notes: A blog by Desmond Cole*, 17 April 2020. https://thatsatruestory.wordpress.com/2020/04/17/remembering-27-black-indigenous-and-racialized-people-killed-by-canadian-police/

Maynard, R. 2017. *Policing Black Lives: State violence in Canada from slavery to the present.* Montréal: Fernwood Publishing.

Myles, B. "Gangs de rue – 10 000 noms dans la banque du SPVM." *Le Devoir*, 1 October 2010.

Pedicelli, G. 1998. *When police kill: Police use of force in Montréal and Toronto.* Montréal: Véhicule Press.

Symons, G. 2002. "Police Constructions of Race and Gender in Street Gangs." In *Crimes of Colour: Racialization and the Criminal Justice System in Canada*, edited by W. Chan and K. Mirchandani. Toronto: University of Toronto Press, pp. 115-126.

Trouillot, M-R. 1995. *Silencing the Past: Power and the Production of History.* Boston, MA: Beacon Press.

WHOSE CITY? CLAIMING JUSTICE FOR INDIGENOUS PEOPLES

CHRISTOPHER CURTIS

We met at funerals.

It was just like that with Nakuset. If you had not seen her at the women's shelter or giving the mayor what for at city hall, you would almost certainly run into her at a memorial service.

Because the truth of it was brutal. Indigenous women die on the streets of Montréal every month. And without Nakuset, we would not have the spaces to honour their memory.

So I would see her at Cabot Square, in a church basement on Parc Ave, or outside the old Anglican chapel on Atwater Ave. After they found Siasi's body near the high-rise buildings west of Concordia University, Nakuset stood up and said she was running out of ways to express her pain.

"I don't know how many more of these I can go to," she said. "I'm tired of being angry, tired of hurting. I'm just tired."

That was four years ago.

There have been dozens more dead since then. So many, in fact, that my memories of them began bleeding into each other a long time ago. Even the inactive social media accounts they left behind start to look alike; one final picture with a child or a boyfriend, one last post about the weather—otherwise unremarkable, but for the posthumous messages dangling underneath.

"I love you."

"I'll always remember you."

"This was our song."

It is easy to let the grief wash over you. To resign yourself to the inevitability of it all. I certainly have. But not Nakuset.

"Hey, you."

Without fail, this is how she would greet me after one of the memorial services: familiar, playful, warm.

"Are we gonna have to start some trouble over this?" Nakuset would say. "We tried giving them an easy out. I guess we'll just have to play hardball. I'm not really a sports person; is that how you use that expression?"

I asked her why she keeps showing up to these funerals.

"Because their lives fucking mattered," she said. "I didn't personally know all of these victims, but we need to honour them, and we do that by fighting. That's all we can do."

Officially, Nakuset is the executive director of the Native Women's Shelter of Montréal. Unofficially, you cannot make a policy decision concerning Indigenous people in this city without first consulting Nakuset. If you want your project to succeed, it goes through Nakuset.

When an Innu man froze to death on Parc Ave last winter, Nakuset had an emergency overnight shelter put in place before the next cold snap. After an outbreak of COVID-19 among the homeless in December 2020, Nakuset fought to get mobile testing at shelters and 2,500 vaccines from the provincial government within weeks.

She pushed for the creation of a reconciliation commissioner at city hall, and for the province to fund a homeless day centre for Indigenous people on Atwater Ave. She also secured federal funding for a project that tracks missing and murdered women in Montréal. And her shelter is overseeing the construction of transitional housing for women looking to leave abusive relationships.

Oh, and there is a play being made about her life. It is based on the CBC documentary *Becoming Nakuset* released earlier this year (2021).

She did not ask for any of this. In a parallel universe, Nakuset would have been allowed to remain in the Cree territory of northern Saskatchewan and be raised with her sisters. That parallel universe Nakuset could live a normal life on the land, passing on the language of her ancestors, and raising her sons in their culture.

But we do not live in that universe. In our world, Nakuset was forcefully taken from her mother at the age of three and adopted into a Jewish family in Montréal, where she would be taught to hide her Indigenous roots.

She would grow up to learn that there were thousands more like her, taken by force and put in families, told to erase whatever traces of the children's Indigenous roots remained.

There was another chilling fact.

"Not all of us made it out," Nakuset said. "There were those who wound up in jail, some were molested by their adopted parents and never the same again, and there were those who took their own lives.

"It's up to those who remained to keep the fight alive."

***

She was chosen from a catalogue.

This is how hundreds of Indigenous children made their way to Montréal in the 1960s and 1970s. They were taken from their homes in the prairies, the west coast, and northern Ontario photographed and marketed to settler families as a sort of humanitarian project.

The Sixties Scoop came to replace the state-sanctioned child abductions that marked the residential school system (in place since the 19th century). As that policy drew to a close, child welfare agencies stepped in to fill the void. They declared tens of thousands of mothers unfit and placed their children in state custody.

Nakuset was three when they took her from her mom and two sisters. She wound up in a Jewish home in Montréal.

"They told me to say I was Israeli if ever anyone asked why my skin was dark," she said. "You had to hide the fact that you were an Indian. It was seen as a shameful thing."

When she enrolled at Concordia University, Nakuset started to find others just like herself.

"We would compare notes, 'What did your parents tell you about being native?' That sort of thing," she said. "So, we started an adoptees group called ANA—Advocacy for Native Adoptees. We met every Sunday, developed programs, and just bonded.

"There were Lakoffs, Waldmans, Rosenbergs, McFarlands; we had all been assigned this new identity. God, I still have the minutes from those meetings. Most of us were from very far away, which was the point of the Sixties Scoop, to separate you from yourself.

"We were treated like aliens. They didn't know what to do with us, so a lot of us acted out. A friend was kicked out of St-George's High School for smoking pot in the bathroom; some ran away from home and ended up in juvenile hall, some were sexually abused.

"Most of our stories were horror stories."

It was a radicalizing moment in Nakuset's life. Then, as she started reconnecting with other adoptees, Nakuset came face to face with a whole new set of problems when she began working at the Native Women's Shelter of Montréal in the late-1990s.

"You start to learn about this horrible cycle of violence so many women have to deal with," Nakuset said. "It starts with forced adoption or abysmal poverty, and it never goes away. Children are taken by youth protection; families are broken apart. The abused become abusers, and you realize there needs to be radical change."

She quickly earned a reputation as someone who got things done at the Native Women's Shelter of Montréal. So when the position of executive director opened up, a colleague suggested that Nakuset apply.

"I laughed; I never in a million years thought that I could become an executive director. Never," she said. "I didn't think I was qualified. But this woman, she saw something in me, and she insisted I apply. So I did.

"I think oftentimes, an executive director is maybe a bit more reserved, a little shy even, and that's not me. So I started reaching out to all these other organizations. I went to Batshaw Youth Services and said, 'I'm an executive director. I want to talk to your executive director. Let's work together.'

"And that's how the network was built."

***

The mayor looked ready to charm his way through another community meeting.

He gave me a wink, a tap on the shoulder, and his trademark *"salut mon vieux"* as he glad-handed his way into the conference room. It was 2017, an election year, and Coderre could not afford to appear callous in the face of growing social problems within Montréal's Indigenous population.

So he turned up his charisma to 11 and led his entourage forward.

The fact that the Montréal Urban Aboriginal Community Network even got a face-to-face meeting with the mayor was, in itself, a sign of their growing influence in the city. Less than 1% of the island's population is Indigenous, so they do not necessarily have any demographic power to sway politicians.

Rather, their strength lay in Nakuset's ability to bring Indigenous community groups together and build coalitions with settlers. They raised awareness about missing and murdered Indigenous women, police brutality, and children in foster care, among so many of the other injustices people face every day in Montréal.

On the day they met with the mayor, Nakuset and the network had just pressured the police into re-opening an investigation into the death of an Inuk sex worker. That came just months after the women's shelter secured funding to hire social workers to patrol Cabot Square—a west downtown park frequented by homeless Indigenous folk.

As the doors closed behind Coderre, a colleague leaned over and whispered.

"You think Nakuset can handle him?" she said.

"I think you have it backwards," I replied.

Coderre emerged from the room about an hour later, looking like a man who had just lost his pay on an ill-advised card game. It occurred to me that he may have unwittingly committed to more than he could deliver.

"I can't tell you exactly what happened in there, but I was blunt with him," Nakuset said at the time. "Talk is cheap. We needed him to commit to specific actions, and we didn't back down."

At the time, gentrification was breathing life back into the western end of downtown.

It had taken decades for the neighbourhood to bounce back after the Canadiens had left the Montréal Forum for bigger, more modern accommodations across town in 1996. With a 17,000-person arena sitting vacant most days, it did not take long for the economy around Atwater Ave to collapse. Entire blocks were shuttered. Once thriving businesses either died or followed the Habs east to survive.

By the late 2000s, developers started buying up abandoned gas stations, movie theatres, and empty low-rise buildings in the area to tear them down and build condo towers in their place. Money came pouring back into the blocks between Guy St and Atwater Ave—a Starbucks, a new branch of the Bank of Montréal, a restaurant and nightclub helmed by star chef Antonio Park, and a brand new police station just a few blocks east.

And now developers were talking about transforming the old Children's Hospital into a massive condo and shopping complex. Cabot Square would also undergo a series of renovations to make it brighter, cleaner, and more welcoming to the area's newest residents.

Left unchecked, the development would have pushed the homeless out of Cabot Square.

So Nakuset laid out a vision to prevent that from happening. Every summer, she worked with the city to host activities that highlighted the neighbourhood's Inuit heritage. Inuit stone carvers gave workshops to local children and the elderly. There were Inuit games, Inuit storytelling, and an annual concert to mark Indigenous Peoples Day on June 21.

"We didn't want them to become invisible; we wanted to highlight who the Inuit are," said Nakuset. "If you know who someone is, it's harder to ignore their suffering. Eventually, you might even have to do something about it."

Of course, the Coderre meeting was ultimately voided by his election loss, so he did not have to hold up his end of whatever bargain he had made. But Nakuset's projects went forward with a new administration at city hall.

The network's influence was undeniable.

Both Coderre and future mayor Valérie Plante fielded an Indigenous candidate in the 2017 municipal election. The city had already committed to hiring a reconciliation commissioner. It had also changed its flag to reflect Montréal's Haudenosaunee roots and put the full weight of the mayor's office behind a quest to find a new location for a day-shelter that catered to Inuit west of downtown.

Over the years, the network provided sensitivity training for downtown police officers. It pushed the municipal court to offer alternative remedies for minor offences that might otherwise have landed women in prison. The network was behind a ground-breaking study into the over-representation of Indigenous youth in Québec's foster care system. And it will be at the table when it comes time to change the way Indigenous families are treated by youth protection services.

"Youth protection had essentially blacklisted us a few years ago because we pushed too hard," Nakuset said. "But they're coming back to the table now because you can't deny it anymore. We're not in the time of residential schools and Sixties Scoop, but we're not that far removed either.

"There are way too many kids being warehoused by the state. We're going to fight until they're safe and until they have access to their culture."

***

This story almost had a happy ending.

Twenty-two years after they had been separated by the state, Nakuset and her sister found each other again. Sonya was living in Ontario, scouring social media to find her little sister.

Nakuset was 25 when they reunited. But the sisters still needed to find Rosemary, who—it seemed—had fallen off the grid in Canada.

After years of amateur detective work, they found her living in Austria, where she had been sent during the Sixties Scoop. When they finally spoke on the phone in 2016, it had been 30 years since they had been in contact.

They kept the relationship going through more phone calls and online correspondence until they could all be together in person.

But that never happened.

It was August 2018 when Nakuset received a video file and an ominous text message from Sonya.

"I love you."

She took her life shortly after sending the message. In the video file, Sonya tried to explain her lifelong struggle with guilt and trauma. She spoke about feeling ashamed that she could not protect her little sisters, about the pain she carried from her own abuse.

"I felt so weak when I heard her say those things," Nakuset said. "She was my hero; she did years of detective work to find us, to bring us back together again."

When we spoke about it on the phone a few years ago, it was the first time I heard Nakuset cry. She had lost a lot of people in the short time we knew each other, but this, she said, was like losing a piece of herself.

Around that time, I was going through my own problems and had to take a few months off work at the newspaper. So I stopped checking in with Nakuset, who had—at that point—evolved from a source to a friend.

One afternoon, after I had been released from the Douglas Mental Health Institute, I got a phone call from a familiar number.

"Hey you."

It was Nakuset, and she just wanted to tell me how much she appreciated me. Pretty soon, we were both laughing about whatever politician Nakuset had just shaken down at city hall.

That call meant more to me than Nakuset will ever know.

You cannot tell the story of Montréal without exploring its abusive relationship with Indigenous people.[1] Whether it is the Mohawks who lived in the St-Lawrence valley long before Europeans arrived on the continent, or the people forced into the city through the displacing effect of colonialism, their destinies and ours are intertwined. And there's no way of telling that story without Nakuset standing squarely in the middle of it.

We still meet at funerals now and again, but there are happy moments too.

"You know they're making my life into a play?" she said the other day. "Little old me, a Jewish Indian on the big stage. What'll they think of next?"

I told her this does not surprise me. She did not dwell on the play. Within a few moments, she was back in planning mode, trying to figure out how to secure three million dollars to open a new shelter near Cabot Square.

"My life is insane," she said. "I guess it's the only way I've ever known it."

---

1. For a history of Indigenous peoples on the island of Montréal and their relationship with European colonists, see the chapter by Pouliot-Thisdale in this book.

PUSHING MUNICIPAL BOUNDARIES: EXPERIENCES OF MONTRÉAL'S IMMIGRANT WORKERS CENTRE

CHEOLKI YOON

INTRODUCTION

In the democratic regimes of ancient Greece, the "city" (*polis*) was considered the political entity fit for democracy *par excellence* (Aristotle [350BCE] 1990). Although it is anachronistic to equate the *polis* with the contemporary city, this model from antiquity is often approached as the archetype of democracy and still inspires our political imagination. While the nation-state presents itself today as the main body framing politics, can the contemporary city still be a significant political sphere? More specifically, from the perspective of social movements, what is the place of the municipal government in the overall strategies of political intervention?

In European history, the modern state emerged from a strong centralization of political powers at the national level, either through a radical unification, as in the French Revolution, or through a compromise between various socio-political sectors, as illustrated by the British tradition. Contrary to this trend, in the 1970s, there was a phase of administrative decentralization in several European and American countries, sometimes echoing the notion of participatory democracy. In this context, the place of municipal governments was revisited, both concerning the sharing of powers and resources between the different levels of government, and concerning citizen participation in politics.

In the modern nation-state system, social movements advocating political change most often target national governments. In the context of Canadian federalism, both federal and provincial governments are the preferred targets.

As the Québécois are recognized as a "nation within a united Canada,"[1] in Québec, the provincial level is treated as more important than in other Canadian provinces. However, the municipal level (i.e., the city) is also an inescapable political sphere, both in Québec and the rest of Canada.

This chapter will explore the potential for mobilization in the urban sphere from the perspective of social movements. To this end, it will focus on the experiences of the Montréal-based Immigrant Workers Centre (IWC). More specifically, the analyses presented here are based on two IWC interventions with the City of Montréal: the struggle to raise the minimum wage to $15 and the debates around the notion of a sanctuary city. But first, we begin with a short section focused on events in the United States that have inspired IWC's strategies.

SUCCESS STORIES IN THE UNITED STATES

Canada is influenced in many ways by its large neighbour to the south, not only in international relations but also in its economy. American social movements also constantly inspire individuals and organizations in Canada. This influence also applies to the fight for a $15 minimum wage and the debates surrounding the idea of providing sanctuary for migrants without immigration status.

In the United States, the fight for $15 began in 2012 and gained momentum in the following years. In most U.S. states, municipal governments have the power to determine the minimum wage in the territory they administer. In fact, following the actions of social movements, the City of Seattle was the first government to approve increasing the minimum wage to $15.

As a result of a popular campaign composed of community, political, student, and labour organizations, the $15 minimum wage became one of the central issues in the 2013 Seattle municipal election. This was particularly highlighted by city council candidate Kshama Sawant of the Socialist Alternative. Ongoing efforts in various settings—including SeaTac Airport and the University of Washington—helped spread the campaign's themes more widely.

The dynamics were similar in several other U.S. cities, including New York and San Francisco. In these and many other cases, social movements have successfully gained recognition for the importance of the cause. They have also successfully pushed for substantial increases in the minimum wage, first at the municipal, and then at the state level. Pressed by social movements, many governments have increased their minimum wage. According to a report

---

1. Hansard; 39th Parliament, 1st Session; No. 087; 27 November 2006, http://www2.parl.gc.ca/HousePublications/

published in December 2019, at least seven states and 40 municipalities have increased their minimum wage to $15 or more (Lathrop 2019).

The word "sanctuary", which in its religious sense refers to a sacred place, is used by universal human rights advocates to refer to a space in which the rights of migrants are protected on an equal footing regardless of their immigration status. However, it should be noted that the connotation is not the same on both sides of the Atlantic. While European sanctuary cities focus on providing settlement services for asylum seekers and refugees, the key to North American sanctuaries is non-cooperation with federal immigration authorities, particularly when it comes to the deportation of people without immigration status.

During the 1980s and 1990s, social movements demanding the protection of undocumented migrants gained momentum in the United States, and increasing numbers of state and municipal governments asserted themselves as sanctuaries. As of March 2020, eleven state governments and more than 160 city and county governments in the U.S. officially present themselves as sanctuaries (Griffith and Vaughan 2020). Beyond non-cooperation with federal authorities, many state and municipal governments also provide public services to their residents regardless of immigration status. That said, the increasing spread of the far-right across the country and the election of Donald Trump as U.S. president have posed significant challenges to sanctuary jurisdictions. President Trump has publicly threatened sanctuary cities on numerous occasions, and several state governments have passed anti-sanctuary laws. The primary means of suppressing sanctuary jurisdictions has been to cut off public funding and bring legal charges against officials.

For the movements associated with these two causes, municipal governments, especially those in metropolitan areas, serve as the main battlegrounds. Municipal governments are also influential players in the expansion of these movements. The broad autonomy granted to U.S. municipalities is an indispensable prerequisite for identifying the dynamics in question. The rest of the chapter will focus on Québec's experiences, inspired by these American struggles, drawing attention to legal and administrative differences and the lessons that can be learned from them.

MONTRÉAL'S SUPPORT FOR THE $15 MINIMUM WAGE

For decades, achieving a decent minimum wage has been a significant concern for workers' organizations in Québec and across Canada. The demand for an increase in the minimum wage has taken on increased importance in the context of the precarious nature of work in the neoliberal era, which encourages the proliferation of workers who are not covered by a collective bargaining agreement.

In 2015, the IWC was one of the first Québec organizations, along with the *Syndicat industriel des travailleurs et travailleuses – Industrial Workers of the World* (SITT-IWW) and Socialist Alternative, to publicly launch a campaign for the $15 minimum wage. The rise of struggles in the United States—marked by the particularly active participation of non-unionized, migrant, and immigrant workers—was a source of inspiration and motivation for Québec organizers. For the IWC, however, wage increases were not the sole objective of the fight. Through its involvement, the IWC also wanted to broaden its alliance network as much as possible and to organize more low-wage workers, especially migrants and immigrants (Yoon and Frozzini 2018). In this perspective, the Centre experimented with various strategies, going beyond the spectrum of its usual practices.

In the Canadian context, the provincial government has the exclusive power to set the minimum wage, so coalitions or campaigns for $15 have mainly been formed at the provincial level. During 2016, provincial campaigns such as "$15 Now", "Minimum 15", and "Campaign 5-10-15" were launched in Québec, with the Québec provincial government as their primary target. However, from the beginning of the IWC's involvement, it also took interest in local governments (cities and boroughs), despite their limited jurisdiction over wages.

That same year, the IWC initiated discussions with councillors from the borough of Cote-des-Neiges-Notre-Dame-de-Grace, where its offices are located, and organized meetings with various organizations in the neighbourhood to discuss the campaign for $15. In collaboration with other groups and individuals, the IWC launched two neighbourhood committees for the $15 minimum wage in 2017—in the Côte-des-Neiges and Parc-Extension neighbourhoods. Three more neighbourhood committees were subsequently organized at the initiative of other organizations. The first objective of the neighbourhood committees was to anchor struggles within the target population (i.e., the working poor) to open up a space for their participation. Also, activists have invested in constructing local bases of solidarity to divert or overcome divisions and rivalries in the context of the multitude of Québec campaigns. In these neighbourhood committees, individuals who joined the different campaigns listed above or who were not associated with them collaborated without any apparent rivalry or tension.

At the initiative of the neighbourhood committees, several organizations fighting for $15 have decided to carry out a series of actions targeting the City of Montréal as part of their campaign strategies. Meetings with elected officials were held in at least two boroughs, and telephone or email messages were sent to elected officials across the city. In the borough of Côte-des-Neiges-Notre-Dame-de-Grâce, the neighbourhood committee, in conjunction with the IWC and Project Genesis, organized a small rally in front of the borough's public meeting in April 2017. Several neighbourhood committee members also attended the session to ask questions and advocate for an increase in the minimum wage. A few days after this session, borough councillor Marvin Rotrand tabled a motion to support the $15 minimum wage at city council. The five neighbourhood committees and several Montréal organizations, unions, community, and student groups circulated a message to the city's elected officials asking them to support this motion. During the municipal session in August, these groups held a press briefing and rally in front of city hall, where the motion was to be put to the vote. City council eventually adopted the motion, and these actions were widely publicized.

In the lead-up to the municipal election in November 2017, a letter was sent on behalf of the five neighbourhood committees to party leaders, asking for concrete actions to be implemented following the motion adopted earlier that summer. The election of Valérie Plante and Projet Montréal was well received by supporters of the fight for $15, as the demand had been included in their electoral platform. Despite this political support, the implementation of concrete measures—in particular, pressure on the provincial government and an increase in the starting wage for all city employees—was delayed.

Undeterred, activists used several strategies to pressure the city: lobbying at the Projet Montréal convention, a few months after their victory in the municipal election, sending a letter from the neighbourhood committees to the mayor, and raising this issue in a meeting between the mayor and the *Comité intersyndical du Montréal métropolitain* (CIMM). At the end of May 2018, the city reiterated its intention to increase the salaries of municipal employees. It also argued for the importance of a decent minimum wage for all of Québec, raising the issue with the Québec government and provincial parties in the months leading up to the 2018 provincial election. Since then, the fight for $15 has continued, though the target has moved primarily to the provincial government.

It is a long struggle, lasting more than five years. The activists involved have had to deal with fluctuating and sometimes stagnant campaigns, and still, the Québec government has not accepted a minimum wage of $15.[2]

Although the provincial government is now the primary target of the struggle and has remained rigid, the municipal front certainly marks a crucial moment in the evolution of Québec's campaigns. Committees were created in neighbourhoods where there is a high concentration of working poor to prioritize the participation of those directly affected by the minimum wage.

2. As of February 2021, the minimum wage is $13.10 per hour in Québec.

This strategy was deliberately designed to combat job insecurity, a phenomenon that poses a major challenge to the organization of workers in their workplace. Through these local structures, the movement's organizers could meet new faces, whether or not they were regularly involved with social movements, in order to organize and mobilize them in local actions. In addition, elected municipal officials are likely to be more accessible than those at the provincial or federal level. This has encouraged the participation of residents, instilling in them confidence in their ability to influence. While it is not possible to accurately measure the impact of the City of Montréal's positioning on the minimum wage issue, it is clear that the actions implemented at the municipal level—and the city's public announcements on the issue—have helped to attract and renew public attention. It has also helped to encourage supporters of the fight for $15.

COMMITMENT OF THE CITY OF MONTRÉAL TO THE PROTECTION OF MIGRANTS WITHOUT IMMIGRATION STATUS

Immigration policies include both selection and integration procedures. The former relates to the selection of temporary and permanent immigrants and the regulation of their entry and exit from the territory. The latter includes the full range of public measures implemented to promote immigrants' integration and harmonize relations between immigrant and non-immigrant populations. In this second set of policies, all levels of government are involved, while it is primarily the federal government that governs selection policies in both Canada and the United States. However, the Québec government has an exceptional power of immigrant selection, unlike other Canadian provinces. Therefore, in the Québec context, immigration is a shared jurisdiction between the federal and provincial governments. For this reason, Québec social movement organizations, including the IWC, intervene on both levels of government when it comes to immigration issues.

The City of Montréal, where immigrants represent 34% of the population (Statistics Canada 2017), has been developing its own integration policies for decades. These have focused on supporting the integration of new immigrants and raising public awareness about racial discrimination. Despite the transfer of jurisdiction from the federal government to Québec in this area over the past decades, the municipal government's scope for intervention remains limited in Canada, and it has no authority over immigrant selection policies.

Despite these limitations, some Canadian municipalities, including Toronto, Hamilton, London, and Vancouver, have designated themselves as sanctuary cities. Former Montréal Mayor Denis Coderre adopted the same position in February 2017, which was then unanimously endorsed by city council. However, this announcement was an embarrassment for organizations fighting to protect migrants without immigration status, as no concrete measures were included in the declaration, and no prior discussions with these organizations had been held. In fact, the municipal election was scheduled for only a few months later, in November 2017. As such, the duty to implement the declaration was passed on to the next administration. In December 2018, when she announced her first action plan on immigration and the integration of newcomers, newly elected Mayor Valérie Plante revoked Montréal's status as a "sanctuary city", thereby recognizing the limits of measures put in place by the city. In this context, the IWC began to engage, in collaboration with the City of Montréal, in a municipal project aimed at protecting migrants without immigration status.

During the city's public consultations on the issues of racial and social profiling held in 2017, the issue of the particular vulnerability of persons without immigration status was raised by several organizations. The *Bureau d'intégration des nouveaux arrivants à Montréal* (BINAM) then initiated an in-depth reflection on this subject in collaboration with other organizations. As stated by the mayor in her speech announcing the revocation of Montréal's sanctuary city status, the city was intending to broaden access to municipal services for all residents, regardless of immigration status.

According to undocumented migrants' advocates, the key to protection at the municipal level lies in non-cooperation with the *Service de police de la Ville de Montréal* (SPVM) and the Canada Border Services Agency (CBSA). In most cases, a police intervention includes verifying the identity of the people concerned. Persons without immigration status in Canada generally do not have valid identification. Therefore, they are concerned that CBSA will be informed of their presence during a police intervention, which may lead to their detention and subsequent deportation. Under the yoke of this well-founded fear, they live in daily anxiety and rarely resort to contacting public authorities, even when they are victims of crime. After a series of discussions, the City of Montréal proposed the "Fearless Access to Municipal Services Policy," which includes issuing a municipal card that would ensure access to available services. Participating organizations insisted that this card be officially recognized as valid identification by all municipal institutions, including the SPVM. However, the SPVM has refused to consent to this.

Within the IWC, the Women's Committee of the *Association des travailleuses-eurs temporaires et d'agences de placement* (ATTAP) actively participated in formulating and implementing this municipal policy. A member of the IWC Board of Directors, and an IWC organizer responsible for ATTAP's Women's Committee, actively participated in these discussions. Per its organizational principles, the most important decisions of the IWC are made by members without immigration status. Some of them came in person to two of the meetings organized by BINAM to share their experiences. These testimonies had a resounding effect on the participants of the meetings. Throughout the process, IWC organizers paid special attention to the safety of non-status members, especially since police officers were often present.

Faced with the city's proposal for a pilot project on this policy, the organizers hesitated to take a stand due to the SPVM's refusal to recognize this municipal access card as a valid identification document during a police intervention. In fact, almost all municipal services are already accessible to residents regardless of immigration status, provided that proof of address is presented. In practical terms, the new card does not grant any new rights, and its effect remains largely symbolic. However, following a request from its non-status members, the IWC has now given its official consent to the pilot project. While they were aware of the policy's limitations, they stressed the importance of being recognized by a public institution. In addition, there was increased confidence among these members in their ability to influence public policy. From consultation to the implementation of the new policy, the entire process was perceived as an experience of empowerment by those who felt isolated and marginalized within Québec society. Furthermore, the involvement of the IWC in managing the issuance of the card offered its organizers an opportunity to meet more undocumented migrants.

Following the outbreak of the COVID-19 pandemic in 2020, the issuance of this municipal card was delayed. The fate of persons without immigration status is, of course, made more bitter. Due to limited access to public benefits, most of them were forced to continue working, being put at risk of infection, in order to meet basic needs. Increased police presence, especially with the introduction of the curfew, intimidates more than unusual the undocumented workers who work at night. In this context, the voices calling for the regularization of immigration status, namely by granting permanent residence to migrants with temporary status or without status, have increased, highlighting their contributions during the crisis. Faced with these voices, the Québec government, following negotiations with the federal government, established the Special Program for Asylum Seekers in the Period of COVID-19 in December 2020; however, eligibility is strictly limited by immigration category (asylum seekers) and work experience (in the health sector during the pandemic).

In February 2021, Giuliana Fumagalli, borough mayor of Villeray–Saint-Michel–Parc-Extension, tabled the *Motion to Support the Regularization of Persons Without Legal Status Living on its Territory*, which was subsequently adopted unanimously by the Montréal city council. The mayor of the borough, where many migrants are concentrated, continued to work closely with the

IWC and other community organizations, particularly during COVID-19. They then contributed to the drafting of the motion and publicly expressed their support for it (CTI 2021). The passage of this motion is another example of the city's political commitment to a cause beyond its administrative jurisdiction, based on local collaboration with its residents and organizations. The effects of the city's positioning on higher levels of government are not evident at this time. It is, however, certainly a motivating factor for the social movement organizations working in this area, and it is their task to incorporate it into their mobilization strategies.

CONCLUSION

Social movements must target the right level of government, depending on the issues they are addressing. Compared to their counterparts in the United States, Canadian municipal governments have limited jurisdiction in many respects. In this context, Canadian social movements rightly organize their municipal-level interventions primarily around issues of municipal jurisdiction, such as housing, urban redevelopment, and public transit.

However, the two IWC experiences discussed here lead us to rethink the place of municipal government in the struggle for social change. While it is true that the minimum wage and immigration are issues that go beyond their municipal framework, the activities organized in collaboration—or in conflict—with the City of Montréal have fostered the involvement of directly affected populations and have contributed to the empowerment of participants. In order to promote grassroots social movements, local actions are indispensable, and municipal institutions are relatively accessible partners—or targets.

Moreover, it is clear that the municipal government is an influential political actor, which is supposed to represent the will of its residents. Even on issues beyond its jurisdiction, it can play an intermediary political role in relation to other levels of government. As such, there is a need to plan actions at the municipal level in line with all strategies aimed at higher levels of government.

Finally, it should be noted that these two experiments were carried out in the context of a political opportunity opened up by the election of a progressive party (Project Montréal) favourable to the demands being put forward. The concrete strategies would have been different if the party in power in Montréal had been different. Society evolves in a constant state of flux, and social movements need to innovate in order to adapt to the conditions encountered on the ground and experiment with new avenues for social change. The municipal sphere is certainly an essential environment for this endless journey and one definitely not to be ignored in crafting a strategy for change.

REFERENCES

Aristotle. (350 BCE) 1990. *Politics*. Translated by P. Pellegrin. Paris: Flammarion.

Centre des travailleurs et travailleuses immigrants (CTI). 2021. "Pour Montréal 'responsable et engage' : appuyant la Motion à soutenir la régularisation des personnes sans statut légal vivant sur sont territoire." Press release, 22 February 2021. https://iwc-cti.ca/fr/pour-montreal-responsable-et-engagee/.

Griffith, B., and Vaughan, J.M. 2020. "Map: Sanctuary Cities, Counties, and States." *Centre for Immigration Studies*, Last modified 23 March 2020. https://cis.org/Map-Sanctuary-Cities-Counties-and-States.

Lathrop, Y. 2019. "Raises from Coast to Coast in 2020: Minimum Wage Will Increase in Record-High 47 States, Cities, and Counties This January." *National Employment Law Project (NELP)*, December 2019. https://s27147.pcdn.co/wp-content/uploads/Report-Minimum-Wage-Raises-From-Coast-to-Coast-2020.pdf.

Statistics Canada. 2017. *Montréal, V [Census subdivision], Québec and Québec [Province]* (table). *Census Profile*. 2016 Census. Statistics Canada Catalogue no. 98-316-X2016001. Ottawa. Released 29 November 2017. https://www12.statcan.gc.ca/census-recensement/2016/dp-pd/prof/index.cfm?Lang=E.

Yoon, C., and Frozzini, J. 2018. "La bataille des 15 dollars de l'heure. L'expérience du Centre des travailleurs et travailleuses immigrants." *Nouveau Cahiers du socialisme* 20: 145-149.

PART VIII.

UPPITY 'HOODS AND THE CITY

MILTON PARC: GRABBING AND KEEPING COMMUNITY CONTROL

NATHAN MCDONNELL

Dedicated to those who have gone before us, and to those who are to come.

INTRODUCTION

The Milton Parc story shows us that we can fight back and win. It also shows that residents can run housing themselves, making it democratic and (with government help) affordable. The community organizing history in Milton Parc shows us that to transform society, we need to both resist and build; we need to oppose injustice and the power structure, and then develop democratic alternatives and sustain ourselves materially and politically. It also shows us the central importance of land and property. In the Milton Parc community housing project, land and housing cannot be bought or sold for profit, effectively abolishing real estate capitalism in a downtown neighbourhood of Canada's second-largest city. The success of the community housing project, and the village-like community that it nurtures, has been a base for the emergence of many other achievements in community control, ecology, and grassroots democratization. Milton Parc is a petri dish for what we can do—for what we must do—to fundamentally confront gentrification, alienation, and disempowerment in cities worldwide.

WHAT DID WE DO?

We saved a total of four city blocks of heritage housing from demolition, took it off the private market, renovated it, and made it a community housing project that is affordable and democratically controlled in perpetuity. It consists of a federation of 22 different housing co-ops and non-profits, with 133 buildings and 645 apartments, housing a total population of about 1,500. It is inclusive, involving families, seniors, low-income residents, a few professionals, the unemployed, immigrants, people of colour, and those who have previously lived on the streets. The project is decentralized into 22 different autonomous housing groups—small is beautiful, and it makes it easier to get to know your neighbour and develop a community. The co-ops themselves are organized according to direct democracy, self-management, and volunteerism. Each member must volunteer six to ten hours per month in different committees like finance, maintenance, member selection, secretarial, leisure, and sometimes conflict resolution and the environment. These autonomous housing groups are federated as a "co-op of co-ops" in the *Communauté Milton Parc* (CMP). The CMP's declaration of co-ownership protects the principles stated above and ensures that the selection of new members prioritizes those with low and modest incomes.

This project is the largest co-operative and non-profit housing project on an urban community land trust in North America. In a community land trust (CLT), the land is owned collectively, and is protected from speculation in perpetuity, to serve community needs. CLTs can be used to protect everything from green spaces to agriculture to historical sites. But the most common usage in cities, where land is very expensive, is to protect housing affordability. This ensures housing availability for those who would otherwise struggle to pay a regular rent or mortgage. In the case of Milton Parc, the CMP is a local innovation on an anti-speculative land ownership model created by cleverly manipulating the condo model (it is legally a *syndicat de copropriété*). In this case, the "co-owners" are not individuals owning private property but housing groups (co-ops and non-profits) that technically own the land beneath their buildings but are governed by strict rules that obstruct its resale.

So how does a community run its own neighbourhood? Next, let us turn to explore how we did it.

HOW DID IT HAPPEN?

Originally built as a bourgeois neighbourhood, Milton Parc declined gradually in the post-WW2 period as middle class and wealthy families moved out. The remaining residents were primarily lower-income people, students, and immigrants. In the mid-1960s, tearing down and rebuilding became the desirable form of urban renewal promoted by city planners and the real estate industry. At the same time, a group of developers (Concordia Estates Ltd.) slowly and secretly bought up 90% of the buildings that stood on the six-block area between Hutchison, Pine, Sainte-Famille, and Milton Streets. They planned to demolish everything and construct a new, shiny, modern "city of the 21st century" (as they called it) with high-rises, offices, and commercial buildings.

The developers declared their grand plan in 1968, a year of global revolutionary tumult, of movements for social justice, and fighting back. The University Settlement community centre on Saint Urbain Street near Prince Arthur was part of this social ferment. From 1968 to 1972, its social workers, community organizers, and users, along with citizen activists from the Milton Parc Citizens' Committee, began to organize to save their neighbourhood. They knocked on doors, signed petitions, demonstrated in the streets, marched to city hall, held street festivals, presented alternatives to high-rises, and held endless meetings—all the while committed to democratic principles. This mobilization occurred alongside the development of self-managed solidarity projects, like the formation of a housing co-operative, a community health clinic, a legal clinic, a daycare, a food-buying co-op, a credit union, and a co-operative laundromat. This activity formed a cohesive vision for creating a cooperative community, sharing democratic values, and anchored in ideals of social justice.

In May 1972, the Milton Parc Citizens' Committee squatted empty dwellings slated for demolition. Simultaneously, a dozen particularly courageous individuals performed a sit-in at the offices of Concordia Estates Ltd. on Parc Avenue. They were arrested and, though acquitted by a jury, this took the wind out of everyone's sails. The developers proceeded with the first phase of the three-stage development, constructing five high-rise buildings and an underground shopping mall that remain to this day: *La Cité*. People were exhausted and were left with a feeling of failure.

Neighbourhood activities came to a standstill. This was until the issue of traffic noise on a small residential street sparked the creation of the Jeanne-Mance Street Committee. The subsequent organizing around traffic calming employed the tried-and-true methods of non-violent activism, supported by experts doing technical research to bolster the argument. This led to small wins, thereby reviving neighbourhood activity, collective confidence, and the recruitment of new citizen activists.

Meanwhile, matters were not going well for the developers. The militant activity of the Citizens' Committee had drawn the attention of some of the developers' financial backers. One major financial supporter of the *La Cité* project, the Ford Foundation, withdrew its funding after activists flew to Chicago to intervene in its Annual General Meeting. The worldwide oil crisis of 1973 and construction activities linked to the 1976 Montréal Olympics caused a massive jump in inflation. This severely decreased the value of the funding planned by Concordia Estates Ltd. for all three phases of the development. By 1977, funding had dried up, and the developers were considering selling the remaining two-thirds of their original project. When the community learned of this, organizers reassessed their strategy. The Milton Parc saga was relaunched, and the timing could not have been better.

The election of the *Parti Québécois* (PQ), and their promise to hold Québec's first sovereignty referendum, was polarizing the province. Many businesses left the province and real estate values began to stagnate or plummet; there was no longer a market for Concordia's old urban housing, and the developers wanted to be relieved of it. The neighbourhood now had nearly ten years of experience in "militant action": working together, understanding the role of non-violent direct action, trusting each other, understanding the need for volunteering, employing the principles of transparency and democracy. They had also developed their ability to analyze how society and the economy function. Many residents wanted to form housing co-operatives. With the help of a grant, professional support, and research on financing, legal requirements, and political strategy, the neighbourhood was ready. On 16 May 1979, the Government of Canada, through its housing agency, the Canada Mortgage and Housing Corporation (CMHC), bought the property for only $5.5 million.[1]

However, CMHC indicated that future rents would be based on market values to account for high interest rates—there was no guarantee the rents would remain affordable. There was also no guarantee that residents would not be permanently displaced. The community was quick to mobilize again, leveraging the support of PQ leader René-Levesque and the imminent May 1980 Québec sovereignty referendum. They used these to effectively blackmail senior CMHC civil servants who were ferried from Ottawa to Montréal in several limousines. The federal government, nervous about any unwanted disruptions, quickly caved in. The neighbourhood would be allowed to charge rents for the renovated units in line with those currently in place, rather than based on the market, and residents would not be forced to vacate following a large rent increase.

The 1980s were a period of hard yet imaginative work. This involved learning about renovations, how to run co-ops and other non-profits, and a commitment to democratic functioning. For years there were weekly meetings in local church basements with intense discussions among residents, supported by professionals, to flesh out their vision of community control for the properties. In discussing the project's social values and governance, the result was a kind of "Federation of Milton-Parc Co-ops" that would be resident-run and not-for-profit. This proposal triumphed after a bitter fight,

---

1. Equivalent to approximately $21.5 million in today's dollars.

as a group of around 40 residents had wanted to own their own homes rather than relinquish them to common property.

The first eight co-ops self-organized through affinity very quickly, formed from the buildings where all the community organizers lived. Then came several years of work to temporarily relocate residents and renovate the apartments to bring them up to the national housing code. Apartments were run down; some did not even have heating. Once the housing project was finally established and functioning, the community gave a collective sigh of relief. Many citizens retreated into political retirement or, as described informally, into their bedrooms to produce children. But the political energy of Milton Parc does not end there. The activist core of Milton Parc moved on to other struggles over the ensuing decades.

THE MOVEMENT CONTINUES

After the success of Milton Parc, there were attempts to export the idea to other Montréal neighbourhoods facing similar struggles. Activists from Milton Parc joined with residents in Overdale (in the Shaughnessy Village on René-Levesque) to save their so-called "slum" housing from demolition—and to organize it collectively. They clashed with the mayor Jean Doré, from the supposedly grassroots left-wing Montréal Citizens' Movement (MCM). Doré and the MCM had cynically argued that the city needed more revenue from property taxes to enact the progressive policies they aspired to implement. The activists were unsuccessful, and the housing was demolished. The land then lay abandoned for over two decades, leaving a tragic scar in the memory of Montréal housing struggles.

Continuing from the early activism around traffic calming in the neighbourhood, Milton Parc activists would continue to blaze a trail pioneering urban ecology initiatives, in particular through the Montréal Urban Ecology Centre/*Centre d'écologie urbain de Montréal* (CEUM). The centre pioneered many participatory planning and ecological practices that are now commonplace: making streets safer for pedestrians and cyclists, composting, urban agriculture and community-supported agriculture, public consultation, and participatory budgeting. Also managed out of the CEUM was the *Place publique*, a bilingual local neighbourhood community newspaper with a circulation of 35,000 readers, which covered urban and social issues. There was also the decades-long (yet eventually successful) struggle to remove the Park-Pine freeway interchange—a concrete monster that scarred the neighbourhood.

At a municipal level, these same activists led the building of a city-wide grassroots citizens' movement. They founded Ecology Montréal, the first municipal ecological political party in North America, which contested municipal elections in 1990 and 1994. These activists also took the lead in organizing five major Montréal Citizens' Summits between 2001 and 2009. These summits brought together many grassroots citizen and worker organizations and up to 1,000 citizens from across Montréal to discuss issues and propose municipal policy changes, very much inspired by the World Social Forum process. This movement left a permanent imprint on the city, particularly through the *Chantier sur la démocratie* and the development of innovative arms-length municipal institutions. These institutions included the Ombudsman and *l'Office de consultation publique de Montréal* (OCPM), an international pioneer in public consultation, and are governed by the Montréal Charter of Rights and Responsibilities, the first city-based declaration of human rights. The Charter has been recognized by UNESCO and cited as a notable example of a tool for citizen involvement. Of note, the Charter allows citizens to force an official and independent OCPM consultation following the collection of enough signatures—the least-known weapon available to citizens.

Other projects created in the neighbourhood include the Milton Parc Recreation Association, a follow-up from the University Settlement, which continues to organize language classes and health and fitness activities at very affordable rates. Other long-running projects included the anarchist-run community cafe, *Café Commun-commune*, and a co-operative hardware store, but both have since closed. The community continues to host an active social life, including the annual events of the *Fête des Voisins* festival (with a potluck in the alley attended by 300 people), a *Cabane à sucre* in the spring, and a Halloween party.

FROM A CULTURE OF SOLIDARITY TO A SOLIDARITY ECONOMY

With an increasing homeless population visible in the neighbourhood, Solidarity Milton Parc (SMP) was created as an all-volunteer citizens' initiative to build meaningful relationships with and provide material support to this homeless community, many of whom are Indigenous. Over the past few years, SMP has served a weekly hot meal (coordinated with other front-line service organizations), organized decolonial popular education activities such as blanket exercises, and advocated for policy change.

When the COVID-19 pandemic hit Montréal, activists from the Milton Parc Citizen's Committee (MPCC) formed the Milton Parc Mutual Aid Network. They have been cooking weekly meals and organizing food banks for low-income residents and members of the homeless community, distributing personal protective equipment (PPE), organizing community visits to harvest vegetables from organic farms, and also partially subsidizing organic basket subscriptions. In addition, they have been organizing social activities such as an outdoor feminist theatre performance, an online Earth Day talent show, and a study group reading Peter Kropotkin's *Mutual Aid*. With these emergency direct aid projects as a base, their ambition is to develop a permanent infrastructure for a democratic food system in Milton Parc. This would include a community café/bistro, a bulk-buying zero-waste food co-op, a sliding scale meals subscription service, collective kitchens, cooking and other practical DIY workshops, urban agriculture, and an education program for discussions of social issues.

In Milton Parc, our community now owns nine commercial and two office spaces. They are owned through the *Société du développement communautaire* (SDC) *de Milton Parc*, which is managed by a board of volunteers delegated from different housing co-ops and non-profits. The SDC can prioritize leasing to businesses that meet community needs. By charging a much cheaper rent, it can support local and democratic businesses that otherwise could not survive in our heavily gentrified neighbourhood. Money generated from these rents can then be democratically invested back into the community. The SDC regularly funds the work of popular education, mobilization, and mutual aid, as well as the *Fête des voisins de Milton Parc*, Solidarity Milton Parc, and other community projects.

Over the last few years, with the mortgages now paid off and a comfortable surplus built up, a fresh SDC leadership is preparing to take greater risks and to be more intentional about using these assets to advance a democratic economy by leasing space to community or worker-run businesses. For example, the SDC hopes to buy the *Bar des Pins*, near the Park-Pine intersection, currently owned by a family that is looking to sell.

NEXT STEPS: A BILLION DOLLARS FOR COMMUNITY DEVELOPMENT

There are enormous possibilities for development projects on several sites in the neighbourhood, representing approximately $1.5-2 billion in potential development.

The provincially owned Hôtel-Dieu hospital has been nearly empty for several years. The MPCC founded the *Communauté Saint Urbain*, a community coalition of 60 organizations advocating for the site to be used for co-operative housing for families, non-profit housing, spaces for community organizations, arts and culture, and urban agriculture. The social architect Ron Rayside[2] has

---

2. See chapter by Rayside and Proulx Cormier elsewhere in this book.

been working with the Hotel-Dieu group for over 15 years and has produced compelling visuals and feasibility studies for the site.

Directly adjacent to the hospital is *La Cité des Hospitalières de Saint Joseph*, a vast complex including a convent and gardens, which was recently purchased by the City of Montréal. The magnificent garden, stretching from Pine Avenue to Duluth Street, still has some remnants of urban agriculture; it will gradually be opened up to the public as a park and, hopefully, more urban farming.

The provincially-owned Royal Victoria Hospital is another large empty building in the neighbourhood. McGill University wants to use about half of the site's buildings for a $700 million campus, and the provincial government is making a master plan for the site. The CCMP co-founded the Royal Vic for the Public Coalition and circulated an open letter signed by 55 community organizations, unions, and student groups insisting that the site remain in public hands and that its future be determined democratically and ecologically for the common good. We are also working on a community consultation and demanding a study on developing community-led projects for the site.

The Montréal Chest Institute was sadly privatized by the provincial government, even though one of the buildings was initially the preferred site for the Open Door homeless shelter. Several different capitalist condo development companies now own all four of its buildings.

The monumental *Institut des Sourdes-Muettes* has sat empty for years. An initiative of the Plateau's *Comité Logement*, the deaf community, and the borough of Le Plateau-Mont-Royal wants to acquire this site. It would be used for social housing, a community centre for the deaf community, and the offices of the Plateau borough.

On Saint Urbain Street, there are also three provincially-owned parking lots that the community seeks to acquire to develop into non-profit seniors housing and indigenous-led housing.

OUR CHALLENGES

Despite the remarkable history and reality of our neighbourhood, the housing project has not physically expanded since the victory of the 1980s. Are we victims of our own success—the idyllic comfort of living downtown in a village of heritage houses with bargain rents? Without a great enemy directly threatening our lives, as we had with Concordia Estates Ltd, a generalized culture of individualism and depoliticization can settle in. This can lead to a lack of engagement in the socio-political struggle against injustice and a lack of ambition to go further. It is the mood of the neo-liberal individualist epoch and a by-product of living comfortable lives; we become disconnected from urgent social needs and the stressful realities of the oppressed, so we forget the need for radical social change. Most residents are not necessarily activists or social developers, and with jobs, kids, and other interests, these issues are no longer a top priority. But they will give their support to initiatives for the common good if someone else takes the first step.

Milton Parc was built by a combination of visionary leadership and an active organizational membership. The two prominent leaders were extraordinary local activists. The first was Lucia Kowaluk, a secular saint, an activist intellectual, and a community organizer extraordinaire. She was a social worker and an ever-cheerful wellspring of humanistic compassion. She was a pioneer of community organizing projects, services for the homelessness, and grassroots-led housing projects, both in the Milton Parc neighbourhood and across the city. Her timeless recipe for winning social change relied on three essential ingredients: mobilizing the people, using allies in high places, and watching the big picture of the larger economy.

The other great pillar of radical leadership in the neighbourhood was Dimitri Roussopoulos, active in local and international social movements and radical publishing, releasing books, journals, and newspapers. Politically initiated in the New Left movements of the 1960s, he migrated towards anarchism and encouraged its development in Québec. Afterwards, he would become a friend and publisher of eco-anarchist intellectual Murray Bookchin, who pioneered social ecology as an innovative anarchist response to the urban and ecological issues of the post-WW2 era. Dimitri would become a leader in radical municipalist struggles in Montréal and pioneer participatory democratic reforms in the city.

It is crucial to build a radical and committed leadership to take the initiative to continue this long tradition. Milton Parc has a 60-year tradition of activism, with some elders remaining to share their wisdom. However, it is necessary to renew political leadership with a new generation—one with the courage to stand against injustice, sharpened by political education, patient, and able to negotiate their differences and misunderstandings (there will be many). They must enjoy their work together and develop a sense of community among themselves while always being humble, open, and inviting for new recruits to join their ranks. They should have a sense of collective self-care concerning each other's needs and boundaries, dreams, and pleasures while also taking the time to celebrate their victories and recharge for future battles. They should have a long-term utopian vision of how society should be structured (a maximum program) while, in the short-term, mobilize around realizable demands that the community can connect to and build together.

REFERENCES

Bemma, A. 2011. "The Milton Parc Affair (1 of 2)". *YouTube*, 18 July 2018, video, 11:48. https://www.youtube.com/watch?v=ASY35siyWco.

Bemma, A. 2011. "The Milton Parc Affair (2 of 2)". *YouTube*, 18 July 2011, video, 10:18. https://www.youtube.com/watch?v=c9K9qRP8814.

Helman, C. 1987. *The Milton Parc Affair: Canada's Largest Citizen-Develop Confrontation*. Montréal: Véhicule Press.

Kowaluk, L., and Piché-Burton, C., eds. 2012. *Communauté Milton-Parc: How We Did It and How It Works Now*. http://www.miltonparc.org/English.pdf

Hawley, J., and Roussopoulos, D., eds. 2019. *Villages in Cities: Community Land Ownership, Cooperative Housing, and the Milton Parc Story*. Montréal: Black Rose Books.

Nozick, M. 1992. "Milton Park Montréal: community ownership of land and housing." In *No Place Like Home – Building Sustainable Communities*, edited by M. Nozick. Ottawa: Canadian Council of Social Development.

POINTE-SAINT-CHARLES: LEGACIES AND CONTINUITY

JOCELYNE BERNIER AND CÉDRIC GLORIOSO-DERAICHE

Several Montréal neighbourhoods are faced with a development logic driven by major real estate developers who build large residential complexes that are often inaccessible to the resident population. Especially in neighbourhoods near the city centre, the few remaining brownfield sites arouse greed. They are the site of a clash between two visions of urban development—one driven by the accumulation of profit in the hands of private developers and one aiming to create an equitable, inclusive, and sustainable city for the benefit of all its residents. How can the citizens of these neighbourhoods resist these forces, which lead to gentrification and exclusion? The struggle to defend the right to the city while improving living conditions has been ongoing in Montréal's Pointe-Saint-Charles neighbourhood for several years. This chapter will present an overview of that struggle.

A BRIEF HISTORY OF POPULAR STRUGGLES IN POINTE-SAINT-CHARLES

Pointe-Saint-Charles is a neighbourhood located between the Lachine Canal, the St Lawrence River, and downtown Montréal. It has a rich industrial past and a history of workers' struggles dating back to the 19th century. This experience of fighting and organizing the workers' movement has created fertile ground for the emergence of citizen movements and the first social animation experiences in Montréal.

Deteriorating living conditions deepened in the neighbourhood with the closure of the Lachine Canal and the departure of several factories. This resulted in a significant decrease and impoverishment of the population. The population's resistance movements, and the creation of the first popular groups, began towards the end of the 1960s, when the Pointe-Saint-Charles Community Clinic, the Community Legal Services of Pointe-Saint-Charles and Little Burgundy, and the *Carrefour d'éducation populaire* were born. Several other groups followed these in the early 1970s. Today, these autonomous community organizations are still spaces for local democracy and experimentation that have influenced the development of public services throughout Québec.[1]

During this period, struggles over housing multiplied, leading to the creation of many housing co-operatives. Organizers also called for defending tenants rights and the rights of small landlords. This pushed groups to start looking beyond their particular scope of action and generating concern about broader issues of urban development. In the early 1980s, the community networks came together in a *Table de concertation, Action Gardien*.

Faced with the first threats of gentrification, the community drafted a manifesto (*Des choix pour la Pointe*) that summarized the neighbourhood's demands in terms of housing, job protection, access to the Lachine Canal, and others (RIL et al. 1986). Even today, these demands remain relevant at a time when the neighbourhood is under increasing pressure from real estate developers. The community also called for public consultations to be led by an independent advisory board (RIL et al. 1986). This movement also encouraged the first foray into the municipal electoral domain, with the election of a municipal councillor who carried these citizens' demands to city hall.[2]

Known for its long-standing activist tradition, the neighbourhood's population and the local community network still defends its right to the surrounding territory with its own identity and struggles. It aims to maintain an inclusive neighbourhood for all. These mobilizations aim to recognize the right to the city and the need and legitimacy for the population to intervene on the associated urban planning issues. Since the early 2000s, Popular Planning Operations (OPA; *Opérations populaires d'aménagement*) have been carried out in the neighbourhood to affirm citizen viewpoints in response to the various municipal consultations on urban planning.

These participatory approaches mobilize residents to develop concrete proposals based on their needs, their knowledge of the environment, and a diagnosis of the targeted sector. They are assisted in the OPA with the aid of resource persons. The first OPA, carried out in 2004, aimed to improve the neighbourhood's living environment; the second, in 2007, proposed a rehabilitation project for the industrial wasteland on the site of the former Canadian National train yards. These initiatives are part of intense struggles

---

1. The Community Clinic is often cited as a pioneer of CLSCs (*centre local de services communautaires*) while the Community Legal Services inspired the creation of the Québec legal aid network.
2. Marcel Sévigny, a local activist, was elected as a councillor and served on city council from 1986 to 2001, first with the Montréal Citizens' Movement (MCM) and then as an independent.

ongoing for more than fifteen years, including multiple lobbying actions and lengthy negotiations with local elected officials and real estate developers (Triolet 2013). The determination, constancy, and concerted action of several groups have made it possible to make gains in this ongoing confrontation with the private interests that shape the city.

These past mobilization experiences have taught us the importance of demanding greater democratic control over the development of the city—development that needs to be directed to benefit residents. Therefore, the ability to organize at the local level, in response to locally identified needs, determines the extent of citizen mobilization.[3] This citizen counter-power is built according to urban struggles and stands in opposition to traditional development actors' indifference to the impact of their interventions on the city and its urban character.[4]

MOBILIZATION FOR THE FUTURE OF THE BRIDGE-BONAVENTURE SECTOR

In Montréal, the right to the city is under serious threat. The expansion of the downtown core and the acceleration of gentrification has had an enormous impact on access to the city, particularly in its central neighbourhoods. Griffintown, a former industrial district in southwestern Montréal, is a prime example of this invasion of a new mode of 'land consumption,'[5] where private interests appropriate land for their own profit at the expense of community members.

Numerous impacts have been observed in neighbouring communities: housing units converted into condos, the erosion of the affordable rental housing stock, and the exodus of families and households with modest incomes to outlying neighbourhoods on the island of Montréal or off-island suburbs. This gentrification process has reached the point that the history of Pointe-Saint-Charles, Little Burgundy, and Saint-Henri is being obscured—we are now destined to live in "The Neighbourhoods of the Canal."[6]

Even today, we are facing a new urban struggle in the Bridge-Bonaventure planning sector, east of the Pointe-Saint-Charles neighbourhood. On the outskirts of the Peel Basin, developers Devimco and Bronfman are targeting public lands owned by the Canada Lands Company (CLC), a federal Crown

---

3. Jake Ryan's chapter in this book explores the development and history of the co-operative housing movement.
4. The urban character here is exemplified by the variation of the density and diversity of the objects which make up the urban space, both in its physical and functional dimensions, and in its various spatial configurations (see Lévy 1999).
5. By "land consumption" we refer to the various practices aimed at making the land value of a site profitable, and at defining the functions and daily uses that should be allowed to take place there according to the interests of individuals or companies, dividing the land up according to their image.
6. See for instance *SDC Les Quartiers du Canal*: http://lesquartiersducanal.com/

corporation. The aim is to develop a mega-project consisting of 4,000 to 5,000 condominium units, a new baseball stadium, and a green technology investment centre. In contrast, the members of the *Table de quartier*—now named the *Corporation de développement communautaire* (CDC) *Action-Gardien*—are proposing a project rooted in the community. This contrasting vision results from an extensive independent citizen consultation exercises in the context of a new OPA.

For almost two decades, the members of *CDC Action-Gardien* have been keeping a watchful eye on the development of the Bridge-Bonaventure sector. This began with their successful resistance to the planned move of the Montréal Casino to the Peel Basin in the early 2000s, a senseless proposal that was subsequently withdrawn. Starting in 2018-2019, guided tours and a booklet on the site's history have been produced by the *Société d'histoire de Pointe-Saint-Charles*. These initiatives have raised residents' awareness of the substantial vacant lots in the vicinity that are attracting the interest of various real estate developers. They have also served to alert public authorities to the impact that massive infrastructure projects under development, including the *Réseau express métropolitain* (REM), the new Samuel de Champlain Bridge, and the redevelopment of the entrance to the city centre (Bonaventure project), will have on the neighbourhood. *CDC Action-Gardien* has carried out various advocacy activities with elected municipal officials and federal authorities to promote the need for comprehensive planning and ensure that the local community's concerns are respected.

A committee composed of community and citizen organizations already involved in monitoring previous OPAs has been trained to guide the analysis and participatory approaches to consult with the local population. Working with UQAM's *Service aux collectivités* and other professionals, an initial analysis of this vast territory was carried out, and thematic fact sheets were produced. These covered urban planning and zoning regulations, land ownership, built heritage, industrial activities and employment, transportation infrastructure, and environmental challenges. The work was presented as part of an open-door event in early summer 2019 to discuss public concerns and mobilizing action. This OPA brought together more than a hundred residents in six work teams for an entire weekend of intense work, ideas workshops, and public presentations. In the presence of a local delegation of elected officials from the Le Sud-Ouest Borough, this exercise allowed neighbourhood residents to come and express their dreams and aspirations for the Pointe and develop proposals for its future. In response to identifying and conceptualizing the neighbourhood's needs and citizen demands, this OPA proposed creating a complete, accessible, and inclusive living environment (Action-Gardien n.d.). This requires social and community housing, local services, a secondary school, outdoor and indoor sports facilities, a *Maison de la culture*, among other needs. The OPA also proposed the creation of an integrated, accessible, and inclusive community centre.

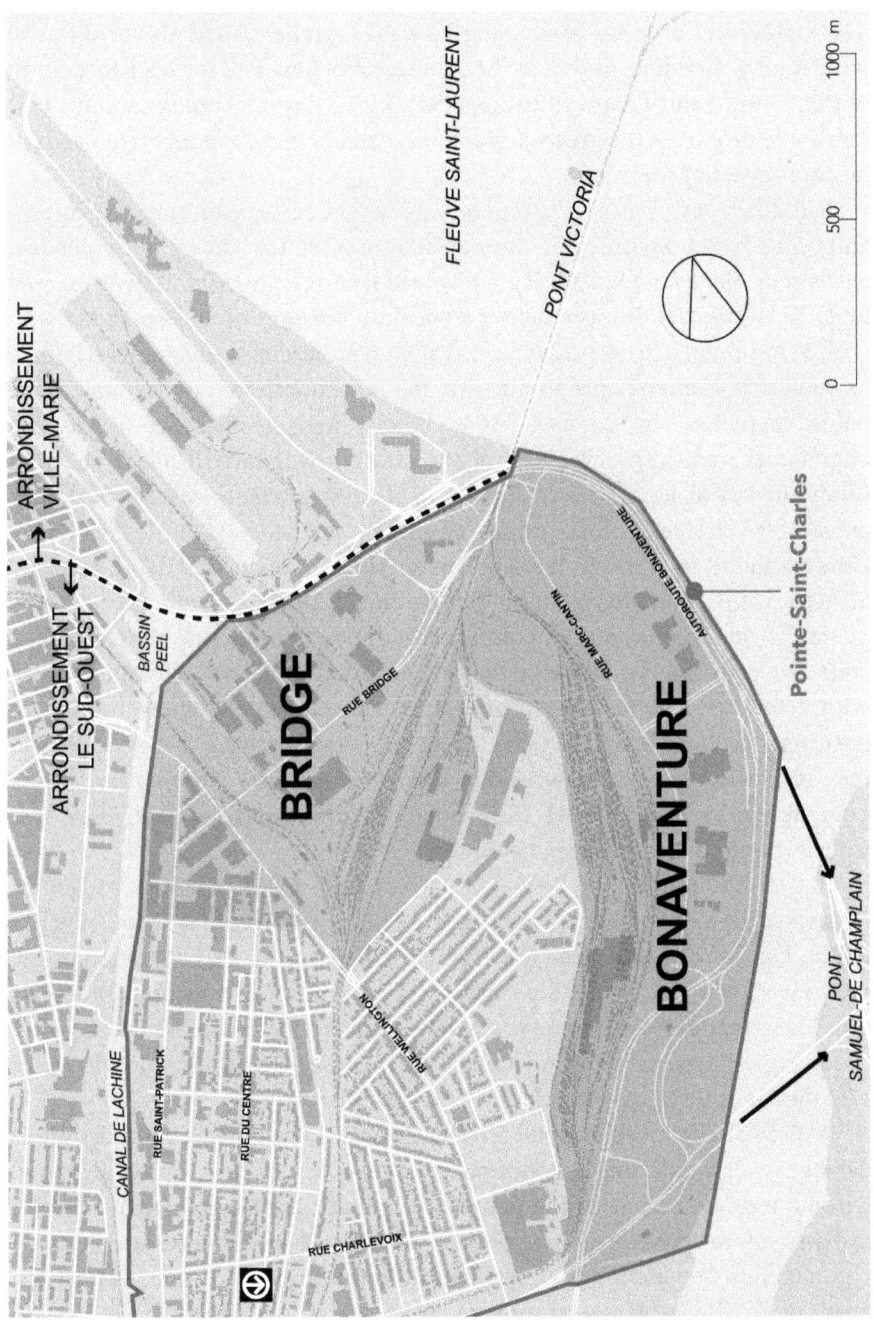

The participants also examined the reconfiguration of the neighbourhood's road infrastructure, suggesting that more space be allocated towards active transportation and public transit. Other proposals addressed by this OPA concern improved access to the St Lawrence River—including the development of a linear park along its banks, greening and the creation of biodiversity corridors, as well as the protection of jobs, and the transformation of the Pointe-Saint-Charles Business Park into a new technological hub. This hub could be part of the green, sustainable, and circular economy that needs to be developed in Montréal.

Fall 2019 was devoted to preparations for the participation of the Pointe-Saint-Charles community in the consultations of the *Office de consultation publique de Montréal* (OCPM). This involved drafting the brief to be presented by *CDC Action-Gardien*, producing a checklist for groups and residents who wished to submit a brief, presentations at OCPM hearings, and media relations to publicize alternative proposals from the neighbourhood. At the same time, public activities in connection with the federal elections made the community's concerns visible. A demonstration was carried out to demand funds for social housing with the *Front d'action populaire en réaménagement urbain* (FRAPRU) and allied groups, ending on public lands in the Peel Basin. Commitments to transfer the land under the National Affordable Housing Strategy were demanded from candidates during a public meeting.

The Bridge-Bonaventure committee continued its work to strengthen collective proposals and develop the case against developers' projects. It began with a tour of neighbourhood groups to consolidate the appropriation of positions resulting from the OPA for Bridge-Bonaventure. This process, and the production of a newspaper for door-to-door distribution, were interrupted by the COVID-19 pandemic; however, these activities will continue and have only been postponed.

In the meantime, on 9 March 2020, the OCPM released its Public Consultation Report on the future of the Bridge-Bonaventure sector (OCPM 2020). Due to the arrival of the pandemic in Canada, its resonance in the media was limited. Despite these circumstances, the OCPM recommendations provide a clear answer to the type of development that could be envisaged in the Bridge-Bonaventure sector: mixed high-density residential development on a human scale (recommendation #41; OCPM 2020).

And what about the baseball stadium project? The OCPM commissioners deemed it irresponsible to pronounce on such a vague project proposal without a study measuring the potential economic, social, and environmental impacts of an infrastructure project of this scale. Instead, the OCPM recommends implementing accessible multi-sport facilities that address the needs of all Montréalers (recommendation #40; OCPM 2020). This is a vision in contrast to the one proposed by Stephen Bronfman and his group during the consultations and his many public appearances.

The OCPM report is unequivocal, embracing the inclusive, affordable, accessible, and human-scale vision that community stakeholders—including *CDC Action-Gardien*—presented during the public consultations. More specifically, the Commission rejects a Griffintown-style development model; instead, it recommends establishing "sound and successful governance of the transformation of the sector" (OCPM 2020, 94) based on the principles of coherence, collaboration, and communication between all stakeholders concerned.

> The definition of a shared vision for the development of the Bridge-Bonaventure sector requires the City to go beyond ad hoc public consultations to **consider the collective interest**. The scope and duration of the project require sustained collaboration based on **an ongoing dialogue between politicians, citizens and various stakeholders**. This collaboration is not a one-way street. It involves long-term participation and commitment on the part of the stakeholders, since a project of this dimension will inevitably lead to planning revisions over the years (OCPM 2020, 95 [emphasis added]).

As for the City of Montréal, its reaction to the OCPM's recommendations was timid. It invited the group behind the Montréal Baseball Project to redo its homework and present an improved project plan accounting for all considerations set out in the OCPM report. Once again, the municipal administration seems to be backing private projects; the mayor has noted her strong interest in a project of this magnitude, which she considers "a great idea" (Boulay 2020). As of spring 2021, the city has yet to take a public position on the OCPM recommendations. Instead, it chose to form a multi-party governance table, bringing together companies operating in the sector as well as public and community actors. Workshops involving all stakeholders will be held to define a vision for the future of the sector. The debate will therefore have to continue within the context of the November 2021 municipal elections. Meanwhile, developers continue to lobby for federal land—and are even seeking out public funding—to build a stadium. At the same time, the current health crisis has increased the need for public services and undermined state finances.

WHO CONTROLS THE DEVELOPMENT OF THE CITY?

Faced with two competing visions that confront each other in determining the future of the redevelopment of the Bridge-Bonaventure sector, the City of Montréal must play a greater political role. The land use plan (*schéma d'aménagement*), the Metropolitan Land Use and Development Plan (PMAD; *Plan métropolitain d'aménagement et de développement du Grand Montréal*), and the Urban Development Plan are indispensable tools that the city must put in place upstream of private developments. Other tools more suited to guiding the development of a particular site, like the *programme particulier d'urbanisme* (PPU), comprehensive development plans, vision documents, and others, are necessary and complementary to ensure an overall holistic vision for the sector. However, the City of Montréal constantly finds itself falling behind regarding major urban planning projects led by private developers. The city may try to introduce nuances or regulatory changes or take advantage of negotiation opportunities without ever affirming its own vision based on its existing planning tools. Recent examples, including the Molson Brewery, Royalmount, Montréal Children's Hospital, and others, show that the city is more reactive in communicating its overall vision for a sector and initiating consultation with stakeholders.

An analysis of these cases shows us that private developers generally determine the nature of major land use projects and shape the city's urban form[7] and urban landscape. In an interview, André Boisclair of the *Institut de développement urbain du Québec* stated that real estate developers are the real builders of the city of tomorrow.[8] While this statement may shock members of the municipal administration and urban planning professionals, it is not far from the truth!

In the absence of a robust municipal vision, the city has let developers undertake piecemeal development with no real overall planning. It then finds itself in an urgent need to manage critical situations on a case-by-case basis. Thus, it is not the city that dictates urban development rules to developers, but rather developers who dictate to the city. Then, the interventions and investments will be targeted to produce maximum benefits for investors according to the profitability of the market, especially that of the real estate market. The needs of citizens and communities will become sidelined.

This weakness in the city's urban planning is partly due to the limited power granted to municipal authorities; the problem is exacerbated when the city limits its political will to adopt binding regulations. In this sense, the case of the city of Berlin provides a remarkable counterexample. The city, tenants' associations, civil society groups, and the media have been reporting for several years now on the severe crisis regarding the lack of affordable housing in the Berlin tenants' market. Rental prices have almost doubled in the last ten years, while incomes have not kept pace. To counter this trend, the municipality has declared a rent freeze for a period of five years, which could affect up to 1.5 million apartments in the German capital (Le Monde 2019).

In Québec, adopting such a policy would be unthinkable today due to the

---

7. By urban form we mean the various social practices which shape the city in the image of its inhabitants and which leave a lasting impression on those who live, move around and consume in it (Gracq 1985; Unwin [1909] 1981).
8. For more details, see the IDU positions on their website: https://www.idu.quebec/fr/engagement

lack of regulatory power given to cities, which are, let us remember, creatures of the provinces. On the other hand, the City of Montréal is reluctant to use its existing powers or cross the boundaries of jurisprudence when tackling fundamental problems such as gentrification, real estate speculation, or conversion of the rental housing stock.

Various measures have been recommended in recent years to address these issues, including several proposed by the *Institut de recherche et d'informations socio-économique* (Gaudreau and Johnson 2019):

1. accelerating the setting aside of buildings for public purposes,
2. guidance in the issuance of conversion permits to safeguard the affordable rental stock, and
3. the use of a new form of zoning to preserve rental tenure in our neighbourhoods.

Several Montréal boroughs (including Le Sud-Ouest) have recently adopted a series of measures to restrict the approval of housing conversion requests—either subdivisions or expansions (Goudreault 2020). This follows the demands coming from many housing committees and allied groups throughout the city. This news is well received by Montréal tenants, who often find themselves at a disadvantage in the face of these "renoviction" projects.[9] However, it is still too early to analyze the impact of these measures on the vitality of the rental housing stock. Several landlord groups have already massively opposed this regulation, the formal adoption of which is slow in coming. Therefore, it is essential to ensure increased vigilance in the face of these strategies for evicting tenants, which border on the edge of legality. The adoption of a moratorium on condo conversions in the early 1990s in Montréal had raised a lot of hope at the time; however, over the ensuing 25 years, this measure has gradually been eroded.

Meanwhile, in Pointe-Saint-Charles, the cost of rents is skyrocketing (23.2% over five years), and property values are increasing at a dizzying rate (474% over five years) (RIL and Action Gardien forthcoming). Additionally, at least 136 affordable housing units have been taken out of the rental market since the 2000s, representing just over 5% of the current private rental stock (RIL and Action Gardien forthcoming). This has been done through the expansion and conversion of existing units. Condominiums now account for one out of every four dwellings in the neighbourhood. The arrival of this new, more affluent population—accompanied by the flow of workers passing through the Nordelec luxury real estate complex and its new start-ups[10]—promotes the transformation of local commercial offerings to meet

---

9. By *renoviction*, we mean the practice of evicting tenants from a dwelling to carry out major renovations, in order to change the use of the dwelling or to significantly increase the monthly rent.
10. This is the largest industrial building in the district that has been converted by a developer, housing,

these emerging needs. All of this occurs at the expense of the traditional local population's basic needs, for instance, local food services, thrift stores, and other necessities. This situation is being repeated in most neighbourhoods surrounding the city centre.

SHAPING THE CITY OF THE FUTURE: A COLLECTIVE CHALLENGE

To defend the right to the city, it is essential to defend the right to the neighbourhood (Gauvreau 2018). Several forms of resistance are being organized at the community and citizen level to halt the transformations discussed above. Some examples include:

- mobilizing and contesting developer initiatives with little local benefit,
- fighting against "renovictions" through political pressure and defending tenants' rights,
- calling for large public landlords to reserve land for collective purposes,
- and promoting access to community premises, particularly on commercial streets.

This does not include the struggle for adequate funding for social housing, which is also essential.

To resist land speculation and the control of private interests over the city's development, it is essential to create a balance of power that can reflect the wants and needs of the resident population. Hence, there is a need to proliferate a range of strategies, including mobilizing the population through information and popular education, and the involvement of social movements. There is also a need for continuous interaction with local elected officials, development of collective projects, and participation in public consultations and media campaigns. Neighbourhood vigilance committees are part of the counter-power to be developed and consolidated for creating inclusive and ecological cities.

A reflection on the modes of public consultation is also necessary in order to evolve towards innovative and inclusive practices. The OCPM has developed an approach that allows the expression of several sometimes-divergent interests and to produce recommendations. However, the OCPM's recommendations are not binding. Instead, the final decision rests with the elected representatives. These representatives need to remain accountable to the population. They should be obligated to explain and present their reasoning when they take decisions on the recommendations of various public and private bodies, notably those of the OCPM.

among others, several start-up companies with a strong potential for economic growth and financial speculation on their future value.

In addition to the urban planning tools that frame the direction of development, municipal elected officials must have the powers and resources to implement these directions and to meet the needs of the population. The *"Réflexe Montréal"* framework agreement signed with the Government of Québec gives the City of Montréal greater flexibility in the areas of infrastructure, school facilities, immigration, housing, homelessness, culture and heritage, and economic development. The city's right of pre-emption for social and community housing development needs to be exercised to deal with the housing crisis. This could be a way to begin to counter the stranglehold of real estate developers who have the means to buy land and whose sole aim is the profit motive. However, to do so will require additional resources, beyond what the city can raise through property taxes and the other limited sources of municipal revenue. What is at stake here is the private ownership of urban space.

However, these measures will not make a difference without the involvement of citizens. Broad participation is needed in the debate over the future of the city. Mobilization remains essential to resist the stranglehold of property developers motivated by the pursuit of private profit. And mobilization is critical for demanding that elected representatives assume their responsibilities to develop a city for the benefit of all, from the perspective of equity, inclusion, and environmental protection.

REFERENCES

Action-Gardien. n.d. "Bridge-Bonaventure." http://www.actiongardien.org/bridge-bonaventure.

Boulay, M. 2020. "Le projet de retour du baseball à Montréal jugé 'controversé.'" *TVA Nouvelles*. https://www.tvanouvelles.ca/2020/03/09/le-projet-de-retour-du-baseball-a-montreal-juge-controverse-1.

Gaudreau, L., and Johnson, M. 2019. "Spéculation immobilière et accès au logement : Trois propositions pour Montréal." Institut de recherche et d'informations socio-économique. https://iris-recherche.qc.ca/publications/logementlocatif.

Gauvreau, C. 2018. "Le droit au quartier: Pour contrer les effets nocifs de la gentrification, Leila Ghaffari prône une revitalisation urbaine inclusive." *Actualités UQAM*. https://www.actualites.uqam.ca/2018/droit-au-quartier-contrer-gentrification.

Goudreault. Z. 2020. "Crise du logement : quatre arrondissements s'attaquer de front aux 'évictions abusives.'" *Journal Métro*, 19 March 2020. https://journalmetro.com/actualites/montreal/2431063/crise-du-logement-quatre-arrondissements-sattaquent-de-front-aux-evictions-abusives.

Gracq, J. 1985. *La forme urbaine*. Paris: Corti.

Le Monde. 2019. "Face à la flambée des prix de l'immobilier, Berlin décrète un gel des loyers." 19 June 2020. https://www.lemonde.fr/economie/article/2019/06/19/face-a-la-flambee-des-prix-de-l-immobilier-berlin-decrete-un-gel-des-loyers_5478370_3234.html.

Lévy, J. 1999. *Le tournant géographique*. Paris: Belin.

Office de consultation publique de Montréal (OCPM). 2020. *Rapport de consultation publique: L'Avenir du Secteur Bridge-Bonaventure*. https://ocpm.qc.ca/sites/ocpm.qc.ca/files/pdf/P103/

rapport_final_bridge-bonaventure.pdf.

Regroupement information Logement (RIL), and Action-Gardien. Forthcoming. *Portrait de l'habitation à Pointe-Saint-Charles.*

RIL, la Clinique communautaire de Pointe-Saint-Charles, and le Programme économique de Pointe-Saint-Charles (PEP). 1986. *Des choix pour la Pointe. Un quartier à améliorer. Une population à respecter.*

Triolet, K. 2013. "Une décennie de luttes urbaines à Pointe-Saint Charles. Vers une réappropriation citoyenne." *Nouveaux cahiers du socialisme* 10: 129-143.

Unwin, R. (1909) 1981. *L'étude pratique des plans de ville. Introduction à l'art de dessiner les plans d'aménagement et d'extension.* Translated by L. Jaussely. Paris: L'équerre. 1st English edition published 1909.

MONTRÉAL-NORD: COMMUNITY POWER CATALYZED BY HOODSTOCK

RUSHDIA MEHREEN, MZWANDILE PONCANA, AND WILL PROSPER

FORGOTTEN BOROUGH

Perched on the north-eastern margin of the island, Montréal-Nord can be considered a forgotten borough of Montréal. Socio-economically, Montréal-Nord is one of Canada's most impoverished neighbourhoods and is home to around 83,000 residents. A significant portion of the borough's population lives below the poverty line; a high proportion is racialized, most of them Black, primarily descendants of Haitian immigrants during the 20th century.

Montréal-Nord was its own city until it was amalgamated into the new megacity of Montréal as a borough in 2001. It stretches just over 11 square kilometres on the southeast bank of the *Rivière des Prairies*. Montréal-Nord is not only far from the city centre, it is also bounded by train tracks to the south and Highway 25 to the east. The borough currently features no subway station.

Compared to other boroughs in the city, Montréal-Nord receives much less city funding. It thus accumulates a deficit at numerous levels, including political, economic, social, technological, and environmental, widening the gap between the boroughs and contributing to further marginalization of its residents. What is less well-known is that Montréal-Nord is also a borough that has organized extensively and has worked to self-empower through collective action.

Montréal-Nord residents protested vigorously, particularly after the killing of Fredy Villanueva in 2008. Marginalization catalyzed the rage and the movement that ensued in the neighbourhood. Twelve years later, the borough that saw lethal racial profiling, and continues to face racism, is still one of the country's poorest but is treading its way towards self-empowerment. More recently, during the early months of COVID-19, the residents of Montréal-Nord once again rose to the occasion when the city neglected them in the face of the pandemic's disproportionate impact on the neighbourhood.

This chapter details the organizing in Montréal-Nord over the last decade and how a small group of people under the umbrella of Montréal-Nord Republik (MNR) initiated a transformation of the borough in a quest for justice, fairness, and self-empowerment. The collective action was iconic, not only in Québec but also nationally and internationally; the word spread as MNR continued to resist the borough's marginalized political and financial situation. We will first shed light on MNR and how it has transformed into a structured organization, Hoodstock. We then focus on the actions and projects taken up by Hoodstock over the years and its role in empowering the most marginalized people in the borough and surrounding areas. Next, we address the work done during the COVID-19 pandemic, when Hoodstock filled the gap left by the city authorities in ensuring the health and safety of the most vulnerable population in the city. Lastly, we highlight areas where the city can step in to fulfill its responsibilities towards the betterment of its most marginalized and oppressed population.

ORIGINS OF MONTRÉAL-NORD REPUBLIK AND HOODSTOCK

Montréal-Nord has risen up repeatedly over the last decade to take back control, demonstrating a resolve for self-determination. The 2008 revolt following the killing of Fredy Villaneuva brought Montréal-Nord into the spotlight.

Fredy Alberto Villanueva, an 18-year-old youngster of Honduran origin, was shot and killed by agent Jean-Loup Lapointe of the Montréal Police Department (SPVM; *Service de police de la Ville de Montréal*) on Saturday, 9 August 2008. Villaneuva's death was part of a larger trend of systemic injustice towards Black people and immigrants in Québec. After Villaneuva's killing, the existing organizations in the Montréal-Nord community fell short of providing an adequate response. Thus, the residents took matters into their own hands—they rose up, protested, and began organizing.

Montréal-Nord Republik (MNR), a collective of Montréal-Nord residents, put forth five demands to local authorities. These demands included: the resignation of the mayor, a public inquiry into the failings of the SPVM, an art piece in memory of Fredy, the end to racial profiling, and the recognition that social insecurity exists as long as there is economic insecurity. MNR directed its focus towards immediate actions to be taken in the face of Villaneuva's death and other social issues such as racial profiling, poverty, school dropouts, and more. Because of the intensity of its rebellious spirit, the MNR was seen as radical—an outlier amongst the other existing community organizations. Its discourse did not ascribe to the status quo; the MNR was perceived as a threat by existing community outfits and the establishment.

Eventually, the demands to establish a public inquiry were met, and shortly after that, MNR organized a public assembly—the first of its kind in the neighbourhood. The assembly gave voice to people who were struggling in various ways and felt forgotten by society. The strength of popular support allowed MNR organizers to continue to organize and keep the struggle alive.

The turbulence following Villanueva's death persisted for several years. On the first anniversary, MNR organized the Hoodstock Social Forum—inspired by the Woodstock festival of the 1960s that mobilized hundreds of thousands of people. Nargess Mustapha, one of the organizers of the social forum, co-founder of Hoodstock and current president of its Board, recalls that it was appropriate to hold the event in a park because Villanueva was killed in a park. On the last day of the Hoodstock Social Forum, a demonstration brought together three mourning families that had lost members to Police killings; along with the family of Fredy Villaneuva were the families of Mohamed Anas Bennis and Quillem Registre.

Out of this social forum, a central core of people solidified it into an organization, also named Hoodstock. As a continuity of MNR, Hoodstock leads the way towards collective empowerment.

Over the last few years, Hoodstock has received project-based funding from various foundations and government programs. They now have three full-time employees, including two project coordinators and fourteen people working on project-based contracts. Despite these differences from MNR, Hoodstock still does not receive the same status as other community organizations regarding access to funding and treatment from different levels of government. As such, Hoodstock faces a precarious and insecure financial situation while doing the work that should be done by the municipal authorities.

SELF-EMPOWERMENT CATALYZED BY HOODSTOCK

Hoodstock breaks the isolation and marginalization of Montréal-Nord's population through a number of initiatives. Even though Hoodstock does not receive core funding as an organization, it has taken up extensive consciousness-raising programs around racial profiling and those building competencies providing practical, employable skills.

In partnership with various organizations, Hoodstock leads several projects ranging from technological literacy and arts (STARTS) to leadership incubation and a legal clinic, among others. Several other initiatives have been carried out or are in the works. These include a campaign against racial profiling, an alternative justice project (*justice hoodistique*), participative defence, youth programs that include participative budgeting and democracy, a centre for sexual assault prevention, and a campaign to defund the police. A few of these initiatives are detailed in the following sections.

STARTS

Soutien technologique et Arts (S.T.ARTS or STARTS) is a technological literacy and arts project offering courses to primary and secondary school students between the ages of 10 and 18, intending to reduce dropout rates. Public schools in Montréal-Nord are extremely underfunded. Some of them, such as the secondary schools Calixa-Lavallé and Henri Bourassa, rank among the last in Montréal school rankings, where dropout rates are much higher. The demographic situation in the borough, where many single-mother households face high levels of poverty and marginalization, results in families with many children living in small apartments lacking sufficient space to study or focus on preparing for exams. After dropping out, youths often resort to working in the service industry, with limited opportunity for a fair chance to develop their careers.

STARTS was custom-made for youth in Montréal-Nord and surrounding areas; it provides them with opportunities for alternative forms of education. By providing writing workshops through hip-hop, or information technology programs, STARTS allows youth to build interest in school and self-confidence to pursue higher education. According to Wissam Mansour, coordinator of the STARTS project:

> The main objective of STARTS is to rebalance youth's chances of succeeding academically and professionally by providing them with the necessary tools for them to develop their skills and competencies to succeed in today's society, and to pursue college and university studies. It is of primary importance that youth living in peripheral neighbourhoods such as Montréal-Nord, Saint-Michel, and Rivière des Prairies have opportunities that allow them to compete with youth from richer parts of the city.

The workshops are offered over an entire semester as part of the French curriculum (e.g., at Henri Bourassa secondary school); they are also offered at the *Maison de culture de Montréal-Nord* as a special series of ten workshops in the afterschool program. In the hip-hop workshops, students learn to develop their creativity and self-confidence through songwriting and performing rap while also improving and practicing their French. The workshops also allow for appropriating and being proud of their culture and interests, otherwise not included in the standard school curriculum.

Information technology workshops for young girls in video game programming is another crucial component of the work of STARTS. Once again, in partnership with schools, workshops equip young girls with employable skills and self-confidence while breaking gender barriers common in the tech sector. It creates options for girls beyond stereotypical 'women's work.' In addition to programming, basic IT skills training and 3D mapping are also offered to reinforce youth's interest in learning, developing creative skills, and continuing their studies.

COMBATTING THE DIGITAL DIVIDE

A blaring digital divide exists in the neighbourhoods of Montréal-Nord, where many households do not have access to the internet nor own equipment such as a computer, laptop, or tablet. Thus, doing any personal work, or researching and applying for jobs is an issue for youth in Montréal-Nord. Montréal, boasting itself as an "Intelligent and Digital City," needs to address this digital divide that furthers the Montréal-Nord community's marginalization. According to the *Centre facilitant la recherche et l'innovation dans les organisations* (CEFRIO), one in five families earned less than $20,000 a year and had no computer or internet access. Moreover, the COVID-19 pandemic (discussed in detail later) showed how lack of access to technology and the internet kept Montréal-Nord at a disadvantage compared to the rest of the city. In Montréal-Nord, access to vital information and essential services was sorely lacking.

EquiTAB

As part of the Combatting the Digital Divide initiative, the EquiTAB project aims to provide digital equipment (tablets) to youth, families, and the elderly and offer digital literacy training. This is especially important to break the isolation of the elderly. As part of the EquiTAB project, Hoodstock collaborated with the Socio-Economic Summit for the Development of Youth in Black Communities (SdesJ; *Sommet socio-économique pour le développement des jeunes des communautés noires*), launched in the summer of 2020. The program coordinates the distribution of equipment and offers digital literacy workshops and educational webinars for families. These efforts are also focused on developing career-related skills and breaking the isolation of youth. However, only 20% of SdesJ's project budget goes to Montréal-Nord households. So far, they have provided equipment and internet access for a few months to over 500 marginalized families, with another 700 families expected to receive the same.

ALTERNATIVE JUSTICE INITIATIVE

The overrepresentation of Black youth and Indigenous people in prisons continues to be alarming; this prison population has increased over the last decade, while the crime rate has not. Alternative justice initiatives are meant as grassroots solutions adapted to the community to counter the chances of police interventions and brutalities that lead to the death of people like Fredy Villanueva, among others.

Hoodstock initiated the Alternative Justice project, based on the concept of restorative justice (*justice reparatrice*), in consultation with other community partners; the aim was to address the roots of the problem affecting the community. If there is an infraction, the idea would be to look into the underlying reasons (e.g., economic, familial, and social), and work to address them alongside other environmental aspects. Such measures would also be beneficial to others in the family and the community. This vision is radically different from the typical incarceration model, where people's lives and dreams are ruined, and their social reintegration is often challenging.

An alternative justice model is inspired by Indigenous approaches to justice and reparation, taking into consideration a holistic view of the person and their environment. It is an innovative approach and allows for considering various perspectives on the problem—and the solution. "Our Restorative Justice project is by and for Black communities, whose goal is to eliminate the over-representation of Black people in prison", explained Marie-Livia Beaugé, the Alternative Justice project coordinator.

Early in 2020, Hoodstock's effort to bring the alternative justice process to Montréal-Nord, *Programme de mesures de rechange général pour adultes* (PMRG), was accepted by Québec's justice ministry as an alternate measure for adults who are charged with certain criminal offences. The provision gives an opportunity to the people involved and the community to "take responsibility for their actions and settle the dispute that brought them into the justice system, following an alternative route that does not involve the usual court proceedings prescribed by the Criminal Code" (Ministère de la Justice 2017). The provision was tested elsewhere in Québec between 2017 and 2019, and Montréal-Nord will be the forerunner on the island of Montréal.

The alternative justice approach includes measures such as mediation, restorative circles to address conflict, and community service. The first step in the direction of alternative justice is to have a legal clinic established in the neighbourhood.

MONTRÉAL-NORD LEGAL CLINIC

One of the project managers of Hoodstock, Me Marie-Livia Beaugé, with the

Black Law Students' Association of UQAM (AEND; *L'Association des étudiants noirs en droit du Canada*) launched the legal clinic in September 2020. The clinic caters to racialized people and immigrant communities who face systemic discrimination. It is instrumental for people who cannot access legal counsel or legal aid due to their immigration status.

The clinic offers free consultations on matters related to immigration, family, and criminal law. It has over 30 volunteers, of which two-thirds are law students. The legal clinic has also taken charge of running popular education campaigns linked to fundamental rights. This includes popular education campaigns related to housing and joint custody, educating on how to face power, and explaining rights when under arrest.

"Hoodstock is a proud collaborator in this project whose mission is to enable Nord-Montréalais's capacity to know their rights and thus obtain better access to justice," noted Hoodstock co-founder Nargess Mustapha.

Participative defence program

In partnership with the legal clinic, the participative defence program helps people who are not covered by legal aid and cannot afford a private criminal lawyer to prepare and defend their case in court. Training is offered to explain the court's rules and equip people in different aspects of criminal law so that those disadvantaged by the system are empowered to represent themselves.

COVID-19 PANDEMIC—ONCE AGAIN, MONTRÉAL-NORD IS ON ITS OWN

The COVID-19 pandemic that hit Québec in early March 2020 left a deep mark on Montréal-Nord. From the very beginning, activists in Montréal-Nord warned that their neighbourhood faced significant health and economic vulnerabilities and should be offered special treatment during the pandemic and recourse provided by government. Hoodstock had forewarned city officials about a potential spike in cases in the borough. Their warnings, however, went unheard, and Montréal-Nord quickly became the neighbourhood with the most infections.[1]

While the intensity of the virus' spread was attributed to the neighbourhood's high population density and its large population of healthcare and other essential workers, the inaction of city officials was also a significant contributor. Yet again, the legacy of the city's ignorance towards Montréal-Nord—the borough is often 'left behind' and treated like 'they don't matter'—was highlighted as a central reason.

With few other options, Hoodstock took matters into its own hands, once

---

1. By March 2021, the borough had a cumulative case rate of nearly 10,000 cases per 100,000 residents, remaining the highest in the city (Santé Montréal 2021).

again. Hoodstock raised over $200,000 online through individual contributions and used that money to buy hand sanitizers, masks, and other essential items to distribute around the neighbourhood to combat the spread of the virus. A call for volunteers was made; both old and new members of Hoodstock provided popular education on virus prevention measures. As Nargess Mustapha detailed: "It's not just about being in distribution mode ... But it's also to provide a certain level of support: to speak to people, to see how they're dealing with this quarantine, how they're living through the reality that today is affecting everyone here in Montréal-Nord."

One of Hoodstock's demands was to set up a COVID-19 testing site in the borough. Following the popular support and the general uproar in the media, the municipal government contributed $10,000 and 2,000 masks. The Montréal-Nord borough finally established their first COVID-19 mobile testing clinic at the *Rivière-Des-Prairies* hospital. Additional prevention measures were adopted, such as partially closing roads to create hygiene corridors to provide pedestrians with the social-distancing space needed.

During the early days of the pandemic, Hoodstock called for collecting data on race, ethnicity, and economic status during testing for COVID-19 to spot infection trends sooner. Had this data been previously collected, it could have helped slow the spread of COVID-19 in Montréal-Nord. Later on, data indeed showed that COVID-19 hit poorer boroughs the hardest[2]. Montréal-Nord, with a median household income of $46,225 and where 22.7% of households are considered low income, bore the brunt of it.

The mobile app, *Colors of Covid*, created by Montréal entrepreneur Thierry Lindor, allowed for anonymous and volunteer data collection. This provided information on some of the pandemic's collateral damage, such as statistics on food insecurity, people's mental health status, and job losses. Hoodstock supported the app's launch, which allowed them to highlight the intersection between the racial and economic factors exasperating the effects of the pandemic.

***

Montréal-Nord rose again in rage and lament following George Floyd's killing, but, more broadly, in reaction to decades of police violence towards Black people both in the United States and Canada. During the rise of the popular global movement surrounding Black Lives Matter, Hoodstock and other Montréal-based organizers responded strongly to the City of Montréal's missteps and the people taking to the street denouncing police violence.

Hoodstock is one of the co-founders of the coalition calling for the

---

2. For further details on COVID-19's disproportionate impact on poor and marginalized citizens, see Leier's chapter in this book.

defunding of Montréal's police force (SPVM), with a list of other demands (the coalition also includes Black Lives Matter—Montréal, the Native Women's Shelter of Montréal, and Stella Montréal). These demands reflect what the most disenfranchized people of Montréal are also calling for, including: cutting the SPVM's budget by half and redirecting that funding to Black, Indigenous, and other oppressed communities; disarming the Montréal police; decriminalising sex work and drugs; and eliminating certain police operations that disproportionately affect marginalized communities such as 'random' police checks.

A WAKE-UP CALL FOR GOVERNMENTS AT ALL LEVELS

As highlighted during the pandemic, the most fundamental underlying problem facing Montréal-Nord is marginalization and being forgotten, thus being disadvantaged. Most stark was the digital divide. Households are not equipped with an essential tool—information technology—which is taken for granted in all measures associated with the pandemic, from instructions on necessary precautions to tracking the virus' spread to applying for emergency funding.

Structural issues mark the reasons why Montréal-Nord is where it is. A study commissioned by the Montréal-Nord borough administration in September 2019 revealed that community organizations in Montréal-Nord are under-financed by the City of Montréal (Arrondissement de Montréal-Nord 2019). Older boroughs enjoy a privileged place in the budget, whereas relatively newly amalgamated boroughs such as Montréal-Nord suffer. Along with other boroughs with marginalized populations such as Côte-des-Neiges and Saint-Michel, organizations in Montréal-Nord are among the lowest funded per low-income person to carry out their mission.

Hoodstock applies and receives funding on a project-by-project basis and is not funded as an organization (*à la mission*). Precarious project-based funding for work on the ground does not allow for long-term planning, investment in infrastructure, or development of human power. Effects of uncertainty can be seen at physical, emotional, and psychological levels, toiling in demanding conditions without job security nor project stability, endangering both the projects and the organization. On the receiving end, people also face non-reliability and uncertainty regarding the services offered.

Funding from private foundations allows for projects to remain afloat. Still, it does not allow for longer-term planning and makes it challenging to fulfill the mission holistically. Project-based yearly funding available through various city programs and other levels of the government does not allow for constancy. It takes up a significant amount of precious time to do paperwork and deal with bureaucratic requirements. Another option suggests Wissam Mansour "could be to offer the project-based funding for longer-term, such as three to five years. That way, we know the funding is available for the full project and provides assurance to our partners too, the schools where we have programs."

Providing stable funding to community organizations like Hoodstock to carry out their mission would allow further empowerment and long-term development of the resources needed to alleviate marginalization and precarity.

CONCLUDING REMARKS

During the pandemic that hit Montréal-Nord the hardest in Canada, the population responded to the cry of solidarity raised by Hoodstock; more than two years' worth of funding by the city was raised in just a few days. However, the urgency mode cannot continue, and support found during the pandemic is not sufficient to provide the means for an organization to survive and thrive in the long term. It is the role of the governments at different levels to be equitable and redistribute wealth fairly so that organizations in the community can cater to the needs of a diverse population. Providing funds on a project-by-project basis or in reaction to fundraising efforts does not allow for stability and reliability. Funding the organization's mission provides the possibility of improving the material conditions of the impoverished population on a sustainable basis.

It is no small feat that twelve years after getting started on the streets amid the popular rage following Fredy Villaneuva's killing by the police, MNR evolved into Hoodstock—an organization with an active board, three full-time paid staff, and several people working on project-based contracts. An organization led mainly by Black people, opening jobs for neighbourhood residents and providing opportunities for numerous projects has many challenges ahead—but also many opportunities.

The next few years are filled with plans and expectations from Hoodstock, the community, local outfits, and institutions. For instance, the secondary schools where Hoodstock provides an alternative and fun way of educating, contributing to reduce dropout rates, expect the program to continue and grow. Meanwhile, the legal aid clinic or the upcoming alternative justice projects need more resources and reliable funding to be substantial. While MNR organizing initially channelled despair and rage through demonstrations and public assemblies, its transformation into Hoodstock, a formal structure with a solid foundation, has proven its potential to fully transform the forgotten borough and its most marginalized population. This building of power through emancipating structures goes hand in hand with the challenge of maintaining radical politics and vision while securing sustainable funding. Therefore, it is high time for the municipal government to seize the moment and provide the stability that Hoodstock and other community organizations need and deserve in light of an equitable distribution of wealth and serving justice.

REFERENCES

Arrondissement de Montréal-Nord. 2019. "Le sous-financement des organismes à Montréal-Nord : 'un lourd constat.'" *Newswire*. https://www.newswire.ca/news-releases/le-sous-financement-des-organismes-a-montreal-nord-un-lourd-constat-821830850.html.

Ministère de la Justice, Gouvernement du Québec. 2017. "General alternative measures program for adults." https://www.justice.gouv.qc.ca/en/programs-and-services/programs/general-alternative-measures-program-for-adults.

Santé Montréal. 2021. "Situation of the coronavirus (COVID-19) in Montréal." Accessed March 21, 2021. https://santemontreal.qc.ca/en/public/coronavirus-covid-19/situation-of-the-coronavirus-covid-19-in-montreal/.

FINAL WORD: PRENONS LA VILLE!

MOSTAFA HENAWAY, JASON PRINCE, AND ERIC SHRAGGE

As we write the conclusion to this book, the Montréal election race is in play. The dominant contenders are Projet Montréal, led by Valérie Plante, who is once again competing with a rebranded Denis Coderre and his *Ensemble Montréal*. However, other municipal parties are forming. The most visible new party is *Mouvement Montréal* led by Balarama Holness.

To further complicate the race, there are also new parties forming at the borough level. For example, Courage, led by borough mayor Sue Montgomery in Côte-des-Neiges–Notre-Dame-de-Grâce, and *Vision politique commune 2021* in Villeray–Saint-Michel–Parc-Extension led by borough mayor Giuliana Fumagalli. As we write these words, it is still too early to see how all of this will play out.

However, our book transcends specific elections, as it is rooted in an analysis of fundamental relations of power. Regardless of who wins the election, the underlying tensions (for example, between pro-growth developers, car-oriented culture, and the majority of people who need decent, affordable housing and solutions to the climate crisis) will remain and will continue to be contested.

There is a lot at stake in this election, including the repositioning of Montréal post-pandemic. The municipal administration that will be elected in 2021 will be crucial not only for the future of the city but also for the planet.

The COVID-19 pandemic revealed some crucial facts.

First, Montréal's stark inequality stood naked for all to see. Who can stay at home and who has to continue going into work—exposed to danger daily—is primarily shaped by class, gender, and race/immigration status. Further, these inequalities have only worsened during the pandemic, with growing financial hardship and displacement through increased rents and gentrification. Existing inequalities and the increasing precarity of labour and housing, already deeply ingrained in the current form of capitalism, have become magnified by COVID-19.

Second, the climate disaster was momentarily stalled as cities around the world shut down due to COVID-19. Some municipal administrations, like ours in Montréal, used the opportunity to increase bike lanes and pedestrian spaces—quite literally rearranging the deck chairs on the Titanic. But this moment of urban calm disappeared quickly, with a return to what is considered 'normal'—increased traffic and congestion.

However, in that short period of calm—when the highways were empty—we witnessed our solution to the problem of carbon emissions.

***

A common lesson from many of the chapters in this book is that power is concentrated and unequally shared; it is heavily weighted toward private capital. And capital shapes our urban landscape. Property, for the most part, is privately owned and treated as a commodity that is there to maximize value and profit. New forms of development—for example, in Griffintown, Mile-Ex, and Mountain Sights—contribute to what Henry Aubin once said 40 years ago: that this investment is tearing apart the very uniqueness and fabric of our city.

This private power plays the long game. It is opportunistic. It prefers to work outside the public realm, and it moves very fast. Some of that private capital is supposedly ours: *our* pension funds and *our* RRSP savings through the *Caisse de dépôt et placement du Québec* or the *FTQ's Fonds de solidarité*, for example. Stein's idea of the "real-estate state" is helpful here for understanding this critical driver that shapes our city (Stein 2019). This is a constant across the globe as private capital sees urban development as a place for growth and private profit.

WHAT IS THE ROLE OF THE CITY?

The city is a junior level of government and is subject to the decisions of the province. Examples are numerous, but two are striking in how they shape urban mobility and growth. The first is the Turcot Interchange replacement project, designed to distribute cars and trucks as efficiently as possible around the urban core (but not people). The second is the imposition of the REM (*Réseau express métropolitain*) light rail project, as a new form of transit in the city, with heavy private funding and links to property development. Both have little relation to the city's transit priorities (for example, as presented in the city's *Plan de transport*). These projects illustrate how the province can override the City of Montréal and impose its vision, in direct contradiction to Montréal's priorities, and with grave consequences for residents and the environment.

In addition, because most of the city's revenues are based on property taxes, this sets up a "trickle down" approach. If the city has more revenue, it can do more; however, this revenue is tied to increased property values. This is played out in the current period of speculation, with real estate as a key commodity for capital investment, further driving this process. It is clear that the city has little power, and the democracy of municipal elections—the right of the city to determine its destiny—is blunted by this reality.

So given these limits, what kind of city administration is possible? What would a progressive city administration look like?

Without any attempt at nuance, here we present three broad approaches to municipal government. In reality, there are overlaps between them, but each represents different priorities and strategies for urban development.

CITY AS GROWTH-MACHINE

The first is the dominant approach. It sees the city as a growth-machine and views the purpose of the municipal administration as supporting the interests and goals of real estate and finance capital. The city—in this view—is a place for investment. Land is treated as a commodity for private, profit-driven development.

Under the growth-machine model, the city competes with other cities to attract private investment for tourism (e.g., the Grand Prix). It invests in infrastructure to attract new economic sectors (e.g., gaming and AI in Montréal). While there might be a limited and decorative environmental aspect to the growth-machine administration, greening the city and innovations in urban transport are seen merely as tools to attract investment and only adopted as long as they do not interfere with the private market.

A growth model is justified because it increases municipal revenues, which are based primarily on property taxes. "Optimized" land use not only contributes more taxes to the city budget, but as a trickle-down/sideways approach to urban development, it also creates jobs.

But it is clear who has power in this approach and how this power is played out.

CITY AS GREEN AND ACTIVE

The second approach, closer to Projet Montréal, is reform-oriented but stays within pre-existing boundaries. As we argued in the introduction, many cities are bringing in green and socially progressive agendas but still playing within the boundaries, with only minimal challenges to the structures of the economy or dominant politics.

In addition to the pressures of private capital, particularly in the case of Montréal, there are barriers and limits inherent in these structures, creating implicit conflicts with the progressive agenda. For example, while Montréal needs at least 50,000 additional units of social and community housing, the city's centrepiece by-law (*règlement pour une métropole mixte*) will only produce a small percentage of these. The additional financial burden on condo-developers is marginal, despite the noise coming from the 'real estate state.'

The city has a powerful bureaucratic structure that transcends elected officials and directs the city. Top civil servants distract, control, and direct administrations in all governments, a lesson on display in political satires like *Yes, Minister*. Even good-hearted administrations, like that under Projet Montréal, are subject to such influence.

In addition, while Green and Active administrations may try to bring in progressive policies and prioritize areas such as green spaces, collective mobility, and social housing, they do not mobilize or engage potential allies, the wider social movements and community organizations described throughout this book. This may be their great failing.

Green and Active city administrations, like Projet Montréal, try to balance the interests of all, at times favouring progressive policies at the expense of large developers but always within a framework of compromise and negotiation with both the private sector and other levels of government.

However, playing within these limits also brings some opportunities. Part of this is connected to the elected representatives themselves. Who are they? What are their politics and orientations? Do they come out of grassroots movements and organizations? What is their connection to these movements and organizations? What are their connections to the private sector? To whom are they accountable?

Finally, we need to consider the political party itself. What role does it play? Montréal is one of the few cities in Canada that has political parties at the municipal level. Some of these parties have become little more than a support mechanism for their mayoralty candidates (and perhaps a few other star candidates), typically pursuing a "growth machine" model. The parties of the left—in striking contrast—have had active membership that formed policies, built platforms, and elected leaders. What is the role of the membership and local associations in pushing the direction of the party, and how accountable are elected officials to these instances? Is the local association active in supporting the municipal administration they worked to elect? Can they play a role after the election in maintaining a mobilized, vibrant connection to the party base and its allies?

This leads us to a third—and our preferred—path forward.

THE ENGAGED OPPOSITION, OR CONFRONTATIONAL ADMINISTRATION

Is there a third path for a municipal government? Such an approach would see itself as the motor of a broader opposition. Capturing municipal government would be another way of challenging the dominant power structure. In overt and ongoing alliance with social movements, community organizations, and its own party base, such a municipal administration becomes a vehicle for education and mobilization to defend environmental, economic, and social policies and programs. It would bring about changes that would be resisted by the forces of capital.

Such an administration would expect strong resistance from the 'real estate state' and the moneyed interests that assume that any municipal administration must shape the city in the interests of (their) profit and growth.

Such a municipal government—echoing the swan song of Plateau mayor Luc Ferrandez—would not shy away from the challenges of our time or confrontation with these private interests but instead would seize them.

Using its powers, and supported by allies, such a municipal government would take direct action to redistribute goods, services, and wealth. It would take land off the market permanently by ceding it to robust partners in the social economy. It would develop the city for the use of its citizens and in an environmentally sane direction. Such a municipal government would be an alliance between city hall and other progressive movements and organizations, both within the city and around the world, to transform the city and act as a counterweight to the forces of capital that shape cities and the wider ecological, social, and economic disasters we face.

***

Elected officials tend to isolate themselves and, once elected, believe that their 'mandate' is all the authority they need. There is no analysis of wider power and what role allies can play in supporting change. The third type of municipal administration would have vibrant and activated links to the wider social movements, progressive unions, and community organizations.

These groups have traditionally played a role to pressure municipal (and other levels of) government to bring in progressive policies that serve the wider collective. The urgent issues we described throughout the book are the collective agenda of these groups.

Mass mobilization, such as the 500,000 people coming out against inaction on climate change, the demands of housing organizations for big and permanent solutions to the housing crisis, and the demands for free public transit are all examples of the ongoing pressure on the city. How does our city government respond? Does it collaborate and support these groups and movements? Does it try to ignore them or co-opt them with small scale and symbolic change? Does it make empty promises during elections? These are crucial questions.

There is a naivety about power in city hall, a belief that the mandates of democratically elected officials are adequate to overcome the power of private (and other forms of) capital that shape the city. They are not.

Our contention is that the only power that has a hope of contesting the capital that controls our city is that which flows from broader alliances.

But what is the source of these alliances?

Community organizations, social movements, and engaged progressives—if mobilized—are the counter-power that can bring change to the city. Their mobilization, their capacity to visualize and articulate alternatives, and their traditions of local action have already shaped the city in important ways and will continue to do so. Also, importantly, there is a growing "collective capital" that is strengthening our capacity to act. Existing community assets and the ability to raise new funds with tools like community bonds may become important under an Engaged Opposition, or Confrontational Administration.

THE CITY AS A TOOL

A fundamental shift has to take place in our city if this change is to come about. We need to see the city as the master tool to achieve the fundamental change we all seek.

Many city-based groups ignore the municipal level and only make demands on higher levels of government. They have not seen the city as a lever to move other levels of government and as a means of pushing demands for social, environmental, and economic justice.

Our movements and organizations must target city hall as a vehicle for profound change. Yes, there are structural limits to city hall. Yes, city hall has limited financial resources. But city hall "represents" the residents of Montréal. It is a legitimate voice for other levels of government. It can be an ally. The city, through its planning powers and land ownership, has the potential to transform the city. It can align itself with movements and community organizations to challenge structural racism, address the climate crisis, the lack of affordable housing and adequate public infrastructure, and influence how land will be developed.

"PRENONS LA VILLE"

A new initiative, launched in February 2021, brings together community and neighbourhood organizations, social and climate justice movements, and activists to build a broad platform to articulate common demands. This new alliance aims to play a role in the election and push popular demands and concerns. No matter who wins the November election, this kind of pressure will be a key element and an alternative voice and—in unity—a source of power to shape the direction of city hall.

Building an alliance and sharing a vision at a grassroots level must be a priority for creating any alternate vision and strategy to build a Montréal that belongs to all of us.

We have a moment during such elections when the spotlight is focused on city hall and municipal politicians. These cycles will come and go, but they can also provide an opportunity to build long-term coalitions and movements that will have an enduring effect on creating change.

Any alliance must also support movements and organizations to build their capacities to win concrete campaigns linked to such a broader vision of the city.

Building solidarity, and with a common understanding of how movements and their members shape power—and how these struggles are linked—will help us to effect and deepen these roots, expand our base and build leadership among communities often marginalized and discarded from the political process and power.

The tension between movements and political parties is not an easy one, but the power of our communities is indispensable for building an inclusive, ecological, and democratic city.

DEMOCRATIZING THE CITY

The ultimate challenge is to democratize the city. In capitalist societies, there is tension between democracy at the political level (formal democracy), based on what in principle is called universal suffrage, and an economy based on private ownership and limited regulation. We live with political democracy and an economy based on very concentrated forms of private ownership, driven by profit and growth.

In the 1960s, Lefebvre used the term "right to the city." Fifty years later, Merrifield (2017) argued that this promotes the city as the site for the democratizing society, gaining and redefining power relations (a *'rapport du force'*).

For Lefebvre, the right to the city was an expression of people trying to shape their own destinies; participation dramatizes urban life. These are rights that stand in opposition to markets. They are collective and rooted in notions of shared purpose. He envisioned the link between the right to the city and broader revolutionary change. He wrote in 1989 that:

> …the right to the city implies nothing less than a revolutionary conception of citizenship…citizenship lies inside and beyond a passport…it doesn't express a legal right bestowed by any institution of the bourgeois nation state…revolutionary citizenship isn't a right at all, it has to be struggled for taken anew- not runner stamped …citizenship without a flag, without a country, without borders…(based on) shared experience- an ever growing mutuality of disadvantage and despair of suffering and perhaps hope. There's an affinity even if it is rarely acknowledged. The right to the city ought to help us identify how this affinity gets recognized how it is mediated, undermined, upended… ought to help us create new forms of organization (Lefebvre 1989).

REFERENCES

Aubin, H. 1977. *City for sale.* Toronto: James Lorimer & Company.

Aubin, H. 1977. *Les vrais propriétaires de Montréal.* Montréal: Éditions l'Étincelle.

Lefebvre, H. 1989. "Quand la ville se perd dans une metamorphose planetaire." *Le monde diplomatique*, May 1989.

Merrifield, A. 2017. "Fifty years on: the right to the city." In *The right to the city: A Verso report.* New York: Verso Books.

Stein, S. 2019. *Capital city: Gentrification and the real estate state.* New York: Verso Books.

TAKE THE CITY! COALITION AGREEMENT

SOCIAL, ECONOMIC, AND ECOLOGICAL JUSTICE

The following document consists of a few parameters for a strategic coalition and an eventual action plan aimed at building grassroots power.

INTRODUCTION

Take the City! (*Prenons la ville!*) is a united front of activists, community groups and social movements to defend and promote our campaigns and demands. We aim to break out of our silos, building connections across Montréal's neighbourhoods and between our various demands for social and ecological justice.

We believe that the city should act on these demands and campaigns to fight climate change and build a city based on equality and social justice.

We recognize that what has become the city of Montréal is located on unceded Kanien'kehá:ka Nation's lands. This place, today, is also home to many racialized and Indigenous communities from across Turtle Island. Within the city, we see the consequences of the process of dispossession and colonization with growing numbers of Indigenous peoples living on the streets of the city. Any process of building basic urban change has to recognize the historic displacement and support their demands for justice.

THE ELECTION

The municipal election will involve political parties and candidates telling the population of Montréal about problems and issues we face and what can be done about them. The assumption is that Montréalers are passive and there only to watch the spectacle. We believe that this is false.

There are hundreds of organizations in the city and many more individuals who make demands for change. What do we expect from the city? Many campaigns have been making demands on city hall in isolation from each other. How will these campaigns—for example, for carbon neutrality, for more and better quality low-income housing, free public transportation, a defunded and accountable police force, increased accessible green spaces, justice for First Nations and racialized minorities—work together to build power and shape our city?

A COLLECTIVE FRONT

Take the City! brings together individuals who are part of many different organizations across the city, who are demanding a green, and socially just city. We believe that city hall should support and act on our demands. Some of these are within the traditional mandate of the city, others involve broader change (provincial, federal, …). In both cases, city hall has to take a lead to promote and support this transition along with diverse social movements and community organizations. Montréalers collectively can build a voice and raise an alternative vision and demands. Let's build a collective voice to fight for the city that meets the needs and the hopes of the majority—a dynamic, green city with social and affordable housing and safe streets for everyone.

Bringing change to the city can only happen if there is a strong, independent, broad alliance of movements and organizations. We are building counter-power. We are building leadership from the ground up. With our collective agendas and campaigns, we can inform and shape the issues of the greatest importance for the majority of Montréalers. Who will define the city? Does the city become the place for property developers and speculators, or social housing and green space, those who put profit and growth before the climate, private transport—roads and cars—over public and other alternatives? We are calling for direct democracy. The real power of Montréalers is to shape their neighbourhoods and the direction of the city. That is what is at stake in this election.

HOW TO CARRY AN ALTERNATIVE AGENDA INTO THE COMING MUNICIPAL ELECTION?

To do this we propose bringing together groups, organizations and individuals campaigning for social, economic and climate justice, who are creating and proposing alternative strategies and projects. We will bring forward an alternative, one that is not shaped by political parties and their communication teams, but by on-the-ground struggles—by those in neighbourhood-based, democratic social movements. We propose to democratize the election by adding our collective voice, by pulling together our demands and vision.

Within the eventual perspective of an Action Plan for "Take the City and Our Neighborhoods" we propose four areas of struggle that are a synthesis of the important struggles that we must undertake. This is not a complete list of demands and campaigns across the city. For more detail, see the "Annex" to this document, which is a living document. We invite groups and individuals to add their campaigns and active demands. The four we have chosen are ones that group together many campaigns and demands and represent urgent issues.

HOUSING

We all need a roof over our heads. This is a right. A number of forces threaten this right, particularly gentrification, speculation, etc. We believe that the question of decent housing, affordable rents free from financial speculation and social housing are at the heart of our priorities in Montréal especially in this period of municipal elections.

Land use is central to housing. Currently, there are several campaigns in the city for the redefinition of public lands and abandoned land for public use including social housing and public green spaces. Examples include the Malting site in St Henri, the former Blue Bonnets in Côte-des-Neiges, the Bridge/Bonaventure in the South-West, *Écoquartier* Louvain Est, and former hospital sites in Milton-Parc and the centre of Montréal. These sites need to be protected and redefined for low-income housing needs and public spaces. Housing is a right.

Keywords: cooperatives, non-profit housing, land trusts, access to housing, social housing, sustainable land use, access to services

CLIMATE CHANGE

500,000 citizens were on the streets of Montréal in 2019. The question of the environment and ecological justice are at the heart of our preoccupations in our daily life as Montréalers, including the need for urban green spaces (among other demands). Our economy, based on growth and profitability, is inherently anti-ecological. Alternative forms of development need support. Of course, the provincial government has a vital role to play, but it is the responsibility of the city to fight and push for the environment to force the National Assembly and Federal government to take action. Ecology is a right.

Keywords: Air and water pollution, soil contamination, carbon emissions, automobile pollution, industrial and corporate pollution, exposure to pollution in the workplace, free public transportation, planning for the conservation of trees in the urban environment, sustainable greening of the city, our parks and bike paths, recycling, composting, community gardens, decontamination of the St. Lawrence River, access to the river.

DEMOCRACY

Which democracy are we talking about? Not a vertical democracy (from top to bottom) practised by traditional parties and even so-called progressive parties. We have to reject this outdated model. We must reflect and develop a new model which will be based on inclusive and direct horizontal democracy. We believe that democracy should be based on autonomous, decision-making assemblies based in each neighbourhood. Elected officials should institute direct consultations as set out in the municipal constitution. Democracy is the means of building a collective voice and power for all Montréalers. Direct democracy is a right.

Keywords: Local decision-making, borough-level decision-making, grassroots power, neighbourhood assemblies, *à nous les quartiers, à nous.*

ECONOMIC and SOCIAL JUSTICE

Economic and social polarization is a huge challenge. Wealth is becoming more concentrated. Indigenous peoples, women, racialized communities, oppressed minorities, migrants, undocumented people, and immigrants are at the top of the list of people living in precariousness and poverty because of the process of wealth creation and redistribution. The pandemic has revealed the polarization of labour. Immigrants who came with the different waves from the end of the 19th century have all contributed to the construction of this city. In a large majority, they are working in the most precarious, difficult, and essential jobs, including a majority of women doing care work. They have a right to decent housing, decent working conditions, a right to unionization, and fair wages. They are full citizens of this city regardless of their formal immigration status, no matter their language, race, religion, political beliefs, sexual orientation, and gender identity. Many of these issues fall outside of the traditional mandate of the city. We want our municipal administration to be part of the campaigns for justice for Montréalers. A decent living is a right.

Keywords: Unionization, workplace organizing, collective negotiations, dignified wages. collective voice, struggles against poverty and inequality, inclusion, economic alternatives, social economy, workplace health and safety.

We recognize that many of the questions outlined above fall beyond the formal jurisdiction of the city. Nonetheless, we demand that the city advocate for these changes.

AUTHOR BIOS

Patrick Barnard worked as an English teacher at Montréal's Dawson College and as a radio journalist for CBC Radio, Radio Canada International, WBAI in New York, and Radio Netherlands in Hilversum. He is a board member of the non-partisan Green Coalition of Montréal, a group dedicated to preserving natural spaces, and the environment in general. He was a board member of The Legacy Fund for the Environment, which facilitates environmental advocacy before Canada's tribunals. He also produces The Pimento Report video blog.

Jocelyne Bernier has lived in Pointe-Saint-Charles for over 40 years. As a citizen, she has been involved in various organizations in the neighbourhood and actively involved in community life. She was general coordinator of the Pointe-Saint-Charles Community Clinic during the 1990s, before working as coordinator of the Chair on Community Approaches and Health Inequalities at the *Institut de recherche en santé publique de l'Université de Montréal* for more than ten years. Currently retired, Jocelyne is active in the Popular Development Operation monitoring committee and the Bridge-Bonaventure committee of CDC *Action-Gardien*.

Christopher Curtis is an award-winning journalist who worked for the Montréal Gazette for nine years, covering Indigenous issues, poverty, cannabis regulation, and municipal, provincial and federal politics. He was nominated for a National Newspaper Award and won a Canadian Association of Journalists award in 2020 for a series of stories on Indigenous issues, including a feature about Air Inuit pilot Melissa Haney. He left the Gazette in 2020 to launch *The Rover* (https://rover.substack.com/), an interactive reporting project in collaboration with Ricochet Media.

Joey El-Khoury is a long-time researcher-activist with the Montréal Climate Coalition. He holds a PhD in applied human sciences from the *Université de Montréal*, studying the role of civil society organizations in urban carbon politics and policy-making for carbon-neutral transitions. He lectures on sustainability and social innovation at HEC Montréal Business School, is a consultant in social impact strategy at the Pôle IDEOS-HEC for social enterprise, and a member of the *Chaire de recherche sur la transition écologique* at UQAM.

Luc Fernandez served as mayor of the Montréal borough of Le Plateau-Mont-Royal from 2009-2019. He was a member of Projet Montréal, where he served as interim party leader from 2014-2016. After Projet Montréal won the 2017 municipal election, he served on the executive committee, responsible for large parks, sustainable development, green spaces, and large projects. The reasons for his 2019 resignation are published in this book as a preface and raise many of the challenges faced by the municipal government.

Luc Gagnon is an energy, transport, and climate change consultant. He has served as Senior Advisor, Climate Change at Hydro-Québec, and Expert Reviewer for the Intergovernmental Panel on Climate Change (IPCC). He also has 14 years of university education to his credit (ETS, UQAM) and was president of Transport2000 in 2008-2009. He is a member of Trainsparence, and also collaborates with the *Groupe de recommandations et d'actions pour un meilleur environnement* (GRAME) and the Montréal Climate Coalition.

Cédric Glorioso-Deraich holds a bachelor's degree and a master's degree in geography from the *Université du Québec à Montréal* (UQAM). Cédric is committed to the development of resilient and supportive communities. Since the fall of 2016, he has been a planning project manager for *Action-Gardien*, the community development corporation (CDC: *Corporation de développement communautaire*) in Pointe-Saint-Charles.

Linda Gyulai is a journalist in Montréal who has covered municipal affairs for 26 years. She started her career writing for alternative weeklies before being hired as a staff reporter at the Montréal Gazette. Her work at the Montréal Gazette over the last 23 years has earned accolades, including the 2009 Michener Award for meritorious public service journalism, which was awarded for her investigations into Montréal's water meter contract. She is a frequent visitor to Québec's access-to-information tribunal.

Mostafa Henaway has been a community/labour organizer at the Immigrant Workers Centre in Montréal since 2008. He began his organizing in Toronto with the Ontario Coalition Against Poverty, organizing taxi drivers. In addition, he has worked in radio at CKUT covering labour issues. He is currently a PhD student at Concordia University in the Department of Geography, Planning, and Environment. He has written extensively on issues of labour and immigration.

Bartek Komorowski is an active mobility professional based in Montréal. He recently joined the Vision Zero team at the City of Montréal and has worked as a project leader in the Consulting Department at Vélo Québec. He is co-author of Vélo Québec's recently released pedestrian and cycling infrastructure design manual, *Aménager pour les piétons et les cyclistes*. Bartek holds a master's degree in Urban Planning from McGill University.

Jean-François Lefebvre is a lecturer in the Department of Urban and Tourism Studies at the *Université du Québec à Montréal* (UQAM) and is also vice-president of Imagine Lachine-Est, a non-profit organization whose mission is to promote practices and policies favoring sustainable and ecological urban development. He also collaborates with the *Groupe de recommandations et d'actions pour un meilleur environnement* (GRAME) and the Montréal Climate Coalition.

Elizabeth Leier is a freelance writer, graduate student, and academic researcher at Concordia University in Montréal. She is a regular contributor to Canadian Dimension, and her writing has also appeared in ROAR Magazine and Truthout.org. She is presently conducting research on international politics and climate justice. She was a co-author of the book *Tisser le Fil Rouge: collected writings on the 2012 Québec Student Strike*, and resides in Montréal.

Robyn Maynard is a Toronto-based award winning, writer and scholar, and doctoral candidate at the University of Toronto. Maynard's most well-known work is *Policing Black Lives: State Violence in Canada from Slavery to the Present*, a national-bestseller that was named "best book of the year" by The Globe and

Mail, The Walrus, and The Hill Times. Her latest work is *Rehearsals for Living*, co-authored with Leanne Betasamosake Simpson, and edited by Lynn Henry, forthcoming in June 2022 with Knopf (Canada), Haymarket: Abolition Papers (U.S.), and Memoire D'encrier (French translation).

Nathan McDonnell is a community activist with the Milton Parc Citizens' Committee (MPCC) and serving as its current president. At its origins, the MPCC built the largest non-profit housing co-operative project on a community land trust in North America. Nathan has co-organized dozens of actions and events over the past years. He also works as a book publisher and intervention worker.

Rushdia Mehreen is an organizer based in Tiohtià:ke/Montréal, a teacher at Vanier College, and a PhD student in Political Science at the *Université du Québec à Montréal* (UQAM). For over a decade, she has been involved in various social justice struggles, including Palestine and anti-colonial solidarity, the Québec student movement, migrant justice, collective care, and anti-racist organizing. She is also a co-founder of the Politics and Care network.

Jon Milton is a student, journalist, and freelancer's union member based in Montréal. His writing and video work has appeared in Briarpatch, Ricochet, Rank and File, Rabble, the Montréal Gazette, the Globe and Mail, the Media Co-op, and The Link. He has also worked as the opinions and managing editor at The Link, Concordia's independent newspaper. His work is primarily focused on grassroots social movements and the mechanics of institutional power.

Claire Morissette (6 April 1950 – 20 July 2007) was a Canadian cycling advocate and fought for the rights of cyclists in Montréal since 1976. She was a member of *Le Monde à Bicyclette* (MAB) and was involved in many of its most memorable stunts and consciousness-raising activities, including the famous die-in on the corner of St Catherine and University. In 1994, she published *Deux roues, un avenir* (Two Wheels, One Future), which promoted the use of bicycles as a mode of urban transportation.

Mzwandile Poncana is a journalist, writer, and researcher based in Montréal/Tiohtià:ke. He specializes in social justice and advocacy journalism. He has covered various social justice actions and organizations, including the movements surrounding prison decarceration and immigration rights. He is currently a staff writer and copy editor for *The Link*, Concordia's independent newspaper.

Eric Pouliot-Thisdale has degrees in history and social science and is a member of the Faculty of Human Sciences at the *Université du Québec à Montréal* (UQAM). He has been a researcher for 20 years in the field of historical and demographic public archives. He is currently a researcher for the Band Council of his nation, Kahnesatake. He is also a freelance writer, including working as a contributing writer and historical columnist for Kahnawake's weekly newspaper, *The Eastern Door* (http://easterndoor.com/).

Jason Prince is an urban planner with nearly three decades of experience in the social economy, working with groups on a range of collective solutions from community housing and daycares to retail and producer co-operatives, as well as community energy projects. Prince teaches part-time at Concordia University and has edited a couple of books on problems facing the city. Prince has two children aged 13 and 14.

Will Prosper is a documentary filmmaker and human rights activist. He is the co-founder of Hoodstock, a space for dialogue and social innovation for the co-creation of more inclusive, safe, and dynamic urban environments. Passionate about cinema from a young age, he has been working on a documentary for the past decade that takes a fresh look at under-represented communities and Afro-descendant cultures in Québec.

Christelle Proulx Cormier holds a bachelor's degree in environmental design and a master's degree in urban studies. Christelle Proulx Cormier is particularly interested in the consolidation of urban living environments and built heritage. She worked for seven years as a senior urban planning project manager for Rayside Labossière before collaborating with various organizations in the Québec development community.

Jean-Pierre Racette is the Founder and Executive Director of the *Société d'habitation populaire de l'Est de Montréal* (SHAPEM), and is a current or former member of numerous boards of directors and several committees. He is engaged in housing and local economic development with a view towards social diversity and the fight against poverty and social exclusion. He holds a master's degree in economics from the *Université de Sherbrooke*, where his thesis was focused on housing in disadvantaged urban areas (*L'habitation en milieu urbain défavorisé. Le cas de Montréal, 1963 à 1986*).

Norma M. Rantisi is a professor in Urban Planning and Geography at Concordia University, with a specialization in economic geography. She is co-chair of the Planners Network and an editor of the online magazine *Progressive City: Radical Alternatives*. Her past research has focused on the social and spatial organization of the apparel industry in Montréal, and on the benefits and limits of work-integration social enterprises (*entreprises d'insertion*) in Montréal and Toronto.

Ron Rayside founded the firm Rayside Architects in 2000, which became Rayside Labossière in 2011. He works with social and community development stakeholders to ensure that urban development addresses social issues and meets the needs and concerns of citizens. His dedication and involvement were recognized in 2019 by the Order of Architects of Québec, which awarded him the first-ever prize for social commitment. In 2013, the *Ordre des urbanistes du Québec* presented him with the Blanche Lemco Van Ginkel Award, and the City of Montréal awarded him the Thérèse Daviau Award for Montréal Personality of the Year.

Jacob Ryan is a graduate student in the Department of Geography, Planning, and Environment at Concordia University in Montréal. His research centres on gentrification, the social economy, and the co-operative movement in Québec. He is a member of the editorial board of the online magazine *Progressive City: Radical Alternatives*. He also sits on the board of directors of The Hive Café Solidarity Cooperative.

Eric Shragge, after many years of academic work, retired to do something relevant. This had included teaching social work at McGill University and acting as the principal of Concordia University's School of Community and Public Affairs. He was a founder and president of the Immigrant Workers Centre in Montréal, where he continues to be an active volunteer. He is an amateur jazz guitarist.

Cheolki Yoon, PhD, is a board member of the Immigrant Workers Centre. He is a researcher affiliated to UNESCO Chair in Communication and Development Technologies (at UQAM), East Asia Observatory (CEIM-UQAM), and the Inter-university and interdisciplinary research group on employment, poverty, and social protection (GIREPS; *Groupe de recherche interuniversitaire et interdisciplinaire sur l'emploi, la pauvreté et la protection sociale*).

Also from Black Rose Books

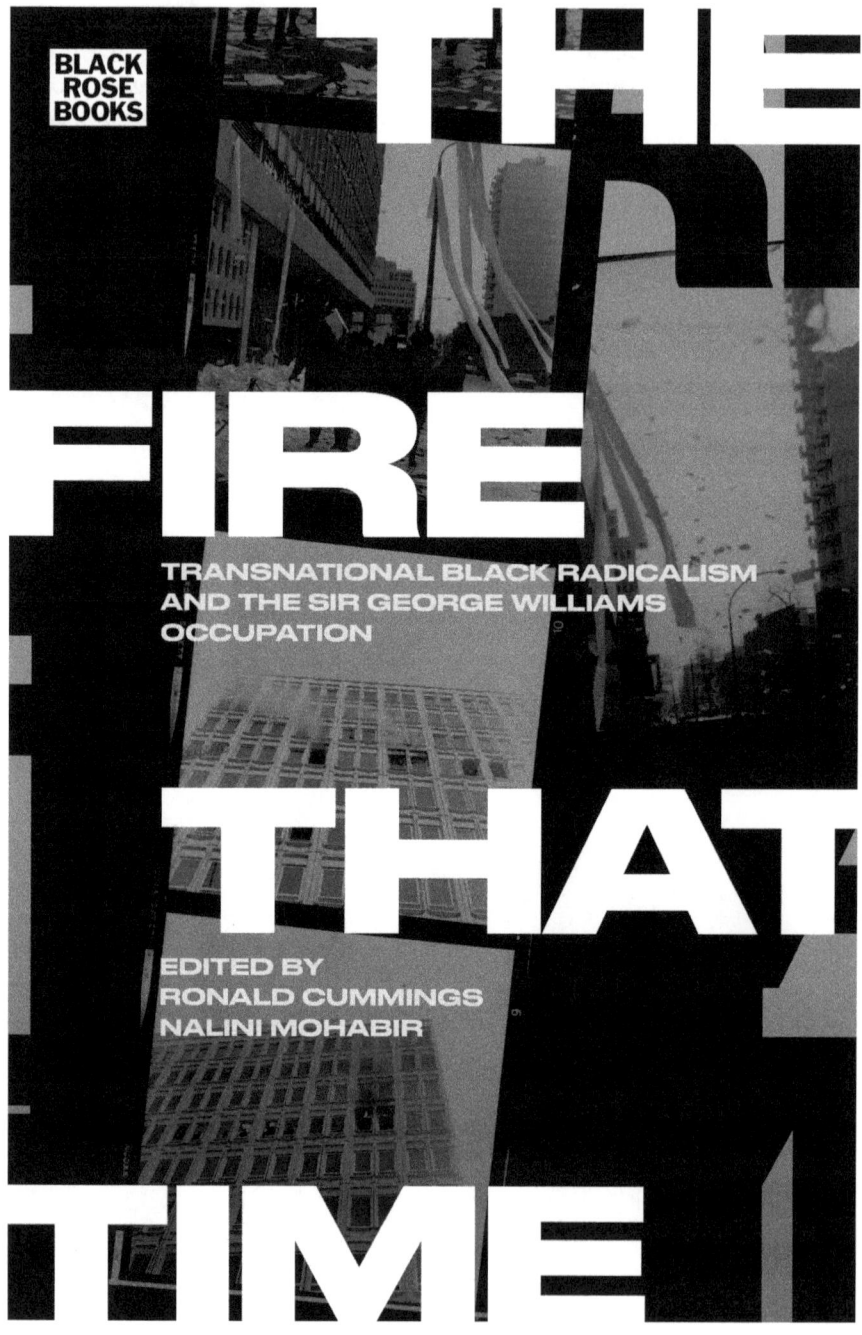

Paperback: 978-1-55164-737-1
Cloth: 978-1-55164-739-5
eBook: 978-1-55164-741-8

Also from Black Rose Books

VILLAGES IN CITIES

Community Land Ownership, Co-operative Housing, and the Milton-Parc Story

JOSHUA HAWLEY • DIMITRIOS ROUSSOPOULOS eds.

Paperback: 978-1-55164-687-9
Cloth: 978-1-55164-688-6
eBook: 978-1-55164-689-3

Also from Black Rose Books

TAKE THE CITY
Voices of Radical Municipalism

Edited by Jason Toney

Paperback: 978-1-55164-727-2
Cloth: 978-1-55164-729-6
eBook: 978-1-55164-731-9

Also from Black Rose Books

Paperback: 978-1-55164-657-2
Cloth: 978-1-55164-659-6
eBook: 978-1-55164-661-9

Also from Black Rose Books

Paperback: 978-1-55164-767-8
Cloth: 978-1-55164-769-2
eBook: 978-1-55164-771-5

Also from Black Rose Books

Paperback: 978-1-55164-334-2
Cloth: 978-1-55164-335-9
eBook: 978-1-55164-615-2

Also from Black Rose Books

Paperback: 978-1-55164-681-7
Cloth: 978-1-55164-683-1
eBook: 978-1-55164-685-5

Lightning Source UK Ltd.
Milton Keynes UK
UKHW021136250322
400602UK00007B/88